Axiomatic Domain Theory in Categories of Partial Maps

Distinguished Dissertations in Computer Science

Edited by
C.J. van Rijsbergen, University of Glasgow

The Conference of Professors of Computer Science (CPCS), in conjunction with the British Computer Society (BCS), selects annually for publication up to four of the best British PhD dissertations in computer science. The scheme began in 1990. Its aim is to make more visible the significant contribution made by Britain – in particular by students – to computer science, and to provide a model for future students. Dissertations are selected on behalf of CPCS by a panel whose members are:

C.B. Jones, Manchester University (Chairman)
S. Abramsky, Imperial College, London
D.A. Duce, Rutherford Appleton Laboratory
M.E. Dyer, University of Leeds
G. Nudd, University of Warwick
V.J. Rayward-Smith, University of East Anglia
Ian Wand, University of York
M.H. Williams, Heriot-Watt University

AXIOMATIC DOMAIN THEORY IN CATEGORIES OF PARTIAL MAPS

MARCELO P. FIORE
Department of Computer Science
University of Edinburgh

CAMBRIDGE
UNIVERSITY PRESS

PUBLISHED BY THE PRESS SYNDICATE OF THE UNIVERSITY OF CAMBRIDGE
The Pitt Building, Trumpington Street, Cambridge, United Kingdom

CAMBRIDGE UNIVERSITY PRESS
The Edinburgh Building, Cambridge CB2 2RU, UK
40 West 20th Street, New York NY 10011–4211, USA
477 Williamstown Road, Port Melbourne, VIC 3207, Australia
Ruiz de Alarcón 13, 28014 Madrid, Spain
Dock House, The Waterfront, Cape Town 8001, South Africa

http://www.cambridge.org

First Published 1996
First paperback edition 2004

A catalogue record for this book is available from the British Library

ISBN 0 521 57188 X hardback
ISBN 0 521 60277 7 paperback

Dedicado
a mis padres, Cristina y Luis, y
a mis hermanos, Verónica y Alejandro.

Table of Contents

Preface

This thesis is an investigation into *axiomatic categorical domain theory* as needed for the denotational semantics of deterministic programming languages.

To provide a direct semantic treatment of non-terminating computations, we make partiality the core of our theory. Thus, we focus on categories of partial maps. We study representability of partial maps and show its equivalence with classifiability. We observe that, once partiality is taken as primitive, a notion of approximation may be derived. In fact, two notions of approximation, contextual approximation and specialisation, based on testing and observing partial maps are considered and shown to coincide. Further we characterise when the approximation relation between partial maps is domain-theoretic in the (technical) sense that the category of partial maps **Cpo**-enriches with respect to it.

Concerning the semantics of type constructors in categories of partial maps, we present a characterisation of colimits of diagrams of total maps; study order-enriched partial cartesian closure; and provide conditions to guarantee the existence of the limits needed to solve recursive type equations. Concerning the semantics of recursive types, we motivate the study of enriched algebraic compactness and make it the central concept when interpreting recursive types. We establish the fundamental property of algebraically compact categories, namely that recursive types on them admit canonical interpretations, and show that in algebraically compact categories recursive types reduce to inductive types. Special attention is paid to **Cpo**-algebraic compactness, leading to the identification of a 2-category of kinds with very strong closure properties.

As an application of the theory developed, enriched categorical models of the metalanguage FPC (a type theory with sums, products, exponentials and recursive types) are defined and two abstract examples of models, including domain-theoretic models, are axiomatised. Further, FPC is considered as a programming language with a call-by-value operational semantics and a denotational semantics defined on top of a categorical model. Operational and denotational semantics are related via a computational soundness result. The interpretation of FPC expressions in domain-theoretic **Poset**-models is observed to be representation-independent. And, to culminate, a computational adequacy result for an axiomatisation of absolute non-trivial domain-theoretic models is proved.

Acknowledgements/Agradecimientos

I will always remain in intellectual debt to my supervisor Gordon Plotkin for having taught me how to do research with his example. Discussing my ideas with him was always —and still is— a pleasure: his suggestions are helpful, and his comments and questions are insightful. This thesis would not have been possible without his stimulating guidance.

I had two second supervisors Barry Jay and John Power from whom I learnt a great deal of category theory and to whom I am grateful for their support and involvement in my work.

In addition, I would like to thank Pietro Cenciarelli, Eugenio Moggi, Wesley Phoa, Andy Pitts, Pino Rosolini and Alex Simpson for conversations on my work.

Also, I am most grateful to Dana Scott and Zhaohui Luo for having examined my thesis.

From October 1992 to October 1993 this work was supported by Fundación Antorchas and The British Council grant ARG 2281/14/6. I am grateful to Monica Paterson for handling the grant with expertise.

A mis padres Cristina y Luis les estoy agradecido porque siempre confiaron en mi, porque siempre me apoyaron en todo y porque les debo todo lo que soy. A mis hermanos Verónica y Alejandro les agradezco su invaluable amistad.

Declaration

This thesis was composed by myself. The work reported herein, unless otherwise stated, is my own.

Edinburgh, June 1994 M.P.F.

Note Added in Print

This book is the author's Ph.D. thesis. Since this work was completed progress in various directions has been made but these new developments have not been incorporated in the text. For a recent overview of the subject, including directions of research, the reader is referred to the expository article [FJM$^+$96, § Axiomatic Domain Theory].

Edinburgh, March 1996 M.P.F.

"Another word about Category Theory: I actually feel that it is particularly significant and important for the theory and for the whole area of semantics. But it must be approached with great caution, for the sheer number of definitions *and* axioms can try the most patient reader. It seems to me to be especially necessary in discussing applications of abstract mathematical ideas to keep the motivation strongly in mind. This is often hard to do if the categories get too thick, but of course it all depends on the writer. Category Theory is especially useful in stating *general* properties of structures and in *characterizing* constructions uniquely; however, there often is a problem actually justifying the *existence* of certain constructions, and a direct approach can be quicker than quoting lots of theorems. But, man cannot live by construction alone: theorems have to be proved in order to get the proper value out of the work. Domain Theory must also be convenient for demonstrating the soundness of various proof rules for properties of recursively defined objects and recursively defined domains, and I think that Category Theory can be helpful here. A step in the right direction has been made in the LCF system (see [GMW79]), which, however, does not take advantage of general Category Theory; but the whole area needs much more development in my opinion."

Dana Scott[1]

[1]In [Sco82].

1 Introduction

The *denotational semantics* approach to the semantics of programming languages understands the language constructions by assigning elements of mathematical structures to them. The structures form so-called *categories of domains* and the study of their closure properties is the subject of *domain theory* [Sco70,Sco82,Plo83a,GS90,AJ94].

Typically, categories of domains consist of suitably complete partially ordered sets together with continuous maps. But, what is a category of domains? Our aim in this thesis is to answer this question by axiomatising the categorical structure needed on a category so that it can be considered a category of domains. Criteria required from categories of domains can be of the most varied sort. For example, we could ask them to

- have fixed-point operators for endomorphisms and endofunctors;
- have a rich collection of type constructors: coproducts, products, exponentials, powerdomains, dependent types, polymorphic types, etc;
- have a Stone dual providing a logic of observable properties [Abr87,Vic89,Zha91];
- have only computable maps [Sco76,Smy77,McC84,Ros86,Pho90a].

The criteria adopted here will be quite modest but rich enough for the denotational semantics of deterministic programming languages. For us a category of domains will be a category with the structure necessary to support the interpretation of the metalanguage FPC (a type theory with sums, products, exponentials and recursive types). And our axiomatic approach will aim not only at clarifying the categorical structure needed on a category for doing domain theory but also at relating such *mathematical* criteria with *computational* criteria.

1.1 Background

This section discusses the topics in domain theory that serve as a basis for our work. The aim is to present the line of research which we explore in this thesis and to outline our approach (a more detailed account is deferred to Sections 1.2 and 1.3). Other *abstract* approaches to domain theory are also mentioned briefly.

1.1.1 Undefinedness in Domain Theory

In domain theory, the traditional treatment of undefinedness (arising from the possibility of non-termination in computation) is to postulate a fictitious element, *undefined*, and code partial functions as total ones. This has been the approach right from the beginning; we quote from [Sco69]:

> "We do not wish to reject a program if the function defined is partial — because as everyone knows it is not possible to predict which programs will 'loop' and which will define total functions.
> The solution to this problem of total vs. partial functions is to make a 'mathematical model' for the theory of partial functions using ordinary total functions."

This approach has been extremely successful but it is not entirely satisfactory. For example, the description of types by universal properties is not always possible (e.g., cartesian closure and fixed-point operators are inconsistent with coproducts —see [HP90]); also, the way of expressing termination of a program p is indirect, $\neg(p = \perp)$, and intuitionistically incorrect (see [Sco79,CS93]).

These considerations lead Gordon Plotkin to reformulate domain theory in terms of partial functions [Plo85]. Technically, this was achieved by eliminating the least element from the domains. Conceptually, the result was the incorporation of partiality, to the notion of approximation, in the foundations of domain theory. As a by-product, the direct treatment of non-termination provided a setting which is computationally more natural; fitting in better with standard formulations of recursion theory. Also, types could be described categorically (via partial cartesian closure [LM84] with coproducts).

1.1.2 Metalanguages for Denotational Semantics

Denotational semantics is always based, generally implicitly, but sometimes explicitly (as in [Sto77] and [Plo85]), on a typed functional *metalanguage*. Examples of metalanguages can be found in [Sto77,Plo83b,Plo85,Abr87,Zha91,CM93]; they typically contain a rich type theory consisting of basic type constructors together with an operator for defining types by recursion.

Metalanguages may themselves be considered as programming languages with an operational and a denotational (or mathematical) semantics. The denotational approach to the semantics of programming languages is then to translate the programming language in consideration into the metalanguage; thus, deriving operational and denotational semantics for the programming language in consideration.

Another aspect of metalanguages is to provide the term language of a *logic* (precursors of such logics are LCF [Sco69] and PPλ [GMW79]). Then, from the translation of a programming language into the metalanguage, a logic for reasoning about the programming language is derived. In this activity it is important that the operational and denotational semantics of the metalanguage be in harmony (see Subsection 1.1.3) since this will guarantee the harmony between *provability* (in the logic) and *validity* (in the model) of operational properties of the programming language.

The metalanguage that will concern us in this thesis is called FPC [Plo85,Gun92] (see Section 8.1). FPC is a typed functional language with sums, products, exponentials and recursive types.

1.1.3 Relating Operational and Denotational Semantics

The investigation of the relation between operational and denotational semantics started with a question of Dana Scott. In [Sco69], he introduced LCF together with its standard semantics and suggested investigating the relation between the model and syntactic reduction. Gordon Plotkin took up Scott's suggestion. In [Plo77], he introduced PCF and proved the *soundness* and *adequacy* of the standard semantics for a call-by-name evaluator. He further showed that due to the presence of parallel functions the standard semantics fails to be *fully abstract*. In [Mil77], Milner constructed a syntactic fully abstract model for PCF and left open the problem of its semantical characterisation. Recently, in [AMR94] and [HO94], *intensionally fully abstract* semantic models (yielding fully abstract models by extensional collapse) have been constructed.

A computational soundness and adequacy result is a correspondence theorem between *operational termination* and *denotational existence*; it generally states that a program terminates according to the operational semantics if and only if its denotational semantics denotes a value.

In [Plo85], the metalanguage FPC was considered as a programming language, with a *call-by-value operational semantics* and a *denotational semantics in* **pCpo** (the category of cpos and partial continuous functions —see page 6). Moreover, the two semantics were related by a computational soundness and adequacy result (inspired by the work of [ML83] —see also [Abr87,Abr90]).

Related results can be found in [MC88]. There, FPC is interpreted in **Cppo**, the category of cppos —small complete pointed partial orders (posets with least element closed under lubs of ω-chains)— and continuous functions. The existence of sound and adequate evaluators for this interpretation is investigated. Two evaluators are proposed: one which is adequate with respect to *observed* types (these are the types with no exponentials); and another one which is adequate for the language without sums. No adequate evaluator for the full language is given.

1.1.4 Recursive Types

The solution of recursive type equations in categories of domains was first treated *abstractly*, in the sense that no commitment to a particular category of domains was required, in [Wan79]. Subsequently this approach was developed in [SP82] and then, further, in [Fre90,Fre92]. The idea is to work with various kinds of *order-enriched categories* (these are categories equipped with an order structure on each hom and such that composition interacts well with it).

The approach was very much appreciated as a *unification* of the techniques for solving recursive type equations in categories of domains, but its *axiomatic* character remained overlooked. For instance, it lead Lehmann and Smyth [LS81] to outline the first abstract setting for specifying both algebraic (in the ADJ jargon) and recursive types, but these ideas were not pursued further.

Recently, a more abstract approach for solving recursive type equations which does not only apply to order-enriched categories was proposed by [Fre91] (see Subsection 1.2.4). This has been a first important step towards an *axiomatic theory of recursive types.*

1.1.5 Abstract Approaches to Domain Theory

Synthetic Domain Theory

Synthetic domain theory [Ros86,Pho90b,Hyl91,Tay91] was proposed by Dana Scott in 1980, with the motivating slogan: *domains are sets* (more exactly, "domains are certain kinds of constructive sets"). The aim is to axiomatise effectivity in a categorical framework suitable for domain theory. The idea of the approach is to assume a *category of sets* (generally a topos; the *effective topos* being the leading example) and identify the domains within this category by means of properties of a classifier of semidecidable properties.

The application of synthetic domain theory to denotational semantics is the subject of current research (see [Pho93]).

Type Theory and Recursion

In the approach of Plotkin [Plo93a,Plo93b], rather than considering directly possible categorical structure, the idea is to work in a *second-order intuitionistic linear type theory* whose primitive type constructors are linear and intuitionistic exponentials, and second order quantification. Then, in the presence of a modified form of Reynold's parametricity the operators of linear logic are derived. Further, initial algebras and final coalgebras for definable endofunctors over the category of linear maps are obtained. One can then consistently add a fixed-point operator for endomorphisms which guarantees algebraic compactness (see Subsection 8.5.2).

In this setting, the connection with operational notions is still unclear.

This Thesis

This thesis is an investigation into *axiomatic categorical domain theory* as needed for the denotational semantics of deterministic programming languages. Our first motivation for this development is to understand the *general principles* underlying categories of domains. Of course, as a by-product, theorems will be established for wide classes of categories of domains yielding a second reason for developing the theory. On more speculative grounds (see Chapter 10), it is also hoped that axiomatisations of categories of domains will suggest new (hopefully non-order-theoretic) models or will provide the basis for setting up a *representation theory*.

Our approach is:

1. *axiomatic*, because we axiomatise certain categories of domains;
2. *categorical*, because our concern is the categorical structure needed on a category to be considered a category of domains; and,
3. *for denotational semantics*, because we particularly consider models of the metalanguage FPC.

The approach is obtained by merging two independent developments (see the chapter dependency on page 16). One of these, the first one in the exposition, deals with *categories of partial maps*, their order-enrichment, and the categorical description of *data types* in them. The other one is that of an *axiomatic theory of recursive types* with emphasis in the solution of recursive type equations in order-enriched categories. The result of their combination provides the mathematical concepts for defining *categorical models* of FPC in which the notion of undefinedness is treated directly.

Consequently, FPC can be considered as a programming language with a call-by-value operational semantics and a denotational semantics defined on top of a categorical model. It happens that the denotational semantics of FPC in *any* model is *computationally sound* for the operational semantics. It is even possible to give an *axiomatisation of domain-theoretic models* for which it is also *computationally adequate*; this constitutes the culmination of this thesis.

Our axiomatic approach and the synthetic approach are different but certainly not incompatible (e.g., as we argue in Section 10.4, from our axiomatic viewpoint we might recover the view of domains as sets advocated by synthetic domain theory). Interaction between the two subjects is bound to be fruitful. For example, the axiomatic approach can influence the synthetic approach by requiring that models of synthetic domain theory comply with axiomatic domain theory. From another perspective, it is conceivable that effectiveness could be incorporated in our framework by doing axiomatic domain theory within synthetic domain theory.

1.2 Our Approach

We discuss our approach to categorical axiomatic domain theory in the light of the paradigmatical example which we will axiomatise, **pCpo**, the category of cpos —small complete partial orders (posets, possibly without least element, closed under lubs of ω-chains)— and partial continuous functions. These are partial functions $u : P \rightharpoonup Q$ such that

1. *Monotonicity*: For every $x, x' \in P$,

$$\text{if } x \sqsubseteq_P x' \text{ then } u(x) \precsim_Q u(x')$$

   where, for two mathematical expressions e and e', we write $e \precsim_Q e'$ to mean that if e denotes some y in Q then e' denotes some y' in Q and $y \sqsubseteq_Q y'$; and

2. *Continuity*: For every ω-chain x in P,

$$\bigsqcup_k u(x_k) \simeq u(\bigsqcup_k x_k)$$

   where the expression on the left is intended to be undefined if every $u(x_k)$ is; or, otherwise, denote $\bigsqcup_{k \geq k_0} u(x_k)$ where k_0 is any index for which $u(x_{k_0})$ is defined, and for two mathematical expressions e and e', $e \simeq e'$ stands for $e \precsim e'$ and $e' \precsim e$.

1.2.1 Partiality

In [Plo85] a revitalised approach to domain theory was initiated by replacing **Cppo** with **pCpo**. Following the main motivation of the reformulation, i.e. to provide a direct treatment of non-termination in the semantics of computation, we postulate categories of partial maps as the primitive universes in which to interpret possibly non-terminating programs.

Our standpoint is to assume a category of *values* (in our case *total maps*) and consider the *notion of computation* we wish to model (in our case *non-termination*) as extra structure on the category of values. The paradigmatical example, **pCpo**, is obtained by taking the category of total maps to be **Cpo** the category of cpos and (total) continuous functions. *Partiality* (the semantical counterpart of non-termination) arises simply by specifying potential domains of definitions for partial functions which will be continuous where defined. Technically, we introduce the subcategory of *admissible monos* $\mathbf{\Sigma}$ consisting of all those full monos in **Cpo** whose induced subobject is Scott-open, and define $p(\mathbf{Cpo}, \mathbf{\Sigma})$ to be the category of cpos and partial functions described by spans consisting of an admissible mono and a total map. It follows that $p(\mathbf{Cpo}, \mathbf{\Sigma}) \cong \mathbf{pCpo}$.

More generally, we have a category $\mathcal{K}$ of total maps (values) together with a subcategory $\mathcal{D}$ of admissible monos (possible domains of definition for partial maps) which induce the category of partial maps (computations) $p(\mathcal{K}, \mathcal{D})$ —see Chapter 3. The basic computational scenario is then given by the faithful inclusion functor $J : \mathcal{K} \to p(\mathcal{K}, \mathcal{D})$ which allows us to regard total maps as partial maps.

Partial continuous functions are *representable* by total continuous ones, in that for every $P \in |\,\mathbf{Cpo}\,|$ and $Q \in |\,\mathbf{pCpo}\,|$,

$$\mathbf{pCpo}(P,Q) \;\cong\; \mathbf{Cpo}(P,Q_\perp) \tag{1.1}$$

where $Q_\perp$ is the cppo obtained from Q by adding a least element. The above bijection is natural in P and Q, and thus establishes that $J : \mathbf{Cpo} \to \mathbf{pCpo}$ has a right adjoint: the *lifting* functor. Requiring this adjunction in the abstract setting, our computational scenario expands to the following

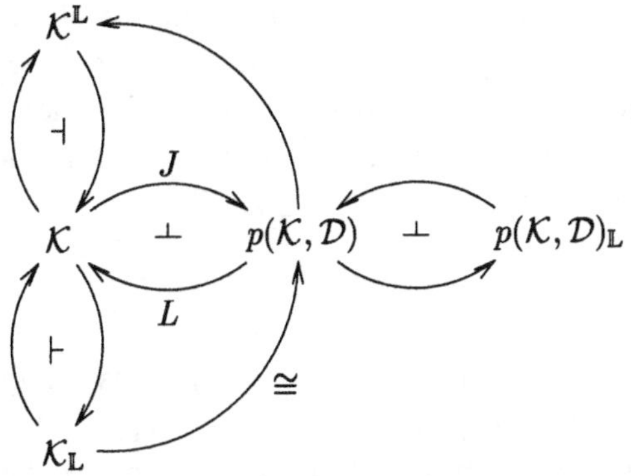

where $\mathcal{K}_{\mathbf{L}}$, $\mathcal{K}^{\mathbf{L}}$ and $p(\mathcal{K},\mathcal{D})_{\mathbf{L}}$ are respectively the Kleisli category, the category of Eilenberg-Moore algebras and the (co)Kleisli category of the (co)monad induced by $J \dashv L$. When $(\mathcal{K},\mathcal{D}) = (\mathbf{Cpo},\mathbf{\Sigma})$ we have $\mathbf{Cpo}_{\mathbf{L}} \cong p(\mathbf{Cpo},\mathbf{\Sigma}) \cong \mathbf{pCpo}$, $\mathbf{Cpo}^{\mathbf{L}} \cong \mathbf{Cppo}_\perp$ (the category of cppos and strict continuous functions), and $p(\mathbf{Cpo},\mathbf{\Sigma})_{\mathbf{L}} \cong \mathbf{Cppo}$.

In this thesis we will mainly focus on the adjunction $J \dashv L : p(\mathcal{K},\mathcal{D}) \to \mathcal{K}$, though we also exploit the isomorphism $p(\mathcal{K},\mathcal{D}) \cong \mathcal{K}_{\mathbf{L}}$. The import of the adjunction is that allows the transfer of properties, constructions, etc. between the category of total maps and the category of partial maps —e.g., it follows that coproducts in $\mathcal{K}$ become coproducts in $p(\mathcal{K},\mathcal{D})$.

Remark. Axiomatising $p(\mathcal{K},\mathcal{D})_{\mathbf{L}}$ and $\mathcal{K}^{\mathbf{L}}$ is the spirit of [Plo93a,Plo93b].

1.2.2 The Approximation Order

Once partiality is treated directly, the notion of approximation may be derived. For $v, v' : Q \rightharpoonup P$ in $\mathbf{pCpo}$ we may state that v approximates v' and write $v \precsim_{Q,P} v'$ (usually omitting the subscripts) if every computable test that the execution of v with some input passes is also passed by the execution of v' with the same input. Formally, we consider partial maps $P \rightharpoonup 1$ in **pCpo** as *computable tests* on P and define $v \precsim v' : Q \rightharpoonup P$ if and only if for every input $x \in Q$ and computable test $u : P \rightharpoonup 1$,

$$u(vx)\downarrow \;\Rightarrow\; u(v'x)\downarrow . \tag{1.2}$$

Note that it would have been equivalent to quantify over more general inputs $Q' \rightharpoonup Q$ and computable tests $P \rightharpoonup P'$. In fact, this will be the approach taken in the abstract setting when defining *contextual approximation*.

An alternative description of approximation is possible. Observe that when $Q = 1$ in (1.1) we have

$$\mathbf{pCpo}(P, 1) \cong \mathbf{Cpo}(P, \Sigma) \cong \mathbf{\Sigma}(P)$$

where $\Sigma = 1_\perp$ and $\mathbf{\Sigma}(P)$ is the set of Scott-open subsets of P; and hence, $\mathbf{\Sigma}(P)$ corresponds to the *semidecidable properties* on P. (In the abstract setting this correspondence will suggest the consideration of subobjects of admissible monos as semidecidable properties). Then, (1.2) can be re-stated as $v \precsim v' : Q \rightharpoonup P$ if and only if for every input $x \in Q$ and every semidecidable property $U \in \mathbf{\Sigma}(P)$,

$$v(x) \in U \Rightarrow v'(x) \in U.$$

The restriction of $\precsim$ to total maps is denoted by $\sqsubseteq$. When $Q = 1$, $\sqsubseteq$ is the *specialisation order* on the T_0-space $(\mid P \mid, \mathbf{\Sigma}(P))$, given on a cpo by the Scott topology. Hence, identifying elements with total maps out of the singleton, we have that

$$x \sqsubseteq_{1,P} x' : 1 \to P \text{ if and only if } x \sqsubseteq_P x';$$

and it also follows that

$$f \sqsubseteq_{Q,P} f' : Q \to P \text{ if and only if for every } x \in Q,\ f(x) \sqsubseteq_P f'(x).$$

The technical appropriateness of the above notions of approximation is that they are *domain-theoretic* in the sense that $(\mathbf{Cpo}(P,Q), \sqsubseteq_{P,Q})$ and $(\mathbf{pCpo}(P,Q), \precsim_{P,Q})$ are cpos, and the composition of maps is a continuous operation (i.e., $\sqsubseteq$ and $\precsim$ provide **Cpo**-enrichments for **Cpo** and **pCpo** respectively).

We stress that $\precsim$ is not *primitive* but derived, as

$$\begin{aligned} v \precsim v' : P \rightharpoonup Q \quad &\Longleftrightarrow \quad \mathrm{dom}(v) \subseteq \mathrm{dom}(v') \;\wedge\; v \restriction \mathrm{dom}(v) \sqsubseteq v' \restriction \mathrm{dom}(v) \\ &\Longleftrightarrow \quad \forall x \in P.\ v(x)\downarrow \Rightarrow \big(v'(x)\downarrow \;\wedge\; v(x) \sqsubseteq v'(x)\big). \end{aligned} \tag{1.3}$$

Remark. Note that the equivalence (1.3) renders the notation of this discussion in harmony with that of page 6.

The above observations support the view that partiality is a *primitive* notion from which the notion of approximation is derived; and that, moreover, the notion of approximation for total maps is more primitive than the notion of approximation for partial maps.

Thus we will study when the notions of approximation for total and partial maps as derived from partiality are domain-theoretic (see Section 4.4). But, for the sake of generality, in our axiomatisation of domain-theoretic models of FPC we will take *both* partiality and $\sqsubseteq$ as primitive, and $\precsim$ as derived. Then the main question, addressed in Chapter 4, is when $\precsim$ is domain-theoretic (as happens in **pCpo**) provided that so is $\sqsubseteq$ (as happens in **Cpo**).

1.2.3 Type Constructors

The type constructors we will be concerned with are sums, products and exponentials (see Chapter 5).

As it is well known, in categories of partial maps cartesian closure does not provide adequate notions of products and exponentials (e.g., consider **Pfn**, the category of small sets and partial functions). Moreover, in general, categories of partial maps are not cartesian closed. This is due to the inconsistency of cartesian closure with zero objects (objects which are both initial and terminal): in a cartesian closed category $\mathcal{C}$ with zero object 0, for every $A \in |\mathcal{C}|$, $0 \cong 0 \times A$ (as 0 is initial) and $0 \times A \cong A$ (as 0 is terminal), thus $\mathcal{C}$ is equivalent to the terminal category **1**. (For more on inconsistencies consult [HP90]). The appropriate categorical structure for interpreting products and exponentials in categories of partial maps is *partial cartesian closure* [LM84].

A category of partial maps is *partial cartesian* if its category of total maps is cartesian. In this case the product functor on total maps extends to a partial-product functor on partial maps. We consider the example of **pCpo**, whose category of total maps, **Cpo**, is cartesian (in fact, cartesian closed but never mind). The product functor $\_ \times = : \mathbf{Cpo} \times \mathbf{Cpo} \to \mathbf{Cpo}$, associating a pair of cpos with the cpo whose underlying set is their cartesian product with the pointwise order, extends to a functor $\_ \otimes = : \mathbf{pCpo} \times \mathbf{pCpo} \to \mathbf{pCpo}$ sending a pair of partial maps $(u, u') : (P, P') \rightharpoonup (Q, Q')$ to the partial map

$$u \otimes u' : P \times P' \rightharpoonup Q \times Q' : \ (x, x') \ \mapsto \ \begin{cases} (u(x), u'(x')) & \text{, if } u(x)\downarrow \text{ and } u'(x')\downarrow. \\ \text{undefined} & \text{, otherwise.} \end{cases}$$

This construction carries over to the abstract setting.

As usual for higher types, exponentiation arises as right adjoint to multiplication. A partial cartesian category of partial maps $p(\mathcal{K}, \mathcal{D})$ is *partial cartesian closed* if, for every $A \in |\mathcal{K}|$, $\_ \otimes A : \mathcal{K} \to p(\mathcal{K}, \mathcal{D})$ has right adjoint $A \rightharpoonup \_ : p(\mathcal{K}, \mathcal{D}) \to \mathcal{K}$. The category

pCpo is partial cartesian closed and $P \rightharpoonup Q$ is the cppo of partial continuous functions from P to Q with the approximation order $\precsim$.

Observe that when the category of total maps has terminal object 1, the *lifting* functor arises from partial cartesian closure because $\_ \otimes 1 \cong J : \mathcal{K} \to p(\mathcal{K}, \mathcal{D})$ and hence $1 \rightharpoonup \_ \cong L : p(\mathcal{K}, \mathcal{D}) \to \mathcal{K}$.

Sums will be interpreted as coproducts in $p(\mathcal{K}, \mathcal{D})$, which in the presence of partial cartesian closure will be given as in $\mathcal{K}$. In **pCpo** coproducts are given by *disjoint unions* and *coproduct injections are admissible monos*. These properties will be shown to hold in the abstract setting as well.

1.2.4 Recursive Types

The traditional way to solve recursive type equations was first established by Scott [Sco72]. It was subsequently developed in the context of **Cpo**-categories by Wand [Wan79], and then by Smyth and Plotkin [SP82]. The method is based on Lambek's Lemma [Lam68] (Lemma 6.1.2), the Basic Lemma [SP82] (Lemma 6.6.4) and the Limit/Colimit Coincidence Theorem [SP82] (Theorem 5.4.5). The idea is to transform **Cpo**-bifunctors $F : \mathcal{C}^{op} \times \mathcal{C} \to \mathcal{C}$ into **Cpo**-endofunctors $F_E : \mathcal{C}_E \to \mathcal{C}_E$ (where $\mathcal{C}_E$ is the category of embeddings in $\mathcal{C}$) such that a fixed-point of F_E is a fixed-point of F. To find a fixed-point for F_E, $\mathcal{C}_E$ is required to have initial object, 0, and colimits of ω-chains so that by the Limit/Colimit Coincidence Theorem the colimit of the ω-chain $\langle {F_E}^n(0), {F_E}^n(0 \to F_E 0) \rangle$ is preserved by F_E and, by the Basic Lemma, is an initial algebra which, by Lambek's Lemma, is an isomorphism.

The ideas behind this method are still the standard way to find fixed-points for bifunctors in categories of domains. However, the approach has some deficiencies: it only applies to **Cpo**-categories and the fixed-points are only canonical in a subcategory of the category of interest.

Recently, Freyd [Fre90,Fre91] has proposed another approach for solving recursive type equations which we develop further (in Chapter 6). He introduced categories appropriate for interpreting *inductive types*. These he called *algebraically complete* [Fre91]; they are those categories such that every endofunctor on them has an initial algebra. The real novelty was his refinement of this notion to *algebraic compactness* [Fre91] by further imposing the axiom that initial algebras are *free* in the sense that their inverses are final coalgebras. In these categories, not only inductive types but also *recursive types* have canonical and minimal interpretations.

The category **pCpo** is **Cpo**-algebraically compact in that every **Cpo**-endofunctor on it has a free algebra. This follows because **pCpo** has the following structure:

1. ep-zero (a zero object such that every morphism with it as source is an embedding and hence every morphism with it as target is a projection); and

2. colimits of ω-chains of embeddings.

Thus, for every **Cpo**-endofunctor F on **pCpo**, by the Basic Lemma, the Limit/Colimit Coincidence Theorem and their dual statements, it follows that the colimit of the ω-chain of embeddings $\langle F^n 0, F^n(0 \rightharpoonup F0)\rangle$ is both an initial algebra and a final coalgebra.

As the above argument applies to any **Cpo**-category with the properties (1) and (2), it is natural to consider the (2-)category of all such small categories. This (2-)category, called **Kind**, besides consisting of **Cpo**-algebraically compact categories will be shown to have very strong closure properties (see Chapter 7).

Finally observe that to solve recursive type equations with this technique in domain-theoretic categories of partial maps, type constructors are required to be **Cpo**-functors. Such considerations are addressed in Chapter 5.

1.2.5 Fixed-point Operators

It is frequently claimed that categories of domains should have fixed-point operators for endomorphisms. But this assertion is just a myth and such an extreme position is not necessary for interpreting recursive programs. To illustrate this point we discuss the interpretation of recursive programs in **pCpo**.

Consider a (call-by-value) language where recursive programs are restricted to higher types with the following syntax:

$$\frac{\Gamma, \mathtt{f} : \tau_1 \rightharpoonup \tau_2, \mathtt{x} : \tau_1 \vdash e : \tau_2}{\Gamma \vdash \mathtt{rec\ f\ in\ } \lambda\mathtt{x}.\, e : \tau_1 \rightharpoonup \tau_2} \,,$$

and operational rule:

$$\mathtt{rec\ f\ in\ } \lambda\mathtt{x}.\, e \leadsto \lambda\mathtt{x}.\, e[\mathtt{f} \mapsto \mathtt{rec\ f\ in\ } \lambda\mathtt{x}.\, e].$$

Then, an adequate interpretation of a recursive program is the total map

$$[\![\vdash \mathtt{rec\ f\ in\ } \lambda\mathtt{x}.\, e : \tau_1 \rightharpoonup \tau_2]\!] : 1 \to [\![\tau_1]\!] \rightharpoonup [\![\tau_2]\!]$$

defined as

$$\mathit{pfix} \circ p\lambda\big(p\lambda([\![\mathtt{f} : \tau_1 \rightharpoonup \tau_2, \mathtt{x} : \tau_1 \vdash e : \tau_2]\!])\big)$$

where, $p\lambda : \mathbf{pCpo}(Q \otimes P_1, P_2) \cong \mathbf{Cpo}(Q, P_1 \rightharpoonup P_2)$ is the natural isomorphism given by the adjunction $\_ \otimes P_1 \dashv P_1 \rightharpoonup \_$; and

$$\mathit{pfix} : \big((P_1 \rightharpoonup P_2) \rightharpoonup (P_1 \rightharpoonup P_2)\big) \to (P_1 \rightharpoonup P_2) : u \mapsto \begin{cases} \bigsqcup_{n \in |\omega|} u^n(\emptyset) & \text{, if } u \text{ is total.} \\ \emptyset & \text{, otherwise.} \end{cases}$$

is the *least total extension* of

$$\mathrm{fix} : \big((P_1 \rightharpoonup P_2) \Rightarrow (P_1 \rightharpoonup P_2)\big) \to (P_1 \rightharpoonup P_2) : f \mapsto \bigsqcup_{n \in |\omega|} f^n(\emptyset),$$

the *least fixed-point operator* in **Cppo**.

However, *pfix* is *not* a fixed-point operator as, in general, $u(\mathit{pfix}\, u) \not\simeq \mathit{pfix}\, u$. It only happens that

$$u(\mathit{pfix}\, u) \downarrow \; \Rightarrow \; u(\mathit{pfix}\, u) = \mathit{pfix}\, u,$$

but *pfix* is still appropriate for our purposes because $u\,(\mathit{pfix}\, u)\, x \simeq (\mathit{pfix}\, u)\, x$ for every x.

In the sequel recursion at the level of programs is *not* considered primitive, instead our viewpoint is that it arises from recursion at the level of types. In fact, the version of FPC adopted in this thesis is not equipped with a fixed-point operator for programs because in the presence of exponentials and recursive types the paradoxical combinators are definable. In particular the *call-by-value fixed-point operator* (see page 149) corresponds to *pfix*.

1.2.6 Models of the Metalanguage FPC

We have exhibited **pCpo** as a

> (parameterised) **Cpo**-algebraically compact partial cartesian closed category with binary coproducts

and, from this perspective, **pCpo** is the prototypical model of type theories with sums, products, exponentials and recursive types (as the metalanguage FPC).

In the abstract setting, models such as **pCpo** will be axiomatised, a denotational semantics defined on top of a categorical model will be given, and soundness and adequacy results will be shown to follow from the categorical structure provided by the models (see Chapters 8 and 9).

1.3 Layout of the Thesis and Summary of Results

Chapter 2 contains the categorical notions outside the scope of [Mac71] used throughout the thesis. The emphasis is on 2-categories (Section 2.1) and order-enriched categories (Section 2.2), though a basic introduction to the general theory of enriched categories [Kel82] (Section 2.3) is also included.

Order-enriched categories play a central role in our approach. Informally an order-enriched category is a category whose homs come equipped with an order (*partial order* in the case of **Poset**-enrichment, *cpo* in the case of **Cpo**-enrichment) and such that composition is a morphism of ordered sets (*monotone* in the case of **Poset**-enrichment, *continuous* in the case of **Cpo**-enrichment). Order-enriched functors between order-enriched categories are functors which are locally morphisms of ordered sets (*locally monotone* in the case of **Poset**-enrichment, *locally continuous* in the case of **Cpo**-enrichment). These mathematical structures and their theory are fundamental for abstractly discussing the notion of approximation, permitting a study of domain theory without committing to particular categories of domains.

2-categories [KS74] are superficially used when discussing categories of kinds (Section 7.3).

Chapter 3 introduces *categories of partial maps* [RR88] (Definition 3.1.2). These are categorical structures in which maps have explicit domains of definition so that it is possible to account for *partiality*. Total maps are then partial maps whose domain of definition coincides with its source. Rather than considering an abstract notion of category of partial maps, for us categories of partial maps will arise from *domain structures* [Ros86, Mog86] (Definition 3.1.1); these consist of a category, the *total maps*, together with a suitably closed subcategory of *admissible monos*, the possible domains of definition.

The *representability* of partial maps as total maps, which amounts to asking for a right adjoint (the *lifting* functor) to the inclusion functor from the category of total maps to the category of partial maps, is studied. It is shown that partial maps can be represented as total ones if and only if they are *classifiable*, in the sense that every partial map determines a unique *characteristic total map* from which the partial map can be recovered by pulling back the classifier (see Definition 3.2.1). This characterisation (Theorem 3.2.6) will be used later, in Sections 4.5 and 5.3, to transfer both order-enrichment and certain colimits from the category of total maps to the category of partial maps.

The direct treatment of non-termination induces *notions of approximation* between partial maps (Section 3.3). Two such notions are introduced, *contextual approximation* (Definition 3.3.1) and *specialisation* (Definition 3.3.3), and shown to coincide (Proposition 3.3.5). The contextual approach is based on *testing* for the totality of partial maps in different contexts; more precisely, a partial map is said to contextually approximate another one if the latter passes the test for all contexts in which the former does. Specialisation is based on *observing* partial maps. Intuitively, a partial map is said to specialise another one if for every observable property on the outputs, whenever the execution of the former with some input satisfies the property then so does the execution of the latter with the same input.

Since the approximation between partial maps can be characterised in terms of the approximation of total maps and test for totality (Proposition 3.3.2), in Chapter 4 we consider the approximation of total maps as the *primitive* notion and treat the approximation of partial maps as derived (see Definition 4.1.1). Thus, we address the question of when the approximation of partial maps is domain-theoretic (in the technical sense that the category of partial maps **Cpo**-enriches with respect to it) provided that so is the approximation of total maps. This study is undertaken in two steps. First, we provide a characterisation of **Poset**-categories of partial maps induced by domain structures with a **Poset**-category of total maps (Theorem 4.2.4). Second, to deal with

Cpo-enrichment, we introduce *uniform* domain structures (Definition 4.3.5) and characterise those **Cpo**-categories of partial maps induced by uniform domain structures with a **Cpo**-category of total maps (Theorem 4.3.9). Intuitively, a domain structure is uniform if lubs of ω-chains of admissible subobjects behave like unions. (The import of this characterisation is discussed in Section 10.4).

In most examples, the categories of total and partial maps are **Poset**-enriched, the inclusion functor from the category of total maps to the category of partial maps is **Poset**-enriched and it has a **Poset**-enriched right adjoint (i.e., the bijective correspondence determined by the adjunction is an isomorphism of posets). This situation is studied in the abstract setting where it is observed that if in addition the category of total maps is **Cpo**-enriched then the category of partial maps **Cpo**-enriches (Corollary 4.5.3).

The above results for transferring order-enrichment from total to partial maps are applied yielding conditions under which the category of partial maps **Cpo**-enriches with respect to specialisation (Proposition 4.4.2 and Theorem 4.5.8).

Chapter 5 is devoted to the study of the categorical structure allowing the interpretation of types in categories of partial maps.

First, *partial cartesian closure* [LM84] (Definition 5.2.3) in the order-enriched setting is discussed. It is shown that the product **Poset**-functor on total maps extends to a partial-product **Poset**-functor on partial maps (Proposition 5.1.2) and conditions under which this extension holds for **Cpo**-enrichment are provided (Proposition 5.1.3). It is also shown that, when the partial-product functor is **Cpo**-enriched, the **Poset**-partial-exponential functor **Cpo**-enriches (Proposition 5.2.1).

Second, we focus on *colimits* in categories of partial maps. We present a characterisation of colimits of diagrams of total maps due to Gordon Plotkin (Theorem 5.3.9) from which it follows that, under mild assumptions, coproducts in categories of partial maps are disjoint and coproduct injections are admissible monos. (This result is relevant to provide a *logical* notion of *representation* (Definition 8.6.1), a formalisation of the notion of implementation, for sum types —see Lemma 8.6.3 (3)). Moreover, assuming the category of total maps has a terminal object and the existence of the lifting functor we provide a method for computing colimits of diagrams of total maps in categories of partial maps provided that the lifted diagram has a colimit in the category of total maps (Theorem 5.3.14).

Finally, we present conditions under which the existence of the colimits needed to solve recursive type equations in **Cpo**-categories of total maps guarantees the existence of such colimits in **Cpo**-categories of partial maps (Theorem 5.4.11).

In Chapter 6 we develop an *axiomatic theory of recursive types*. Following Peter Freyd, we start by introducing categories which are appropriate for interpreting *inductive types*. These he called *algebraically complete* [Fre91] and are those categories such that every endofunctor on them has an initial algebra. Algebraic completeness (Definition 6.1.4) and a *parameterised* version of the concept (Definition 6.1.7) are considered in the enriched setting. (Parameterisation is needed for interpreting types defined by mutual recursion). The basic properties of (parameterised) algebraically complete categories are established: in particular, from the observation that Bekič's Lemma (Lemma 6.1.13) holds for them we conclude the Product Theorem for Parameterised Algebraically Complete Categories (viz., that parameterised algebraically complete categories are closed under finite products —Theorem 6.1.14) and the dinaturality of the functor delivering initial algebras (Proposition 6.1.15). Again following Peter Freyd, with the intention of interpreting general *recursive types*, algebraically complete categories are refined to *algebraically compact categories* [Fre91] by further imposing the axiom that initial algebras are *free* in the sense that their inverses are final coalgebras. After motivating the compactness axiom, we introduce the concept together with its parameterised version in the enriched setting (Definition 6.2.2). Bekič's Lemma together with its corollaries are observed to hold. More importantly, the Fundamental Property of Algebraically Compact Categories (viz., that every endofunctor on an algebraically compact category has a canonical and minimal fixed-point —Theorem 6.4.1) is established and extended to parameterised algebraic compactness (Theorem 6.4.4). Further evidence for the suitability of the compactness axiom is provided by showing that in algebraically compact categories *recursive types reduce to inductive types* (Corollary 6.5.2 and Proposition 6.5.3). Finally, supercompleteness and supercompactness axioms, guaranteeing closure under exponentiation are discussed briefly (Section 6.6).

Cpo-algebraic completeness and compactness is the topic of Chapter 7. The **Cpo**-enriched setting is particularly well behaved as **Cpo**-algebraic completeness and compactness coincide with their parameterised versions (Theorem 7.1.12). Exploiting the Limit/Colimit Coincidence in **Cpo**-categories [SP82] (Theorem 5.4.5), we identify a 2-category, **Kind** (Definition 7.3.11), of parameterised **Cpo**-algebraically compact categories with very strong closure properties: we show that it is 2-cartesian-closed, closed under taking opposite categories, closed under the formation of categories of algebras and coalgebras with *lax*-homomorphisms (Definition 7.1.8), and has a unique *uniform* (up to isomorphism) fixed-point operator —viz., the functor delivering free algebras (Theorem 7.3.12). Thus, **Kind** is appropriate for interpreting type systems with kinds built by recursion from products, exponentials, algebras and coalgebras; but neither such a system nor its interpretation is discussed here.

The theory is applied in Chapters 8 and 9. The metalanguage FPC is considered as a programming language with a *call-by-value* operational semantics (Section 8.2). *Categorical* models of FPC are defined to be parameterised enriched algebraically compact partial cartesian closed categories with binary coproducts (Definition 8.3.1) and a *denotational semantics* defined on top of a categorical model is given (Section 8.4). Two *axiomatic* classes of models, for which **pCpo** is the paradigmatical example, are presented: *domain-theoretic* models (Subsection 8.5.1) and $\mathcal{K}_*$*-models* (Subsection 8.5.2).

Domain-theoretic models are **Cpo**-models arising from domain structures with a **Cpo**-category of partial maps in which **Cpo**-algebraic compactness is obtained from the Limit/Colimit Coincidence (see Corollary 7.2.4). $\mathcal{K}_*$-models are enriched over $\mathcal{K}_*$ (intuitively, the full subcategory of the category of total maps consisting of all those objects with a *least element* (see Definitions 8.5.4 and 8.5.6)), and algebraic compactness is obtained by postulating *special* fixed-points for endofunctors on the category of partial maps together with a parameterised uniform fixed-point operator in $\mathcal{K}_*$.

A first study of the denotational semantics of FPC is carried out in Section 8.6 where it is shown that **Poset**-models arising from domain structures with a **Poset**-category of total maps are *parametric with respect to representations* [Rey74] (see Definition 8.6.1 and Theorem 8.6.6). Secondly, operational and denotational semantics are related. It is shown that the interpretation of FPC expressions is *computationally sound* (Theorem 9.1.4). We culminate by proving that non-trivial domain-theoretic models satisfying an *absoluteness axiom* (which holds in **pCpo**) are *computationally adequate* (Theorem 9.2.19). It follows that the domain-theoretic model specified by $(\mathbf{Cpo}, \Sigma)$ —as well as many similar *classical* models specified by a category of predomains and the Scott-open subsets— is computationally adequate. Other examples are functor categories over **Cpo** (see Corollary 9.2.20).

In Chapter 10 we discuss further directions of research.

The chapter dependency is as follows:

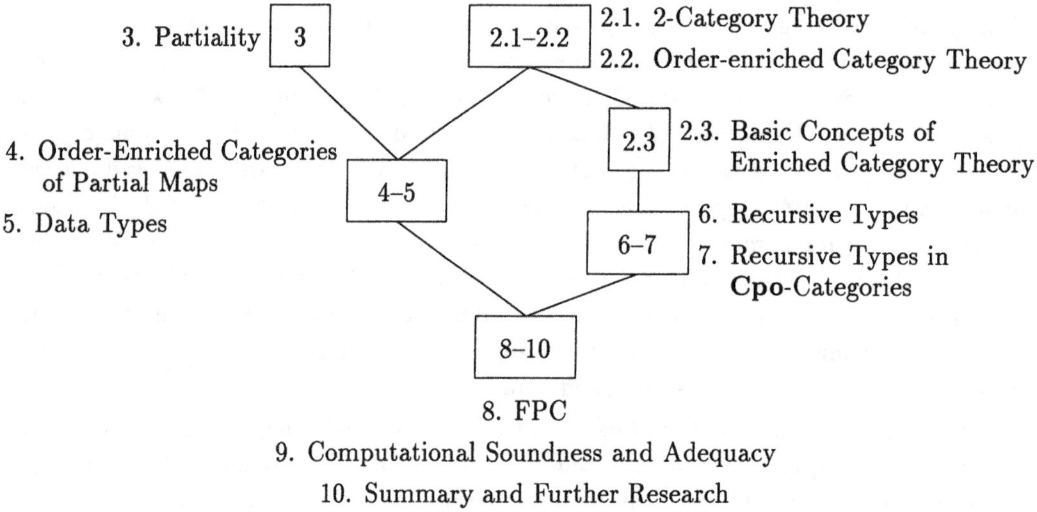

2 Categorical Preliminaries

The category-theoretic notions outside the scope of [Mac71] but used throughout the thesis are reviewed. Section 2.1 is a summary of [KS74] and introduces 2-categories and cartesian closure for them. Section 2.2 introduces order-enriched categories and the elementary notions needed to define order-enriched adjunctions and order-enriched colimits. Both Sections 2.1 and 2.2 are examples of the theory of enriched categories (introduced in Section 2.3 which condenses the first three chapters of [Kel82]).

Familiarity with Sections 2.1 and 2.2 is essential for reading Chapters 4 and 5 whilst familiarity with Section 2.3 is required in Chapters 6–9.

2.1 2-Category Theory

A *2-category* $\mathcal{C}$ has *objects* or *0-cells* $A, B, \ldots$; *arrows* or *morphisms* or *1-cells* $f : A \to B$, $\ldots$; and *2-cells*

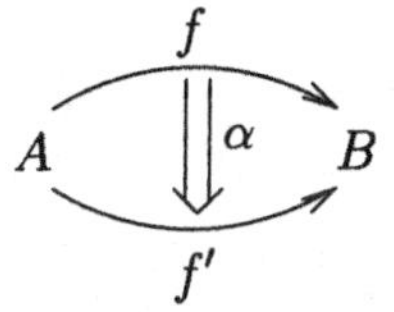

The objects and the arrows form a category $\mathcal{C}_0$, called the *underlying category of* $\mathcal{C}$, with identities $\mathrm{Id}_A : A \to A$. When unambiguous, we sometimes write $\mathcal{C}$ for $\mathcal{C}_0$.

For fixed A and B, the arrows $A \to B$ and the 2-cells between them form a category $\mathcal{C}(A, B)$ under the operation known as *vertical composition*

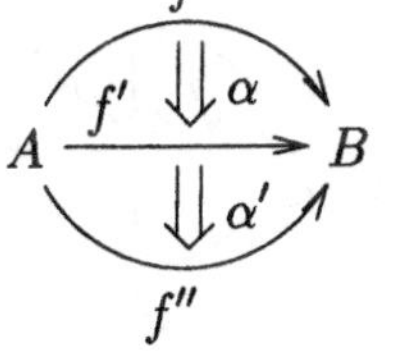

The vertical composite $f \Rightarrow f''$ above is denoted by $\alpha' \circ \alpha$; its identities are denoted by

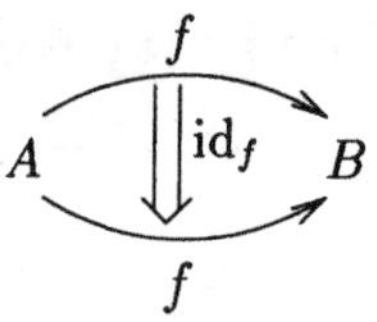

There is also a *horizontal composition* of 2-cells, whereby from 2-cells

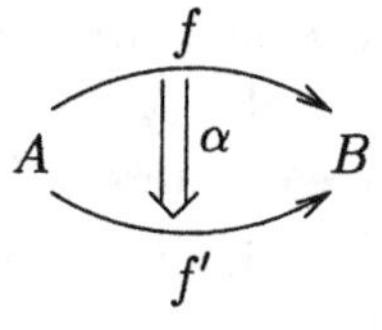

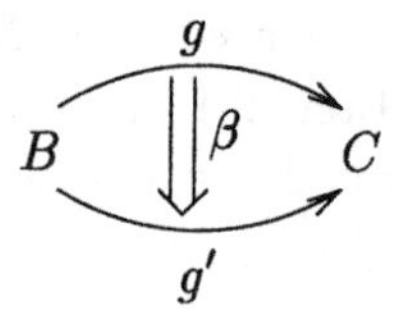

we get a 2-cell

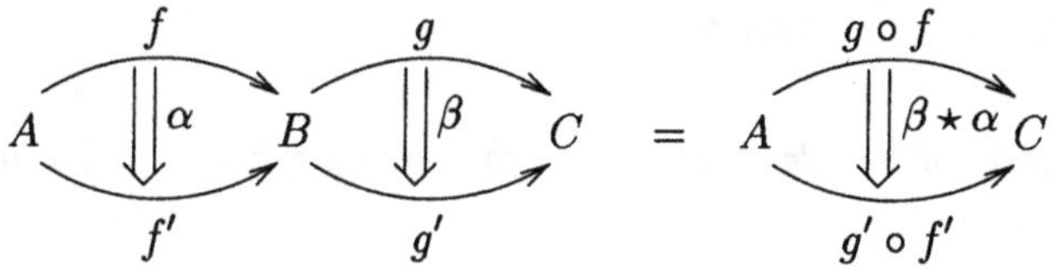

Under this operation 2-cells form a category, with identities

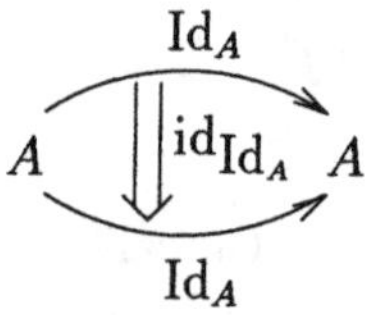

We require finally that, in the situation

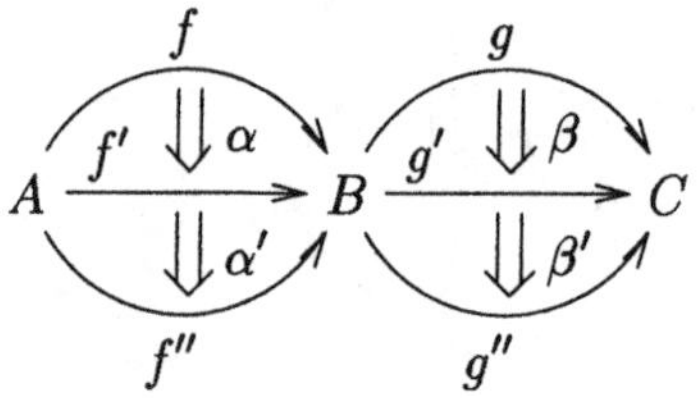

the composites $(\beta' \star \alpha') \circ (\beta \star \alpha)$ and $(\beta' \circ \beta) \star (\alpha' \circ \alpha)$ coincide; and that in the situation

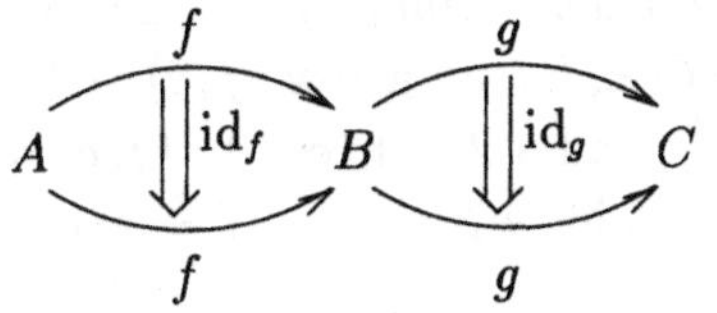

we have $\mathrm{id}_g \star \mathrm{id}_f = \mathrm{id}_{g \circ f}$.

As a convention, in the situation

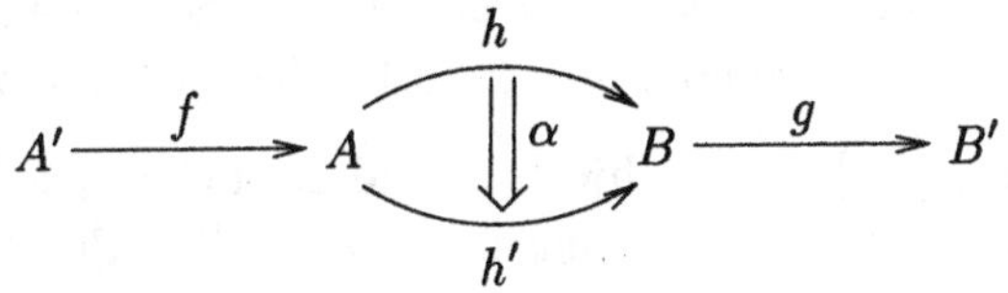

we write $g \circ \alpha \circ f$ or simply $g\alpha f$ for $\mathrm{id}_g \star \alpha \star \mathrm{id}_f : g \circ h \circ f \Rightarrow g \circ h' \circ f : A' \to B'$.

For examples of 2-categories, the paradigmatic ones are **Cat** and **CAT**. The objects are *small categories* and *locally small categories* respectively, the arrows are functors, and the 2-cells are natural transformations. **Cat** is locally small (has small hom-categories) whilst **CAT** is not.

A *2-functor* $F : \mathcal{A} \to \mathcal{B}$ sends objects of $\mathcal{A}$ to objects of $\mathcal{B}$, arrows of $\mathcal{A}$ to arrows of $\mathcal{B}$, and 2-cells of $\mathcal{A}$ to 2-cells of $\mathcal{B}$, preserving domains and codomains and all types of identity and composition.

A trivial example is the "constantly **1**" 2-functor $K\mathbf{1}$ from any 2-category to **CAT**.

A *2-natural transformation* $\eta : F \dot{\to} G : \mathcal{A} \to \mathcal{B}$ assigns to each object A of $\mathcal{A}$ an arrow $\eta_A : FA \to GA$ in $\mathcal{B}$, which is not only natural in the ordinary sense that, for $f : A \to B$, we have $\eta_B \circ Ff = Gf \circ \eta_A$, but also 2-natural in the sense that, for each 2-cell $\alpha : f \Rightarrow f' : A \to B$ in $\mathcal{A}$, we have

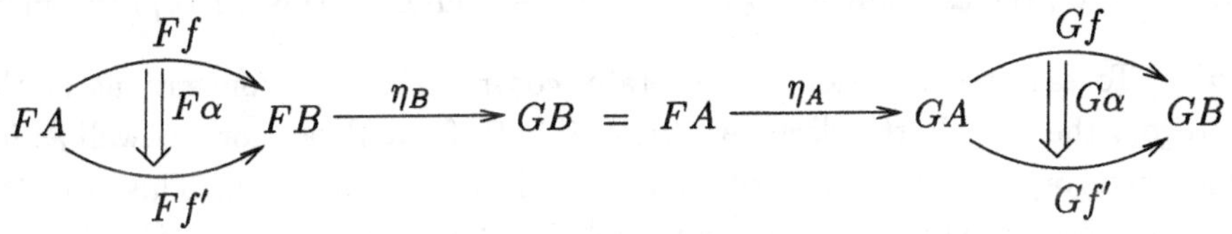
Ff
FA
Fα
FB
η_B
GB
=
FA
η_A
GA
Gf
Gα
GB
Ff′
Gf′

The *dual*, $\mathcal{C}^{op}$, of a 2-category $\mathcal{C}$ has $\mathcal{C}^{op}(A, B) = \mathcal{C}(B, A)$, so that 1-cells are reversed but not 2-cells.

For 2-categories $\mathcal{A}$ and $\mathcal{B}$ we have a *product* 2-category $\mathcal{A} \times \mathcal{B}$, with set of objects $|\,\mathcal{A} \times \mathcal{B}\,| = |\,\mathcal{A}\,| \times |\,\mathcal{B}\,|$, and with $(\mathcal{A} \times \mathcal{B})\big((A, B), (A', B')\big) = \mathcal{A}(A, A') \times \mathcal{B}(B, B')$. Identities and composition are given pointwise.

Every 2-category $\mathcal{C}$ induces a hom 2-functor $\mathcal{C}(\_, =) : \mathcal{C}^{op} \times \mathcal{C} \to \mathbf{CAT}$, sending an object (A, B) to the category $\mathcal{C}(A, B)$, an arrow $(f, g) : (A, B) \to (A', B')$ to the functor $g \circ \_ \circ f : \mathcal{C}(A, B) \to \mathcal{C}(A', B')$, and a 2-cell $(\alpha, \beta) : (f, g) \Rightarrow (f', g') : (A, B) \to (A', B')$ to the natural transformation $\alpha \star \mathrm{id}_\_ \star \beta : g \circ \_ \circ f \Rightarrow g' \circ \_ \circ f' : \mathcal{C}(A, B) \to \mathcal{C}(A', B')$.

A 2-category $\mathcal{C}$, is *2-cartesian-closed* if it has terminal object, binary 2-products and 2-exponentials in the following sense:

- An object 1 of $\mathcal{C}$ is *terminal* if there is a 2-natural isomorphism $\mathcal{C}(\_, 1) \cong K\mathbf{1}$.
- The *2-product* of two objects A and B of $\mathcal{C}$ is specified by an object $A \times B$ of $\mathcal{C}$ together with a 2-natural isomorphism $\mathcal{C}(\_, A \times B) \cong \mathcal{C}(\_, A) \times \mathcal{C}(\_, B)$.
- The *2-exponential* $[A, B]$ of two objects A and B of $\mathcal{C}$ is specified by an object of $\mathcal{C}$ together with a 2-natural isomorphism $\mathcal{C}(\_ \times A, B) \cong \mathcal{C}(\_, [A, B])$ which is also natural in B.

2.2 Order-enriched Category Theory

Throughout this section let $\mathcal{V}$ denote either **Poset** (the category of small partially ordered sets and monotone functions) or **Cpo**.

A **Poset**-category (**Cpo**-category) is a locally small category whose hom-sets come equipped with a partial order (complete partial order) respect to which composition of morphisms is a monotone (continuous) operation.

The immediate examples of **Poset**-categories are **Poset** and **Cpo** where each hom-set is ordered pointwise; even more, **Cpo** is a **Cpo**-category. More examples are obtained from the observation that every category $\mathcal{K}$ *freely* induces a $\mathcal{V}$-category $\mathcal{K}_\mathcal{V}$ by discretely ordering each hom-set.

For $\mathcal{V}$-categories $\mathcal{K}$ and $\mathcal{L}$, a $\mathcal{V}$-functor $F : \mathcal{K} \to \mathcal{L}$ is a functorial mapping such that for every $A, B \in |\mathcal{K}|$ the assignment $F_{A,B} : \mathcal{K}(A, B) \to \mathcal{L}(FA, FB)$ is a morphism in $\mathcal{V}$.

Convention. To ease the notation we generally contravene some conventions of the enriched-category theorist. Particularly, we write $\mathcal{X}$ both for a $\mathcal{V}$-category as well as for its underlying category $\mathcal{X}_0$ where the order structure has been forgotten. This is in the vein of the usual convention of using the same notation for a poset or cpo as well as for its underlying set. A similar convention is adopted for $\mathcal{V}$-functors.

$\mathcal{V}$-**Cat** is the 2-category of small $\mathcal{V}$-categories, $\mathcal{V}$-functors, and natural transformations. It is 2-cartesian-closed, and the structure can be described as follows:

- The terminal $\mathcal{V}$-category **1** has a singleton set of objects while the only hom is the terminal object in $\mathcal{V}$.

- The product, $\mathcal{K} \times \mathcal{L}$, of the $\mathcal{V}$-categories $\mathcal{K}$ and $\mathcal{L}$, is the $\mathcal{V}$-category with set of objects $|\mathcal{K} \times \mathcal{L}| = |\mathcal{K}| \times |\mathcal{L}|$, and homs defined as

$$(\mathcal{K} \times \mathcal{L})((A,X),(B,Y)) \quad = \quad \mathcal{K}(A,B) \times \mathcal{L}(X,Y)$$

  where the operation on the right hand side is the product in $\mathcal{V}$.

- For $\mathcal{V}$-categories $\mathcal{K}$ and $\mathcal{L}$ the functor category $[\mathcal{K},\mathcal{L}]$ is the $\mathcal{V}$-category with the $\mathcal{V}$-functors $\mathcal{K} \to \mathcal{L}$ as the set of objects, and where the hom $[\mathcal{K},\mathcal{L}](F,G)$ is the poset with underlying set $\mathrm{Nat}(F,G)$ of natural transformations $F \dot{\to} G$ ordered pointwise.

For a $\mathcal{V}$-category $\mathcal{K}$ its dual, $\mathcal{K}^{op}$, is the $\mathcal{V}$-category with the same objects as $\mathcal{K}$, but with $\mathcal{K}^{op}(A,B) = \mathcal{K}(B,A)$. (Notice that the order in each hom remains unchanged.)

A $\mathcal{V}$-adjunction $\chi : F \dashv U : \mathcal{K} \to \mathcal{L}$ is given by $\mathcal{V}$-categories $\mathcal{K}$ and $\mathcal{L}$, $\mathcal{V}$-functors $F : \mathcal{L} \to \mathcal{K}$ and $U : \mathcal{K} \to \mathcal{L}$, and a natural isomorphism

$$\chi : \mathcal{K}(F\_,=) \cong \mathcal{L}(\_,U=) : \mathcal{L}^{op} \times \mathcal{K} \to \mathcal{V}.$$

For a category $\mathcal{G}$ and a $\mathcal{V}$-category $\mathcal{K}$, a diagram Γ in $\mathcal{K}$ of type $\mathcal{G}$ is a $\mathcal{V}$-functor $\mathcal{G}_{\mathcal{V}} \to \mathcal{K}$. We have a "constant diagram" $\mathcal{V}$-functor $K : \mathcal{K} \to [\mathcal{G}_{\mathcal{V}},\mathcal{K}]$ defined as the composite

$$\mathcal{K} \cong [\mathbf{1},\mathcal{K}] \xrightarrow{[U,\mathrm{Id}]} [\mathcal{G}_{\mathcal{V}},\mathcal{K}]$$

where U is the unique $\mathcal{V}$-functor $\mathcal{G}_{\mathcal{V}} \to \mathbf{1}$.

A $\mathcal{V}$-colimit of a diagram Γ is given by an object C of $\mathcal{K}$ and a natural transformation $\gamma : \Gamma \dot{\to} KC : \mathcal{G}_{\mathcal{V}} \to \mathcal{K}$ such that for every $A \in |\mathcal{K}|$,

$$[\mathcal{G}_{\mathcal{V}},\mathcal{K}](\gamma,\mathrm{id}) \circ K_{C,A} : \mathcal{K}(C,A) \to [\mathcal{G}_{\mathcal{V}},\mathcal{K}](\Gamma,KA)$$

is an isomorphism in $\mathcal{V}$.

Remark. The treatment of $\mathcal{V}$-colimits offered above is far from been complete and just concerns a restricted class of *conical* colimits [Kel82].

Proposition 2.2.1 Let $\mathcal{G}$ be a category, $\mathcal{K}$ be a **Cpo**-category, and Γ be a diagram in $\mathcal{K}$ of type $\mathcal{G}$. Then, the following are equivalent:

1. (C,γ) is a **Cpo**-colimit of Γ.
2. (C,γ) is a **Poset**-colimit of Γ.
3. (C,γ) is a colimit of Γ and for every $f,g : C \to A$, if $f \circ \gamma \leq g \circ \gamma$ then $f \leq g$. □

For $\mathcal{V}$-functors $F, G : \mathcal{K} \to \mathcal{L}$, a *lax natural transformation* $\eta : F \overset{\cdot}{\underset{\leq}{\to}} G : \mathcal{K} \to \mathcal{L}$ is an $|\mathcal{K}|$-indexed family of components $\eta_A : FA \to GA$ in $\mathcal{L}$ such that for every $f : A \to B$ in $\mathcal{K}$,

$$\begin{array}{ccc} FA & \xrightarrow{\eta_A} & GA \\ {\scriptstyle Ff}\downarrow & \leq & \downarrow{\scriptstyle Gf} \\ FB & \xrightarrow[\eta_B]{} & GB \end{array} \quad .$$

2.3 Basic Concepts of Enriched Category Theory

Subsection 2.3.1 begins by introducing symmetric monoidal closed categories $\mathcal{V}$, examining their elementary properties, and defining the 2-category $\mathcal{V}$-**CAT** of $\mathcal{V}$-categories, $\mathcal{V}$-functors, and $\mathcal{V}$-natural transformations, together with the forgetful 2-functor $(\_)_0 : \mathcal{V}\text{-}\mathbf{CAT} \to \mathbf{CAT}$. Next the basic structure of $\mathcal{V}$-**CAT** —the dual of a $\mathcal{V}$-category, $\mathcal{V}$ itself as a $\mathcal{V}$-category, representable $\mathcal{V}$-functors, and the Yoneda lemma— is developed. With this done, adjunctions in $\mathcal{V}$-**CAT** are discussed.

Subsection 2.3.2 develops more of the basic structure of $\mathcal{V}$-**CAT** —tensor products of $\mathcal{V}$-categories and extraordinary $\mathcal{V}$-natural transformations— in order to present the closed structure of $\mathcal{V}$-**CAT**, given by $\mathcal{V}$-functor categories.

Subsection 2.3.3 considers limits for $\mathcal{V}$-categories in the case of cartesian closed $\mathcal{V}$. (The treatment offered here is far from been complete.)

2.3.1 The Elementary Notions

A *monoidal category* $\mathcal{V} = (\mathcal{V}_0, \otimes, I, l, r, a)$ consists of a category $\mathcal{V}_0$, a functor $\otimes : \mathcal{V}_0 \times \mathcal{V}_0 \to \mathcal{V}_0$, an object $I \in |\mathcal{V}_0|$, and natural isomorphisms $l_X : I \otimes X \to X$, $r_X : X \otimes I \to X$, $a_{X,Y,Z} : (X \otimes Y) \otimes Z \to X \otimes (Y \otimes Z)$ subject to two coherence axioms:

$$\begin{array}{ccccc} ((W \otimes X) \otimes Y) \otimes Z & \xrightarrow{a} & (W \otimes X) \otimes (Y \otimes Z) & \xrightarrow{a} & W \otimes (X \otimes (Y \otimes Z)) \\ {\scriptstyle a \otimes \mathrm{id}}\downarrow & & & & \downarrow{\scriptstyle \mathrm{id} \otimes a} \\ (W \otimes (X \otimes Y)) \otimes Z & & \xrightarrow[a]{\qquad\qquad} & & W \otimes ((X \otimes Y) \otimes Z) \end{array}$$

and

$$\begin{array}{ccc} (X \otimes I) \otimes Y & \xrightarrow{\;a\;} & X \otimes (I \otimes Y) \\ & {\scriptstyle r \otimes \mathrm{id}} \searrow \quad \swarrow {\scriptstyle \mathrm{id} \otimes l} & \\ & X \otimes Y & \end{array}$$

A special kind of example is given by taking for $\mathcal{V}_0$ any *cartesian category* (i.e., a category with finite products), for $\otimes$ and I the product $\times$ and the terminal object 1, and for a, l, r the canonical isomorphisms. Important cases of this are the categories **Set**, **Cat**, **Gpd**, **Poset**, **Cpo**, **Top** of small sets, categories, groupoids, posets, cpos and topological spaces; here "small" refers to a chosen universe, which we suppose given once for all. Other cartesian examples are obtained by taking for $\mathcal{V}_0$ a poset with finite meets, such as the ordinal $\mathbf{2} = (0 \to 1)$. All these examples are symmetric in the sense of page 26, and all the named ones except **Top** are closed in the sense of page 27.

A collection of non-cartesian (symmetric, closed) examples is given by the categories **Ab**, R-**Mod**, of small abelian groups, R-modules for a commutative ring R, each with its usual tensor product as $\otimes$; the ordered set $\overline{\mathbb{R}}_+$ of non-negative reals with $+\infty$, with the reverse of the usual order, and with $+$ as $\otimes$; and the category $\mathbf{Cppo}_\perp$ with the smash product for $\otimes$.

A non-symmetric example is the category of endofunctors of a small category, with composition as $\otimes$; here a, l, r are identities, so the monoidal category is called *strict*.

In general we call $\otimes$ the *tensor product* and I the *unit object.*

We suppose henceforth given a monoidal $\mathcal{V}$ such that $\mathcal{V}_0$ is locally small (has small hom-sets). We then have the representable functor $\mathcal{V}_0(I, \_) : \mathcal{V}_0 \to \mathbf{Set}$, denoted by V. In such cases as **Set**, **Poset**, **Cpo**, **Top**, it is the ordinary "underlying-set" functor; in these cases V is faithful, while in **Set** it is even conservative (i.e., isomorphism-reflecting). Yet V is not faithful in general; in the cases **Cat** and **Gpd**, $V\mathcal{X}$ is the set of objects of $\mathcal{X}$.

In spite of the failure of V to be faithful in general, it is convenient to call an element f of VX, i.e., a map $f : I \to X$ in $\mathcal{V}_0$, an element f of X.

A $\mathcal{V}$-category $\mathcal{A}$ consists of a set $|\,\mathcal{A}\,|$ of objects, a hom-object $\mathcal{A}(A, B) \in |\,\mathcal{V}_0\,|$ for each pair of objects of $\mathcal{A}$, a composition $M_{A,B,C} : \mathcal{A}(B, C) \otimes \mathcal{A}(A, B) \to \mathcal{A}(A, C)$ for each triple of objects, and an identity element $j_A : I \to \mathcal{A}(A, A)$ for each object; subject to the associativity and unit axioms expressed by

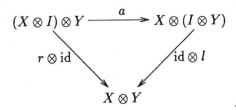

$$\begin{array}{ccc}
(\mathcal{A}(C,D)\otimes\mathcal{A}(B,C))\otimes\mathcal{A}(A,B) & \xrightarrow{\ a\ } & \mathcal{A}(C,D)\otimes(\mathcal{A}(B,C)\otimes\mathcal{A}(A,B))\\
{\scriptstyle M\otimes \mathrm{id}}\downarrow & & \downarrow{\scriptstyle \mathrm{id}\otimes M}\\
\mathcal{A}(B,D)\otimes\mathcal{A}(A,B) & & \mathcal{A}(C,D)\otimes\mathcal{A}(A,C)\\
& {\scriptstyle M}\searrow \qquad \swarrow{\scriptstyle M} & \\
& \mathcal{A}(A,D) &
\end{array}$$

and

$$\begin{array}{ccccc}
\mathcal{A}(B,B)\otimes\mathcal{A}(A,B) & \xrightarrow{\ M\ } & \mathcal{A}(A,B) & \xleftarrow{\ M\ } & \mathcal{A}(A,B)\otimes\mathcal{A}(A,A)\\
{\scriptstyle j\otimes \mathrm{id}}\uparrow & \nearrow{\scriptstyle l} & & \nwarrow{\scriptstyle r} & \uparrow{\scriptstyle \mathrm{id}\otimes j}\\
I\otimes\mathcal{A}(A,B) & & & & \mathcal{A}(A,B)\otimes I
\end{array}\quad .$$

Taking $\mathcal{V} = \mathbf{Set}, \mathbf{Cat}, \mathbf{2}, \overline{\mathbb{R}}_+$ we re-find the classical notions of locally small ordinary category, 2-category, preorder and generalised metric spaces. For a general reference on 2-categories, see [KS74]; and for the generalised metric spaces, see [Law73]. We call the $\mathcal{V}$-category $\mathcal{A}$ *small* if $\mid \mathcal{A} \mid$ is small.

For $\mathcal{V}$-categories $\mathcal{A}$ and $\mathcal{B}$, a $\mathcal{V}$*-functor* $F : \mathcal{A} \to \mathcal{B}$ consists of a function $F : \mid \mathcal{A} \mid \to \mid \mathcal{B} \mid$ together with, for each pair $A, B \in \mid \mathcal{A} \mid$ a map $F_{A,B} : \mathcal{A}(A,B) \to \mathcal{B}(FA, FB)$, subject to the preservation of composition and identities:

$$\begin{array}{ccc}
\mathcal{A}(B,C)\otimes\mathcal{A}(A,B) & \xrightarrow{\ M\ } & \mathcal{A}(A,C)\\
{\scriptstyle F\otimes F}\downarrow & & \downarrow{\scriptstyle F}\\
\mathcal{B}(FB,FC)\otimes\mathcal{B}(FA,FB) & \xrightarrow[\ M\ ]{} & \mathcal{B}(FA,FC)
\end{array}$$

and

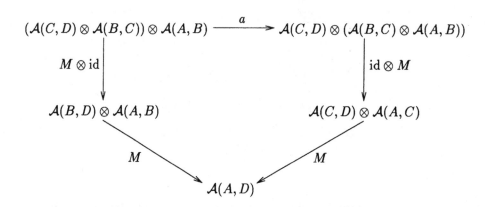

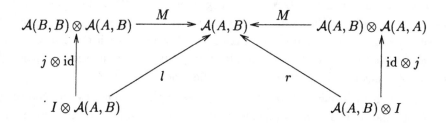

$$\begin{array}{ccc} & & \mathcal{A}(A,A) \\ & \overset{j}{\nearrow} & \\ I & & \Big\downarrow F \\ & \underset{j}{\searrow} & \\ & & \mathcal{B}(FA,FA) \end{array} \quad .$$

In the four examples above we re-find the classical notions of functor, 2-functor, increasing function, and contracting map.

For $\mathcal{V}$-functors $F, G : \mathcal{A} \to \mathcal{B}$, a *$\mathcal{V}$-natural transformation* $\alpha : F \dot{\to} G : \mathcal{A} \to \mathcal{B}$ is an $| \mathcal{A} |$-indexed family of components $\alpha_A : I \to \mathcal{B}(FA, GA)$ satisfying the $\mathcal{V}$-naturality condition expressed by

$$\begin{array}{ccccc} & I \otimes \mathcal{A}(A,B) & \xrightarrow{\alpha_B \otimes F} & \mathcal{B}(FB,GB) \otimes \mathcal{B}(FA,FB) & \\ {\scriptstyle l^{-1}} \nearrow & & & & \searrow {\scriptstyle M} \\ \mathcal{A}(A,B) & & & & \mathcal{B}(FA,GB) \\ {\scriptstyle r^{-1}} \searrow & & & & \nearrow {\scriptstyle M} \\ & \mathcal{A}(A,B) \otimes I & \xrightarrow[G \otimes \alpha_A]{} & \mathcal{B}(GA,GB) \otimes \mathcal{B}(FA,GA) & \end{array} \quad .$$

The "vertical composite" $\beta \circ \alpha$ of $\alpha : F \dot{\to} G : \mathcal{A} \to \mathcal{B}$ and $\beta : G \dot{\to} H : \mathcal{A} \to \mathcal{B}$ has the component $(\beta \circ \alpha)_A$ given by

$$I \cong I \otimes I \overset{\beta_A \otimes \alpha_A}{\longrightarrow} \mathcal{B}(GA, HA) \otimes \mathcal{B}(FA, GA) \overset{M}{\longrightarrow} \mathcal{B}(FA, HA).$$

The composite of α above with $U : \mathcal{B} \to \mathcal{C}$ has for its component $(U\alpha)_A$ the composite

$$I \overset{\alpha_A}{\longrightarrow} \mathcal{B}(FA, GA) \overset{U}{\longrightarrow} \mathcal{C}(UFA, UGA)$$

while the composite of α with $T : \mathcal{C} \to \mathcal{A}$ has for its component $(\alpha T)_C$ simply α_{TC}.

It is easy to verify that $\mathcal{V}$-categories, $\mathcal{V}$-functors, and $\mathcal{V}$-natural transformations constitute a 2-category $\mathcal{V}$-**CAT**; which may not be locally small unless some restriction is placed on the size, as in the 2-category $\mathcal{V}$-**Cat** of *small* $\mathcal{V}$-categories. When $\mathcal{V} =$ **Set**, $\mathcal{V}$-**CAT** reduces to the 2-category **CAT** of *locally small* ordinary categories.

Convention. Since a $\mathcal{V}$-category $\mathcal{A}$ has no "morphisms", we harmlessly call a map $A \to B$ in $\mathcal{A}_0$, which is an element of $\mathcal{A}(A, B)$, "a map $A \to B$ in $\mathcal{A}$".

To speak of a $\mathcal{V}$-functor $F : \mathcal{A} \to \mathcal{B}$ carries the implication that $\mathcal{A}$ and $\mathcal{B}$ are $\mathcal{V}$-categories. Similarly, to speak of a $\mathcal{V}$-natural transformation $\alpha : F \dot{\to} G$ presupposes that F and G are $\mathcal{V}$-functors.

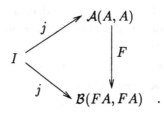

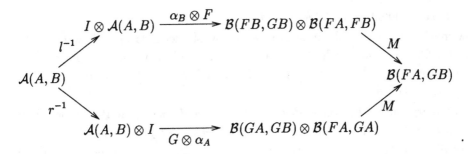

Denoting by $\mathcal{I}$ the *unit $\mathcal{V}$-category* with one object 0 and with $\mathcal{I}(0,0) = I$, we write $(\_)_0 : \mathcal{V}\text{-}\mathbf{CAT} \to \mathbf{CAT}$ for the representable 2-functor $\mathcal{V}\text{-}\mathbf{CAT}(I, \_)$; which we now describe in more elementary terms.

A $\mathcal{V}$-functor $A : \mathcal{I} \to \mathcal{A}$ may be identified with an object A of the $\mathcal{V}$-category $\mathcal{A}$; and a $\mathcal{V}$-natural $f : A \dot{\to} B : \mathcal{I} \to \mathcal{A}$ consists of a single component $f : I \to \mathcal{A}(A, B)$. Thus the ordinary category $\mathcal{A}_0$, which is called the *underlying category* of $\mathcal{A}$, has the same objects as $\mathcal{A}$, while a map $f : A \to B$ in $\mathcal{A}_0$ is just an element $f : I \to \mathcal{A}(A, B)$ of $\mathcal{A}(A, B)$. Otherwise put, $\mathcal{A}_0(A, B) = V\mathcal{A}(A, B)$. The composite $g \circ f$ in $\mathcal{A}_0$ is given by the composite

$$I \cong I \otimes I \xrightarrow{g \otimes f} \mathcal{A}(B, C) \otimes \mathcal{A}(A, B) \xrightarrow{M} \mathcal{A}(A, C)$$

in $\mathcal{V}_0$, whilst the identity in $\mathcal{A}_0(A, A)$ is j_A.

How much information about $\mathcal{A}$ is retained by $\mathcal{A}_0$ depends upon how faithful V is. When $\mathcal{V} = \mathbf{Cat}$, V is not faithful; $\mathcal{A}$ is a 2-category, and $\mathcal{A}_0$ is the category obtained by discarding the 2-cells. When $\mathcal{V} = \mathbf{Cpo}$, V is faithful, and $\mathcal{A}_0$ has lost only the order on the hom-objects of $\mathcal{A}$.

The ordinary functor $F_0 : \mathcal{A}_0 \to \mathcal{B}_0$ induced by (or *underlying*) the $\mathcal{V}$-functor $F : \mathcal{A} \to \mathcal{B}$ sends $A : \mathcal{I} \to \mathcal{A}$ to FA and sends $f : A \dot{\to} B : \mathcal{I} \to \mathcal{A}$ to Ff.

The ordinary natural transformation $\alpha_0 : F_0 \dot{\to} G_0 : \mathcal{A}_0 \to \mathcal{B}_0$ induced by the $\mathcal{V}$-natural $\alpha : F \dot{\to} G : \mathcal{A} \to \mathcal{B}$ has for its A-component $\alpha_{0A} \in \mathcal{B}_0(FA, GA)$ the A-component $\alpha_A : I \to \mathcal{B}(FA, GA)$ of α; so that it is not necessary to distinguish α from α_0. The $\mathcal{V}$-naturality condition for $\alpha : F \dot{\to} G$ becomes the usual naturality condition for $\alpha : F \dot{\to} G$ when V is applied to it. Hence the naturality of $\alpha : F_0 \dot{\to} G_0$, while weaker in general than the $\mathcal{V}$-naturality of $\alpha : F \dot{\to} G$, is equivalent to it when V is faithful.

A *symmetry* for a monoidal category $\mathcal{V}$ is a natural isomorphism $c_{X,Y} : X \otimes Y \to Y \otimes X$ satisfying the *coherence axioms*

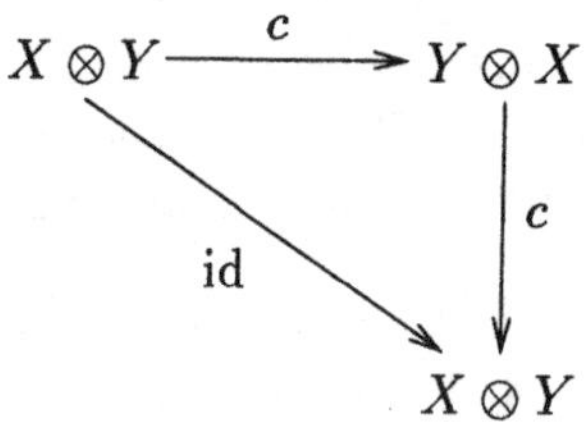

and

$$\begin{array}{ccccc}
(X \otimes Y) \otimes Z & \xrightarrow{a} & X \otimes (Y \otimes Z) & \xrightarrow{c} & (Y \otimes Z) \otimes X \\
\Big\downarrow{\scriptstyle c \otimes \mathrm{id}} & & & & \Big\downarrow{\scriptstyle a} \\
(Y \otimes X) \otimes Z & \xrightarrow[a]{} & Y \otimes (X \otimes Z) & \xrightarrow[\mathrm{id} \otimes c]{} & Y \otimes (Z \otimes X)
\end{array} .$$

A monoidal category $\mathcal{V}$ together with a symmetry is called a *symmetric monoidal category.* We now suppose $\mathcal{V}$ to be such.

To each $\mathcal{V}$-category $\mathcal{A}$ we can associate a *dual*, or *opposite*, $\mathcal{V}$-category $\mathcal{A}^{op}$, with the same objects as $\mathcal{A}$, but with $\mathcal{A}^{op}(A, B) = \mathcal{A}(B, A)$. The composition

$$M : \mathcal{A}^{op}(B, C) \otimes \mathcal{A}^{op}(A, B) \to \mathcal{A}^{op}(A, C)$$

is just the composite

$$\mathcal{A}(C, B) \otimes \mathcal{A}(B, A) \xrightarrow{c} \mathcal{A}(B, A) \otimes \mathcal{A}(C, B) \xrightarrow{M} \mathcal{A}(C, A)$$

whilst the unit element $I \to \mathcal{A}^{op}(A, A)$ is that of $\mathcal{A}$. A functor $\mathcal{A}^{op} \to \mathcal{B}$ may be called a *contravariant* functor from $\mathcal{A}$ to $\mathcal{B}$. From $\alpha : F \stackrel{.}{\to} G : \mathcal{A} \to \mathcal{B}$ we get, with evident definitions, $\alpha^{op} : F^{op} \stackrel{.}{\to} G^{op} : \mathcal{A}^{op} \to \mathcal{B}^{op}$; note that $(\_)^{op}$ reverses 2-cells but not 1-cells. Of course $(\_)^{op}$ is an involution: $(\_^{op})^{op} = \mathrm{Id}$.

The monoidal category $\mathcal{V}$ (symmetric or not) is *closed* (*cartesian closed*, when $\mathcal{V}$ is cartesian) if each functor $\_ \otimes Y : \mathcal{V}_0 \to \mathcal{V}_0$ has a right adjoint $[Y, \_]$; so that we have an adjunction

$$\lambda : \ \mathcal{V}_0(X \otimes Y, Z) \ \cong \ \mathcal{V}_0(X, [Y, Z]) \tag{2.1}$$

with counit (called *evaluation*)

$$\varepsilon : [Y, Z] \otimes Y \to Z.$$

Putting $X = I$ in (2.1), using the isomorphism $l : I \otimes Y \cong Y$, and recalling that $V = \mathcal{V}_0(I, \_) : \mathcal{V}_0 \to \mathbf{Set}$, we get a natural isomorphism

$$\mathcal{V}_0(Y, Z) \ \cong \ V[Y, Z]. \tag{2.2}$$

Since $[Y, Z]$ is thus exhibited as a lifting through V of the hom-set $\mathcal{V}_0(Y, Z)$, it is called the *internal hom* of Y and Z.

From now on we suppose that our given $\mathcal{V}$ is symmetric monoidal closed, with $\mathcal{V}_0$ locally small.

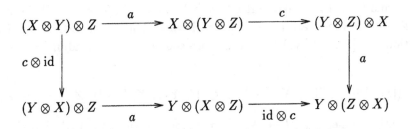

The internal-hom of $\mathcal{V}$ "makes $\mathcal{V}$ itself into a $\mathcal{V}$-category". There is a $\mathcal{V}$-category, which we call $\mathcal{V}$, whose objects are those of $\mathcal{V}_0$, and whose hom-object $\mathcal{V}(X,Y)$ is $[X,Y]$. Its composition $M : [Y,Z] \otimes [X,Y] \to [X,Z]$ corresponds under the adjunction (2.1) to the composite

$$([Y,Z] \otimes [X,Y]) \otimes X \xrightarrow{a} [Y,Z] \otimes ([X,Y] \otimes X) \xrightarrow{\mathrm{id} \otimes \varepsilon} [Y,Z] \otimes Y \xrightarrow{\varepsilon} Z$$

and its identity element $j_X : I \to [X,X]$ corresponds under (2.1) to $l : I \otimes X \to X$. It is easily verified that (2.2) gives an isomorphism between $\mathcal{V}_0$ and the underlying ordinary category of the $\mathcal{V}$-category $\mathcal{V}$; we henceforth identify these two ordinary categories by this isomorphism thus rendering the notation $\mathcal{V}_0$ consistent with the notation $\mathcal{A}_0$.

Next we observe that, for each $\mathcal{V}$-category $\mathcal{A}$ and each object $A \in |\mathcal{A}|$, we have the *representable* $\mathcal{V}$-functor $\mathcal{A}(A,\_) : \mathcal{A} \to \mathcal{V}$, sending $B \in |\mathcal{A}|$ to $\mathcal{A}(A,B) \in |\mathcal{V}|$, and with

$$\mathcal{A}(A,\_)_{B,C} : \mathcal{A}(B,C) \to [\mathcal{A}(A,B), \mathcal{A}(A,C)]$$

corresponding under the adjunction (2.1) to $M : \mathcal{A}(B,C) \otimes \mathcal{A}(A,C) \to \mathcal{A}(A,C)$. Replacing $\mathcal{A}$ by $\mathcal{A}^{op}$ gives the *contravariant representable* $\mathcal{V}$-functor $\mathcal{A}(\_,B) : \mathcal{A}^{op} \to \mathcal{V}$.

The form of the Yoneda Lemma we give here is a weak one, in that it asserts a bijection of sets rather than an isomorphism of objects of $\mathcal{V}$.

Consider a $\mathcal{V}$-functor $F : \mathcal{A} \to \mathcal{V}$ and an object A of $\mathcal{A}$. To each $\mathcal{V}$-natural transformation $\alpha : \mathcal{A}(A,\_) \dot{\to} F$ we can assign the element $a : I \to FA$ of FA given by the composite

$$I \xrightarrow{j_A} \mathcal{A}(A,A) \xrightarrow{\alpha_A} FA.$$

The Yoneda Lemma asserts that this gives a bijection between the set $\mathcal{V}\text{-Nat}(\mathcal{A}(A,\_),F)$ of $\mathcal{V}$-natural transformations and the set $\mathcal{V}_0(I,FA)$ $(= VFA)$ of elements of FA; the component α_X being given in terms of a as the composite

$$\mathcal{A}(A,X) \xrightarrow{F_{A,X}} [FA,FX] \xrightarrow{[a,\mathrm{id}]} [I,FX] \xrightarrow{\lambda(r)^{-1}} FX. \tag{2.3}$$

It is worth noting an alternative way of writing (2.3) when F has the form $\mathcal{B}(B,U\_)$ for a $\mathcal{V}$-functor $U : \mathcal{A} \to \mathcal{B}$, so that $a : I \to \mathcal{B}(B,UA)$ is then a map $a : B \to UA$ in $\mathcal{B}_0$ (in fact, the image of id_A under $V\alpha_A : \mathcal{A}_0(A,A) \to \mathcal{B}_0(B,UA)$). Then α_X is the composite

$$\mathcal{A}(A,X) \xrightarrow{U_{A,X}} \mathcal{B}(UA,UX) \xrightarrow{\mathcal{B}(a,\mathrm{id})} \mathcal{B}(B,UX). \tag{2.4}$$

In particular, every $\mathcal{V}$-natural $\alpha : \mathcal{A}(A,\_) \to \mathcal{A}(X,\_)$ is $\mathcal{A}(f,\_)$ for a unique $f : X \to A$; and clearly f is an isomorphism if and only if α is.

As in any 2-category (see [KS74]) an adjunction $\eta, \varepsilon : F \dashv U : \mathcal{A} \to \mathcal{B}$ in $\mathcal{V}$-**CAT** between $U : \mathcal{A} \to \mathcal{B}$ (the right adjoint) and $F : \mathcal{B} \to \mathcal{A}$ (the left adjoint) consists of

$\eta : \mathrm{Id} \dot{\to} UF$ (the unit) and $\varepsilon : FU \dot{\to} \mathrm{Id}$ (the counit) satisfying the triangular equations $U\varepsilon \circ \eta U = \mathrm{id}$ and $\varepsilon F \circ F\eta = \mathrm{id}$. By the Yoneda Lemma, such adjunctions in $\mathcal{V}$-**CAT** are in bijection with $\mathcal{V}$-natural isomorphisms

$$\chi : \ \mathcal{A}(FB, A) \ \cong \ \mathcal{B}(B, UA)$$

for by (2.4) a $\mathcal{V}$-natural map $\chi : \mathcal{A}(FB, A) \to \mathcal{B}(B, UA)$ has the form $\chi = \mathcal{B}(\eta, \mathrm{id})U$ for a unique η, while a $\mathcal{V}$-natural map $\chi' : \mathcal{B}(B, UA) \to \mathcal{A}(FB, A)$ has the form $\chi' = \mathcal{A}(\mathrm{id}, \varepsilon)F$ for a unique ε, and the equations $\chi' \circ \chi = \mathrm{id}$ and $\chi \circ \chi' = \mathrm{id}$ reduce by Yoneda to the triangular equations. The 2-functor $(\_)_0 : \mathcal{V}\text{-}\mathbf{CAT} \to \mathbf{CAT}$ carries such an adjunction into an ordinary adjunction $\eta, \varepsilon : F_0 \dashv U_0 : \mathcal{A}_0 \to \mathcal{B}_0$ in **CAT**. The corresponding isomorphism of hom-sets is

$$V\chi : \ \mathcal{A}_0(FB, A) \ \cong \ \mathcal{B}_0(B, UA).$$

The unit and counit of this ordinary adjunction are the same η and ε, now seen as natural rather than $\mathcal{V}$-natural.

2.3.2 Functor Categories

Suppose that $\mathcal{V}$ is symmetric monoidal closed and that the underlying ordinary category $\mathcal{V}_0$ is locally small. Then to each pair $\mathcal{A}, \mathcal{B}$ of $\mathcal{V}$-categories we can associate a *tensor product* $\mathcal{A} \otimes \mathcal{B}$, with object-set $\mid \mathcal{A} \mid \times \mid \mathcal{B} \mid$, and with

$$(\mathcal{A} \otimes \mathcal{B})((A, B), (A', B')) \ = \ \mathcal{A}(A, A') \otimes \mathcal{B}(B, B').$$

The composition is given by

$$\begin{array}{ccc}
(\mathcal{A}(A', A'') \otimes \mathcal{B}(B', B'')) \otimes (\mathcal{A}(A, A') \otimes \mathcal{B}(B, B')) & \xrightarrow{\ M\ } & \mathcal{A}(A, A'') \otimes \mathcal{B}(B, B'') \\
\Big\downarrow m & & \Big\uparrow M \otimes M \\
 & (\mathcal{A}(A', A'') \otimes \mathcal{A}(A, A')) \otimes (\mathcal{B}(B', B'') \otimes \mathcal{B}(B, B')) &
\end{array}$$

where $m : (W \otimes X) \otimes (Y \otimes Z) \cong (W \otimes Y) \otimes (X \otimes Z)$ is the *middle-four interchange* defined by any suitable composite of instances of a and c. The identity element is the composite

$$I \cong I \otimes I \xrightarrow{j_A \otimes j_B} \mathcal{A}(A, A) \otimes \mathcal{B}(B, B).$$

With the obvious definitions of $F \otimes G : \mathcal{A} \otimes \mathcal{B} \to \mathcal{A}' \otimes \mathcal{B}'$ and of $\alpha \otimes \beta : F \otimes G \to F' \otimes G'$, we have a 2-functor $\otimes : \mathcal{V}\text{-}\mathbf{CAT} \times \mathcal{V}\text{-}\mathbf{CAT} \to \mathcal{V}\text{-}\mathbf{CAT}$; and we have coherent 2-natural isomorphisms $(\mathcal{A} \otimes \mathcal{B}) \otimes \mathcal{C} \cong \mathcal{A} \otimes (\mathcal{B} \otimes \mathcal{C})$, $\mathcal{I} \otimes \mathcal{A} \cong \mathcal{A} \cong \mathcal{A} \otimes \mathcal{I}$, and $\mathcal{A} \otimes \mathcal{B} \cong \mathcal{B} \otimes \mathcal{A}$ (where $\mathcal{I}$ is the unit $\mathcal{V}$-category). Thus $\mathcal{V}$-**CAT** is a *symmetric monoidal 2-category.*

A functor $T : \mathcal{A} \otimes \mathcal{B} \to \mathcal{C}$ may be thought of as a *functor of two variables*. Such a T gives rise to functors $T(A, \_) : \mathcal{B} \to \mathcal{C}$ for each $A \in |\mathcal{A}|$ and $T(\_, B) : \mathcal{A} \to \mathcal{C}$ for each $B \in |\mathcal{B}|$. Here $T(A, \_)$ is the composite

$$\mathcal{B} \cong \mathcal{I} \otimes \mathcal{B} \xrightarrow{A \otimes \mathrm{Id}} \mathcal{A} \otimes \mathcal{B} \xrightarrow{T} \mathcal{C}$$

from which can be read off the value $T(A, \_)_{B,B'}$.

By *(extraordinary)* $\mathcal{V}$*-naturality* for an $|\mathcal{A}|$-indexed family of maps $\varepsilon_A : Z \to T(A, A)$ in $\mathcal{B}_0$, where $Z \in |\mathcal{B}|$ and $T : \mathcal{A}^{op} \otimes \mathcal{A} \to \mathcal{B}$, we mean the commutativity of each diagram

$$\begin{array}{ccc} \mathcal{A}(A,B) & \xrightarrow{T(A,\_)} & \mathcal{B}(T(A,A),T(A,B)) \\ {\scriptstyle T(\_,B)}\downarrow & & \downarrow{\scriptstyle \mathcal{B}(\varepsilon_A,\mathrm{id})} \\ \mathcal{B}(T(B,B),T(A,B)) & \xrightarrow[\mathcal{B}(\varepsilon_B,\mathrm{id})]{} & \mathcal{B}(Z,T(A,B)) \end{array} \tag{2.5}$$

.

Henceforth we add the further assumption that $\mathcal{V}_0$ is *complete*, in the sense that it admits all small limits.

Consider a $\mathcal{V}$-functor $T : \mathcal{A}^{op} \otimes \mathcal{A} \to \mathcal{V}$. If there exists a *universal* $\mathcal{V}$-natural family $\varepsilon_A : Z \to T(A, A)$, in the sense that every $\mathcal{V}$-natural $\gamma_A : C \to T(A, A)$ is given by $\gamma_A = \varepsilon_A \circ h$ for a unique $h : C \to Z$, we call (Z, ε) the *end* of T; clearly, when it exists, it is unique up to isomorphism. We write $\int_{X \in |\mathcal{A}|} T(X, X)$ for the object Z, and by the usual abuse of language also call this *object* the end of T: then the universal $\mathcal{V}$-natural $\varepsilon_A : \int_X T(X, X) \to T(A, A)$ may be called the *counit* of this end.

The $\mathcal{V}$-naturality condition (2.5), in the case $\mathcal{B} = \mathcal{V}$, transforms under the adjunction $\mathcal{V}_0(W, [X, Y]) \cong \mathcal{V}_0(W \otimes X, Y) \cong \mathcal{V}_0(X, [W, Y])$ into

$$\begin{array}{ccc} Z & \xrightarrow{\varepsilon_A} & T(A,A) \\ {\scriptstyle \varepsilon_B}\downarrow & & \downarrow{\scriptstyle \alpha_{A,B}} \\ T(B,B) & \xrightarrow[\beta_{A,B}]{} & [\mathcal{A}(A,B),T(A,B)] \end{array}$$

where $\alpha_{A,B}$ and $\beta_{A,B}$ are the transforms of $T(A, \_)_{A,B}$ and $T(\_, B)_{B,A}$. When $\mathcal{A}$ is small, the end $\int_{A \in |\mathcal{A}|} T(A, A)$ exists, and is given as the equaliser

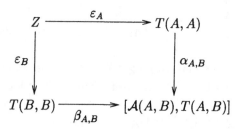

$$\textstyle\int_{A\in|\mathcal{A}|} T(A,A) \xrightarrow{\ \lambda\ } \prod_{A\in|\mathcal{A}|} T(A,A) \underset{\beta}{\overset{\alpha}{\rightrightarrows}} \prod_{A,B\in|\mathcal{A}|} [\mathcal{A}(A,B), T(A,B)].$$

For $\mathcal{V}$-functors $F, G : \mathcal{A} \to \mathcal{B}$ we introduce the notation

$$[\mathcal{A},\mathcal{B}](F,G) \;=\; \int_A \mathcal{B}(FA,GA)$$

for the end on the right, whenever it exists; and we write the counit as

$$\varepsilon_A = \varepsilon_A^{F,G} : \; [\mathcal{A},\mathcal{B}](F,G) \;\to\; \mathcal{B}(FA,GA).$$

We write $[\mathcal{A},\mathcal{B}]_0(F,G)$ for the set $V[\mathcal{A},\mathcal{B}](F,G)$ of *elements* $\alpha : I \to [\mathcal{A},\mathcal{B}](F,G)$ of this end. These correspond to $\mathcal{V}$-natural families

$$\alpha_A = \varepsilon_A \circ \alpha : \; I \;\to\; \mathcal{B}(FA,GA)$$

which are precisely the $\mathcal{V}$-natural transformations $\alpha : F \dot{\to} G : \mathcal{A} \to \mathcal{B}$.

When $[\mathcal{A},\mathcal{B}](F,G)$ exists for all $F, G : \mathcal{A} \to \mathcal{B}$, as it does if $\mathcal{A}$ is small, it is the hom-object of a $\mathcal{V}$-category $[\mathcal{A},\mathcal{B}]$ with all the $F : \mathcal{A} \to \mathcal{B}$ as objects. The composition of $[\mathcal{A},\mathcal{B}]$ is uniquely determined by the commutativity of

$$\begin{array}{ccc}
[\mathcal{A},\mathcal{B}](G,H) \otimes [\mathcal{A},\mathcal{B}](F,G) & \xrightarrow{\quad M \quad} & [\mathcal{A},\mathcal{B}](F,H) \\
{\scriptstyle \varepsilon_A \otimes \varepsilon_A}\downarrow & & \downarrow{\scriptstyle \varepsilon_A} \\
\mathcal{B}(GA,HA) \otimes \mathcal{B}(FA,GA) & \xrightarrow[\quad M \quad]{} & \mathcal{B}(FA,HA)
\end{array}$$

and its identity elements are similarly determined by $\varepsilon_A \circ j_F = j_{FA}$.

We call $[\mathcal{A},\mathcal{B}]$, when it exists, the *functor category*; its underlying category $[\mathcal{A},\mathcal{B}]_0$ is the ordinary category of all $\mathcal{V}$-functors $\mathcal{A} \to \mathcal{B}$ and all $\mathcal{V}$-natural transformations between them —that is,

$$[\mathcal{A},\mathcal{B}]_0 = \mathcal{V}\text{-}\mathbf{CAT}(\mathcal{A},\mathcal{B}).$$

There is a $\mathcal{V}$-functor $E : [\mathcal{A},\mathcal{B}] \otimes \mathcal{A} \to \mathcal{B}$, called *evaluation*, sending (F,A) to FA and with $E_{(F,A),(G,B)}$ as the composite

$$[\mathcal{A},\mathcal{B}](F,G) \otimes \mathcal{A}(A,B) \xrightarrow{\varepsilon_B \otimes F} \mathcal{B}(FB,GB) \otimes \mathcal{B}(FA,FB) \xrightarrow{M} \mathcal{B}(FA,GA);$$

which induces, for each $\mathcal{V}$-category $\mathcal{C}$, an ordinary functor

$$\mathcal{V}\text{-}\mathbf{CAT}(\mathcal{C},[\mathcal{A},\mathcal{B}]) \longrightarrow \mathcal{V}\text{-}\mathbf{CAT}(\mathcal{C}\otimes\mathcal{A},\mathcal{B}) \tag{2.6}$$

sending $F:\mathcal{C}\to[\mathcal{A},\mathcal{B}]$ to the composite

$$\mathcal{C}\otimes\mathcal{A}\xrightarrow{F\otimes\mathrm{Id}}[\mathcal{A},\mathcal{B}]\otimes\mathcal{A}\xrightarrow{E}\mathcal{B}$$

and sending $\alpha : F \overset{\cdot}{\to} G : \mathcal{C}\to[\mathcal{A},\mathcal{B}]$ to the composite $E(\alpha\otimes\mathrm{id})$. *The map (2.6) is 2-natural in $\mathcal{C}$; and in fact is an isomorphism of categories.*

We have called the $\mathcal{V}$-functors $\mathcal{A}(A,\_) : \mathcal{A}\to\mathcal{V}$ *representable*. More generally, a $\mathcal{V}$-functor $F:\mathcal{A}\to\mathcal{V}$ is called representable if there is some $A\in|\mathcal{A}|$ and an *isomorphism* $\alpha:\mathcal{A}(A,\_)\overset{\cdot}{\to}F$. Then the pair (A,α) is a *representation* of F; it is essentially unique if it exists, in the sense that any other representation $\beta:\mathcal{A}(B,\_)\overset{\cdot}{\to}F$ has the form $\beta=\alpha\circ\mathcal{A}(f,\_)$ for a unique isomorphism $f:A\to B$. The corresponding $a:I\to FA$ is called the *unit* of the representation. (We call a the counit when we are representing a contravariant $F:\mathcal{A}^{op}\to\mathcal{V}$ in the form $\mathcal{A}(\_,A)$).

Now let $F:\mathcal{B}^{op}\otimes\mathcal{A}\to\mathcal{V}$ be such that each $F(B,\_):\mathcal{A}\to\mathcal{V}$ admits a representation $\alpha_B:\mathcal{A}(RB,\_)\overset{\cdot}{\to}F(B,\_)$. Then there is *exactly one way of defining a map $R_{B,C}:\mathcal{B}(B,C)\to\mathcal{A}(RB,RC)$ that makes R a $\mathcal{V}$-functor for which the isomorphism $\alpha_{BA}:\mathcal{A}(RB,A)\to F(B,A)$ is $\mathcal{V}$-natural in B as well as A.*

It follows that, if it exists, $[\mathcal{A},\mathcal{B}]$ is uniquely 2-functorial in $\mathcal{A}$ and $\mathcal{B}$ in such a way that (2.6) is 2-natural in every variable. For $F:\mathcal{A}'\to\mathcal{A}$ and $G:\mathcal{B}\to\mathcal{B}'$, the $\mathcal{V}$-functor $[F,G]:[\mathcal{A},\mathcal{B}]\to[\mathcal{A}',\mathcal{B}']$ sends T to GTF and is determined on hom-objects by

$$\begin{array}{ccc}
[\mathcal{A},\mathcal{B}](T,U) & \xrightarrow{[F,G]_{T,U}} & [\mathcal{A}',\mathcal{B}'](GTF,GUF) \\
\downarrow{\scriptstyle \varepsilon_{FA}} & & \downarrow{\scriptstyle \varepsilon'_A} \\
\mathcal{B}(TFA,UFA) & \xrightarrow[G_{TFA,UFA}]{} & \mathcal{B}'(GTFA,GUFA)
\end{array}$$

while the $\mathcal{V}$-natural transformation $[\alpha,\beta]:[F,G]\overset{\cdot}{\to}[F',G']$ is given by

$$[\alpha,\beta]_T=\beta T\alpha : GTF\to G'TF'.$$

The 2-natural isomorphism (2.6) exhibits $[\mathcal{A},\mathcal{B}]$, when it exists, as a representing object for the 2-functor $\mathcal{V}\text{-}\mathbf{CAT}(\_\otimes\mathcal{A},\mathcal{B})$. It is conversely true that, if this 2-functor is representable by some $\mathcal{D}$, then $[\mathcal{A},\mathcal{B}]$ exists and is isomorphic to $\mathcal{D}$ —at least if $\mathcal{V}_0$ has an initial object 0. For taking $\mathcal{C}$ to be $\mathcal{I}$ in (2.6), with $[\mathcal{A},\mathcal{B}]$ replaced by $\mathcal{D}$, we identify the objects of $\mathcal{D}$ with the $\mathcal{V}$-functors $\mathcal{A} \to \mathcal{B}$; while taking $\mathcal{C}$ to be the $\mathcal{V}$-category with two objects 0 and 1, with $\mathcal{C}(0,0) = \mathcal{C}(1,1) = I$, with $\mathcal{C}(1,0) = 0$, and with $\mathcal{C}(0,1)$ an arbitrary object X of $\mathcal{V}$, we easily see that $\mathcal{D}(F,G) = \int_A \mathcal{B}(FA, GA)$.

The 2-functor $\_ \otimes \mathcal{A} : \mathcal{V}\text{-}\mathbf{CAT} \to \mathcal{V}\text{-}\mathbf{CAT}$ has a right adjoint $[\mathcal{A}, \_]$ when $[\mathcal{A}, \mathcal{B}]$ exists for *all* $\mathcal{B}$; and by the above, only then, if $\mathcal{V}_0$ has an initial object. This right adjoint exists when $\mathcal{A}$ is small. In this sense the symmetric monoidal 2-category $\mathcal{V}$-**Cat** of *small* $\mathcal{V}$-categories is closed.

2.3.3 Limits

Suppose that $\mathcal{V}$ is *cartesian* closed and that $\mathcal{V}_0$ is locally small, complete and cocomplete.

Then, the ordinary functor $V = \mathcal{V}_0(I, \_) : \mathcal{V}_0 \to \mathbf{Set}$ has a left adjoint $(\_) \cdot I$, sending the set A to the coproduct $A \cdot I$ of A copies of I in $\mathcal{V}_0$. This functor sends the cartesian product in **Set** to the tensor product in $\mathcal{V}_0$, in that we have

$$(A \times B) \cdot I \cong (A \cdot I) \otimes (B \cdot I), \qquad 1 \cdot I \cong I. \tag{2.7}$$

The 2-functor $(\_)_0 : \mathcal{V}\text{-}\mathbf{CAT} \to \mathbf{CAT}$ now has a left adjoint $(\_)_{\mathcal{V}}$. The *free* $\mathcal{V}$*-category* $\mathcal{G}_{\mathcal{V}}$ on the ordinary locally-small category $\mathcal{G}$ has the same objects as $\mathcal{G}$, and has hom-objects $\mathcal{G}_{\mathcal{V}}(X,Y) = \mathcal{G}(X,Y) \cdot I$; its composition and its identities are induced from those of $\mathcal{G}$ using the isomorphisms (2.7).

It also happens that $I = 1$ in $\mathcal{V}_0$, so that the $\mathcal{V}$-categories $\mathcal{I}$ and $\mathbf{1}$ coincide; then, for every pair of $\mathcal{V}$-categories $\mathcal{A}$ and $\mathcal{B}$, there is, for any $A \in |\mathcal{A}|$, a "constant $\mathcal{V}$-functor" $KA : \mathcal{B} \to \mathbf{1} \to \mathcal{A}$ with this value.

For any ordinary category $\mathcal{G}$, we may think of a $\mathcal{V}$-functor $\Gamma : \mathcal{G}_{\mathcal{V}} \to \mathcal{A}$ as a diagram in $\mathcal{A}$ of type $\mathcal{G}$. For each $A \in |\mathcal{A}|$, we can consider the existence in $\mathcal{V}$ of the object $[\mathcal{G}_{\mathcal{V}}, \mathcal{A}](KA, \Gamma)$. If this exists for all A —as it does when $\mathcal{G}$ is small— it is the value of a $\mathcal{V}$-functor $\mathcal{A}^{op} \to \mathcal{V}$. If this $\mathcal{V}$-functor not only exists but admits a representation

$$\mathcal{A}(A, \lim \Gamma) \cong [\mathcal{G}_{\mathcal{V}}, \mathcal{A}](KA, \Gamma)$$

with counit

$$\pi_A : 1 \to \mathcal{A}(\lim \Gamma, \Gamma A)$$

we call the representation $(\lim \Gamma, \pi)$ the *limit of* Γ.

3 Partiality

Categorical structures suitable for describing partial maps, viz. *domain structures*, are introduced and their induced *categories of partial maps* are defined.

The representation of partial maps as total ones is addressed. In particular, the *representability* (in the categorical sense) and the *classifiability* (in the sense of topos theory) of partial maps are shown to be equivalent (Theorem 3.2.6).

Finally, two notions of approximation, *contextual approximation* and *specialisation*, based on testing and observing partial maps are considered and shown to coincide. It is observed that the approximation of partial maps is definable from testing for totality and the approximation of total maps; providing evidence for taking the approximation of total maps as primitive.

3.1 Categories of Partial Maps

To motivate the definition of a partial map, observe that a partial function $u : A \rightharpoonup B$ is determined by its domain of definition $\mathrm{dom}(u) \subseteq A$ and the total function $\mathrm{dom}(u) \to B$ induced by the mapping $a \mapsto u(a)$. Thus, every partial function $A \rightharpoonup B$ can be described by a pair consisting of an injection $D \rightarrowtail A$ and a total function $D \to B$ with the same source. These *descriptions* are not unique, for (m, f) and (n, g) describe the same partial function if and only if

$$m = n \circ i \text{ and } f = g \circ i, \text{ for some isomorphism } i. \tag{3.1}$$

Following the above reformulation, given a category whose morphisms are to be thought of as total maps, a pair $(m : D \rightarrowtail A, f : D \to B)$ will be a description of a partial map $[m, f] : A \rightharpoonup B$; and conversely, every partial map $A \rightharpoonup B$ will be described by some pair $(D \rightarrowtail A, D \to B)$. Formally, the descriptions (m, f) and (n, g) are regarded as equivalent whenever (3.1) holds; and a partial map is defined to be an equivalence class of descriptions.

When working with partial maps it is usual just to deal with their descriptions and observe that the arguments or constructions involved are independent of the chosen descriptions. For example, in a category with enough pullbacks, the composition of the partial map $v = [n, g] : B \rightharpoonup C$ with the partial map $u = [m, f] : A \rightharpoonup B$ is defined to be the partial map $v \circ u = [m \circ f^{-1}(n), g \circ (n^*f)] : A \rightharpoonup C$ where

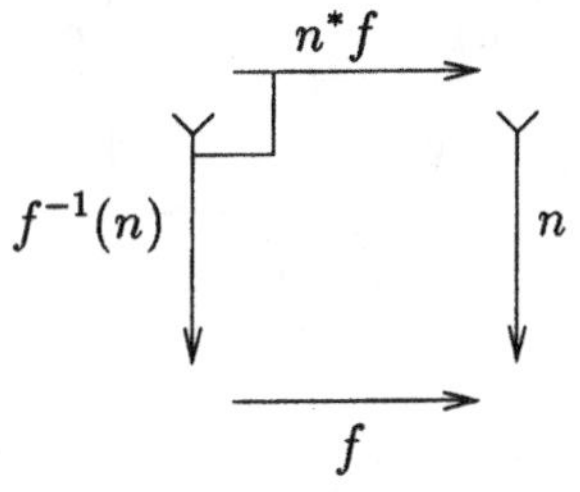

(3.2)

is a pullback.

The suspicious reader should check that the above definition is independent of any choice of descriptions for the partial maps, as well as for the required pullback. It is also easy to see that composition is associative, and that the partial map [id, id] is a unit for it. Before defining categories of partial maps it will be necessary to refine the notion of partial map as the following examples show.

Let **pPoset** be the category whose objects are small posets and whose morphisms $u : P \rightharpoonup Q$ are *partial monotone* functions, in the sense that, for every $x, x' \in P$,

$$\text{if } x \sqsubseteq x' \text{ then } u(x) \mathrel{\underset{\sim}{\sqsubset}} u(x') \tag{3.3}$$

where, for two mathematical expressions e and e', we write $e \mathrel{\underset{\sim}{\sqsubset}} e'$ to mean that if e denotes some y in Q then e' denotes some y' in Q and $y \sqsubseteq y'$. We further write $e \simeq e'$ whenever both $e \mathrel{\underset{\sim}{\sqsubset}} e'$ and $e' \mathrel{\underset{\sim}{\sqsubset}} e$. Further let **pCpo** be the subcategory of **pPoset** whose objects are cpos and whose morphisms $u : P \rightharpoonup Q$ are *partial continuous* functions, in the sense that, for every ω-chain x in P,

$$\bigsqcup_{k \in |\omega|} u(x_k) \;\simeq\; u(\bigsqcup_{k \in |\omega|} x_k) \tag{3.4}$$

where the expression on the left is intended to be undefined if every $u(x_k)$ is; or, otherwise, denote $\bigsqcup_{k \geq k_0} u(x_k)$ where k_0 is any index for which $u(x_{k_0})$ is defined. In these two categories, the domain of definition of a morphism $P \rightharpoonup Q$ cannot be *any* subobject of P: in **pPoset**, by (3.3), the only possible domains of definitions are the upper-closed subsets of P, whilst in **pCpo**, by (3.4), they are the Scott-open subsets of P.

To include such a possibility, descriptions of partial maps are to be pairs (m, f) where m is confined to a class of *admissible* monos. The category of total maps together with such a class constitute a *domain structure*.

Definition 3.1.1 ([Ros86,Mog86]) A *domain structure* is a pair $(\mathcal{K}, \mathcal{D})$ consisting of a well-powered category $\mathcal{D}$ and a category $\mathcal{K}$, such that $\mathcal{D}$ is a full-on-objects subcategory of $\mathcal{K}$ all of whose morphisms are monos in $\mathcal{K}$, with the following closure property: every diagram $\xrightarrow{f}\overset{n}{\leftarrowtail}$ with $f \in \mathcal{K}$ and $n \in \mathcal{D}$ has a pullback in $\mathcal{K}$ and whenever

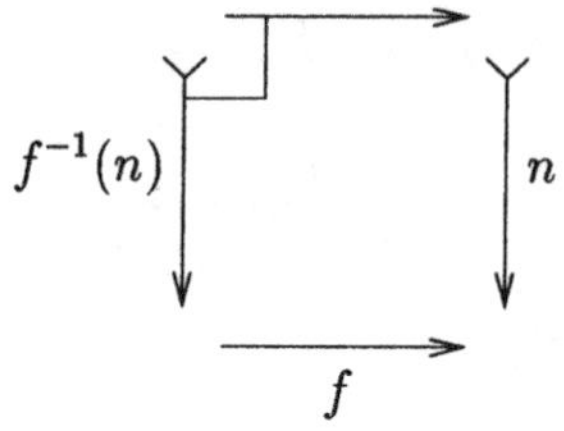

is a pullback then $f^{-1}(n) \in \mathcal{D}$. □

Convention. $\mathcal{K}$ is called the *category of total maps* and $\mathcal{D}$ is called the category of *admissible* monos. For every $A \in |\mathcal{D}|$, we write $\mathcal{D}(A)$ for the representative small set of subobjects of A in $\mathcal{D}$ guaranteed by well-powerness.

Categories of admissible monos are closed under isomorphisms, for every isomorphism i appears in the pullback

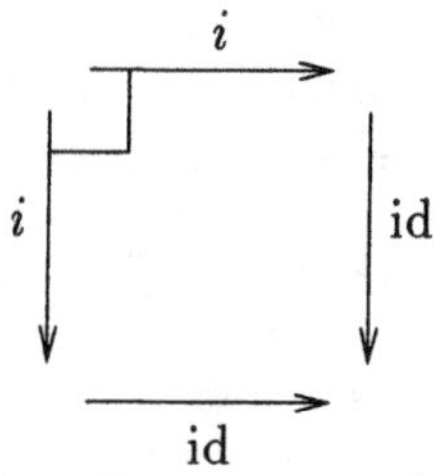

For monos m and n, we write $[m] \subseteq_i [n]$ ($m \subseteq_i n$) and say that i realises the inequality $[m] \subseteq [n]$ ($m \subseteq n$) whenever $m = n \circ i$. Realisers of inequalities between admissible subobjects are admissible, for consider the equivalence:

$[m] \subseteq_i [n] \iff$

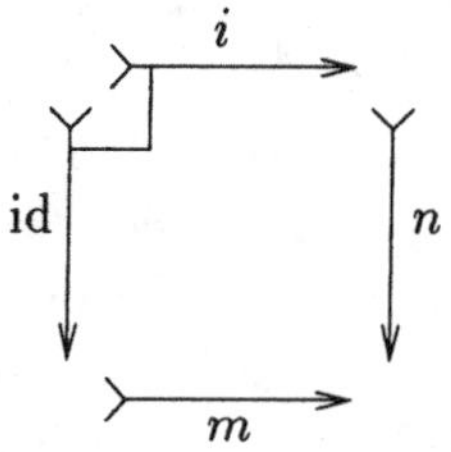

Convention. For a category $\mathcal{X}$ and a set $O \subseteq |\mathcal{X}|$, the full subcategory of $\mathcal{X}$ with set of objects O is denoted as $\mathcal{X} \restriction O$.

It is time for some examples. Every well-powered category $\mathcal{K}$ appears in two domain structures: a minimal one, $(\mathcal{K}, \mathbf{Isos}_{\mathcal{K}})$ where $\mathbf{Isos}_{\mathcal{K}}$ is the category of all isomorphisms in $\mathcal{K}$; and a maximal one, $(\mathcal{K}, \mathbf{Monos}_{\mathcal{K}})$ where $\mathbf{Monos}_{\mathcal{K}}$ is the category of all monomorphisms in $\mathcal{K}$.

To obtain further examples, we show how to construct new domain structures from old ones. Let $(\mathcal{K}, \mathcal{D})$ be a domain structure and let $\mathcal{L}$ be a full subcategory of $\mathcal{K}$ whose objects are closed under taking the source of admissible monos (i.e., for every $X \in |\mathcal{L}|$ and $D \in |\mathcal{D}|$, if $D \rightarrowtail X$ in $\mathcal{D}$ then $D \in |\mathcal{L}|$). Then $(\mathcal{L}, \mathcal{D} \restriction |\mathcal{L}|)$ is a domain structure. In particular, every domain structure $(\mathcal{K}, \mathcal{D})$ and set $O \subseteq |\mathcal{K}|$ induce the domain structure $(\mathcal{K} \restriction O', \mathcal{D} \restriction O')$ where $O' = \bigcup_{A \in O}\{D \mid D \rightarrowtail A \text{ in } \mathcal{D}\}$.

A more tangible example of domain structure is $(\mathbf{Top}, \mathbf{Open})$ where $\mathbf{Open}$ consists of all those monos $m : (X, \mathcal{O}X) \rightarrowtail (Y, \mathcal{O}Y)$ in $\mathbf{Top}$ such that $(m(X), \mathcal{P}(mX) \cap \mathcal{O}Y)$ is a topological space isomorphic to $(X, \mathcal{O}X)$. The above construction applied to $\mathcal{K} = \mathbf{Top}$, $\mathcal{D} = \mathbf{Open}$, and $\mathcal{L} = \mathbf{Poset}$ (resp. $\mathbf{Cpo}$), viewed as the full subcategory of $\mathbf{Top}$ whose objects are posets (resp. cpos) with the Alexandrov (resp. Scott) topology, yields the domain structure $(\mathbf{Poset}, \mathbf{Open})$ $\big($resp. $(\mathbf{Cpo}, \mathbf{Open}) = (\mathbf{Cpo}, \mathbf{\Sigma})\big)$.

Definition 3.1.2 The *category of partial maps* $p(\mathcal{K}, \mathcal{D})$ induced by a domain structure $(\mathcal{K}, \mathcal{D})$ has the same objects as $\mathcal{K}$, a morphism is an equivalence class of descriptions in $\mathcal{D} \times \mathcal{K}$, and composition and identities are given as detailed above. □

Convention. Whenever we write $p(\mathcal{K}, \mathcal{D})$ it is assumed that $(\mathcal{K}, \mathcal{D})$ is a domain structure; when $\mathcal{D}$ is clear from the context we simply write $p\mathcal{K}$.

To distinguish total maps (i.e., morphisms in $\mathcal{K}$) from partial maps (i.e., morphisms in $p\mathcal{K}$) we denote the former with $\rightarrow$ and the latter with $\rightharpoonup$.

The categories of partial maps induced by some of our examples of domain structures are: $p(\mathcal{K}, \mathbf{Isos}_{\mathcal{K}}) \cong \mathcal{K}$, $p(\mathbf{Set}, \mathbf{Monos}) \cong \mathbf{Pfn}$, $p(\mathbf{Poset}, \mathbf{Open}) \cong \mathbf{pPoset}$, and $p(\mathbf{Cpo}, \mathbf{\Sigma}) \cong \mathbf{pCpo}$. A non-standard example is $\boldsymbol{\omega}\mathbf{+1} = p(\omega + 1, \mathbf{Monos})$, which is isomorphic to the category with object-set $\omega + 1$, hom-sets $\mathrm{Hom}(k, l) = \min(k, l) + 1$, identities $\mathrm{id}_k = k$, and composition $(j \xrightarrow{m} k \xrightarrow{n} l) = (j \xrightarrow{\min(m,n)} l)$.

The category of total maps can be viewed as a full-on-objects subcategory of the category of partial maps by identifying $\mathcal{K}$ with its image under the faithful *inclusion* functor $J : \mathcal{K} \rightarrow p\mathcal{K}$ which acts as the identity on objects and sends a total map f to the partial map $[\mathrm{id}, f]$. It should then be clear what is meant by a *total* partial map and by the composition of a total map with a partial map. To indicate that a partial map u is total we write $u\downarrow$. Totality and composition interact in the desirable way: e.g., for partial maps u and v,

$$(v \circ u)\downarrow \;\Rightarrow\; u\downarrow .$$

When the category of total maps has a terminal object, we say that totality is *extensional* if for all $u : A \rightharpoonup B$,

$$u\downarrow \iff (u \circ x)\downarrow \text{ for every } x : 1 \rightarrow A.$$

There is a *partial-inclusion* functor $(\_)^R : \mathcal{D}^{op} \to p\mathcal{K}$ which acts as the identity on objects and sends $m : D \rightarrowtail A$ in $\mathcal{D}$ to $m^R = [m, \mathrm{id}] : A \rightharpoonup D$. Partial inclusions have nice equational properties, in particular

$$m^R = n^R \iff [m] = [n],$$

$$m^R \circ m = \mathrm{id}, \quad (3.5)$$

$$[m, f] = f \circ m^R. \quad (3.6)$$

While (3.5) justifies the terminology, (3.6) shows that every partial map can be factored as a partial inclusion followed by a total map. In fact, as observed by John Power, this determines a *factorisation system* [FK72]. Partial inclusions also provide a simple equational characterisation for the pullbacks we are interested in, as

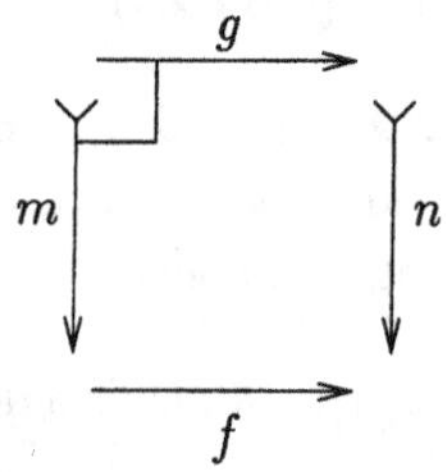

$$\iff n^R \circ f = g \circ m^R.$$

The adopted description of partial maps allows the definition of the *inverse image*, $u^{-1}[n]$, of an admissible subobject $[n] \in \mathcal{D}(B)$ along a partial map $u = [m, f] : A \rightharpoonup B$, simply as the admissible subobject $[m \circ f^{-1}(n)] \in \mathcal{D}(A)$. In fact, we have an inverse-image functor $\mathcal{D} : p\mathcal{K}^{op} \to$ **Poset** sending $A \in |\, p\mathcal{K}\,|$ to $\mathcal{D}(A)$ and $u : A \rightharpoonup B$ to $u^{-1}(\_) : \mathcal{D}(B) \to \mathcal{D}(A)$. Its restriction to total maps is $\mathcal{D} \circ J^{op} : \mathcal{K}^{op} \to$ **Poset**. As a convention, for $u : A \rightharpoonup B$ and $[m : D \rightarrowtail B] \in \mathcal{D}$ we write $u^{-1}(m) : u^{-1}(D) \rightarrowtail A$ for a representative of $u^{-1}[m] \in \mathcal{D}(A)$. Notice that, for $f : A \to B$, the convention agrees with the already adopted notation, $f^{-1}(m)$, for any mono obtained by pulling back m along f. Also, extending the n^*f notation of diagram (3.2) to partial maps, so that $n^*[m, f] = n^*f$, we have:

Proposition 3.1.3 The commuting square

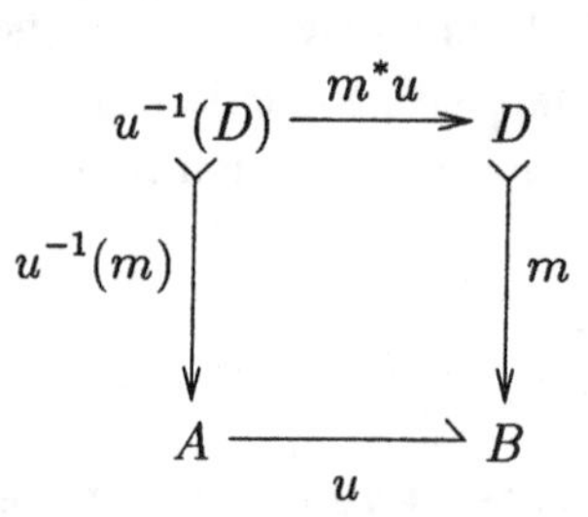

is a pullback for total maps. That is, for every $A \xleftarrow{f} C \xrightarrow{g} D$ satisfying $u \circ f = m \circ g$ there exists a unique $h : C \to u^{-1}(D)$ such that $f = u^{-1}(m) \circ h$ and $g = (m^*u) \circ h$. $\square$

From the inverse image of a partial map we can obtain its *domain of definition* by setting

$$\mathrm{dom}_{A,B}(\_) = (\_)^{-1}[\mathrm{id}_A] : p\mathcal{K}(A,B) \to \mathcal{D}(A)$$

for every $A, B \in |\, p\mathcal{K}\,|$. It follows then that a partial map is total if and only if its domain of definition is the maximal subobject.

3.2 Representing and Classifying Partial Maps

Partial maps are frequently represented as total maps. This section studies this kind of *representability*. The purpose is not to reduce partial maps to total ones, but to deepen the understanding of their relationship; we aim at establishing a connection which will allow the transfer of properties, constructions, etc. between total and partial maps.

The intuition of the representation is simple: a partial map $A \rightharpoonup B$ is represented by a total map $A \to LB$ where LB (read as "B lifted") arises from B by *adjoining undefinedness* to it. For sets and partial functions, LB is B with a new element, usually written $\perp$, symbolising undefinedness. Here, a partial function $u : A \rightharpoonup B$ is represented by the total function

$$\begin{array}{rccl} \chi(u): & A & \longrightarrow & LB \\ & a & \longmapsto & \begin{cases} u(a) & \text{, if } a \in \mathrm{dom}(u) \\ \perp & \text{, otherwise} \end{cases} \end{array}$$

In this way, χ determines a bijection, natural in A, between $\mathbf{Pfn}(A,B)$ and $\mathbf{Set}(A,LB)$.

This kind of representability is categorical. Recall that a *representation of a functor* $F : \mathcal{K}^{op} \to \mathbf{Set}$ is a pair (R, ρ) consisting of a *representing object* $R \in |\,\mathcal{K}\,|$ and a natural isomorphism $\rho : \mathcal{K}(\_, R) \stackrel{\cdot}{\to} F : \mathcal{K}^{op} \to \mathbf{Set}$. The *counit of the representation* is determined by the Yoneda bijection $\Upsilon : \mathrm{Nat}(\mathcal{K}(\_, R), F) \to FR$ as $\Upsilon(\rho) = \rho(\mathrm{id}_R) \in FR$. In the above example LB is a representing object of $\mathbf{Pfn}(\_, B) : \mathbf{Set}^{op} \to \mathbf{Set}$, with counit the partial inclusion $(B \rightarrowtail LB)^R : LB \rightharpoonup B$ only undefined for $\perp$.

Representations of partial functions can be characterised equationally. As the reader should check, for a partial function $u : A \rightharpoonup B$, its representation $\chi(u) : A \to LB$ is the unique total function satisfying

$$\chi(u)^{-1}(B) = \mathrm{dom}(u), \quad \text{and} \quad \forall x \in \mathrm{dom}(u).\ \chi(u)(x) = u(x). \tag{3.7}$$

In topos theoretic terms (3.7) says that u is *classified* by $B \rightarrowtail LB$:

Definition 3.2.1 (c.f. [Joh77]) Let $(\mathcal{K}, \mathcal{D})$ be a domain structure. A *classifier of partial maps with target* B is a mono $n : B \rightarrowtail LB$ in $\mathcal{D}$ such that for every partial map $[m, f] : A \rightharpoonup B$, there exists a unique total map $\chi_{[m,f]} : A \to LB$, called the *characteristic map* of $[m, f]$, making

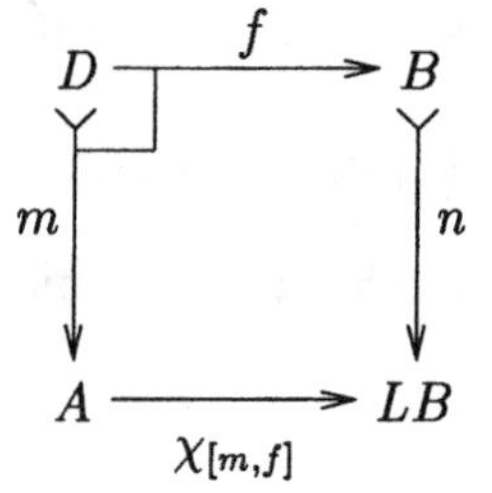

a pullback. □

Convention. An $| p\mathcal{K} |$-indexed collection η is called a *partial map classifier* if for every $B \in | p\mathcal{K} |$ the component η_B is a classifier of partial maps with target B.

When $\mathcal{K}$ has a terminal object, the classifier of partial maps with target 1 classifies admissible monos and so is called a *$\mathcal{D}$-classifier*.

The representing object of $\mathbf{pPoset}(\_, Q) : \mathbf{Poset}^{op} \to \mathbf{Set}$, usually denoted $Q_\perp$, is the poset Q with a new least element. Not surprisingly, the representations are as defined for sets and partial functions. And thus (3.7) also characterises representations of partial monotone functions. Similarly this characterisation extends to partial continuous functions; and in fact, it holds for any category of partial maps:

Theorem 3.2.2 For $B \in | p\mathcal{K} |$, the functor $p\mathcal{K}(\_, B) : \mathcal{K}^{op} \to \mathbf{Set}$ is representable if and only if there is a classifier of partial maps with target B. □

If $\mathcal{K}$ has a terminal object we have that $\mathcal{D}(\_) \cong p\mathcal{K}(\_, 1) : \mathcal{K}^{op} \to \mathbf{Set}$, hence:

Corollary 3.2.3 When $\mathcal{K}$ has a terminal object, the functor $\mathcal{D}(\_) : \mathcal{K}^{op} \to \mathbf{Set}$ is representable if and only if there is a $\mathcal{D}$-classifier. □

Theorem 3.2.2 is a consequence of the following two propositions which correspond to each direction of the theorem.

Proposition 3.2.4 If $\rho : \mathcal{K}(\_, LB) \cong p\mathcal{K}(\_, B) : \chi$ then

1. $\chi(\mathrm{id}_B) : B \to LB$ is admissible,
2. the counit $\rho(\mathrm{id}_{LB}) : LB \rightharpoonup B$ is $\chi(\mathrm{id}_B)^R$,
3. $\chi(\mathrm{id}_B)$ classifies partial maps with target B, and
4. $\chi[m, f]$ is the characteristic map of $[m, f]$.

PROOF: To prove that the counit of the representation ρ is a partial inclusion we show that if $\rho(\mathrm{id}_{LB}) = [n, g]$ then g is an isomorphism; so that $\rho(\mathrm{id}_{LB}) = (n \circ g^{-1})^R$.

As ρ and χ are inverses to each other,

for every object $A \in |\mathcal{K}|$ and every partial map $[m, f] \in p\mathcal{K}(A, B)$, the total map $\chi[m, f] \in \mathcal{K}(A, LB)$ is the unique such that (3.8)

$$[m, f] \;=\; \rho(\chi[m, f]) \;=\; \rho(\mathrm{id}_{LB}) \circ \chi[m, f].$$

Recalling that $\rho(\mathrm{id}_{LB}) = [n, g]$, the above equation states that

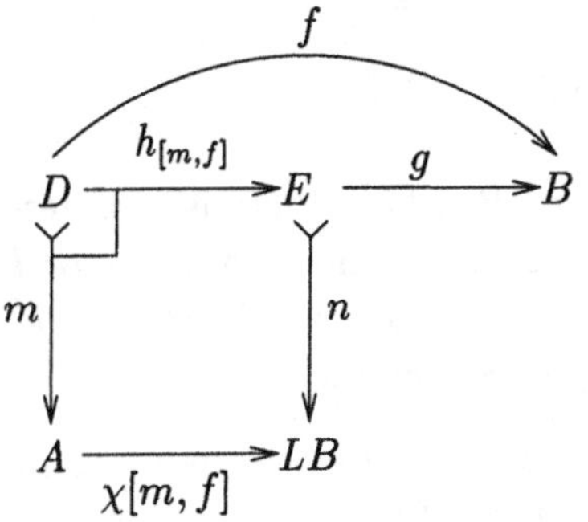

for some $h_{[m,f]}$.

In particular, for every $A \in |\mathcal{K}|$ and $f \in \mathcal{K}(A, B)$ there exists $h_f \in \mathcal{K}(A, E)$ such that $f = g \circ h_f$. Moreover, it is unique because as for every $h : A \to E$, $[n, g] \circ n \circ h = g \circ h$ then, if $g \circ h = f$ it follows that $n \circ h_f = \chi_f = n \circ h$ and hence $h_f = h$. Therefore, $g \circ \_ : \mathcal{K}(\_, E) \dot{\to} \mathcal{K}(\_, B) : \mathcal{K}^{op} \to \mathbf{Set}$ is a natural isomorphism and, by the Yoneda Lemma, g is an isomorphism.

The equality

$$(n \circ g^{-1})^R \circ \chi(\mathrm{id}_B) \;=\; \rho(\mathrm{id}_{LB}) \circ \chi(\mathrm{id}_B) \;=\; \rho(\chi(\mathrm{id}_B)) \;=\; \mathrm{id}_B$$

stands for

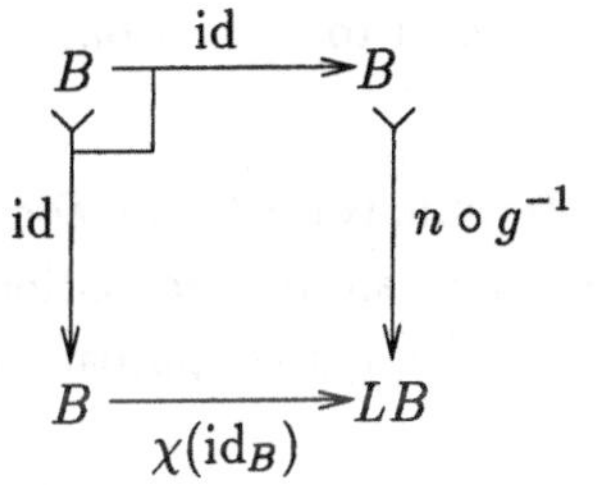

and implies both that $\chi(\mathrm{id}_B)$ is admissible and

$$\rho(\mathrm{id}_{LB}) = \chi(\mathrm{id}_B)^R. \qquad (3.9)$$

Finally, (3.8) and (3.9) establish that $\chi(\mathrm{id}_B)$ classifies partial maps with target B, and that $\chi[m, f]$ is the characteristic map of $[m, f]$. □

Proposition 3.2.5 If $n : B \rightarrowtail LB$ classifies partial maps with target B, then $\Upsilon^{-1}(n^R) = n^R \circ \_ : \mathcal{K}(\_, LB) \dot{\to} p\mathcal{K}(\_, B)$ represents $p\mathcal{K}(\_, B) : \mathcal{K}^{op} \to \mathbf{Set}$.

PROOF: Since n classifies partial maps with target B, it follows that for every $A \in |\mathcal{K}|$ and every $[m, f] \in p\mathcal{K}(A, B)$ there exists a unique $\chi_{[m,f]} \in \mathcal{K}(A, LB)$ such that

$$\begin{aligned} [m, f] &= n^R \circ \chi_{[m,f]} \\ &= \Upsilon^{-1}(n^R)(\chi_{[m,f]}). \end{aligned}$$

Hence $\Upsilon^{-1}(n^R)$ is an isomorphism. □

As is well-known, if for every $B \in |\mathcal{K}|$ there is a representing object $LB \in |p\mathcal{K}|$ of $p\mathcal{K}(\_, B) : \mathcal{K}^{op} \to \mathbf{Set}$ then L can be extended to a functor $L : p\mathcal{K} \to \mathcal{K}$, called the *lifting* functor, which is right adjoint to the inclusion functor $J : \mathcal{K} \to p\mathcal{K}$. This adjunction can be characterised from the previous analysis.

Theorem 3.2.6 $\eta, \varepsilon : J \dashv L : p\mathcal{K} \to \mathcal{K}$ if and only if η is a partial map classifier, $\varepsilon = \eta^R$ and, for every $[m, f] : A \rightharpoonup B$, $L[m, f]$ is the characteristic map of $[\eta_A \circ m, f]$. □

Remark. The action of the lifting functor on partial maps can be described as a characteristic map because, as follows from Proposition 3.2.4 (4), the natural isomorphism $\chi : p\mathcal{K}(\_, =) \dot{\to} \mathcal{K}(\_, L=) : \mathcal{K}^{op} \times p\mathcal{K} \to \mathbf{Set}$ induced by the adjunction provides the characteristic map of a partial map; and for every $[m, f] : A \rightharpoonup B$,

$$\begin{aligned} L[m, f] &= \chi([m, f] \circ \varepsilon_A) && \text{, by a well-known formula} \\ &= \chi[\eta_A \circ m, f] && \text{, using } \varepsilon_A = {\eta_A}^R. \end{aligned}$$

(Another possible explanation is by naturality of $\varepsilon : JL \dot{\to} \mathrm{Id} : p\mathcal{K} \to p\mathcal{K}$).

Succinctly, to have a lifting functor is equivalent to have a partial map classifier. It should be stressed that this alternative viewpoint is essential when transferring structure like enrichment and colimits from total to partial maps (see Section 4.5 and Theorem 5.3.14).

Among all classifiers, when $\mathcal{K}$ has a terminal object, the $\mathcal{D}$-classifier plays a central role as it can encode all the others. This allows an axiomatisation of the lifting in terms of the classification of admissible monos; which is the approach taken in *synthetic domain theory* [Ros86,Pho90b,Hyl91,Tay91].

Proposition 3.2.7 Assume $\mathcal{K}$ has terminal object and let $t : 1 \rightarrowtail \Sigma$ be admissible. If the right adjoint Π_t of $t^* : \mathcal{K}/\Sigma \to \mathcal{K}$ exists then it is full and faithful.

PROOF: We show that the counit ϵ of the adjunction $t^* \dashv \Pi_t$ is an isomorphism.

By the universal property of ϵ we have that for every $a : A \to \Sigma$ in $|\mathcal{K}/\Sigma|$ and every $f : t^*a \to B$ in $\mathcal{K}$ there exists a unique $\overline{f} : a \to \Pi_t B$ in $\mathcal{K}/\Sigma$ such that

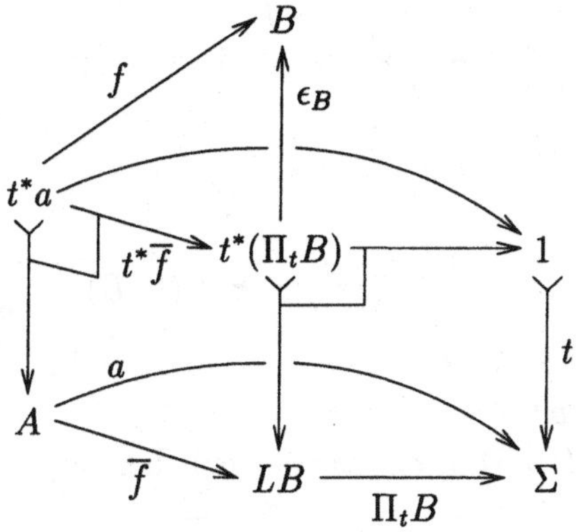

In particular, taking a to be $B \to 1 \overset{t}{\rightarrowtail} \Sigma$ and f to be the canonical isomorphism in

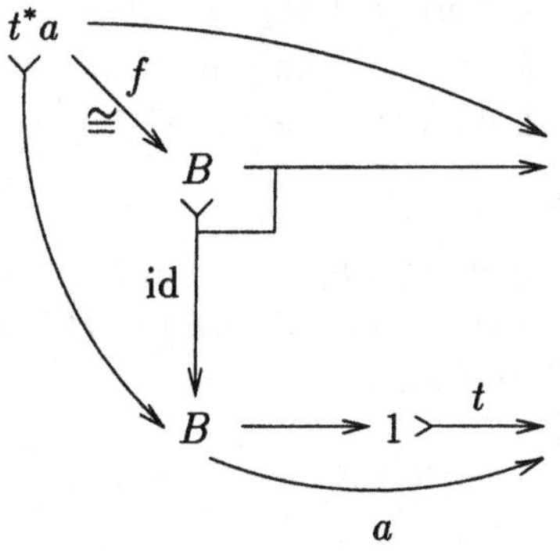

we have that $\epsilon_B \circ (t^*\overline{f})$ is an isomorphism; and hence ϵ_B is split epi.

Finally, we show that ϵ_B is mono. For every $x : A \to t^*(\Pi_t B)$, writing f for the canonical isomorphism $t^*(A \to 1 \overset{t}{\rightarrowtail} \Sigma) \cong A$ and n_B for $t^*(\Pi_t B) \rightarrowtail LB$ we have that

$$\overline{\epsilon_B \circ x \circ f} \quad = \quad n_B \circ x$$

because

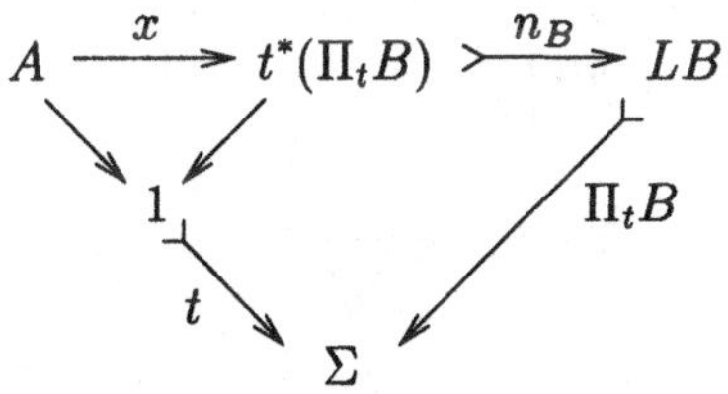

and

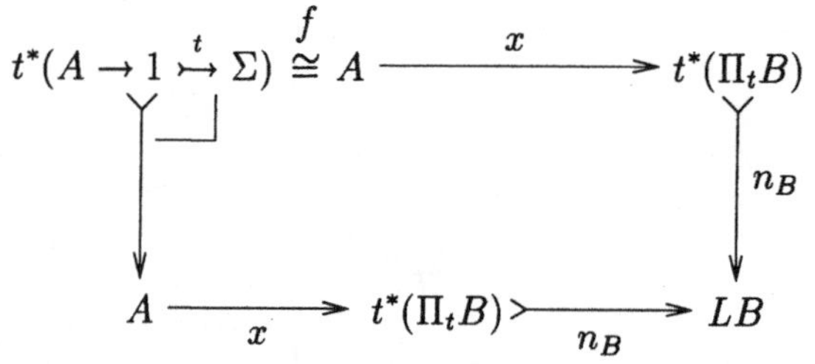

so that $\epsilon_B \circ t^*(n_B \circ x) = \epsilon_B \circ x \circ f$.

Hence, for $x, y : A \to t^*(\Pi_t B)$, if $\epsilon_B \circ x = \epsilon_B \circ y$ then

$$n_B \circ x \;=\; \overline{\epsilon_B \circ x \circ f} \;=\; \overline{\epsilon_B \circ y \circ f} \;=\; n_B \circ y$$

and, as n_B is mono, $x = y$. □

Theorem 3.2.8 Assume $\mathcal{K}$ has terminal object. Then $t : 1 \rightarrowtail \Sigma$ is a $\mathcal{D}$-classifier and $t^* : \mathcal{K}/\Sigma \to \mathcal{K}$ has a right adjoint if and only if $J : \mathcal{K} \to p\mathcal{K}$ has a right adjoint and, writing η for the unit of the adjunction, $\eta_1 \cong t$ in $\mathcal{K}^{\cdot\to\cdot}$.

PROOF:

($\Rightarrow$) Let $\Pi_t : \mathcal{K} \to \mathcal{K}/\Sigma$ be right adjoint to t^*. For every $B \in |\mathcal{K}|$ define η_B to be the composite $B \cong t^*(\Pi_t B) \rightarrowtail LB$ where $\epsilon_B : t^*(\Pi_t B) \cong B$ is the counit of the adjunction $t^* \dashv \Pi_t$ (see Proposition 3.2.7) and where

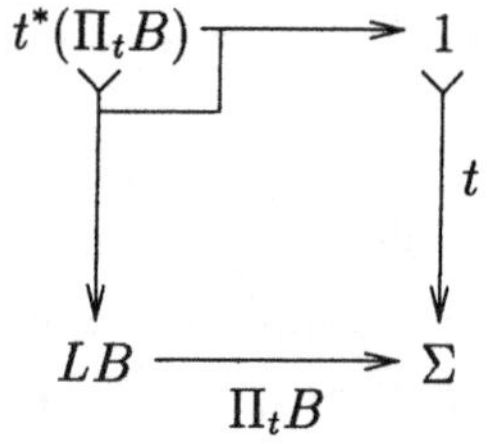

Then we have that

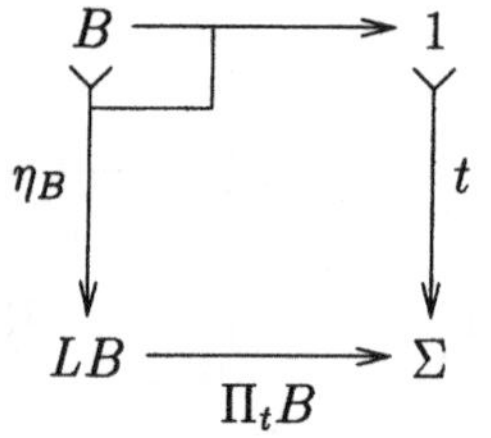

and that η_B classifies partial maps with target B as we now show.

For $[m, f] : A \rightharpoonup B$ we have

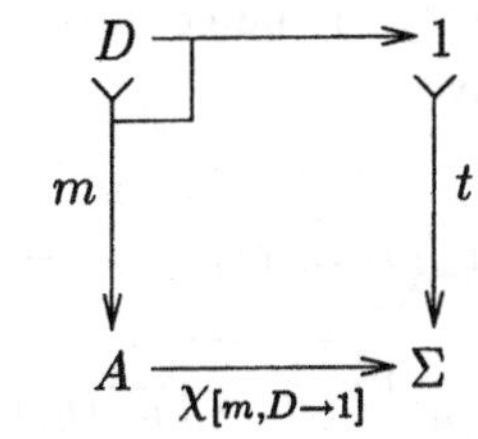

Then, $D \cong t^*\chi_{[m,D\to 1]}$, and the transpose of the map $t^*\chi_{[m,D\to 1]} \cong D \xrightarrow{f} B$ gives a unique $\varphi : \chi_{[m,D\to 1]} \to \Pi_t B$ such that $\epsilon_B \circ (t^*\varphi) = (t^*\chi_{[m,D\to 1]} \cong D \xrightarrow{f} B)$ and

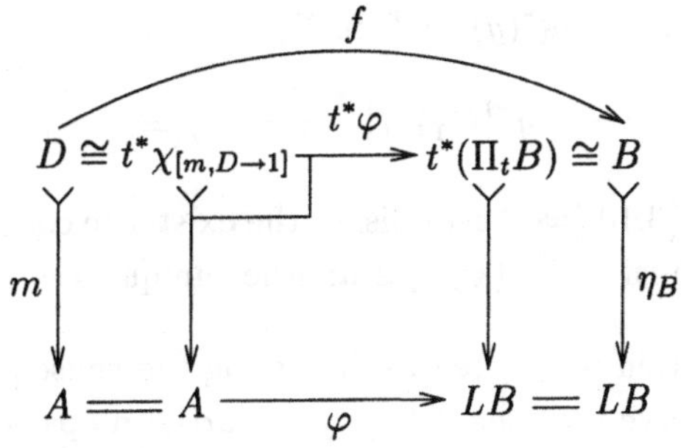

Thus φ is the characteristic map of $[m, f]$.

($\Leftarrow$) As $t \cong \eta_1$ in $\mathcal{K}^{\cdot\to\cdot}$ we have both that t is a $\mathcal{D}$-classifier and that $t^* \cong {\eta_1}^*$. Therefore we only need show that ${\eta_1}^*$ has right adjoint.

Let L be the lifting functor. For $B \in |\, \mathcal{K}\,|$, $L(B \to 1) \in |\, \mathcal{K}/L1\,|$ is the cofree object on B with counit $\epsilon_B : {\eta_1}^*(L(B \to 1)) \cong B$ defined as the mediating morphism between the following two pullbacks

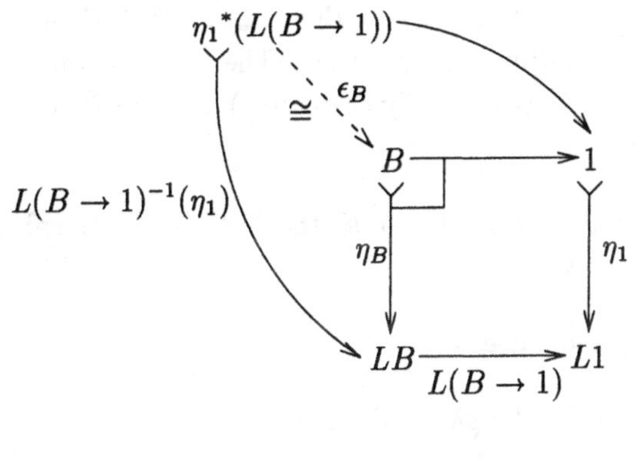

Recall that the square is a pullback because $L(B \to 1)$ is the characteristic map of $[\eta_B, B \to 1]$ (see Theorem 3.2.6 and the remark after it).

We now check the universal property of the counit. Let $B \in |\mathcal{K}|$, $g \in |\mathcal{K}/L1|$ and $h : g \longrightarrow L(B \to 1)$ in $\mathcal{K}/L1$. We have,

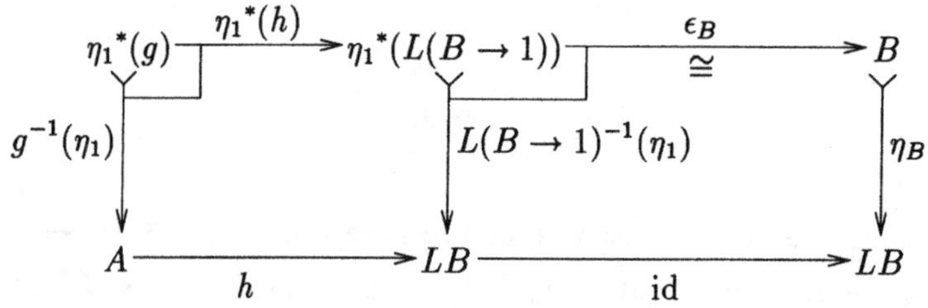

and therefore, for every $f : {\eta_1}^*(g) \to B$ in $\mathcal{K}$,

$$h = \chi[g^{-1}(\eta_1), f] \iff f = \epsilon_B \circ {\eta_1}^*(h). \tag{3.10}$$

Finally, observe that $\big(3.10\ (\Rightarrow)\big)$ establishes the existence condition of the universal property of the counit, whilst $\big(3.10\ (\Leftarrow)\big)$ establishes uniqueness. □

The rest of the section is devoted to discussing the consequences of having the lifting functor. We first observe that the category of partial maps is the Kleisli category of the monad induced by the adjunction. This simply happens because the inclusion functor is bijective on objects.

Proposition 3.2.9 (Kleisli) If $\eta, \varepsilon : F \dashv U : \mathcal{L} \to \mathcal{K}$ and F is bijective (essentially surjective) on objects then $\mathcal{L}$ is isomorphic (equivalent) to $\mathcal{K}_{\mathbb{T}}$, the Kleisli category of the monad $\mathbb{T} = (UF, U\varepsilon F, \eta) : \mathcal{K} \to \mathcal{K}$.

PROOF: Recall that there is an adjunction $F_{\mathbb{T}} \dashv U_{\mathbb{T}} : \mathcal{K}_{\mathbb{T}} \to \mathcal{K}$ such that there exists a unique *comparison* functor $\mathcal{K}_{\mathbb{T}} \to \mathcal{L}$ acting as F on objects and sending $f \in \mathcal{K}_{\mathbb{T}}(A, B)$ to $\rho(f) \in \mathcal{L}(FA, FB)$, where $\rho : \mathcal{K}(\_, U\_) \dot{\to} \mathcal{L}(F\_, \_) : \mathcal{K}^{op} \times \mathcal{L} \to \mathbf{Set}$ is the natural isomorphism induced by the adjunction $F \dashv U$. The comparison functor is full and faithful, and when F is bijective (essentially surjective) on objects, it is an isomorphism (equivalence) of categories. □

Corollary 3.2.10 If $\eta, \varepsilon : J \dashv L : p\mathcal{K} \to \mathcal{K}$ then $p\mathcal{K}$ is (isomorphic to) the Kleisli category of $\mathbb{L} = (LJ, L\varepsilon J, \eta) : \mathcal{K} \to \mathcal{K}$. □

Further miscellaneous consequences are:

Proposition 3.2.11 If $\eta, \varepsilon : J \dashv L : p\mathcal{K} \to \mathcal{K}$ then

1. η is a *cartesian* natural transformation (i.e., the commuting square defining naturality is a pullback).

2. Every admissible mono is regular. In particular, η_A is the equaliser of the pair $L\eta_A, \eta_{LA} : LA \to L^2A$.

3. L is faithful.

4. L reflects isomorphisms.

PROOF:

(1) By naturality of $\varepsilon J : JLJ \dot{\to} J : \mathcal{K} \to p\mathcal{K}$.

(2) Every admissible mono $m : D \rightarrowtail B$ is the equaliser of $\chi[m,m], \eta_B : B \to LB$. In particular, $\chi[\eta_A, \eta_A] = L\eta_A$.

(3) Because ε is epi, as $\varepsilon_A \circ \eta_A = \text{id}$ for every $A \in |\, p\mathcal{K}\,|$.

(4) Assume $L[m,f]$ is an isomorphism.

First we show that f is an isomorphism: if $L[m,f]$ has inverse h, then defining g as the mediating morphism in the diagram

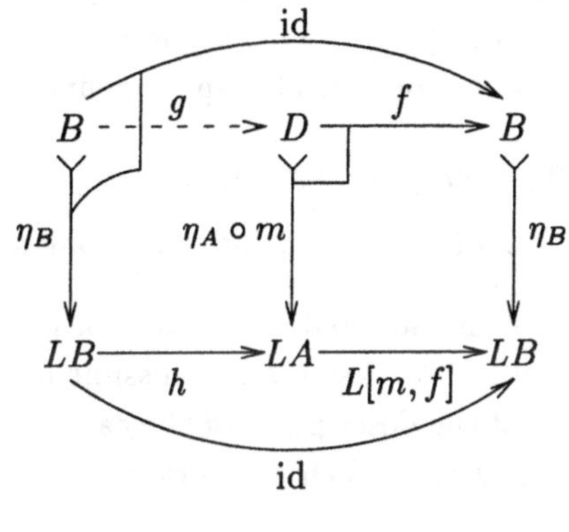

it follows that $f \circ g = \text{id}$. Moreover, $g \circ f = \text{id}$, because the following rectangle is a pullback,

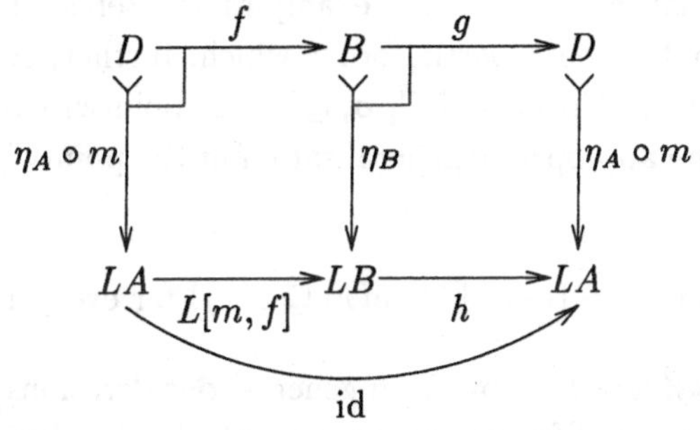

Second we show that m is an isomorphism (for which we need only check that $m \circ m^R = \mathrm{id}$): $L[m, f] = L(f) \circ L(m^R)$ and since $L[m, f]$ and Lf are both isomorphisms it follows that so is $L(m^R)$. Moreover, $L(m^R) \circ L(m) = L(m^R \circ m) = \mathrm{id}$ and hence $(Lm)^{-1} = L(m^R)$. Thus, $L(m \circ m^R) = \mathrm{id}$ and, as L is faithful, $m \circ m^R = \mathrm{id}$. □

3.3 Testing and Observing Partial Maps

The capability of observing that an input/output program terminates serves as the basis for discriminating between programs. For example, in the *contextual* approach, a program e is said to approximate a program e' (written $e \precsim^c e'$) if, in every program in which e occurs, e can be safely replaced by e' in the sense that new non-terminating behaviour will not happen.

The explicit distinction between partial and total maps induces an approximation relation in which contexts are used to discriminate between maps based on their terminating behaviour. Following the informal description of a context as a "program with a hole"; in a category of partial maps, a context is described as a "partial map with a hole". Formally, contexts are *incomplete* composites $u \circ \_ \circ v$ where u and v are partial maps. The *contextual approximation* relation for partial maps is defined as follows,

Definition 3.3.1 (Plotkin) For every $u, v : A \rightharpoonup B$,

$$u \precsim^c v \text{ if and only if } C[u]\downarrow \Rightarrow C[v]\downarrow \text{ for every context } C[\_]. \qquad \square$$

Remark. Observe that because of the adopted description of partial maps it is enough to consider contexts of the form $m^R \circ \_ \circ f$ for m an admissible mono and f a total map. But the definition is independent of the description of the category of partial maps, and thus, makes sense in any axiomatisation of such categories.

The restriction of $\precsim^c$ to total maps gives a contextual approximation relation on total maps which we denote $\sqsubseteq^c$. Both $\sqsubseteq^c$ and $\precsim^c$ are preorders and, in general, they are not partial orders.

Justifying our computational intuition, in the examples of interest the contextual approximation relation turns out to be a partial order which, further, coincides with the usual notion of approximation. In **Poset** and **Cpo**, $\sqsubseteq^c$ is the pointwise order $\sqsubseteq$; whilst in **pPoset** and **pCpo**, $\precsim^c$ is the appropriate generalisation of the pointwise order, namely for $u, v : P \rightharpoonup Q$,

$$u \precsim v \text{ if and only if } u(x)\downarrow \Rightarrow \big(v(x)\downarrow \wedge\ u(x) \sqsubseteq v(x)\big) \text{ for every } x \in P. \qquad (3.11)$$

Instead of checking these facts, which follow from general considerations (see the remark after Proposition 3.3.5), we exemplify the use of contexts to discriminate maps. Let

$f, g : P \to Q$ in **Poset** be such that there exists $v \in P$ for which $fv \sqsubset gv$, and let $C[\_]$ be the context in **pPoset**, $U^R \circ \_ \circ v$, where $v : 1 \to P : * \mapsto v$ and $U = Q \backslash \{y \in Q \mid y \sqsubseteq fv\}$. Then, with respect to termination, $C[\_]$ distinguishes f and g, as $C[f] \uparrow$ and $C[g] \downarrow$.

In **pPoset** (**pCpo**), (3.11) reduces the order on partial monotone (continuous) functions to the test for definedness and the order on elements. As the next proposition shows this is a general phenomenon and sustains a claim that testing for totality and the approximation of total maps are primitive concepts, whilst the approximation of partial maps is a derived one.

Proposition 3.3.2 For every $u, v : A \rightharpoonup B$,

$$u \precsim^c v \text{ if and only if } u \circ x \downarrow \Rightarrow (v \circ x \downarrow \wedge u \circ x \sqsubseteq^c v \circ x) \text{ for every } x : X \to A.$$

Moreover, when the category of total maps has terminal object and totality is extensional (in the sense of page 37) the above can be strengthened to

$$u \precsim^c v \text{ if and only if } u \circ x \downarrow \Rightarrow (v \circ x \downarrow \wedge u \circ x \sqsubseteq^c v \circ x) \text{ for every } x : 1 \to A. \qquad \square$$

Remark. In the proposition, it would make no difference to allow x to range over partial maps, as $u \circ x \downarrow \Rightarrow x \downarrow$. Moreover, this property is central to the (omitted) proof.

Further evidence for the suitability of contextual approximation is that it interacts well with composition: *the contextual approximation relation is a preorder with respect to which composition is a monotone operation.*

The description of partial maps based on domain structures provides another computationally natural notion of approximation. For this purpose, admissible monos are regarded as predicates describing *observable properties*.

A program e is said to *specialise* a program e' (written $e \precsim^s e'$) if the observable properties of the outputs of e are also satisfied by the outputs of e'. Put it in another way, for any observable property U, the weakest precondition ensuring that every execution of e satisfies U is a precondition ensuring that every execution of e' satisfies U. Thus, an observer content with the input/output behaviour of e should also be content with the input/output behaviour of e'. The *specialisation* relation for partial maps is defined as follows,

Definition 3.3.3 $u \precsim^s v : A \rightharpoonup B$ in $p\mathcal{K}$ if and only if $u^{-1}(\_) \subseteq v^{-1}(\_) : \mathcal{D}(B) \to \mathcal{D}(A)$ in **Poset**. $\square$

The specialisation relation generalises the one from topology. Recall that for a T_0-space

$(X, \mathcal{O}(X))$, its specialisation order $\leq \subseteq X \times X$ is defined as

$$x \leq y \text{ if and only if } x \in U \Rightarrow y \in U \text{ for every } U \in \mathcal{O}(X).$$

Then, by identifying elements with functions out of the singleton, the above definition can be put in a form resembling Definition 3.3.3:

$$x \leq y \text{ if and only if } x^{-1}(U) \subseteq y^{-1}(U) \text{ for every } U \in \mathcal{O}(X).$$

Pleasantly enough, the notions of approximation obtained by testing and by observing partial maps coincide.

Lemma 3.3.4 For $f \in \mathcal{K}(X, A)$, $u \in p\mathcal{K}(A, B)$ and $m \in \mathcal{D}(D, B)$,

$$m^R \circ u \circ f \downarrow \iff f \text{ factors through } u^{-1}(m).$$

PROOF:

($\Rightarrow$) For every $n \in \mathcal{D}(E, Y)$ and $g \in \mathcal{K}(X, Y)$, $n^R \circ g \downarrow \Rightarrow g = n \circ n^R \circ g$.

Thus, assuming $m^R \circ u \circ f \downarrow$ we have that $u \circ f = m \circ (m^R \circ u \circ f)$, and since $A \overset{u^{-1}(m)}{\leftarrowtail} u^{-1}(D) \overset{m^* u}{\longrightarrow} D$ is a pullback of $A \overset{u}{\rightharpoonup} B \overset{m}{\leftarrowtail} D$ for total maps (see Proposition 3.1.3) we are done.

($\Leftarrow$) Assume $f = u^{-1}(m) \circ g$. Then, g is total and

$$\begin{aligned} m^R \circ u \circ f &= m^R \circ u \circ u^{-1}(m) \circ g \\ &= m^R \circ m \circ (m^* u) \circ g \\ &= (m^* u) \circ g. \end{aligned}$$

□

Proposition 3.3.5 Contextual approximation and specialisation coincide.

PROOF:

($\precsim^c \subseteq \precsim^s$) Let $u \precsim^c v : A \rightharpoonup B$. Then,

$$\begin{aligned} u \precsim^c v &\implies \forall [m] \in \mathcal{D}(B). \\ &\qquad (m^R \circ u \circ u^{-1}(m) \downarrow \Rightarrow m^R \circ v \circ u^{-1}(m) \downarrow) \\ &\iff \forall [m] \in \mathcal{D}(B).\ m^R \circ v \circ u^{-1}(m) \downarrow \\ &\qquad\qquad , \text{ as } m^R \circ u \circ u^{-1}(m) = m^* u \downarrow \\ &\iff \forall [m] \in \mathcal{D}(B).\ u^{-1}(m) \text{ factors through } v^{-1}(m) \\ &\qquad\qquad , \text{ by Lemma 3.3.4} \\ &\iff u \precsim^s v. \end{aligned}$$

($\precsim^s \subseteq \precsim^c$) Let $u \precsim^s v : A \rightharpoonup B$. Then,

$$\begin{array}{rcl} u \precsim^s v & \iff & \forall [m] \in \mathcal{D}(B).\ u^{-1}(m) \subseteq v^{-1}(m) \\ & \iff & \forall [m] \in \mathcal{D}(B).\ u^{-1}(m) \text{ factors through } v^{-1}(m) \\ & \implies & \forall f \in \mathcal{K}(X, A).\ \forall [m] \in \mathcal{D}(B). \\ & & \quad \big(f \text{ factors through } u^{-1}(m) \Rightarrow f \text{ factors through } v^{-1}(m)\big) \\ & \implies & \forall f \in \mathcal{K}(X, A).\ \forall [m] \in \mathcal{D}(B). \\ & & \quad (m^R \circ u \circ f \downarrow \Rightarrow m^R \circ v \circ f \downarrow) \qquad \text{, by Lemma 3.3.4} \\ & \iff & u \precsim^c v. \end{array}$$

□

Remark. In **Poset** (resp. **Cpo**), the contextual approximation relation, the specialisation relation, and the pointwise order are equal, by Proposition 3.3.5 and the well-known fact that, for $f, g : P \to Q$,

$f \sqsubseteq g$ if and only if $f^{-1}(U) \subseteq g^{-1}(U)$ for every upper-closed (resp. Scott-open) $U \subseteq Q$.

Moreover, the equality extends to **pPoset** and **pCpo**, by Propositions 3.3.2 and 3.3.5.

4 Order-Enriched Categories of Partial Maps

Motivated by the discussion in Section 3.3, the approximation order between total maps ($\sqsubseteq$) is adopted as primitive and is used to derive the notion of approximation between partial maps ($\precsim$). Afterwards, the main goal is to understand when $\precsim$ is domain theoretic, in the technical sense that the category of partial maps **Cpo**-enriches with respect to it. For simplicity we undertake this study in two steps: first, we characterise **Poset**-categories of partial maps induced by domain structures with a **Poset**-category of total maps; second, we restrict our attention to *uniform* domain structures (Definition 4.3.5) with a **Cpo**-category of total maps, and provide necessary and sufficient conditions so that the induced category of partial maps **Cpo**-enriches. As an example, these characterisations are used when the approximation order is specialisation.

Finally, the transference of **Cpo**-enrichment from the category of total maps to the category of partial maps is revisited in the light of representability and, again, the example when the approximation order is specialisation is discussed.

Convention. For $\mathcal{V}$ = **Poset** or **Cpo**, a domain structure with a $\mathcal{V}$-category of total maps is called a $\mathcal{V}$-domain-structure and the order on total maps is denoted $\sqsubseteq$.

4.1 Ordering Partial Maps

A **Poset**-domain-structure induces an order on partial maps (denoted $\precsim$) whose definition is motivated by Proposition 3.3.2.

Definition 4.1.1 Given a **Poset**-domain-structure, for every $u, v : A \rightharpoonup B$,

$$u \precsim v \text{ if and only if for every } x : X \to A,\ u \circ x \downarrow \Rightarrow (v \circ x \downarrow\ \wedge u \circ x \sqsubseteq v \circ x). \qquad \square$$

Remark. The relation $\precsim$ is clearly reflexive and transitive. That it is antisymmetric follows from Proposition 4.1.2 below.

The intuition behind the definition is that a possibly non-terminating input/output program e approximates another one e' provided that under all possible inputs, the outputs of e approximate the outputs of e'. Thus, in particular, whenever e outputs, so does e'. In symbols,

$$\mathrm{dom}(e) \subseteq \mathrm{dom}(e') \quad \wedge \quad e \restriction \mathrm{dom}(e) \sqsubseteq e' \restriction \mathrm{dom}(e).$$

This intuition is technically correct:

Proposition 4.1.2 Given a **Poset**-domain-structure, for every $[m, f], [n, g] : A \rightharpoonup B$,

$$[m, f] \underset{\sim}{\sqsubset} [n, g] \iff m \subseteq_i n \wedge f \sqsubseteq g \circ i \text{ for a unique } i.$$

(In diagram form:

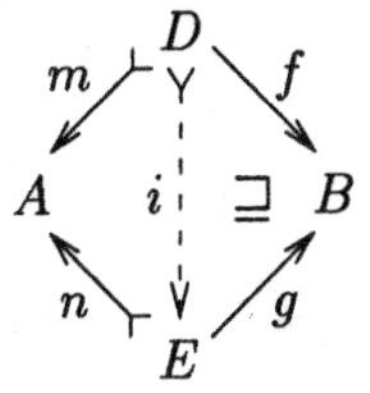

.)

PROOF:
($\Rightarrow$) Assume $[m, f] \underset{\sim}{\sqsubset} [n, g]$. Since $[m, f] \circ m = f$ is total then so is $[n, g] \circ m$ and therefore there exists a unique i for which

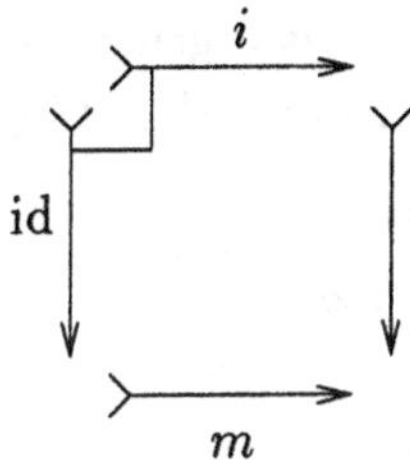

and $\quad f = [m, f] \circ m \sqsubseteq [n, g] \circ m = g \circ i.$

($\Leftarrow$) Let $m \subseteq_i n$ and $f \sqsubseteq g \circ i$ for some i. For $x : X \to A$, if $[m, f] \circ x \downarrow$ then

$$\begin{aligned} [\mathrm{id}] &= \mathrm{dom}([m, f] \circ x) \\ &= x^{-1}[m] \\ &\subseteq x^{-1}[n] \\ &= \mathrm{dom}([n, g] \circ x) \end{aligned}$$

and therefore $[n, g] \circ x \downarrow$.

Moreover, we have

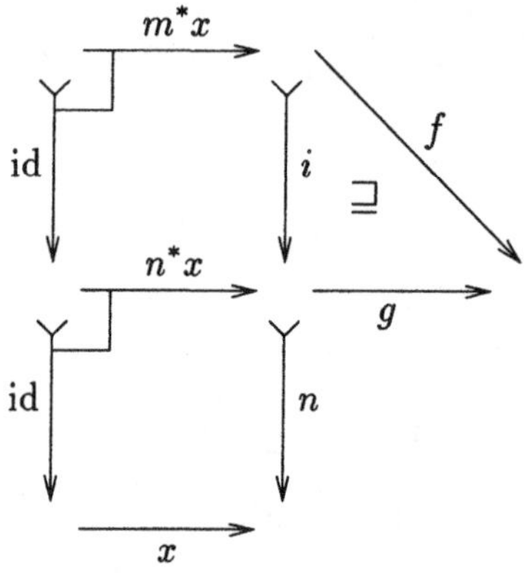

and hence, $[m, f] \circ x \;=\; f \circ (m^*x) \;\sqsubseteq\; g \circ i \circ (m^*x) \;=\; [n, g] \circ x.$ □

Convention. We introduce the notation $[m, f] \precsim_i [n, g]$ to indicate that i realises the inequality between the representatives (i.e., $m \subseteq_i n$ and $f \sqsubseteq g \circ i$). Clearly, if $[m, f] \precsim [n, g]$ and $m \subseteq_i n$ then $[m, f] \precsim_i [n, g]$.

An example of the order induced by a **Poset**-domain-structure is a generalisation of the *graph inclusion order*; denoted $\subseteq$, and defined to be the order induced by $(\mathcal{K}_{\mathbf{Poset}}, \mathcal{D})$ where $(\mathcal{K}, \mathcal{D})$ is a domain structure. Explicitly,

$$[m, f] \subseteq_i [n, g] \text{ if and only if } m \subseteq_i n \text{ and } f = g \circ i.$$

Justifying the terminology, when $(\mathcal{K}, \mathcal{D}) = (\mathbf{Set}, \mathbf{Monos})$,

$$u \subseteq v \text{ if and only if } \mathrm{graph}(u) \subseteq \mathrm{graph}(v),$$

and when $(\mathcal{K}, \mathcal{D}) = \big(\omega + 1, \mathbf{Monos}\big)$,

$$[m \rightarrowtail k, m \to l] \subseteq [n \rightarrowtail k, n \to l] \text{ if and only if } m \subseteq n.$$

The characterisation of $\precsim$, provided by Proposition 4.1.2, is more convenient to work with than its definition and thus, from now on, the definition will be forgotten. For example, using this characterisation the following is straightforward:

Proposition 4.1.3 Let $(\mathcal{K}, \mathcal{D})$ be a **Poset**-domain-structure. Then, for $A, B \in |\, \mathcal{K} \,|$,

1. $(p\mathcal{K}(A, B), \precsim)$ is a poset.

2. $J_{A,B} : (\mathcal{K}(A, B), \sqsubseteq) \hookrightarrow (p\mathcal{K}(A, B), \precsim)$ is a full functor. Therefore, $f \sqsubseteq g : A \to B$ if and only if $Jf \precsim Jg : A \rightharpoonup B$.

3. $\mathcal{K}(A, B)$ is upper-closed in $(p\mathcal{K}(A, B), \precsim)$; i.e., for every $f : A \to B$ and $u : A \rightharpoonup B$, if $f \precsim u$ then $u \downarrow$.

4. $J_{A,B}$ preserves lubs.

5. $\mathrm{dom}_{A,B} : (p\mathcal{K}(A, B), \precsim) \to (\mathcal{D}(A), \subseteq)$ is monotone. □

Remark. From (2) and (3) above, it follows that $J_{A,B}$ is a *full* and *upper-closed* morphism in **Poset**, in the sense that, for every $f : A \to B$ and $u : A \rightharpoonup B$, if $Jf \precsim u$ then there exists a unique $g : A \to B$ such that $f \sqsubseteq g$ and $Jg = u$. And this property together with monotonicity imply (4).

Full and upper-closed morphisms play a central role in the next section.

4.2 Poset-Categories of Partial Maps

We have seen that the category of partial maps induced by a **Poset**-domain-structure has hom-posets with respect to the induced order. Thus, it would be **Poset**-enriched if composition (or equivalently, composition on the right and composition on the left) was monotone.

Checking for monotonicity, and also continuity (as will be seen in the next section), of composition on the right is easier than for composition on the left due to the asymmetry in the diagram

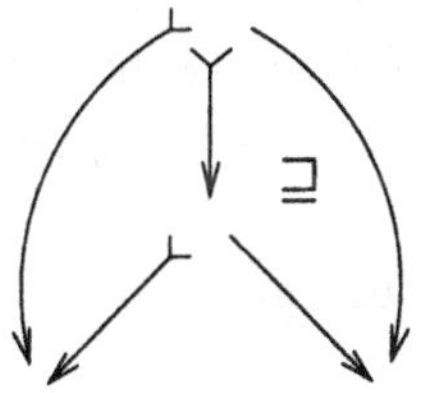

(4.1)

expressing the inequality between two partial maps. When the order on partial maps is the graph inclusion order, the situation in (4.1) is symmetric (as both triangles commute) and *potentially* more manageable.

Monotonicity of composition on the right is immediate:

Lemma 4.2.1 For a **Poset**-domain-structure, $p\mathcal{K}(\_, A)$ is a functor $p\mathcal{K}^{op} \to$ **Poset** for every $A \in |\, p\mathcal{K}\,|$.

PROOF: Let $[m, f] : X \rightharpoonup Y$. Assume $[n', g'] \precsim_i [n, g] : Y \rightharpoonup A$, then the diagram

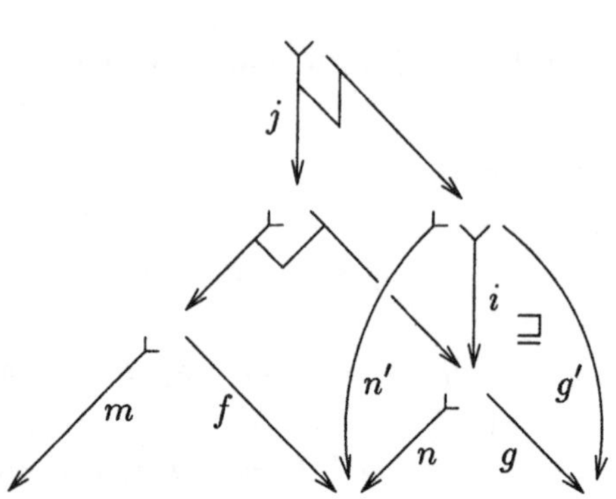

states that j realises the inequality $[n', g'] \circ [m, f] \lesssim [n, g] \circ [m, f]$. □

Aiming at characterising monotonicity of composition on the left, some domain-theoretic concepts in the context of **Poset**-categories, due to Barry Jay, are introduced.

Definition 4.2.2 (Jay) In a **Poset**-category $\mathcal{C}$, a morphism $m : A \to B$ is said to be

1. *full* if for every $C \in |\mathcal{C}|$, the monotone map $m \circ \_ : \mathcal{C}(C, A) \to \mathcal{C}(C, B)$ is full as a functor (i.e., for every $x, y : C \to A$, $m \circ x \leq m \circ y \Rightarrow x \leq y$).
2. *upper-closed* if for every $x : C \to A$ and $y : C \to B$, whenever $m \circ x \leq y$ there exists a $z : C \to A$ such that $m \circ z = y$. □

In **Poset**, a morphism $m : P \to Q$ is full if and only if establishes an isomorphism between P and $m(P)$ ordered as in Q. Further, if $f : P \to Q$ is upper-closed then $f(P)$ is an upper-closed subset of Q. The converse need not hold, but whenever $m : P \to Q$ is full and such that $m(P)$ is an upper-closed subset of Q then m is an upper-closed morphism. Therefore, the full and upper-closed subobjects of a poset are exactly its upper-closed subsets with the induced order.

Full and upper-closed morphisms can be characterised along the lines of the remark after Proposition 4.1.3.

Proposition 4.2.3 In a **Poset**-category, a morphism $m : A \to B$ is full and upper-closed if and only if it is a mono and for every $x : C \to A$ and $y : C \to B$, if $m \circ x \leq y$ then there exists a (necessarily unique) $z : C \to A$ such that $x \leq z$ and $m \circ z = y$. □

In **pPoset** every admissible mono is full and upper-closed. This is not accidental:

Theorem 4.2.4 Given a **Poset**-domain-structure $(\mathcal{K}, \mathcal{D})$, the following are equivalent:

1. $p(\mathcal{K}, \mathcal{D})$ **Poset**-enriches with respect to $\lesssim$.
2. $p\mathcal{K}(A, \_)$ is a functor $p\mathcal{K} \to$ **Poset** for every $A \in |p\mathcal{K}|$.

3. For every $A \in |\mathcal{K}|$ and $m : D \rightarrowtail B$ in $\mathcal{D}$, the map

$$m^R \circ \_ : \ \mathcal{K}(A,B) \longrightarrow p\mathcal{K}(A,D)$$

is monotone.

4. Every admissible mono is full and upper-closed.

PROOF:

(1) ⇒ (2) Vacuously.

(2) ⇒ (1) By Lemma 4.2.1.

(2)⇒(3) Obvious.

(3)⇒(4) Let $m \in \mathcal{D}$, and assume that $m \circ x \sqsubseteq y$. Then,

$$x = m^R \circ m \circ x \sqsubseteq_{\sim} m^R \circ y.$$

In diagram form,

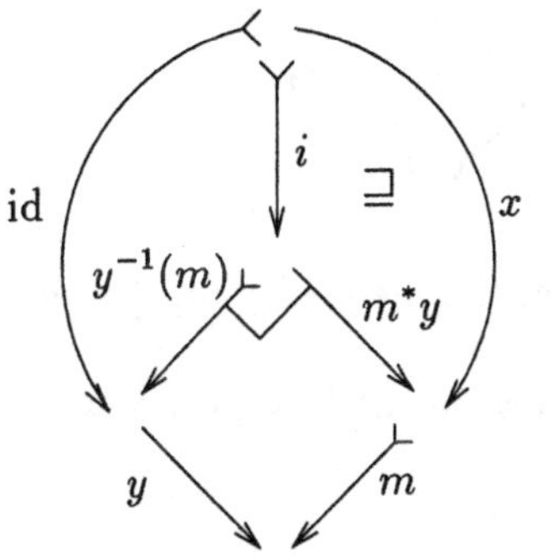

for some i.

Therefore, $x \sqsubseteq (m^*y) \circ i$ and $m \circ (m^*y) \circ i = y$.

(4) ⇒ (2) Let $[n,g] : X \rightharpoonup Y$. Assume $[m',f'] \sqsubseteq_i [m,f] : A \rightharpoonup X$, then

$$n \circ (n^*f') = f' \circ f'^{-1}(n) \sqsubseteq f \circ i \circ f'^{-1}(n).$$

Since n is full and upper-closed, it follows that there exists a unique z such that

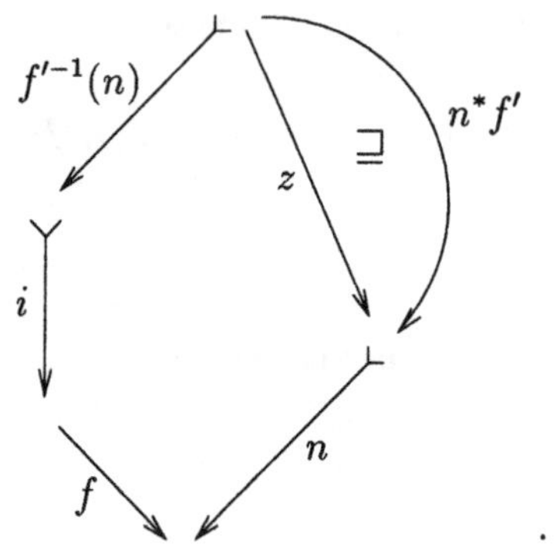

Then, by the universal property of pullbacks, there exists a unique j such that

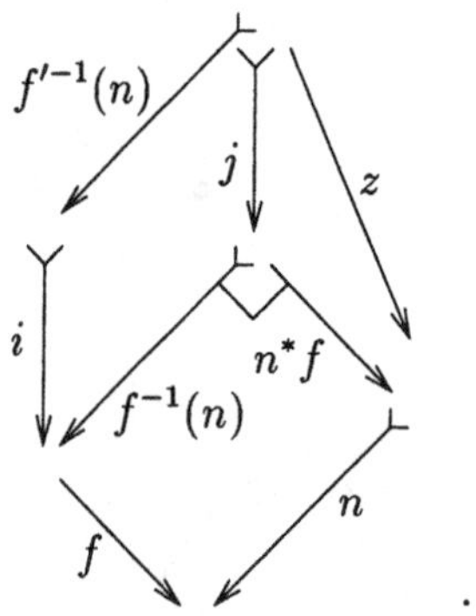

And finally, it follows that j realises the inequality $[n,g] \circ [m',f'] \sqsubseteq [n,g] \circ [m,f]$. □

Corollary 4.2.5 $p(\mathcal{K},\mathcal{D})$ **Poset**-enriches with respect to $\subseteq$. □

4.3 Cpo-Categories of Partial Maps

We start the investigation on **Cpo**-categories of partial maps focusing on the properties enforced by the enrichment. In this respect, two important points are: the fact that the class of admissible subobjects of a **Cpo**-domain-structure inducing a **Cpo**-category of partial maps ought to be locally a cpo, and a *trick* which reduces lubs of arbitrary partial maps to lubs of *graph included* partial maps (Subsection 4.3.1). Afterwards, with the purpose of obtaining lubs of admissible subobjects and lubs of partial maps in a canonical way, *uniform* domain structures are introduced and their properties studied (Subsection 4.3.2). This, together with the given characterisation of **Poset**-categories of partial maps, will provide a characterisation of **Cpo**-categories of partial maps induced by uniform **Cpo**-domain-structures (Subsection 4.3.3). Finally, as an application, a recipe for computing lubs of ω-chains of partial maps in these categories is given (Subsection 4.3.4).

Convention. Whenever we say that a category of partial maps is **Cpo**-enriched we assume that so is the domain structure that induces it and that the order is $\sqsubseteq$.

4.3.1 Properties of Cpo-Categories of Partial Maps

Convention. We regard lubs (of subobjects and partial maps) as colimits. Thus we sometimes write $\bigsqcup\langle[m_k] \subseteq [m_{k+1}]\rangle = \langle[m_k] \subseteq [m]\rangle$ to mean that $\langle[m_k] \subseteq [m_{k+1}]\rangle$ is an ω-chain with lub $[m]$. (An analogous notation is used for partial maps.)

Proposition 4.3.1 Let $(\mathcal{K}, \mathcal{D})$ be a **Cpo**-domain-structure. If $p(\mathcal{K}, \mathcal{D})$ has hom-cpos then $\mathcal{D}$ is locally a cpo (i.e., for every $A \in |\mathcal{D}|$, $(D(A), \subseteq)$ is a cpo).

PROOF: If $\langle[m_k] \subseteq [m_{k+1}]\rangle$ is an ω-chain in $\mathcal{D}(A)$ then $\langle[m_k, m_k] \subseteq [m_{k+1}, m_{k+1}]\rangle$ is an ω-chain in $p\mathcal{K}(A, A)$. And, if $\bigsqcup[m_k, m_k] = [m, f]$, it follows that $\bigsqcup[m_k] = [m]$. □

The local completeness of the class of admissible subobjects has interesting consequences:

Proposition 4.3.2 Given a domain structure, if $\mathcal{D}$ is locally a cpo then

1. If $\langle[m_k] \subseteq_{i_k} [m_{k+1}]\rangle$ is an ω-chain in $\mathcal{D}(A)$ with lub $\langle[m_k] \subseteq_{\mu_k} [m : D \rightarrowtail A]\rangle$ then $\langle[\mu_k] \subseteq_{i_k} [\mu_{k+1}]\rangle$ is an ω-chain in $\mathcal{D}(D)$ with lub $[\mathrm{id}_D]$.
2. For every $n : D \rightarrowtail A$ in $\mathcal{D}$, the mapping $[n \circ \_] : \mathcal{D}(D) \to \mathcal{D}(A)$ is continuous.
3. dom preserves lubs of ω-chains.

PROOF:

(1) Clearly $\langle[\mu_k] \subseteq_{i_k} [\mu_{k+1}]\rangle$ is an ω-chain in $\mathcal{D}(D)$, and $\bigsqcup[\mu_k] = [\mathrm{id}_D]$ because for every $[n] \in \mathcal{D}(D)$,

$$\begin{aligned} \forall k \in |\omega|.\ \mu_k \subseteq n &\iff \forall k \in |\omega|.\ m_k = m \circ \mu_k \subseteq m \circ n \\ &\iff m \subseteq m \circ n \\ &\iff [n] = [\mathrm{id}_D]. \end{aligned}$$

(2) First, observe that for every $[m] \in \mathcal{D}(D)$ and $[n'] \in \mathcal{D}(A)$,

$$n \circ m \subseteq n' \iff m \subseteq n^{-1}(n'). \tag{4.2}$$

Now, let $\langle[m_k] \subseteq [m_{k+1}]\rangle$ be an ω-chain in $\mathcal{D}(D)$ with lub $[m]$. Then, for every $[n'] \in \mathcal{D}(A)$,

$$\begin{aligned} \forall k \in |\omega|.\ n \circ m_k \subseteq n' &\iff \forall k \in |\omega|.\ m_k \subseteq n^{-1}(n') && \text{, by (4.2)} \\ &\iff m \subseteq n^{-1}(n') \\ &\iff n \circ m \subseteq n' && \text{, by (4.2).} \end{aligned}$$

(3) Let $\langle [m_k, f_k] \underset{\sim}{\sqsubset} [m_{k+1}, f_{k+1}] \rangle$ be an ω-chain. If $\bigsqcup [m_k, f_k] = \langle [m_k, f_k] \underset{\sim}{\sqsubset}_{\mu'_k} [m', f] \rangle$ and $\bigsqcup [m_k] = \langle [m_k] \subseteq_{\mu_k} [m] \rangle$ then we are required to prove that $[m] = [m']$.

The admissible subobject $[m']$ is an upper bound of the ω-chain $\langle [m_k] \subseteq [m_{k+1}] \rangle$ and then $[m] \subseteq_i [m']$. For every $k \in |\,\omega\,|$, since $[m_k] \subseteq_{\mu_k} [m] \subseteq_i [m']$ and $[m_k] \subseteq_{\mu'_k} [m']$, it follows that $\mu'_k = i \circ \mu_k$. Therefore, $[m, f \circ i]$ is an upper bound of the ω-chain $\langle [m_k, f_k] \underset{\sim}{\sqsubset} [m_{k+1}, f_{k+1}] \rangle$, and then, $[m'] \subseteq [m]$. □

Convention. Let $\langle i_k : D_k \to D_{k+1} \rangle$ be an ω-chain, then

1. we write $\langle m_k \rangle : \langle i_k \rangle \stackrel{\cdot}{\to} A$ to indicate that $\langle m_k : D_k \to A \rangle$ is a cone for $\langle i_k \rangle$ (that is, $m_k = m_{k+1} \circ i_k$ for all $k \in |\,\omega\,|$);

2. we write $\langle f_k \rangle : \langle i_k \rangle \stackrel{\cdot}{\underset{\le}{\to}} B$ to indicate that $\langle f_k : D_k \to B \rangle$ is a *lax* cone for $\langle i_k \rangle$ (that is, $f_k \sqsubseteq f_{k+1} \circ i_k$ for all $k \in |\,\omega\,|$); and,

3. for cones $\langle \mu_k \rangle : \langle i_k \rangle \stackrel{\cdot}{\to} D$ and $\langle m_k \rangle : \langle i_k \rangle \stackrel{\cdot}{\to} A$, we write $m : \langle \mu_k \rangle \to \langle m_k \rangle$ to indicate that $m : D \to A$ is a morphism of cones (that is, $m \circ \mu_k = m_k$ for all $k \in |\,\omega\,|$).

We now analyse ω-chains of partial maps and their lubs. Let $\langle [m_k, f_k] \underset{\sim}{\sqsubset}_{i_k} [m_{k+1}, f_{k+1}] \rangle$ be an ω-chain in $p\mathcal{K}(A, B)$. Then we have that $\langle i_k \rangle$ is an ω-chain in $\mathcal{D}$, $\langle m_k \rangle : \langle i_k \rangle \stackrel{\cdot}{\to} A$, and $\langle f_k \rangle : \langle i_k \rangle \stackrel{\cdot}{\underset{\le}{\to}} B$. In diagram form,

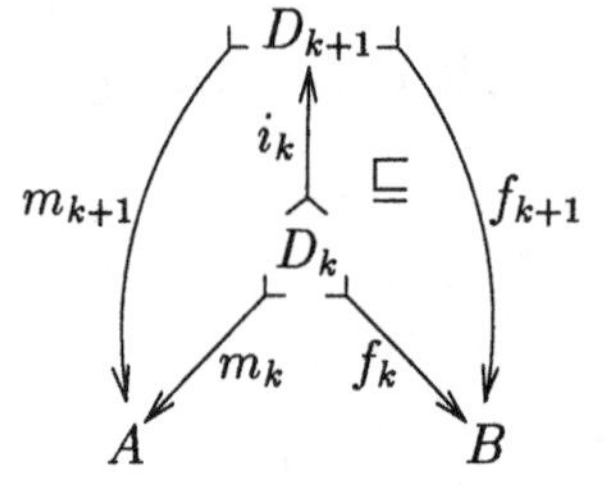

$(k \in |\,\omega\,|)$.

The **Cpo**-enrichment of $\mathcal{K}$ allows us to replace lax cones by cones. In fact, the *lax cone* $\langle f_k \rangle : \langle i_k \rangle \stackrel{\cdot}{\underset{\le}{\to}} B$ induces a *cone* $\langle F_k \rangle : \langle i_k \rangle \stackrel{\cdot}{\to} B$ such that —as we see below— the lub of the ω-chain of *graph inclusions* $\langle [m_k, F_k] \subseteq_{i_k} [m_{k+1}, F_{k+1}] \rangle$ equals the lub of the original ω-chain $\langle [m_k, f_k] \underset{\sim}{\sqsubset}_{i_k} [m_{k+1}, f_{k+1}] \rangle$.

Intuitively, F_k improves f_k by taking into account the information of the f_l's, for $l \geq k$, restricted to D_k. Formally, define $F_k = \bigsqcup_{l \geq k} f_l \circ i_{k,l}$ where we write $i_{k,l}$ for the composite $i_{l-1} \circ \ldots \circ i_k$. Then, $\langle F_k \rangle : \langle i_k \rangle \stackrel{\cdot}{\to} B$ because, for every $k \in |\,\omega\,|$,

$$\begin{aligned} F_k &= \bigsqcup_{l\geq k+1} f_l \circ i_{k,l} &&= \bigsqcup_{l\geq k+1}(f_l \circ i_{k+1,l} \circ i_k) \\ &= (\bigsqcup_{l\geq k+1} f_l \circ i_{k+1,l}) \circ i_k &&= F_{k+1} \circ i_k. \end{aligned}$$

Technically, F_k may not be f restricted to D_k, as $F_k \sqsubseteq f \circ \mu_k$ (see Proposition 4.3.3 (1)) but the equality *need not* hold (in Subsection 4.3.2 this oddity is removed by imposing a *uniformity* condition on the domain structure).

With the above notation we have:

Proposition 4.3.3 1. $\bigsqcup[m_k, f_k]$ exists if and only if so does $\bigsqcup[m_k, F_k]$ and they are equal.

2. For $[n, g] : X \rightharpoonup A$, $\bigsqcup([m_k, f_k]\circ[n, g])$ exists if and only if so does $\bigsqcup([m_k, F_k]\circ[n, g])$ and they are equal.

PROOF:

(1) Observe that for every $k \in |\,\omega\,|$,

$$[m_l, f_l] \precsim_{\mu_l} [m, f] \text{ for every } l \geq k \;\Rightarrow\; [m_k, F_k] \precsim_{\mu_k} [m, f] \tag{4.3}$$

because assuming the antecedent, $f_l \sqsubseteq f \circ \mu_l$ and then, $f_l \circ i_{k,l} \sqsubseteq f \circ \mu_l \circ i_{k,l} = f \circ \mu_k$ for $l \geq k$, yielding $F_k \sqsubseteq f \circ \mu_k$.

Moreover, since for every $k \in |\,\omega\,|$, $[m_k, f_k] \precsim_{\mathrm{id}} [m_k, F_k]$ it follows that

$$[m_k, f_k] \precsim_{\mu_k} [m, f] \text{ for all } k \in |\,\omega\,| \iff [m_k, F_k] \precsim_{\mu_k} [m, f] \text{ for all } k \in |\,\omega\,|$$

and we are done.

(2) By Proposition 4.3.3 (1), $\bigsqcup([m_k, f_k]\circ[n, g]) = \bigsqcup[n\circ g^{-1}(m_k), f_k\circ(m_k{}^*g)]$ exists if and only if so does $\bigsqcup[n \circ g^{-1}(m_k), H_k]$ and they are equal, where $H_k = \bigsqcup_{l\geq k} f_l \circ (m_l{}^*g) \circ j_{k,l}$ and $[n \circ g^{-1}(m_k), f_k \circ (m_k{}^*g)] \precsim_{j_k} [n \circ g^{-1}(m_{k+1}), f_{k+1} \circ (m_{k+1}{}^*g)]$ as indicated in the following diagram

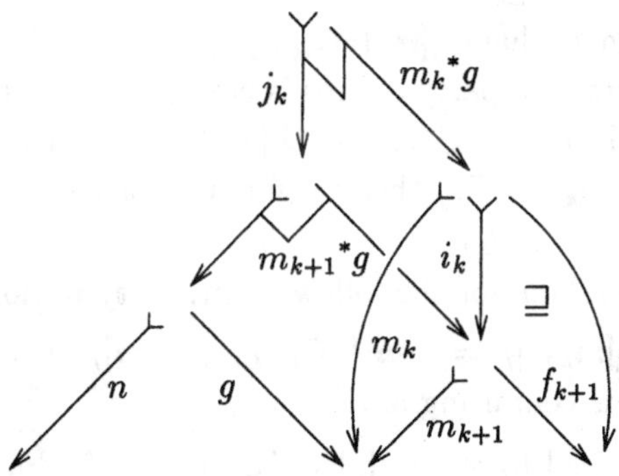

(4.4)

To conclude the proof it is enough to show that $H_k = F_k \circ ({m_k}^* g)$ because then $[n \circ g^{-1}(m_k), H_k] = [n \circ g^{-1}(m_k), F_k \circ ({m_k}^* g)] = [n, g] \circ [m_k, F_k]$.

But from (4.4), by induction, it follows that $({m_l}^* g) \circ j_{k,l} = i_{k,l} \circ ({m_k}^* g)$ for every $l \geq k$ and hence $H_k = \bigsqcup_{l \geq k} f_l \circ ({m_l}^* g) \circ j_{k,l} = \bigsqcup_{l \geq k} f_l \circ i_{k,l} \circ ({m_k}^* g) = F_k \circ ({m_k}^* g)$. □

As mentioned at the beginning of Section 4.2, checking for continuity of composition on the left is more difficult than checking for continuity of composition on the right. This is reflected in the fact that the technique used to prove Proposition 4.3.3 does not extend to prove that $\bigsqcup([n, g] \circ [m_k, f_k]) = \bigsqcup([n, g] \circ [m_k, F_k])$ for every $[n, g] : B \rightharpoonup Y$. For instance, a straight reduction of this equality to Proposition 4.3.3 (1) —as done for proving Proposition 4.3.3 (2)— is not possible because, for a start, there is no reason for which $\mathrm{dom}([n, g] \circ [m_k, f_k]) = [m_k \circ {f_k}^{-1}(n)]$ equals $\mathrm{dom}([n, g] \circ [m_k, F_k]) = [m_k \circ {F_k}^{-1}(n)]$.

4.3.2 Uniform Domain Structures

There are **Cpo**-categories of partial maps in which lubs do not behave as expected, the worst case being that the lub of an ω-chain of partial identities need not be a partial identity (i.e., for every $A \in |\mathcal{K}|$, the *partial-identity* mapping $[\_, \_] : \mathcal{D}(A) \to p\mathcal{K}(A, A)$ need not be continuous). For an example, consider the **Cpo**-category $\mathcal{K}$ pictured as

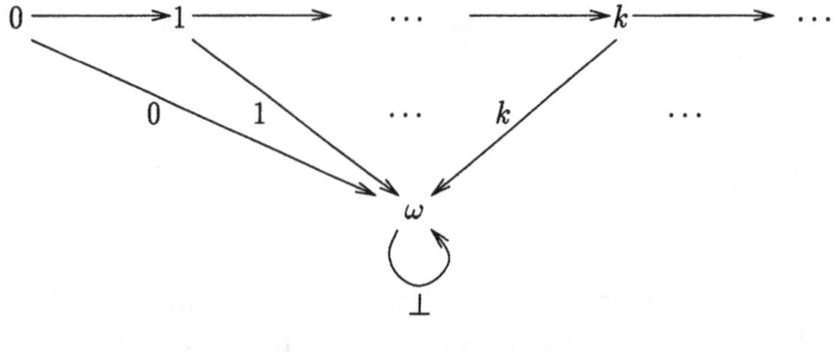

$(k \in |\omega|)$

where $\perp \sqsubset \omega$, and hence forced to be idempotent. Then $\mathbf{Monos}_{\mathcal{K}} = \mathcal{K} \setminus \{\perp\}$ and $p(\mathcal{K}, \mathbf{Monos})$ **Cpo**-enriches. The only infinite chain is $\langle [k, k] \subseteq [k+1, k+1] \rangle$ in $p\mathcal{K}(\omega, \omega)$ and, contradicting all expectations, $\bigsqcup [k, k] = [\omega, \perp] \sqsubset [\omega, \omega]$.

The problem is that for an ω-chain $\langle [m_k] \subseteq_{i_k : D_k \rightarrowtail D_{k+1}} [m_{k+1}] \rangle$ in $\mathcal{D}(A)$ with lub $\langle [m_k] \subseteq_{\mu_k : D_k \rightarrowtail D} [m] \rangle$ the universal property of lubs is not enough to capture the intuition that $D = \bigcup D_k$. Pursuing this intuition, given an $|\omega|$-indexed family $\langle f_k : D_k \to B \rangle$ such that f_{k+1} extends f_k (i.e., $f_k = f_{k+1} \restriction D_k$) there ought to be a *unique uniform extension* $f : D \to B$ of the f_k's (i.e., $f_k = f \restriction D_k$).

In categorical terms, we are asking for the following property to hold:

$$\text{If } \bigsqcup \langle [m_k] \subseteq_{i_k} [m_{k+1}] \rangle = \langle [m_k] \subseteq_{\mu_k : D_k \rightarrowtail D} [m] \rangle \text{ then } \langle \mu_k \rangle : \langle i_k \rangle \stackrel{\cdot}{\to} D \text{ is colimiting in } \mathcal{K}. \tag{4.5}$$

A colimit as in (4.5) can be used to obtain lubs of ω-chains of admissible subobjects:

Lemma 4.3.4 Let $\langle [m_k] \subseteq_{i_k} [m_{k+1}] \rangle$ be an ω-chain in $\mathcal{D}(A)$, and let $\langle \mu_k \rangle$ be a colimit in $\mathcal{K}$ for $\langle i_k \rangle$. If the unique mediating morphism $m : \langle \mu_k \rangle \to \langle m_k \rangle$ is admissible, then $\bigsqcup [m_k] = [m]$.

PROOF: The cone $\langle \mu_k \rangle : \langle i_k : m_k \to m_{k+1} \rangle \dot{\to} m$ is colimiting in $\mathcal{D}/A$ because the forgetful functor $U_A : \mathcal{D}/A \to \mathcal{K}$ reflects colimits. □

When (4.5) holds for all ω-chains of admissible subobjects, the domain structure is said to be uniform.

Definition 4.3.5 A domain structure $(\mathcal{K}, \mathcal{D})$ is said to be *uniform* if the forgetful functor $U : \Sigma_{A \in |\mathcal{D}|} \mathcal{D}/A \to \mathcal{K}$ preserves colimits of ω-chains. □

The following should help in understanding uniformity:

Lemma 4.3.6 The domain structure $(\mathcal{K}, \mathcal{D})$ is uniform and $\mathcal{D}$ is locally a cpo if and only if $p(\mathcal{K}_{\mathbf{Poset}}, \mathcal{D})$ has hom-cpos.

PROOF:

($\Rightarrow$) $\bigsqcup \langle [m_k, f_k] \subseteq [m_{k+1}, f_{k+1}] \rangle = [m, f]$ where $\bigsqcup [m_k] = \langle [m_k] \subseteq_{\mu_k} [m] \rangle$ and $f : \langle \mu_k \rangle \to \langle f_k \rangle$.

($\Leftarrow$) By Proposition 4.3.1, $\mathcal{D}$ is locally a cpo. Let $\langle [m_k] \subseteq [m_{k+1}] \rangle$ be an ω-chain in $\mathcal{D}(A)$ with lub $\langle [m_k] \subseteq_{\mu_k} [m] \rangle$, and let $\langle f_k \rangle : \langle \mu_k \rangle \dot{\to} B$ in $\mathcal{K}$. Then the ω-chain $\langle [m_k, f_k] \subseteq [m_{k+1}, f_{k+1}] \rangle$ in $p\mathcal{K}(A, B)$ has lub $\langle [m_k, f_k] \subseteq_{\mu_k} [m, f] \rangle$ for some f (because if $\bigsqcup [m_k, f_k] = [n, g]$ then $[m] = \bigsqcup [m_k] = [n]$). Clearly $f : \langle \mu_k \rangle \to \langle f_k \rangle$. To see that it is the unique such, let $g : \langle \mu_k \rangle \to \langle f_k \rangle$ then $[m_k, f_k] \subseteq [m, g]$ for every $k \in |\, \omega \,|$ and therefore $[m, f] \subseteq [m, g]$. Thus, $f = g$. □

It follows from the lemma that $(\mathbf{Set}, \mathbf{Monos})$, $(\mathbf{Poset}, \mathbf{Open})$, and $(\mathbf{Cpo}, \mathbf{\Sigma})$ are uniform. A non-example was given at the beginning of the subsection.

The next proposition exhibits the appropriateness of uniformity by showing that, for uniform domain structures, the partial-identity mapping is continuous. Various other consequences are also presented.

Proposition 4.3.7 Let $(\mathcal{K}, \mathcal{D})$ be a uniform **Poset**-domain-structure. If $p\mathcal{K}$ has hom-cpos, then for every $A \in |\, \mathcal{K} \,|$, the partial-identity mapping $[\_, \_] : \mathcal{D}(A) \to p\mathcal{K}(A, A)$ is continuous.

PROOF: Monotonicity is clear. For preservation of lubs, let $\langle [m_k] \subseteq [m_{k+1}] \rangle$ be an ω-chain in $\mathcal{D}(A)$.

Assume that $\bigsqcup [m_k, m_k] = \langle [m_k, m_k] \mathrel{\underset{\sim}{\sqsubset}}_{\mu_k} [m, f] \rangle$. Then, by Proposition 4.3.1, $\bigsqcup [m_k] = [m]$ and therefore we just need to check that $f = m$.

Since, $[m, m]$ is an upper bound of the ω-chain $\langle [m_k, m_k] \subseteq [m_{k+1}, m_{k+1}] \rangle$ it follows that $[m, f] \mathrel{\underset{\sim}{\sqsubset}} [m, m]$ and therefore $f \sqsubseteq m$. Thus, $f \circ \mu_k \sqsubseteq m \circ \mu_k$ and since $m \circ \mu_k = m_k \sqsubseteq f \circ \mu_k$, we get $m \circ \mu_k = f \circ \mu_k$; invoking uniformity the proof is finished. □

Proposition 4.3.8 Let $(\mathcal{K}, \mathcal{D})$ be a uniform **Cpo**-domain-structure. If $p\mathcal{K}$ **Cpo**-enriches, then

1. $\mathcal{D}(\_)$ is a **Cpo**-functor $\mathcal{K}^{op} \to$ **Cpo**.

2. If $\langle [m_k] \subseteq [m_{k+1}] \rangle$ is an ω-chain in $\mathcal{D}(A)$ with lub $[m]$, then for every $f, g : A \to B$,

$$f \circ m_k \sqsubseteq g \circ m_k \text{ for every } k \in |\, \omega \,| \text{ if and only if } f \circ m \sqsubseteq g \circ m.$$

3. $\subseteq$ is a subcpo of $\mathrel{\underset{\sim}{\sqsubset}}$.

PROOF:

(1) By Proposition 4.3.1, $\mathcal{D}$ is locally a cpo. And $\mathcal{D}(\_)(=)$ is a composition of continuous maps, namely, $\mathrm{dom}([=, =] \circ \_)$ —by Propositions 4.3.2 (3) and 4.3.7.

(2) ($\Rightarrow$) For every $k \in |\, \omega \,|$, $f \circ m_k \sqsubseteq g \circ m_k$ implies $f \circ [m_k, m_k] \mathrel{\underset{\sim}{\sqsubset}} g \circ [m_k, m_k]$. Then, $f \circ [m, m] = \bigsqcup f \circ [m_k, m_k] \mathrel{\underset{\sim}{\sqsubset}} \bigsqcup g \circ [m_k, m_k] = g \circ [m, m]$ and therefore $f \circ m \sqsubseteq g \circ m$.

($\Leftarrow$) For every $k \in |\, \omega \,|$, let $[m_k] \subseteq_{\mu_k} [m]$. Then,

$$f \circ m_k = f \circ m \circ \mu_k \sqsubseteq g \circ m \circ \mu_k = g \circ m_k.$$

(3) For every $A, B \in |\, p\mathcal{K} \,|$, by Propositions 4.3.1 and 4.3.6, $(p\mathcal{K}(A, B), \subseteq)$ is a cpo. As $\subseteq$ is a subposet of $\mathrel{\underset{\sim}{\sqsubset}}$, we only need to show that for every ω-chain $\langle [m_k, f_k] \subseteq [m_{k+1}, f_{k+1}] \rangle$ with lub $\langle [m_k, f_k] \subseteq_{\mu_k} [m, f] \rangle$ in $(p\mathcal{K}(A, B), \subseteq)$

$$[m_k, f_k] \mathrel{\underset{\sim}{\sqsubset}}_{\nu_k} [n, g] \text{ for every } k \in |\, \omega \,| \;\Rightarrow\; [m, f] \mathrel{\underset{\sim}{\sqsubset}} [n, g].$$

Assuming the antecedent, $[m_k] \subseteq_{\nu_k} [n]$ for every $k \in |\, \omega \,|$ and, because $\bigsqcup [m_k] = [m]$, we have that $[m] \subseteq_i [n]$. Finally, to show that $f \sqsubseteq g \circ i$ observe that $[m_k] \subseteq_{\nu_k} [n]$ and $[m_k] \subseteq_{\mu_k} [m] \subseteq_i [n]$ imply $\nu_k = i \circ \mu_k$. Then, $f \circ \mu_k = f_k \sqsubseteq g \circ \nu_k = g \circ i \circ \mu_k$ and since, by Proposition 4.3.2 (1), $\bigsqcup [\mu_k] = [\mathrm{id}]$, using Proposition 4.3.8 (2) we are done. □

4.3.3 Characterisation of Cpo-Categories of Partial Maps induced by Uniform Domain Structures

Theorem 4.3.9 Let $(\mathcal{K}, \mathcal{D})$ be a uniform **Cpo**-domain-structure. Then,

$p(\mathcal{K}, \mathcal{D})$ **Cpo**-enriches with respect to $\precsim$

if and only if

1. $p(\mathcal{K}, \mathcal{D})$ **Poset**-enriches with respect to $\precsim$,
2. $\mathcal{D}(\_)$ is a **Cpo**-functor $\mathcal{K}^{op} \to$ **Cpo**, and
3. the colimits of ω-chains preserved by the forgetful functor $U : \Sigma_{A \in |\mathcal{D}|} \mathcal{D}/A \to \mathcal{K}$ are **Poset**-colimits. □

That the three conditions above are necessary follows from Propositions 4.3.8 (1), 4.3.8 (2), 4.3.2 (1) and 2.2.1. We show that they are sufficient in a series of steps.

Remark. The idea behind the proof is simple though one has to go through a series of long calculations.

- For showing that every hom-poset is a cpo, by Proposition 4.3.3 (1), we reduce the general case to finding lubs of chains of graph inclusions. Intuitively, the lub of a chain of graph inclusions is the partial map with domain of definition the union of the domains of definition of the partial maps in the chain, and with total component the unique uniform extension of the total components of the partial maps in the chain. (Recall that such extensions exist by the uniformity of the domain structure.)
- For showing that composition on the right is continuous, by Proposition 4.3.3 (2), the general case is reduced to the graph inclusion case which, in turn, is proved by calculating the relevant lub with the above recipe.
- For showing that composition on the left is continuous the problem is broken down in more subcases. We show that composition on the left with total maps is continuous, and that composition on the left with partial inclusions is continuous for total maps. This allows us to reduce the general case to the graph inclusion case. Then, after proving that composition on the left is continuos for chains of graph inclusions the general case is established.

Until the end of this subsection, let $(\mathcal{K}, \mathcal{D})$ be a uniform **Cpo**-domain-structure.

Hom-posets are cpos

Lemma 4.3.10 (The graph inclusion case) Let $\mathcal{D}$ be locally a cpo, and let $\mathcal{K}$ be **Poset**-enriched. Assume that U maps colimits of ω-chains to **Poset**-colimits. For an ω-chain $\langle [m_k, f_k] \subseteq [m_{k+1}, f_{k+1}] \rangle$,

$$\bigsqcup [m_k, f_k] = \langle [m_k, f_k] \mathrel{\sqsubseteq\!\!\!\!\!\sim}_{\mu_k} [m, f] \rangle \iff \bigsqcup [m_k] = \langle [m_k] \subseteq_{\mu_k} [m] \rangle \text{ and } f : \langle \mu_k \rangle \to \langle f_k \rangle.$$

PROOF:

($\Rightarrow$) $\bigsqcup [m_k] = \langle [m_k] \subseteq_{\mu_k} [m] \rangle$ because dom preserves lubs of ω-chains —see Proposition 4.3.2 (3). Since U preserves colimits of ω-chains, it follows that $\langle \mu_k \rangle$ is a colimiting cone. Let $g : \langle \mu_k \rangle \to \langle f_k \rangle$, then $[m, g]$ is an upper bound of the ω-chain $\langle [m_k, f_k] \subseteq [m_{k+1}, f_{k+1}] \rangle$ and therefore $f \sqsubseteq g$. Thus, $f \circ \mu_k \sqsubseteq g \circ \mu_k = f_k$, and since $f_k \sqsubseteq f \circ \mu_k$, it follows that $f : \langle \mu_k \rangle \to \langle f_k \rangle$.

($\Leftarrow$) By construction, $[m, f]$ is an upper-bound of $\langle [m_k, f_k] \subseteq [m_{k+1}, f_{k+1}] \rangle$. It is also the least, for assuming that $[m_k, f_k] \mathrel{\sqsubseteq\!\!\!\!\!\sim}_{\nu_k} [n, g]$, it follows that $[m_k] \subseteq_{\nu_k} [n]$, and therefore $[m] \subseteq_i [n]$. Thus, $\nu_k = i \circ \mu_k$ and then $f \circ \mu_k \sqsubseteq g \circ i \circ \mu_k$ for every $k \in |\, \omega \,|$. Finally, since $\langle \mu_k \rangle$ is a **Poset**-colimit, we conclude that $f \sqsubseteq g \circ i$. □

Proposition 4.3.11 (Hom-posets are cpos) Let $\mathcal{D}$ be locally a cpo, and let $\mathcal{K}$ be **Cpo**-enriched. If U maps colimits of ω-chains to **Poset**-colimits, then every hom-poset in $p\mathcal{K}$ is a cpo.

PROOF: Follows from Lemma 4.3.10 and Proposition 4.3.3 (1). □

Composition on the right is continuous

Proposition 4.3.12 Let $\mathcal{K}$ be **Cpo**-enriched. Assume that U maps colimits of ω-chains to **Poset**-colimits, and that $\mathcal{D}(\_)$ is a functor $\mathcal{K}^{op} \to$ **Cpo**. Then,

1. **(Composition on the right is continuous for ω-chains of graph inclusions)** for every ω-chain $\langle [m_k, f_k] \subseteq [m_{k+1}, f_{k+1}] \rangle$ in $p\mathcal{K}(B, C)$, and every $[n, g] : A \rightharpoonup B$,

$$(\bigsqcup [m_k, f_k]) \circ [n, g] \;=\; \bigsqcup ([m_k, f_k] \circ [n, g]).$$

2. **(Composition on the right is continuous)** $p\mathcal{K}(\_, A)$ is a functor $p\mathcal{K}^{op} \to$ **Cpo** for every $A \in |\, p\mathcal{K} \,|$.

PROOF:

(1) Let $\bigsqcup [m_k, f_k] = \langle [m_k, f_k] \mathrel{\sqsubseteq\!\!\!\!\!\sim}_{\mu_k} [m, f] \rangle$. By Lemma 4.3.10, $\bigsqcup [m_k] = \langle [m_k] \subseteq_{\mu_k} [m] \rangle$ and $f : \langle \mu_k \rangle \to \langle f_k \rangle$.

By Corollary 4.2.5, $\langle [m_k, f_k] \circ [n, g] \subseteq [m_{k+1}, f_{k+1}] \circ [n, g] \rangle$ is an ω-chain. To prove

$$\bigsqcup [n \circ g^{-1}(m_k), f_k \circ (m_k{}^* g)] \;=\; [n \circ g^{-1}(m), f \circ (m^* g)]$$

we will, again, use Lemma 4.3.10.

First,

$$\bigsqcup [n \circ g^{-1}(m_k)] = [n \circ g^{-1}(m)]$$

by Proposition 4.3.2 (2) and the continuity of $\mathcal{D}(g)$.

Second, assume that $n \circ g^{-1}(m_k) \subseteq_{\nu_k} n \circ g^{-1}(m)$. Since $f : \langle \mu_k \rangle \to \langle f_k \rangle$, it follows that

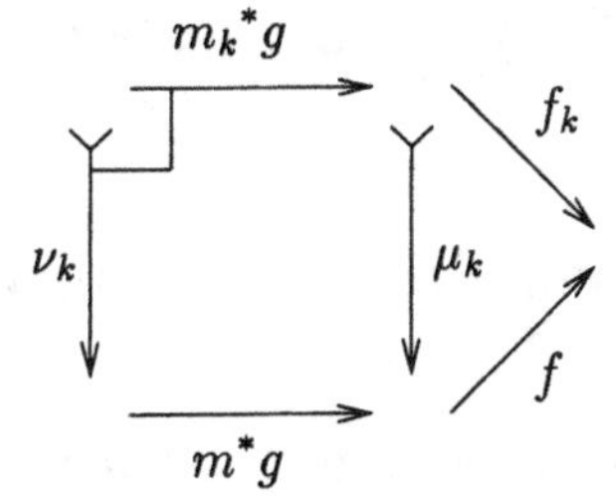

and therefore $f \circ (m^*g) : \langle \nu_k \rangle \to \langle f_k \circ (m_k{}^*g) \rangle$.

(2) For every ω-chain $\langle [m_k, f_k] \sqsubseteq [m_{k+1}, f_{k+1}] \rangle$ in $p\mathcal{K}(C, A)$ and $[n, g] : B \rightharpoonup C$, by Lemma 4.2.1, $\langle [m_k, f_k] \circ [n, g] \sqsubseteq [m_{k+1}, f_{k+1}] \circ [n, g] \rangle$ is an ω-chain in $p\mathcal{K}(B, A)$. And, we have

$$\begin{aligned} (\bigsqcup [m_k, f_k]) \circ [n, g] &= (\bigsqcup [m_k, F_k]) \circ [n, g] &&, \text{by Proposition 4.3.3 (1)} \\ &= \bigsqcup ([m_k, F_k] \circ [n, g]) &&, \text{by Proposition 4.3.12 (1)} \\ &= \bigsqcup ([m_k, f_k] \circ [n, g]) &&, \text{by Proposition 4.3.3 (2).} \end{aligned}$$ □

Composition on the left is continuous

Proposition 4.3.13 Let $\mathcal{D}$ be locally a cpo, let $\mathcal{K}$ be **Cpo**-enriched, and let $p\mathcal{K}$ be **Poset**-enriched. Assume that U maps colimits of ω-chains to **Poset**-colimits. Then,

1. **(Composition on the left with total maps is continuous)** $p\mathcal{K}(A, \_)$ is a functor $\mathcal{K} \to$ **Cpo** for every $A \in |\, p\mathcal{K}\,|$.

2. **(Composition on the left with partial inclusions is continuous for total maps)** For $A \in |\, \mathcal{K}\,|$ and $m \in \mathcal{D}(D, B)$, if the mapping $\mathcal{D}(\_)[m] : \mathcal{K}(A, B) \to \mathcal{D}(A)$ is continuous, then so is the mapping $m^R \circ \_ : \mathcal{K}(A, B) \to p\mathcal{K}(A, D)$.

3. **(Reduction to the graph inclusion case)** If $\mathcal{D}(\_)$ is a **Cpo**-functor $\mathcal{K}^{op} \to$ **Cpo**, then for every ω-chain $\langle [m_k, f_k] \sqsubseteq_{i_k} [m_{k+1}, f_{k+1}] \rangle$ in $p\mathcal{K}(A, B)$ and $[n, g] : B \rightharpoonup C$,

$$\bigsqcup ([n, g] \circ [m_k, f_k]) = \bigsqcup ([n, g] \circ [m_k, F_k])$$

where $F_k = \bigsqcup_{l \geq k} f_l \circ i_{k,l}$.

PROOF:

(1) Let $\langle [m_k, f_k] \mathrel{\underset{\sim}{\sqsubset}}_{i_k} [m_{k+1}, f_{k+1}] \rangle$ be an ω-chain in $p\mathcal{K}(A, B)$.

By Proposition 4.3.3 (1) and Lemma 4.3.10, we have that $\bigsqcup [m_k, f_k] = [m, f]$ where $\bigsqcup [m_k] = \langle [m_k] \subseteq_{\mu_k} [m] \rangle$ and $f : \langle \mu_k \rangle \to \langle \bigsqcup_{l \geq k} f_l \circ i_{k,l} \rangle$.

Then, $g \circ f : \langle \mu_k \rangle \to \langle \bigsqcup_{l \geq k} (g \circ f_l) \circ i_{k,l} \rangle$ and, again by Proposition 4.3.3 (1) and Lemma 4.3.10, $\bigsqcup [m_k, g \circ f_k] = [m, g \circ f]$.

(2) $m^R \circ \_$ is monotone because $p\mathcal{K}$ is **Poset**-enriched.

For the preservation of lubs, if $\langle f_k \rangle$ is an ω-chain in $\mathcal{K}(A, B)$, writing f for $\bigsqcup f_k$, we must prove

$$\bigsqcup [{f_k}^{-1}(m), m^* f_k] \quad = \quad [f^{-1}(m), m^* f].$$

The ω-chain $\langle [{f_k}^{-1}(m), m^* f_k] \mathrel{\underset{\sim}{\sqsubset}} [{f_{k+1}}^{-1}(m), m^* f_{k+1}] \rangle$ in $p\mathcal{K}(A, D)$ has $[f^{-1}(m), m^* f]$ as an upper bound because the composition of partial maps is monotone. To see that it is the least, assume $[{f_k}^{-1}(m), m^* f_k] \mathrel{\underset{\sim}{\sqsubset}}_{\mu_k} [f^{-1}(m), m^* f]$ and $[{f_k}^{-1}(m), m^* f_k] \mathrel{\underset{\sim}{\sqsubset}}_{\nu_k} [n, g]$.

First, $[{f_k}^{-1}(m)] \subseteq_{\nu_k} [n]$ and therefore, $[f^{-1}(m)] \subseteq_i [n]$, by the continuity of $\mathcal{D}(\_)[m]$.

Second, we will show that $m^* f \sqsubseteq g \circ i$.

The inequalities $[{f_k}^{-1}(m)] \subseteq_{\mu_k} [f^{-1}(m)] \subseteq_i [n]$ and $[{f_k}^{-1}(m)] \subseteq_{\nu_k} [n]$, imply $\nu_k = i \circ \mu_k$. So we have

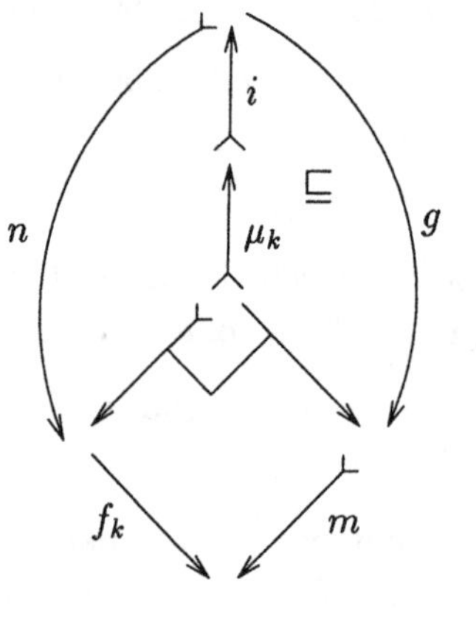

Thus, $f_k \circ n \circ i \circ \mu_k \sqsubseteq m \circ g \circ i \circ \mu_k$ for every $k \in |\, \omega \,|$, and since $\langle \mu_k \rangle$ is a **Poset**-colimit, we conclude that $m \circ g \circ i$ is an upper bound of the ω-chain $\langle f_k \circ n \circ i \rangle$. On the other hand, $\bigsqcup (f_k \circ n \circ i) = f \circ n \circ i = f \circ f^{-1}(m) = m \circ (m^* f)$.

Then, $m \circ (m^* f) \sqsubseteq m \circ g \circ i$, and since m is full we are done.

(3) We proceed via two calculations:
First,

$$\begin{aligned}
\bigsqcup_{k\geq 0}(n^R \circ [m_k, F_k]) &= \bigsqcup_{k\geq 0}(n^R \circ (\bigsqcup_{l\geq k} f_l \circ i_{k,l}) \circ {m_k}^R) \\
&= \bigsqcup_{k\geq 0}\left((\bigsqcup_{l\geq k} n^R \circ f_l \circ i_{k,l}) \circ {m_k}^R\right) &&\text{, by Proposition 4.3.13 (2)} \\
&= \bigsqcup_{k\geq 0}\bigsqcup_{l\geq k}(n^R \circ f_l \circ i_{k,l} \circ {m_k}^R) &&\text{, by Proposition 4.3.12 (2)} \\
&= \bigsqcup_{k\geq 0}(n^R \circ f_k \circ {m_k}^R) \\
&= \bigsqcup_{k\geq 0}(n^R \circ [m_k, f_k]).
\end{aligned}$$

Second,

$$\begin{aligned}
\bigsqcup([n,g] \circ [m_k, f_k]) &= \bigsqcup(g \circ n^R \circ [m_k, f_k]) \\
&= g \circ \bigsqcup(n^R \circ [m_k, f_k]) &&\text{, by Proposition 4.3.13 (1)} \\
&= g \circ \bigsqcup(n^R \circ [m_k, F_k]) &&\text{, by the previous calculation} \\
&= \bigsqcup(g \circ n^R \circ [m_k, F_k]) &&\text{, by Proposition 4.3.13 (1)} \\
&= \bigsqcup([n,g] \circ [m_k, F_k]).
\end{aligned}$$

□

Proposition 4.3.14 (Composition on the left is continuous for ω-chains of graph inclusions) Let $\mathcal{K}$ be **Cpo**-enriched. Assume that U maps colimits of ω-chains to **Poset**-colimits, and that $\mathcal{D}(\_)$ is a functor $\mathcal{K}^{op} \to$ **Cpo**. Then, for every ω-chain $\langle [m_k, f_k] \subseteq_{i_k} [m_{k+1}, f_{k+1}] \rangle$ in $p\mathcal{K}(A, B)$ and $[n, g] : B \rightharpoonup C$,

$$\bigsqcup([n,g] \circ [m_k, f_k]) \;=\; [n,g] \circ \bigsqcup [m_k, f_k].$$

PROOF: Let $\bigsqcup [m_k, f_k] = \langle [m_k, f_k] \precsim_{\mu_k} [m, f] \rangle$.

By Corollary 4.2.5, $\langle [n,g] \circ [m_k, f_k] \subseteq [n,g] \circ [m_{k+1}, f_{k+1}] \rangle$ is an ω-chain. To prove

$$\bigsqcup [m_k \circ {f_k}^{-1}(n), g \circ (n^* f_k)] \;=\; [m \circ f^{-1}(n), g \circ (n^* f)]$$

we will use Lemma 4.3.10.

If $[m_k \circ {f_k}^{-1}(n)] \subseteq_{j_k} [m_{k+1} \circ {f_{k+1}}^{-1}(n)]$ then to show $\bigsqcup [m_k \circ {f_k}^{-1}(n)] = [m \circ f^{-1}(n)]$, by Lemma 4.3.4, it is enough to find a colimiting cone for $\langle j_k \rangle$, say $\langle \nu_k \rangle$, such that $m \circ f^{-1}(n) : \langle \nu_k \rangle \to \langle m_k \circ {f_k}^{-1}(n) \rangle$.

We have

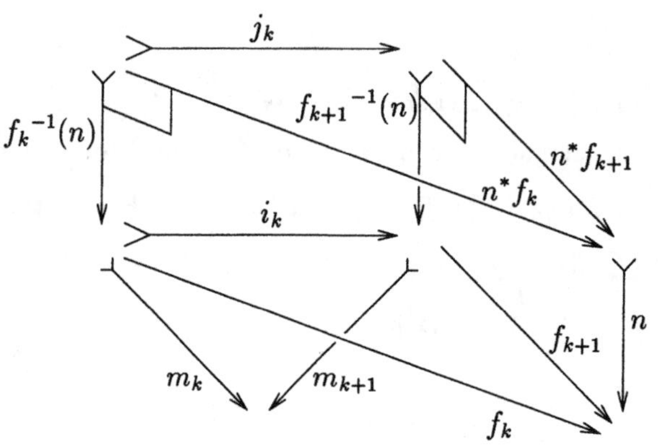

and so

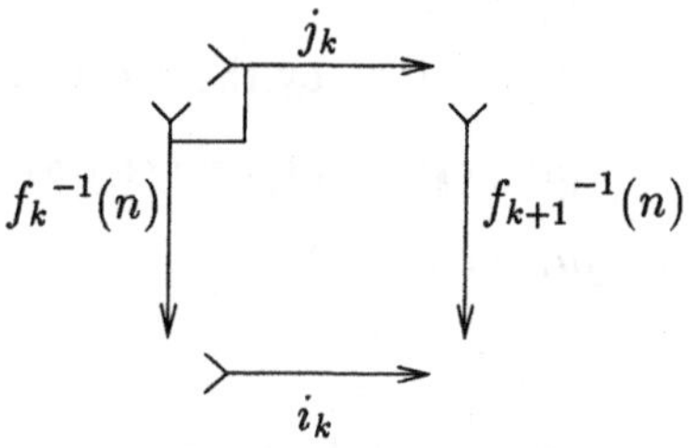

Moreover, by Lemma 4.3.10, $f : \langle \mu_k \rangle \to \langle f_k \rangle$, and therefore for every $k \in |\, \omega \,|$ we have

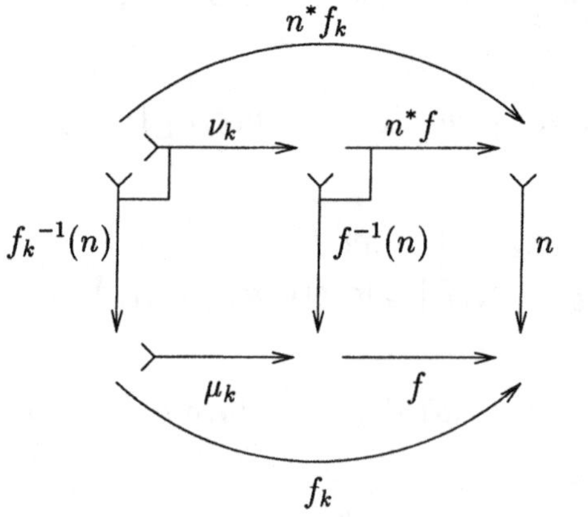

(4.6)

for some unique ν_k.

The complete picture is as follows

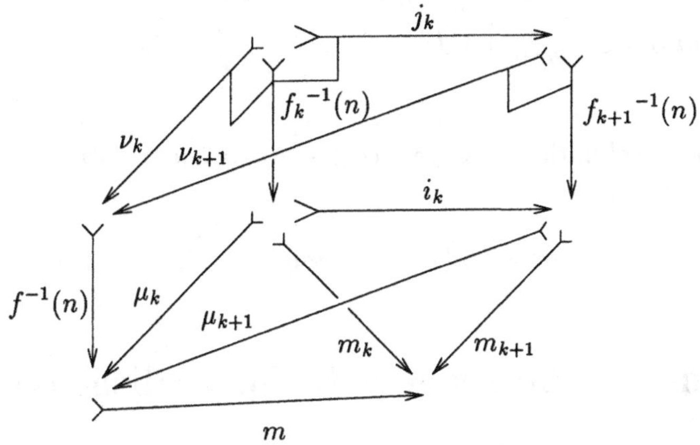

Thus, $\langle \nu_k \rangle$ is a cone for $\langle j_k \rangle$ and $m \circ f^{-1}(n) : \langle \nu_k \rangle \to \langle m_k \circ f_k{}^{-1}(n) \rangle$.

Finally, recall that by Lemma 4.3.10, $\bigsqcup [m_k] = \langle [m_k] \subseteq_{\mu_k} [m] \rangle$ and so, by Proposition 4.3.2 (1), $\bigsqcup [\mu_k] = [\mathrm{id}]$. Since, by construction, ν_k is obtained by pulling back μ_k along $f^{-1}(n)$, and $\mathcal{D}(f^{-1}(n))$ is continuous, it follows that $\bigsqcup [\nu_k] = [\mathrm{id}]$. Hence, since U preserves colimits of ω-chains, $\langle \nu_k \rangle$ is a colimit for $\langle j_k \rangle$.

To complete the proof, by Lemma 4.3.10, we need only check whether $g \circ (n^* f) : \langle \nu_k \rangle \to \langle g \circ (n^* f_k) \rangle$. This follows because $(n^* f) \circ \nu_k = n^* f_k$ —see diagram (4.6). □

Proposition 4.3.15 (Composition on the left is continuous) Let $\mathcal{K}$ be **Cpo**-enriched and let $p\mathcal{K}$ be **Poset**-enriched. Assume that U maps colimits of ω-chains to **Poset**-colimits and that $\mathcal{D}(\_)$ is a **Cpo**-functor $\mathcal{K}^{op} \to$ **Cpo**. Then, $p\mathcal{K}(A, \_)$ is a functor $p\mathcal{K} \to$ **Cpo** for every $A \in |\, p\mathcal{K} \,|$.

PROOF: Because for every ω-chain $\langle [m_k, f_k] \sqsubseteq [m_{k+1}, f_{k+1}] \rangle$ in $p\mathcal{K}(A, B)$, and every $[n, g] : B \rightharpoonup C$, we have

$$\begin{aligned} [n,g] \circ \bigsqcup [m_k, f_k] &= [n,g] \circ \bigsqcup [m_k, F_k] && \text{, by Proposition 4.3.3 (1)} \\ &= \bigsqcup ([n,g] \circ [m_k, F_k]) && \text{, by Proposition 4.3.14} \\ &= \bigsqcup ([n,g] \circ [m_k, f_k]) && \text{, by Proposition 4.3.13 (3).} \end{aligned}$$

□

4.3.4 Computing Lubs of ω-Chains of Partial Maps

A by-product of the above characterisation is a recipe for computing lubs of ω-chains of partial maps in **Cpo**-categories of partial maps induced by uniform **Cpo**-domain-structures:

Proposition 4.3.16 Let $(\mathcal{K}, \mathcal{D})$ be a uniform **Cpo**-domain-structure such that $p\mathcal{K}$ **Cpo**-enriches. For every ω-chain $\langle [m_k, f_k] \precsim_{i_k} [m_{k+1}, f_{k+1}] \rangle$,

$$\bigsqcup [m_k, f_k] = \langle [m_k, f_k] \precsim_{\mu_k : D_k \rightarrowtail D} [m, f] \rangle$$

if and only if

> $\langle \mu_k \rangle : \langle i_k \rangle \dot{\to} D$ is colimiting in $\mathcal{K}$, $m : \langle \mu_k \rangle \to \langle m_k \rangle$ and $f : \langle \mu_k \rangle \to \langle F_k \rangle$ where $F_k = \bigsqcup_{l \geq k} f_l \circ i_{k,l}$.

PROOF: Follows from Proposition 4.3.3 (1) and Lemma 4.3.10. □

4.4 Enrichment with respect to Specialisation

In this section the characterisation theorem of **Cpo**-categories of partial maps (Theorem 4.3.9) is applied when the order is specialisation. As will be shown, **Poset**-enrichment is immediate, whilst **Cpo**-enrichment requires that the operation of pulling back admissible monos along arbitrary maps be continuous.

Proposition 4.4.1 Let $(\mathcal{K}, \mathcal{D})$ be a domain structure. Then, $\mathcal{K}$ and $p\mathcal{K}$ **Preorder**-enrich with respect $\sqsubseteq^s$ and $\precsim^s$ respectively.

Thus, if $\sqsubseteq^s$ is antisymmetric, $\mathcal{K}$ and $p\mathcal{K}$ **Poset**-enrich with respect $\sqsubseteq^s$ and $\precsim^s$ respectively.

PROOF: It is enough to see that $p\mathcal{K}$ **Preorder**-enriches with respect to $\precsim^s$.

This follows because $\precsim^s$ is a preorder and, for $u : X \rightharpoonup A$, $v \precsim^s v' : A \rightharpoonup B$ and $w : B \rightharpoonup Y$, we have that

$$\begin{aligned} v \precsim^s v' &\iff \mathcal{D}(v) \subseteq \mathcal{D}(v') \\ &\implies \mathcal{D}(w \circ v \circ u) = \mathcal{D}(u) \circ \mathcal{D}(v) \circ \mathcal{D}(w) \subseteq \mathcal{D}(u) \circ \mathcal{D}(v') \circ \mathcal{D}(w) \\ &\iff w \circ v \circ u \precsim^s w \circ v' \circ u. \end{aligned}$$

□

Proposition 4.4.2 Let $(\mathcal{K}, \mathcal{D})$ be a uniform domain structure. If $\mathcal{D}$ is locally a cpo, $\mathcal{K}$ has hom-cpos with respect to $\sqsubseteq^s$, and for every $A, B \in |\mathcal{K}|$, the mapping $\mathcal{D}(\_)(=) : \mathcal{K}(A, B) \times \mathcal{D}(B) \to \mathcal{D}(A)$ is continuous, then $\mathcal{K}$ and $p\mathcal{K}$ **Cpo**-enrich with respect to $\sqsubseteq^s$ and $\precsim^s$ respectively.

PROOF: By Proposition 4.4.1, $\mathcal{K}$ **Poset**-enriches. By hypothesis every hom in $\mathcal{K}$ is a cpo. Moreover, using the fact that $\mathcal{D}(\_) : \mathcal{K}(A, B) \to \mathbf{Cpo}(\mathcal{D}(B), \mathcal{D}(A))$ is injective, we have that

- since for every $m : D \rightarrowtail B$ in $\mathcal{D}$, the mapping $\mathcal{D}(\_)[m] : \mathcal{K}(A, B) \to \mathcal{D}(A)$ is continuous, then so is composition on the left in $\mathcal{K}$; and,

- since, in addition, for every $f : A \to B$, the mapping $\mathcal{D}(f) : \mathcal{D}(B) \to \mathcal{D}(A)$ is continuous, it follows that so is composition on the right in $\mathcal{K}$.

Therefore, $\mathcal{K}$ **Cpo**-enriches.

By Proposition 4.4.1, $p\mathcal{K}$ **Poset**-enriches.

Finally, for every ω-chain $\langle [m_k] \subseteq [m_{k+1}] \rangle$ for which $[m_k] \subseteq_{\mu_k : D_k \to D} \bigsqcup [m_k]$ we show that for $f, f' : D \to B$,

$$f \circ \mu_k \sqsubseteq^s f' \circ \mu_k \text{ for every } k \in |\,\omega\,| \;\Rightarrow\; f \sqsubseteq^s f'. \tag{4.7}$$

This will establish item (3) of Theorem 4.3.9 and, by invoking this theorem, conclude the proof of the proposition.

For $[m] \in \mathcal{D}(B)$, let $\mathcal{D}(f)[m] = [n]$ and let $\mathcal{D}(f')[m] = [n']$. Assuming the antecedent of (4.7), it follows that $\mathcal{D}(\mu_k)[n] = \mathcal{D}(f \circ \mu_k)[m] \subseteq \mathcal{D}(f' \circ \mu_k)[m] = \mathcal{D}(\mu_k)[n']$ and therefore $[n \circ n^{-1}(\mu_k)] = [\mu_k \circ {\mu_k}^{-1}(n)] \subseteq [\mu_k \circ {\mu_k}^{-1}(n')] = [n' \circ n'^{-1}(\mu_k)]$. Then,

$$\begin{aligned}
\mathcal{D}(f)[m] &= \bigsqcup [n \circ n^{-1}(\mu_k)] \quad \text{, because } [n \circ _] \text{ and } \mathcal{D}(n) \text{ are continuous,} \\
&\qquad\qquad\qquad\qquad \bigsqcup [\mu_k] = [\mathrm{id}] \text{ and } n^{-1}[\mathrm{id}] = [\mathrm{id}]. \\
&\subseteq \bigsqcup [n' \circ n'^{-1}(\mu_k)] \\
&= \mathcal{D}(f')[m].
\end{aligned}$$

□

4.5 Cpo-Categories of Partial Maps Revisited

Cpo-categories of partial maps are revisited in the light of representability. The idea is to regard $p\mathcal{K}$ as a subcategory of $\mathcal{K}$ via the lifting functor and see whether the **Cpo**-enrichment of $\mathcal{K}$ restricts to this subcategory.

We know, by Proposition 4.1.3 (4), that $J : \mathcal{K} \to p\mathcal{K}$ locally preserves lubs of ω-chains but, what about its right adjoint?

Proposition 4.5.1 If $\chi : J \dashv L : p\mathcal{K} \to \mathcal{K}$ is a **Poset**-adjunction, then L locally preserves lubs.

PROOF: By Theorem 3.2.6, $\varepsilon_A = {\eta_A}^R$. So for every $A, B \in |\, p\mathcal{K}\,|$,

$$\_ \circ \varepsilon_A \dashv \_ \circ \eta_A : p\mathcal{K}(LA, B) \to p\mathcal{K}(A, B)$$

and thus $\_ \circ \varepsilon_A$ preserves lubs. Since also $\chi_{A,B}$ preserves lubs (as it is an isomorphism in **Poset**), and $L_{A,B}(\_) = \chi_{A,B}(\_ \circ \varepsilon_A)$ we are done. □

Now let $\chi : J \dashv L : p\mathcal{K} \to \mathcal{K}$ be a **Poset**-adjunction. Then,

- **hom-posets are cpos**, as: for every ω-chain $\langle u_k \rangle$ in $p\mathcal{K}(A,B)$,

$$\bigsqcup_{p\mathcal{K}} u_k = \varepsilon_B \circ \big(\bigsqcup_{\mathcal{K}} \chi(u_k)\big);$$

- **composition on the left is continuous**, as: for every ω-chain $\langle u_k \rangle$ in $p\mathcal{K}(A,B)$ and $v : B \rightharpoonup Y$,

$$\begin{aligned}\textstyle\bigsqcup_{p\mathcal{K}}(v \circ u_k) &= \varepsilon_Y \circ \big(\textstyle\bigsqcup_{\mathcal{K}} \chi(v \circ u_k)\big) &= \varepsilon_Y \circ \big(\textstyle\bigsqcup_{\mathcal{K}}(Lv) \circ \chi(u_k)\big) \\ &= \varepsilon_Y \circ (Lv) \circ (\textstyle\bigsqcup_{\mathcal{K}} \chi u_k) &= v \circ \varepsilon_B \circ (\textstyle\bigsqcup_{\mathcal{K}} \chi u_k) \\ &= v \circ (\textstyle\bigsqcup_{p\mathcal{K}} u_k).\end{aligned}$$

- **composition on the right is continuous**, as: for every ω-chain $\langle u_k \rangle$ in $p\mathcal{K}(A,B)$ and $v : X \rightharpoonup A$,

$$\begin{aligned}\textstyle\bigsqcup_{p\mathcal{K}}(u_k \circ v) &= \varepsilon_B \circ \big(\textstyle\bigsqcup_{\mathcal{K}} \chi(u_k \circ v)\big) \\ &= \varepsilon_B \circ (\textstyle\bigsqcup_{\mathcal{K}} L(u_k) \circ \chi v) \\ &= \varepsilon_B \circ \big(\textstyle\bigsqcup_{\mathcal{K}} L(u_k)\big) \circ \chi v \\ &= \varepsilon_B \circ L(\textstyle\bigsqcup_{p\mathcal{K}} u_k) \circ \chi v \qquad \text{, because } L \text{ locally preserves lubs} \\ &= (\textstyle\bigsqcup_{p\mathcal{K}} u_k) \circ \varepsilon_A \circ \chi v \\ &= (\textstyle\bigsqcup_{p\mathcal{K}} u_k) \circ v.\end{aligned}$$

As the next proposition shows, all these calculations can be avoided.

Proposition 4.5.2 Let $F \dashv U : \mathcal{L} \to \mathcal{K}$ be a **Poset**-adjunction with F bijective on objects. If $\mathcal{K}$ is **Cpo**-enriched and UF is a **Cpo**-functor, then $\mathcal{L}$ **Cpo**-enriches.

PROOF: Let $\mathbb{T}$ be the monad induced by $F \dashv U$. By a **Poset**-enriched version of Proposition 3.2.9, we have that $\mathcal{L} \cong \mathcal{K}_{\mathbb{T}}$ in **Poset-CAT**. Since UF is a **Cpo**-functor, it follows that $\mathcal{K}_{\mathbb{T}}$ is **Cpo**-enriched and therefore so is $\mathcal{L}$. □

Corollary 4.5.3 If $J \dashv L : p\mathcal{K} \to \mathcal{K}$ is a **Poset**-adjunction and $\mathcal{K}$ is **Cpo**-enriched then $p\mathcal{K}$ **Cpo**-enriches. □

Unfortunately, not every adjunction $J \dashv L : p\mathcal{K} \to \mathcal{K}$ in **CAT** enriches to one in **Poset-CAT**. For example, $\chi : J \dashv L : \mathbf{Pfn} \to \mathbf{Set}$ is not a **Poset**-adjunction because $\chi_{A,B}$ is not a monotone function $(\mathbf{Pfn}(A,B), \subseteq) \to (\mathbf{Set}(A, LB), =)$. In fact, this is all that can fail:

Proposition 4.5.4 Let $\mathcal{K}$ and $p\mathcal{K}$ be **Poset**-enriched and let $\chi : J \dashv L : p\mathcal{K} \to \mathcal{K}$, then $J \dashv L$ is a **Poset**-adjunction if and only if for every $A, B \in |\mathcal{K}|$, the bijection $\chi_{A,B}$ is monotone.

PROOF:

($\Rightarrow$) Obvious.

($\Leftarrow$) Because for every $A, B \in |\mathcal{K}|$, $\chi_{A,B}^{-1} = \varepsilon_B \circ \_ : \mathcal{K}(A, LB) \to p\mathcal{K}(A, B)$ is monotone. □

Again we pay particular attention to enrichment with respect to specialisation. For this purpose we consider *maximal* partial map classifiers.

Definition 4.5.5 Let $\eta, \varepsilon : J \dashv L : p\mathcal{K} \to \mathcal{K}$. Then, η is said to be *maximal* if for every $A \in |\mathcal{K}|$, η_A is maximal among all *proper* (i.e., non-maximal) admissible monos of LA. □

With the purpose of characterising maximal units we introduce some notation: for a poset P, let $P^\top$ denote the poset resulting from adjoining a new top element to P; and, for every poset with top element Q and every monotone $f : P \to Q$, let $f^\# : P^\top \to Q$ denote the unique top-preserving monotone extension of f.

Proposition 4.5.6 Let $\eta, \varepsilon : J \dashv L : p(\mathcal{K}, \mathcal{D}) \to \mathcal{K}$. Then, η is maximal if and only if for every $A \in |\mathcal{K}|$, either $[\eta_A] = [\mathrm{id}_{LA}]$ or $[\eta_A \circ \_]^\# : \mathcal{D}(A)^\top \to \mathcal{D}(LA)$ is an isomorphism in **Poset**.

PROOF:

($\Rightarrow$) Let $A \in |\mathcal{K}|$.

If $[\eta_A] = [\mathrm{id}_{LA}]$ we are done.

Assume $\eta_A \subset \mathrm{id}_{LA}$. By maximality, for all proper $m \in \mathcal{D}/LA$ there exists a unique $i \in \mathcal{D}/A$ such that $\eta_A \circ i = m$ and therefore $[\eta_A \circ \_] : \mathcal{D}(A) \to \mathcal{D}(LA) \setminus \{ [\mathrm{id}_{LA}] \}$ is a bijection. It is monotone and so is its inverse because, for every $i, j \in \mathcal{D}/A$,

$$i \subseteq j \iff \eta_A \circ i \subseteq \eta_A \circ j.$$

Hence, $[\eta_A \circ \_]^\# : \mathcal{D}(A)^\top \to \mathcal{D}(LA)$ is an isomorphism in **Poset**.

($\Leftarrow$) For every $A \in |\mathcal{K}|$, either $[\eta_A] = [\mathrm{id}_{LA}]$ and therefore η_A is maximal, or the isomorphism $[\eta_A \circ \_]^\#$ restricts to a bijection from $\mathcal{D}(A)$ to $\mathcal{D}(LA) \setminus \{ [\mathrm{id}_{LA}] \}$, establishing the maximality of η_A. □

It follows then, that the unit of $J \dashv L :$ **Pfn** $\to$ **Set** is not maximal, and that the units of $J \dashv L :$ **pPoset** $\to$ **Poset** and $J \dashv L :$ **pCpo** $\to$ **Cpo** are.

Observe that the condition $[\eta_A] = [\mathrm{id}_{LA}]$ in the characterisation is not vacuous since, for example, $J \dashv L : p(\mathcal{K}, \mathbf{Isos}_\mathcal{K}) \cong \mathcal{K}$ has a maximal unit $\eta \cong \mathrm{id}$. The other condition, $[\eta_A \circ \_]^\# : \mathcal{D}(A)^\top \cong \mathcal{D}(LA)$, is appealing as it states that the observable properties of LA are the observable properties of A together with a new observable property, $[\mathrm{id}_{LA}]$, providing no information. This yields an appropriate computational interpretation of lifting; internalising the operation on locales corresponding to lifting of cpos (viz., to add a new top element —see [Rob87]). (For a discussion on how this approach might extend to powerdomains see Section 10.6.)

The main property of maximal units follows:

Proposition 4.5.7 Let $\chi : J \dashv L : p\mathcal{K} \to \mathcal{K}$. If the unit of this adjunction is maximal, then for every $A, B \in |\mathcal{K}|$, the bijection $\chi_{A,B}$ preserves the specialisation preorder.

PROOF: Let $u \precsim^s v : A \rightharpoonup B$. We need show that $\mathcal{D}(\chi u)[m] \subseteq \mathcal{D}(\chi v)[m]$ for every $[m] \in \mathcal{D}(LB)$.

The case $[m] = [\mathrm{id}]$ is vacuously satisfied. Assume m is a proper mono and let $m \subseteq_i \eta_B$. Then, as $p\mathcal{K}$ is **Preorder**-enriched with respect to $\precsim^s$ (see Proposition 4.4.1) we have that

$$m^R \circ \chi u \;=\; i^R \circ {\eta_B}^R \circ \chi u \;=\; i^R \circ u \precsim^s i^R \circ v \;=\; m^R \circ \chi v$$

and the result follows. □

Finally, we have:

Theorem 4.5.8 Let $\mathcal{K}$ be **Cpo**-enriched with respect to $\sqsubseteq^s$. If $\eta, \varepsilon : J \dashv L : p\mathcal{K} \to \mathcal{K}$ and η is maximal, then $p\mathcal{K}$ **Cpo**-enriches with respect to $\precsim^s$.

PROOF: Follows from Proposition 4.5.7, Proposition 4.5.4, and Corollary 4.5.3. □

5 Data Types

In this chapter we study the categorical constructions for interpreting data types. We start by observing that the notion of pairing in a category of partial maps (with a minimum of structure) cannot be the categorical product. The appropriate interpretation for product types (*partial products*) is the categorical product in the category of total maps endowed with a pairing operation on partial maps extending the pairing of total maps. Once the notion of product is established, *partial exponentials* are defined as usual, and some properties of **Poset**-partial-exponentials are presented. Next *colimits* are studied. The situation is completely different from that of limits. For example, an object is initial in the category of total maps if and only if it is so in the category of partial maps. A characterisation of certain colimits (including coproducts) in a category of partial maps, due to Gordon Plotkin, is given. We further relate colimits in the category of total maps and colimits in the category of partial maps by means of the lifting functor. Finally, we provide conditions on a **Cpo**-category of partial maps under which *ω-chains of embeddings* have colimits. This is done in the presence of the lifting functor, and for arbitrary categories of partial maps.

5.1 Partial Binary Products

The data type for pairing in $p\mathcal{K}$ cannot be the categorical product because, under reasonable assumptions, this would lead to inconsistency. For example, if $p\mathcal{K}$ has a zero object (which we think of modelling the recursive data type μT.T) and is cartesian closed, then for every $A \in |\, p\mathcal{K}\,|$,

$$\begin{aligned} A &\cong 0 \times A \quad &&\text{, because 0 is terminal and } \times \text{ is the categorical product} \\ &\cong 0 &&\text{, because 0 is initial and } \_ \times A \text{ preserves colimits.} \end{aligned}$$

Then, $p\mathcal{K} \simeq \mathbf{1}$. (In particular, as every algebraically compact category has a zero object (see Definition 6.2.2 (1) and Proposition 6.2.4), it follows that cartesian closure is inconsistent with algebraic compactness.)

Writing $A_1 \otimes A_2$ for the data type representing pairs of elements of A_1 and A_2, we expect that to give a pair of *generalised elements*, $(X \to A_1, X \to A_2)$, of A_1 and A_2 corresponds precisely to give a generalised element, $X \to A_1 \otimes A_2$, of $A_1 \otimes A_2$. That is, $A_1 \otimes A_2$ is the categorical product in the category of total maps. But, this is meaningful because there is a pairing operation for partial maps: in the situation

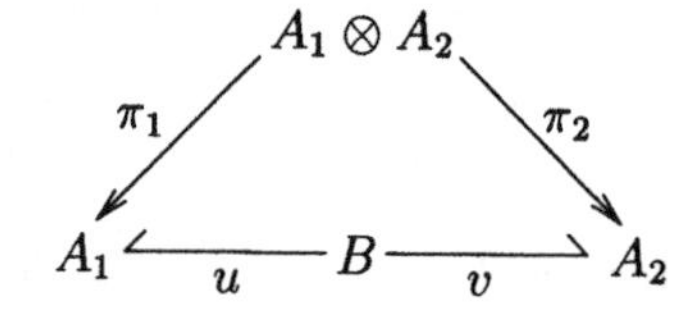

$$
\begin{array}{ccc}
& A_1 \otimes A_2 & \\
\pi_1 \swarrow & & \searrow \pi_2 \\
A_1 \xleftarrow{\;u\;} B \xrightarrow{\;v\;} A_2 &
\end{array}
\tag{5.1}
$$

the *partial pairing* of $u = [m, f]$ and $v = [n, g]$ is the partial map

$$
\langle\!\langle u, v \rangle\!\rangle = [m \cap n, \langle f \circ m^{-1}(n), g \circ n^{-1}(m)\rangle] : B \rightharpoonup A_1 \otimes A_2
\tag{5.2}
$$

where $\langle \_, = \rangle$ is the pairing of total maps and π_i $(i = 1, 2)$ are the corresponding projections. Intuitively,

$$
\langle\!\langle u, v \rangle\!\rangle(x) = \begin{cases} \big(u(x), v(x)\big) & , \text{if } x \in \mathrm{dom}(u) \cap \mathrm{dom}(v). \\ \text{undefined} & , \text{otherwise.} \end{cases}
$$

so that the pairing is *strict*.

By definition, *the partial pairing extends the pairing of total maps* as, for $f : B \to A_1$ and $g : B \to A_2$, it follows that $\langle f, g \rangle = \langle\!\langle f, g \rangle\!\rangle$.

Combining (5.1) and (5.2) into one diagram we obtain

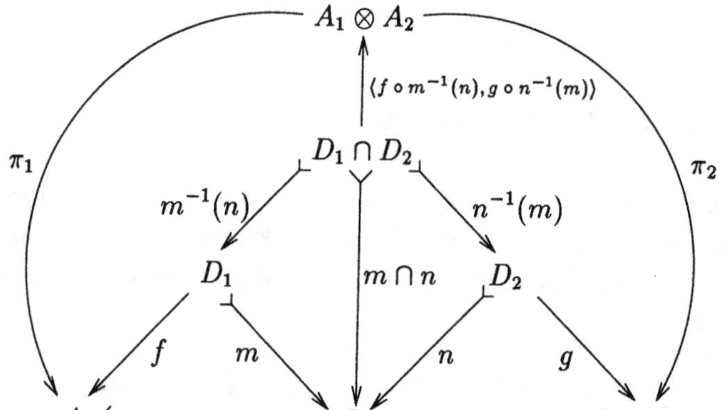

showing that

$$
\pi_1 \circ \langle\!\langle [m, f], [n, g] \rangle\!\rangle = [m \cap n, f \circ m^{-1}(n)],
\tag{5.3}
$$

$$
\pi_2 \circ \langle\!\langle [m, f], [n, g] \rangle\!\rangle = [m \cap n, g \circ n^{-1}(m)].
\tag{5.4}
$$

Convention. For the sake of readability we will write $[D \rightarrowtail B, D \to A]$ for a partial map $B \rightharpoonup A$ whenever the maps $D \rightarrowtail B$ and $D \to A$ are clear from the context. Thus, for example, with this notation the above two equations become

$$\pi_1 \circ \langle\!\langle [D_1 \rightarrowtail B, D_1 \to A_1], [D_2 \rightarrowtail B, D_2 \to A_2] \rangle\!\rangle = [D_1 \cap D_2 \rightarrowtail B, D_1 \cap D_2 \rightarrowtail D_1 \to A_1],$$

$$\pi_2 \circ \langle\!\langle [D_1 \rightarrowtail B, D_1 \to A_1], [D_2 \rightarrowtail B, D_2 \to A_2] \rangle\!\rangle = [D_1 \cap D_2 \rightarrowtail B, D_1 \cap D_2 \rightarrowtail D_2 \to A_2].$$

The following properties of the partial pairing are *folklore*:

Proposition 5.1.1 Let $u_i : B \rightharpoonup A_i$, $v_i : A_i \rightharpoonup A'_i$ $(i = 1, 2)$, and $v : B' \rightharpoonup B$. Then,

1. $\pi_1 \circ \langle\!\langle u_1, u_2 \rangle\!\rangle = \pi_2 \circ \langle\!\langle u_2, u_1 \rangle\!\rangle$.
2. $\pi_i \circ \langle\!\langle u_1, u_2 \rangle\!\rangle \subseteq u_i$ $(i = 1, 2)$.
3. $\mathrm{dom}(u_1) \subseteq \mathrm{dom}(u_2) \iff \pi_1 \circ \langle\!\langle u_1, u_2 \rangle\!\rangle = u_1$.
4. $u_i : B \to A_i$ $(i = 1, 2) \iff \langle\!\langle u_1, u_2 \rangle\!\rangle : B \to A_1 \otimes A_2$.
5. $\langle\!\langle u_1, u_2 \rangle\!\rangle \circ v = \langle\!\langle u_1 \circ v, u_2 \circ v \rangle\!\rangle$.
6. $\langle\!\langle v_1 \circ \pi_1 \circ \langle\!\langle u_1, u_2 \rangle\!\rangle, v_2 \circ \pi_2 \circ \langle\!\langle u_1, u_2 \rangle\!\rangle \rangle\!\rangle = \langle\!\langle v_1 \circ u_1, v_2 \circ u_2 \rangle\!\rangle$.
7. The product functor $\_ \times = : \mathcal{K} \times \mathcal{K} \to \mathcal{K}$ extends to a functor $\_ \otimes = : p\mathcal{K} \times p\mathcal{K} \to p\mathcal{K}$ sending a pair of objects (A, B) to $A \times B$ and a pair of partial maps (u, v) to $\langle\!\langle u \circ \pi_1, v \circ \pi_2 \rangle\!\rangle$. Moreover, $[m, f] \otimes [n, g] = [m \times n, f \times g]$.

PROOF:

(1)–(3) Follow from (5.3) and (5.4).

(4) ($\Rightarrow$) Clear as the partial pairing extends the pairing of total maps.

($\Leftarrow$) By Proposition 5.1.1 (2), $\pi_i \circ \langle\!\langle u_1, u_2 \rangle\!\rangle \subseteq u_i$, and since $\pi_i \circ \langle\!\langle u_1, u_2 \rangle\!\rangle$ is total, then so is u_i.

(5) Let $u_i = [D_i \rightarrowtail B, D_i \to A_i]$ $(i = 1, 2)$ and $v = [E \rightarrowtail B', E \to B]$.

From the diagram

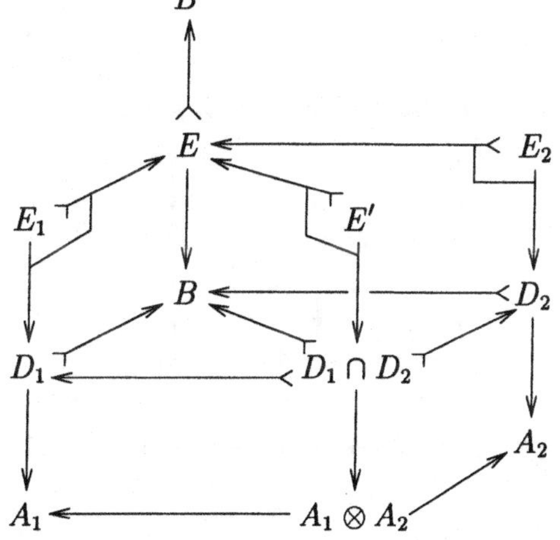

it follows that $\langle\langle u_1, u_2\rangle\rangle \circ v = [E' \rightarrowtail E \rightarrowtail B', E' \to D_1 \cap D_2 \to A_1 \otimes A_2]$ and that, for $i = 1, 2$, there exists a unique $E' \rightarrowtail E_i$ for which

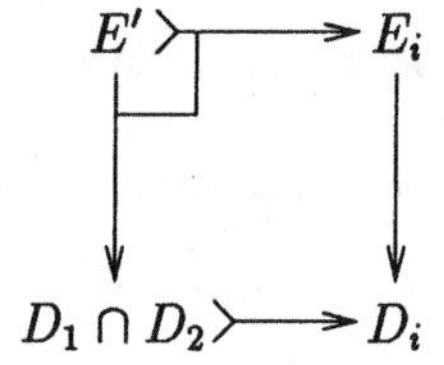

is a pullback.

Thus, in the following cube

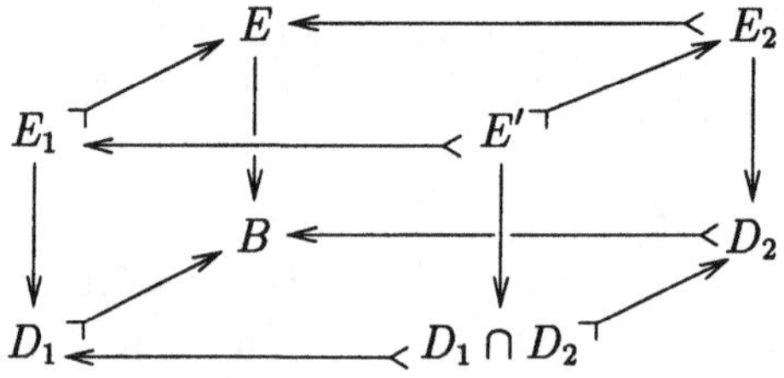

every face, except for the top one, is known to be a pullback. But then the top face is a pullback as well, and therefore so is

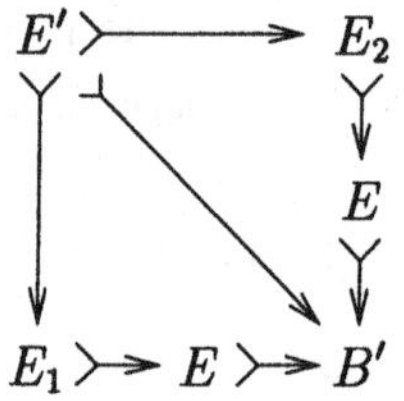

Moreover, as

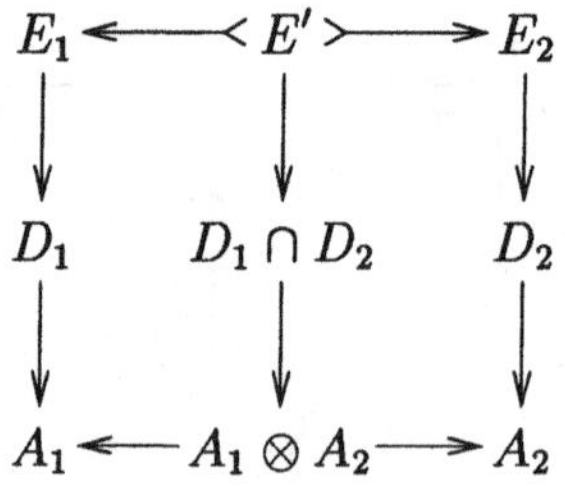

we conclude that $\langle\langle u_1 \circ v, u_2 \circ v\rangle\rangle = [E' \rightarrowtail B', E' \to D_1 \cap D_2 \to A_1 \otimes A_2]$.

(6) The proof is essentially given by the following diagram

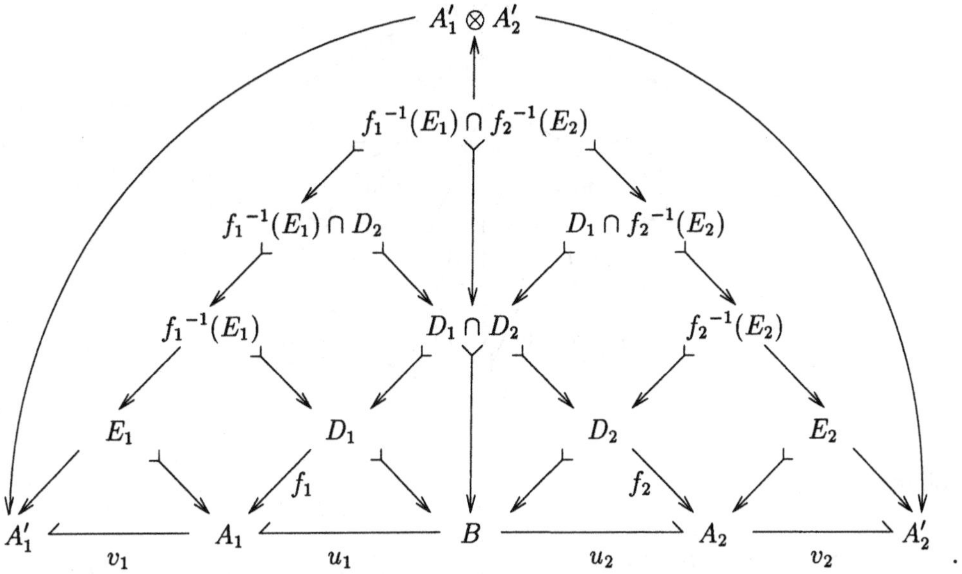

As it implies that

- $\pi_i \circ \langle\!\langle u_1, u_2 \rangle\!\rangle = [D_1 \cap D_2 \rightarrowtail B, D_1 \cap D_2 \rightarrowtail D_i \to A_i]$ $(i = 1, 2)$.
- $v_1 \circ \pi_1 \circ \langle\!\langle u_1, u_2 \rangle\!\rangle = [f_1{}^{-1}(E_1) \cap D_2 \rightarrowtail B, f_1{}^{-1}(E_1) \cap D_2 \rightarrowtail f_1{}^{-1}(E_1) \to E_1 \to A'_1]$.
- $v_2 \circ \pi_2 \circ \langle\!\langle u_1, u_2 \rangle\!\rangle = [D_1 \cap f_2{}^{-1}(E_2) \rightarrowtail B, D_1 \cap f_2{}^{-1}(E_2) \rightarrowtail f_2{}^{-1}(E_2) \to E_2 \to A'_2]$.

And therefore,

$$\begin{aligned} &\langle\!\langle v_1 \circ \pi_1 \circ \langle\!\langle u_1, u_2 \rangle\!\rangle, v_2 \circ \pi_1 \circ \langle\!\langle u_1, u_2 \rangle\!\rangle \rangle\!\rangle \\ &\quad = [f_1{}^{-1}(E_1) \cap f_2{}^{-1}(E_2) \rightarrowtail B, f_1{}^{-1}(E_1) \cap f_2{}^{-1}(E_2) \to A'_1 \otimes A'_2] \\ &\quad = \langle\!\langle v_1 \circ u_1, v_2 \circ u_2 \rangle\!\rangle. \end{aligned}$$

(7) The operation $\otimes$ extends $\times$, because $\langle\!\langle -, = \rangle\!\rangle$ extends $\langle -, = \rangle$, and therefore preserves identities. It preserves composition by Proposition 5.1.1 (5) and (6).

Finally, let $[m, f] : A \rightharpoonup X$ and $[n, g] : B \rightharpoonup Y$. From the following diagram,

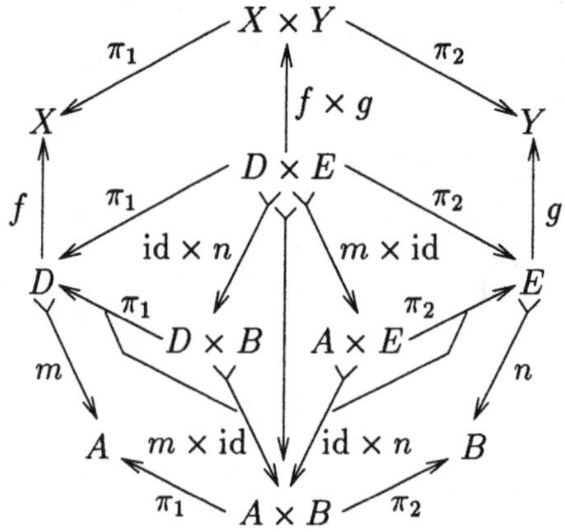

it follows that

$$[m, f] \circ \pi_1 = \pi_1 \circ [m \times n, f \times g], \quad \text{and} \quad [n, g] \circ \pi_2 = \pi_2 \circ [m \times n, f \times g].$$

Thus,

$$\begin{aligned} [m, f] \otimes [n, g] &= \langle\!\langle [m, f] \circ \pi_1, [n, g] \circ \pi_2 \rangle\!\rangle \\ &= \langle\!\langle \pi_1 \circ [m \times n, f \times g], \pi_2 \circ [m \times n, f \times g] \rangle\!\rangle \\ &= \langle\!\langle \pi_1, \pi_2 \rangle\!\rangle \circ [m \times n, f \times g] && \text{, by Proposition 5.1.1 (5)} \\ &= [m \times n, f \times g] \end{aligned}$$

□

As the order-enriched case is the one that concern us, from now on we consider $\mathcal{K}$ and $p\mathcal{K}$ to be **Poset**-enriched w.r.t. $\sqsubseteq$ and $\precsim$ respectively, and assume that $\mathcal{K}$ has binary **Poset**-products.

Proposition 5.1.2 Let A_i $(i = 1, 2)$, $B \in |\, p\mathcal{K}\,|$. Then, the partial pairing operation $\langle\!\langle -, = \rangle\!\rangle : p\mathcal{K}(B, A_1) \times p\mathcal{K}(B, A_2) \to p\mathcal{K}(B, A_1 \otimes A_2)$ is monotone.

And hence, $- \otimes = : p\mathcal{K} \times p\mathcal{K} \to p\mathcal{K}$ is a **Poset**-functor.

PROOF: Let $u = [m, f] \precsim [m', f'] = u' : B \rightharpoonup A_1$ and $v = [n, g] : B \rightharpoonup A_2$.

Then we have the following situation,

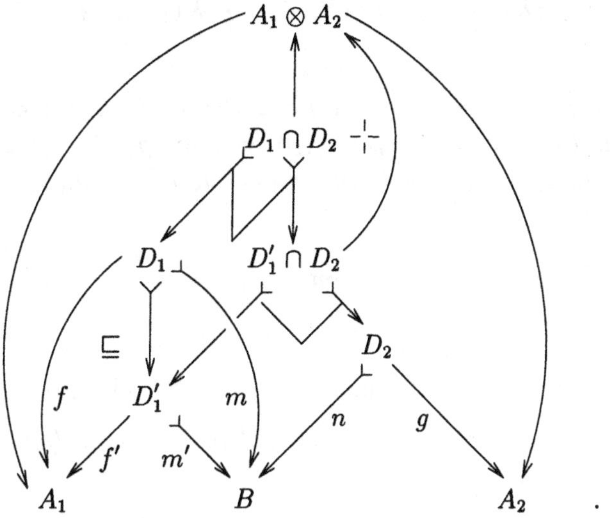

(5.5)

So that

$$\langle\!\langle u, v \rangle\!\rangle = [D_1 \cap D_2 \rightarrowtail B, D_1 \cap D_2 \to A_1 \otimes A_2]$$

and

$$\langle\!\langle u', v \rangle\!\rangle = [D'_1 \cap D_2 \rightarrowtail B, D'_1 \cap D_2 \to A_1 \otimes A_2].$$

Since $(D_1 \cap D_2 \rightarrowtail B) = (D_1 \cap D_2 \rightarrowtail D'_1 \cap D_2 \rightarrowtail B)$, to show that $\langle\!\langle u, v \rangle\!\rangle \sqsubseteq \langle\!\langle u', v \rangle\!\rangle$ we just need to establish that

$$(D_1 \cap D_2 \to A_1 \otimes A_2) \sqsubseteq (D_1 \cap D_2 \rightarrowtail D'_1 \cap D_2 \to A_1 \otimes A_2). \tag{5.6}$$

Chasing the diagram (5.5), it follows that

$$(D_1 \cap D_2 \to A_1 \otimes A_2 \to A_1) \sqsubseteq (D_1 \cap D_2 \rightarrowtail D'_1 \cap D_2 \to A_1 \otimes A_2 \to A_1)$$

and

$$(D_1 \cap D_2 \to A_1 \otimes A_2 \to A_2) = (D_1 \cap D_2 \rightarrowtail D'_1 \cap D_2 \to A_1 \otimes A_2 \to A_2).$$

Thus, since products in $\mathcal{K}$ are **Poset**-enriched, (5.6) holds.

The monotonicity of the partial pairing in the second argument follows, because

$$\langle\!\langle v, u \rangle\!\rangle = \langle\!\langle \pi_2, \pi_1 \rangle\!\rangle \circ \langle\!\langle u, v \rangle\!\rangle \sqsubseteq \langle\!\langle \pi_2, \pi_1 \rangle\!\rangle \circ \langle\!\langle u', v \rangle\!\rangle = \langle\!\langle v, u' \rangle\!\rangle. \qquad \square$$

Proposition 5.1.3 Let $(\mathcal{K}, \mathcal{D})$ be a uniform **Cpo**-domain-structure such that $p\mathcal{K}$ **Cpo**-enriches. If $\_ \times = : \mathcal{K} \times \mathcal{K} \to \mathcal{K}$ is a **Cpo**-product functor such that, for every $A \in |\mathcal{K}|$, the functor $\_ \times A : \mathcal{K} \to \mathcal{K}$ preserves colimits of ω-chains in $\mathcal{D}$ then the partial-product functor $\_ \otimes = : p\mathcal{K} \times p\mathcal{K} \to p\mathcal{K}$ **Cpo**-enriches.

PROOF: By Proposition 5.1.2 we need only show that

$$\_ \otimes = : p\mathcal{K}(B_1, A_1) \times p\mathcal{K}(B_2, A_2) \rightarrow p\mathcal{K}(B_1 \otimes B_2, A_1 \otimes A_2)$$

is continuous.

First we show that $\_ \otimes =$ preserves lubs of ω-chains of graph included partial maps. Consider ω-chains $\langle [m_k, f_k] \subseteq_{i_k} [m_{k+1}, f_{k+1}] \rangle$ and $\langle [n_k, g_k] \subseteq_{j_k} [n_{k+1}, g_{k+1}] \rangle$ such that $\bigsqcup [m_k, f_k] = \langle [m_k, f_k] \sqsubseteq_{\mu_k} [m, f] \rangle$ and $\bigsqcup [n_k, g_k] = \langle [n_k, g_k] \sqsubseteq_{\eta_k} [n, g] \rangle$.

By Proposition 4.3.16,

$$\bigsqcup [m_k \times n_k, f_k \times g_k] \;=\; [m \times n, f \times g] \;=\; [m, f] \otimes [n, g]$$

because

$$\begin{aligned} \operatorname{colim}_k \langle i_k \times j_k \rangle &\cong \operatorname{colim}_l \operatorname{colim}_k \langle i_k \times j_l \rangle &&\cong \operatorname{colim}_l \langle (\operatorname{colim}_k i_k) \times j_l \rangle \\ &\cong \operatorname{colim}_k \langle i_k \rangle \times \operatorname{colim}_l \langle j_l \rangle &&\cong \langle \mu_k \rangle \times \langle \eta_l \rangle \\ &\cong \langle \mu_k \times \eta_k \rangle, \end{aligned}$$

$m \times n : \langle \mu_k \times \eta_k \rangle \rightarrow \langle m_k \times n_k \rangle$ and $f \times g : \langle \mu_k \times \eta_k \rangle \rightarrow \langle f_k \times g_k \rangle$.

Second, for arbitrary ω-chains $\langle [m_k, f_k] \sqsubseteq_{i_k} [m_{k+1}, f_{k+1}] \rangle$ and $\langle [n_k, g_k] \sqsubseteq_{j_k} [n_{k+1}, g_{k+1}] \rangle$, by Proposition 4.3.3 (1), we have that

$$\bigsqcup [m_k, f_k] \otimes \bigsqcup [n_k, g_k] \;=\; \bigsqcup [m_k, F_k] \otimes \bigsqcup [n_k, G_k] \;=\; \bigsqcup [m_k \times n_k, F_k \times G_k]$$

where $F_k = \bigsqcup_{l \geq k} f_l \circ i_{k,l}$ and $G_k = \bigsqcup_{l \geq k} g_l \circ j_{k,l}$. Also, by Proposition 4.3.3 (1),

$$\bigsqcup [m_k, f_k] \otimes [n_k, g_k] \;=\; \bigsqcup [m_k \times n_k, f_k \times g_k] \;=\; \bigsqcup [m_k \times n_k, H_k]$$

where

$$\begin{aligned} H_k &= \textstyle\bigsqcup_{l \geq k} (f_l \times g_l) \circ (i_{k,l} \times j_{k,l}) &&= \textstyle\bigsqcup_{l \geq k} (f_l \circ i_{k,l}) \times (g_l \circ j_{k,l}) \\ &= \textstyle\bigsqcup_{l \geq k} (f_l \circ i_{k,l}) \times \bigsqcup_{l \geq k} (g_l \circ j_{k,l}) &&= F_k \times G_k. \end{aligned}$$

And the result follows. □

The terminal object in $\mathcal{K}$ (when it exists) becomes a *partial terminal object* in $p\mathcal{K}$, in the sense that, for every $A \in |\, p\mathcal{K} \,|$ there exists a unique $A \rightarrow 1$ which is maximal among all $A \rightharpoonup 1$. Notice that this maximality condition can be imposed by requiring $(A \rightharpoonup B \rightarrow 1) \subseteq (A \rightarrow 1)$ for every $A \rightharpoonup B$, since then $(A \rightharpoonup 1) = (A \rightharpoonup 1 \rightarrow 1) \subseteq (A \rightarrow 1)$.

Definition 5.1.4 A category of partial maps is *partial cartesian* if its subcategory of total maps is cartesian. □

Remark. A definition based on partial maps would ask for the category of partial maps to have *finite partial products*. What this may mean is under investigation (see [Jay91]).

A miscellaneous result concerning partial cartesian structure and lifting:

Proposition 5.1.5 Let $p\mathcal{K}$ be partial cartesian. If $\chi : J \dashv L : p\mathcal{K} \to \mathcal{K}$, then the monad $\mathbb{L} = (LJ, \eta, L\varepsilon J) : \mathcal{K} \to \mathcal{K}$ has a *tensorial strength* [Koc70]

$$t_{A,B} = \chi(\mathrm{id}_A \otimes \varepsilon_B) : A \times LB \to L(A \times B). \qquad \square$$

We close the section indicating the kind of algebraic structure induced by a partial cartesian structure on a category of partial maps.

Definition 5.1.6 ([Car86]) A *bicategory of partial maps* is a symmetric monoidal structure on a **Poset**-category $\mathcal{B}$ such that

1. the tensor product is a **Poset**-functor,
2. there is a unique cocommutative comonoid structure $t_B : B \to I$, $\Delta_B : B \to B \otimes B$ on each $B \in |\mathcal{B}|$, and
3. $t : \mathrm{Id} \xrightarrow{\cdot}_{\lesssim} I : \mathcal{B} \to \mathcal{B}$ and $\Delta : \mathrm{Id} \xrightarrow{\cdot} \_ \otimes \_ : \mathcal{B} \to \mathcal{B}$. $\square$

Proposition 5.1.7 If $\mathcal{K}$ is **Poset**-cartesian and $p\mathcal{K}$ is **Poset**-enriched then the canonical symmetric monoidal structure on $\mathcal{K}$ extends to a symmetric monoidal structure on $p\mathcal{K}$, with the partial product as the tensor product, making it a bicategory of partial maps.$\square$

5.2 Partial Exponentials

Throughout this section let $\mathcal{K}$ and $p\mathcal{K}$ be **Poset**-enriched w.r.t. $\sqsubseteq$ and $\lesssim$ respectively, and let $\mathcal{K}$ have binary **Poset**-products.

As usual for higher types, exponentiation arises as a right adjoint to multiplication. In our case, for every $A \in |\mathcal{K}|$, we set

$$\_ \otimes A \dashv A \rightharpoonup \_ : p\mathcal{K} \to \mathcal{K} \text{ in } \mathbf{Poset\text{-}CAT}. \tag{5.7}$$

This corresponds to our intuitions, for if $\mathcal{K}$ is cartesian then the global elements of $A \rightharpoonup B$ are the partial maps $A \rightharpoonup B$ (because $p\mathcal{K}(A, B) \cong p\mathcal{K}(1 \otimes A, B) \cong \mathcal{K}(1, A \rightharpoonup B)$). Thus, $A \rightharpoonup B$ *internalises* the partial maps $A \rightharpoonup B$.

Convention. We write ε and $p\lambda$ respectively for the *counit* $(A \rightharpoonup \_) \otimes A \xrightarrow{\cdot} \mathrm{Id}$ and the *natural isomorphism* $p\mathcal{K}(\_ \otimes A, =) \cong \mathcal{K}(\_, A \rightharpoonup =)$ determined by the adjunction (5.7).

Proposition 5.2.1 **Poset**-partial-exponentials extend to a **Poset**-functor $\_ \rightharpoonup = : p\mathcal{K}^{op} \times p\mathcal{K} \to p\mathcal{K}$ sending pairs of objects (A, B) to $A \rightharpoonup B$ and pairs of partial maps (u, v) to $p\lambda(v \circ \varepsilon \circ (\mathrm{id} \otimes u))$.

Moreover, if $\mathcal{K}$ and $p\mathcal{K}$ are **Cpo**-enriched and $\_ \otimes = : p\mathcal{K} \times p\mathcal{K} \to p\mathcal{K}$ is a **Cpo**-functor then $\rightharpoonup$ is a **Cpo**-functor.

PROOF: That $\Rightarrow$ preserves identities is clear; that preserves composition is proved as usual, namely by the diagram

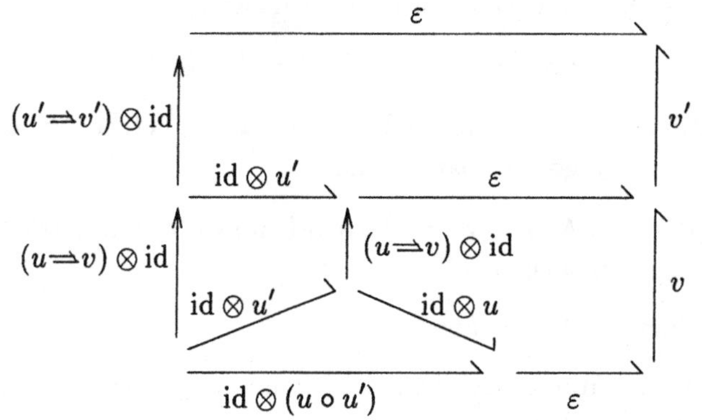

The functor $\Rightarrow$ is **Poset**-enriched because it is locally defined as a composition of monotone operations.

Moreover, if $\mathcal{K}$ and $p\mathcal{K}$ are **Cpo**-enriched then $p\lambda$ is continuous (as it is an isomorphism in **Poset** between cpos); so, if in addition $\otimes$ is a **Cpo**-functor, it follows that $\Rightarrow$ is **Cpo**-enriched because it is locally defined as a composition of continuous operations. $\square$

Some properties of **Poset**-partial-exponentials that will be used later (especially Proposition 5.2.2 (3)) are:

Proposition 5.2.2 In a category of partial maps with partial exponentials the following hold:

1. For $u = [m, f] : C \rightharpoonup A \Rightarrow B$, we have that $f = p\lambda\big(\varepsilon \circ (u \otimes \mathrm{id})\big) \circ m$, and therefore $u \subseteq p\lambda\big(\varepsilon \circ (u \otimes \mathrm{id})\big)$.

2. Whenever $v^L \dashv v$ (i.e., $\mathrm{id} \sqsubseteq v \circ v^L$ and $v^L \circ v \sqsubseteq \mathrm{id}$),

$$
\begin{array}{ccc}
(A \Rightarrow B) \otimes A & \xrightarrow{\ \varepsilon\ } & B \\
{\scriptstyle (v^L \Rightarrow u) \otimes v}\ \Big\downarrow & {\scriptstyle \sqsubseteq} & \Big\downarrow\ {\scriptstyle u} \\
(A' \Rightarrow B') \otimes A' & \xrightarrow[\ \varepsilon\ ]{} & B'
\end{array}
$$

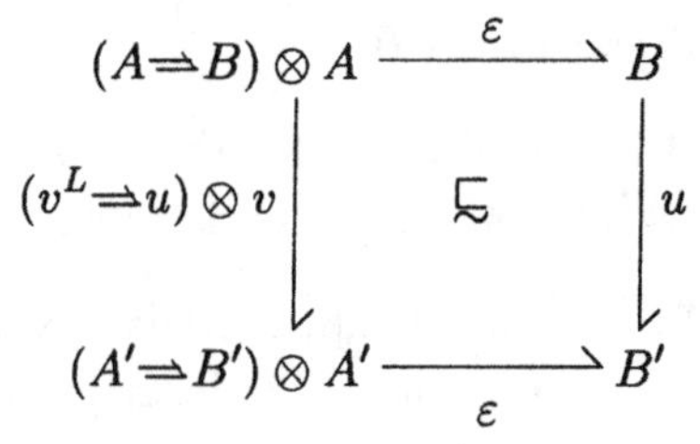

3. Whenever $v^L \dashv v$,

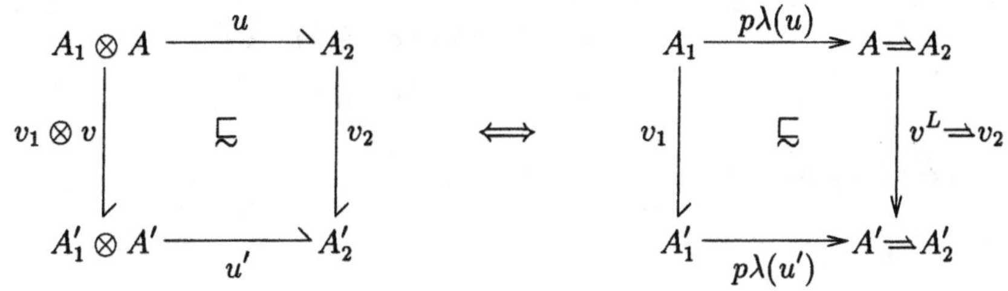

.

PROOF:

(1) Since $f = u \circ m$ is total, it follows that $f = p\lambda\big(\varepsilon \circ (u \otimes \mathrm{id}) \circ (m \otimes \mathrm{id})\big)$, and using the naturality of $p\lambda$, we conclude that $f = p\lambda\big(\varepsilon \circ (u \otimes \mathrm{id})\big) \circ m$.

(2) Because

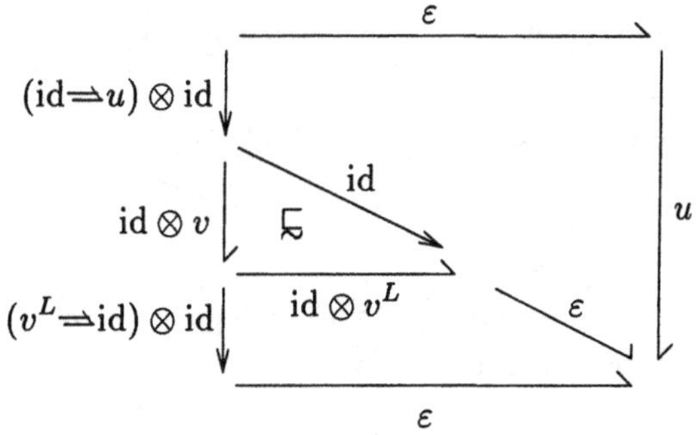

.

(3)($\Rightarrow$) As the following diagram shows, $\varepsilon \circ \Big(\big((v \rightharpoonup \mathrm{id}) \circ p\lambda(u') \circ v_1\big) \otimes \mathrm{id}\Big) = u' \circ (v_1 \otimes v)$

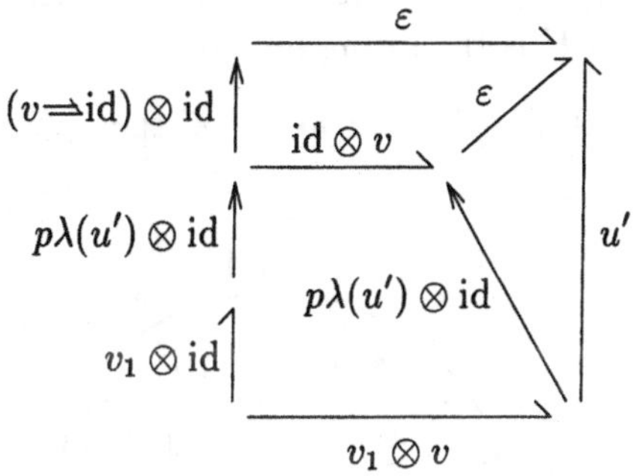

and therefore

$$
\begin{array}{rcll}
(v \rightharpoonup \mathrm{id}) \circ p\lambda(u') \circ v_1 & \subseteq & p\lambda\big(u' \circ (v_1 \otimes v)\big) & \text{, by Proposition 5.2.2 (1)} \\
 & \sqsubseteq & p\lambda(v_2 \circ u) & \text{, by hypothesis since } p\lambda \text{ is monotone} \\
 & = & (\mathrm{id} \rightharpoonup v_2) \circ p\lambda(u). &
\end{array}
$$

Now, post-composing both sides of the inequality with $v^L \rightharpoonup \mathrm{id}$, we are done:

$$\begin{aligned} p\lambda(u') \circ v_1 & \underset{\sim}{\sqsubset} (v^L \rightharpoonup \mathrm{id}) \circ (v \rightharpoonup \mathrm{id}) \circ p\lambda(u') \circ v_1 \\ & \underset{\sim}{\sqsubset} (v^L \rightharpoonup \mathrm{id}) \circ (\mathrm{id} \rightharpoonup v_2) \circ p\lambda(u) \\ & = (v^L \rightharpoonup v_2) \circ p\lambda(u). \end{aligned}$$

($\Leftarrow$) Because

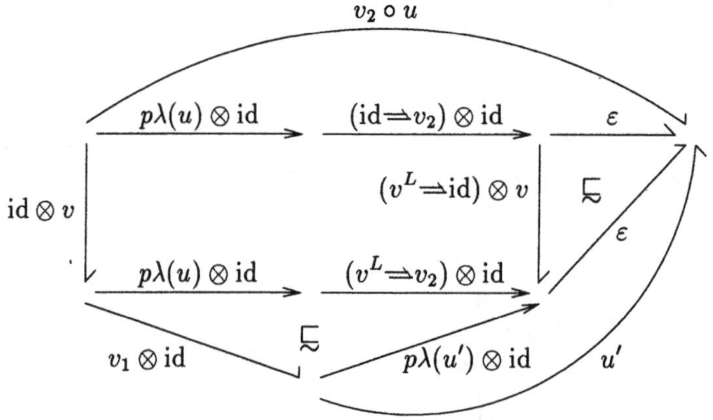

. □

Definition 5.2.3 ([LM84]) A partial cartesian category of partial maps is *partial cartesian closed* if it has all partial exponentials. □

We close the section with some comments on the relations between lifting, partial exponentials and exponentials.

1. Lifting is a partial exponential: if $\mathcal{K}$ is cartesian then $\_ \otimes 1 \cong J : \mathcal{K} \to p\mathcal{K}$ and therefore $1 \rightharpoonup \_ : p\mathcal{K} \to \mathcal{K}$ is the lifting functor.
2. If $\mathcal{K}$ is cartesian closed and $J \dashv L : p\mathcal{K} \to \mathcal{K}$ then $p\mathcal{K}$ is partial cartesian closed, because

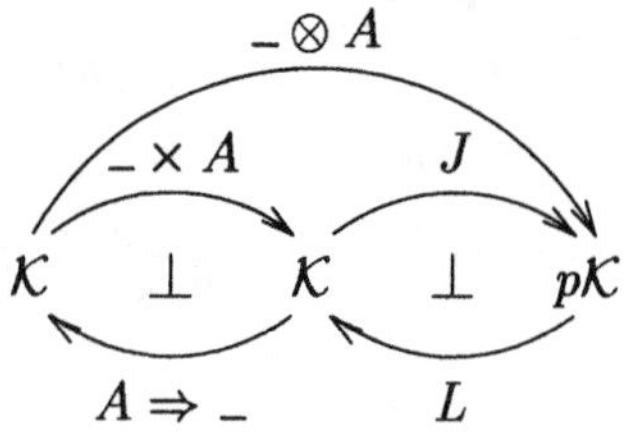

.

3. The existence of lifting and partial exponentials does not imply the existence of exponentials.

Let ω**AlgCpo** and **p**ω**AlgCpo** denote, respectively, the full subcategories of **Cpo** and **pCpo** of ω-algebraic cpos. Then, $J \dashv L$: **p**ω**AlgCpo** $\rightarrow$ ω**AlgCpo** and $\_ \otimes \mathbb{N} \dashv \mathbb{N} \rightharpoonup \_$: **p**ω**AlgCpo** $\rightarrow$ ω**AlgCpo** but $\_ \times \mathbb{N}$: ω**AlgCpo** $\rightarrow$ ω**AlgCpo** does not have a right adjoint.

4. Despite $p\mathcal{K}$ being partial cartesian closed, $\mathcal{K}$ need not be cartesian closed.
   Let **Dom** and **pDom** denote, respectively, the full subcategories of **Cpo** and **pCpo** of consistently complete ω-algebraic cpos. Then, **Dom** is not cartesian closed whilst **pDom** is partial cartesian closed.

5. If $\mathcal{K}$ has equalisers and $p\mathcal{K}$ is partial cartesian closed then $\mathcal{K}$ is cartesian closed (see [Rom89]).

6. **Proposition 5.2.4** If $\mathcal{K}$ has a terminal object then the inclusion functor $J : \mathcal{K} \rightarrow p\mathcal{K}$: (a) reflects, and (b) creates colimits.

PROOF: Let Δ be a diagram in $\mathcal{K}$.

(a) We need show that if $\gamma : \Delta \dot\rightarrow C$ is colimiting in $p\mathcal{K}$ then it is also colimiting in $\mathcal{K}$. Equivalently, assuming γ is colimiting in $p\mathcal{K}$ we show that for every cone $\chi : \Delta \dot\rightarrow X$ the unique mediating partial map $\gamma \rightharpoonup \chi$ is total.

Note that $(X \rightarrow 1) \circ (\gamma \rightharpoonup \chi) = C \rightarrow 1$ because both maps mediate between γ and $\Delta \dot\rightarrow 1$. Thus, $(X \rightarrow 1) \circ (\gamma \rightharpoonup \chi)$ is total and therefore so is $\gamma \rightharpoonup \chi$.

(b) We need show that if $\gamma : \Delta \dot\rightharpoonup C$ is colimiting in $p\mathcal{K}$ then γ is both pointwise-total and colimiting in $\mathcal{K}$.

By Proposition 5.2.4 (a) it is enough to show that γ is pointwise-total. This follows because there exists a unique $C \rightharpoonup 1$ such that $\Delta \dot\rightharpoonup C \rightharpoonup 1$ equals the unique pointwise-total cone $\Delta \dot\rightarrow 1$ so that $\Delta \dot\rightharpoonup C \rightharpoonup 1$ is pointwise-total and therefore so is $\Delta \dot\rightharpoonup C$. □

Corollary 5.2.5 If $p\mathcal{K}$ is partial cartesian closed then, for every $A \in |\mathcal{K}|$, the functor $\_ \times A : \mathcal{K} \rightarrow \mathcal{K}$ preserves colimits.

PROOF: Follows form Proposition 5.2.4 (a) because for every $A \in |\mathcal{K}|$ the functor $\_ \otimes A : \mathcal{K} \rightarrow p\mathcal{K}$ preserves colimits as it has right adjoint. □

Hence, by The Freyd Adjoint Functor Theorem, if $\mathcal{K}$ is cocomplete and $p\mathcal{K}$ is partial cartesian closed then $\mathcal{K}$ is cartesian closed if and only if every $\_ \times A$ satisfies the solution set condition.

5.3 Colimits

We begin by showing some properties of an initial object in a category of partial maps. The aim is to illustrate the difference from limits and to analyse the interaction with partial cartesian closure.

Proposition 5.3.1 An object is initial in $\mathcal{K}$ if and only if it is so in $p\mathcal{K}$.

PROOF:

($\Rightarrow$) Every $D \rightarrowtail 0$ in $\mathcal{D}$ is an isomorphism because it is split epi as $(0 \to D \rightarrowtail 0) = \mathrm{id}$.

($\Leftarrow$) Let $u = [m, f] : 0 \rightharpoonup A$. Then, m is an isomorphism with inverse m^R and therefore u is total. □

Partial cartesian closure constrains initial objects:

Proposition 5.3.2 Let $\mathcal{K}$ have binary products and $p\mathcal{K}$ have partial exponentials. If 0 is initial in $p\mathcal{K}$ then

1. 0 is strict in $\mathcal{K}$ (i.e., for every $A \in |\,\mathcal{K}\,|$, $\mathcal{K}(A, 0) \neq \emptyset \;\Rightarrow\; A \cong 0$), and
2. for every $A \in |\,\mathcal{K}\,|$, $0 \mathrel{=\!\!\rightharpoonup} A$ is terminal in $\mathcal{K}$.

PROOF:

(1) Since initial objects in $\mathcal{K}$ and $p\mathcal{K}$ coincide and, for every $A \in |\,\mathcal{K}\,|$, the functor $\_ \otimes A$ preserves colimits it follows that 0 and $0 \otimes A$ are initial in $\mathcal{K}$.

Then every $f : A \to 0$ is split mono because

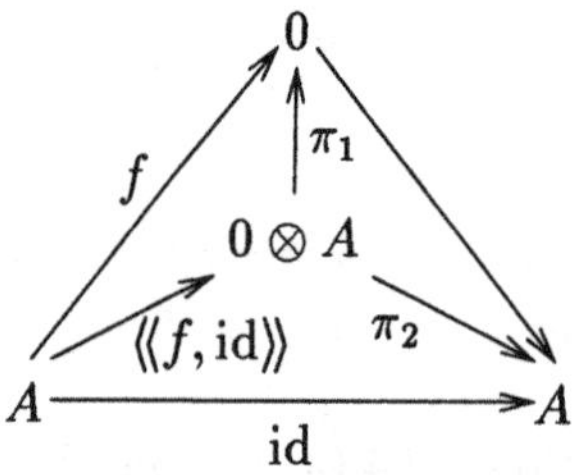

(2) $\mathcal{K}(X, 0 \mathrel{=\!\!\rightharpoonup} A) \cong p\mathcal{K}(X \otimes 0, A) \cong p\mathcal{K}(0, A) \cong 1$. □

Proposition 5.3.3 If 0 is strict initial in $\mathcal{K}$ then 0 is a zero object in $p\mathcal{K}$ if and only if $0 \to A$ is admissible.

PROOF: For every $[m, f] : A \rightharpoonup 0$, by strictness, f is an isomorphism. Therefore,

($\Rightarrow$) $(A \to 0) = m \circ f^{-1} \in \mathcal{D}$.

($\Leftarrow$) $[m, f] = (0 \rightarrowtail A)^R$. □

Corollary 5.3.4 Let $\mathcal{K}$ have binary products and $p\mathcal{K}$ have partial exponentials. Then, 0 is a zero object in $p\mathcal{K}$ if and only if 0 is initial in $\mathcal{K}$ and $0 \to A$ is admissible. □

From now on we will be concern with colimits of diagrams of total maps in categories of partial maps. The restriction to this kind of diagram is not severe as we include the one we need to consider, viz. coproducts and ω-chains of embeddings. The first thing to ask is whether colimiting cones for this kind of diagram ought to be pointwise-total. In general, this will not be the case. Consider the following simple but artificial counterexample: let $\mathcal{K}$ be

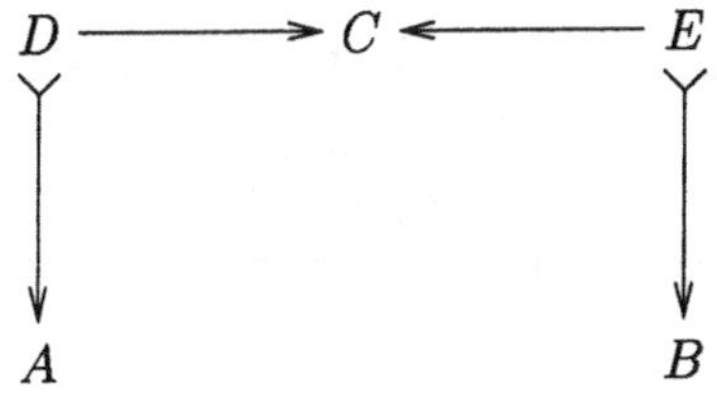

and let $\mathcal{D}$ consist of the specified monos. Then, $p\mathcal{K}$ is

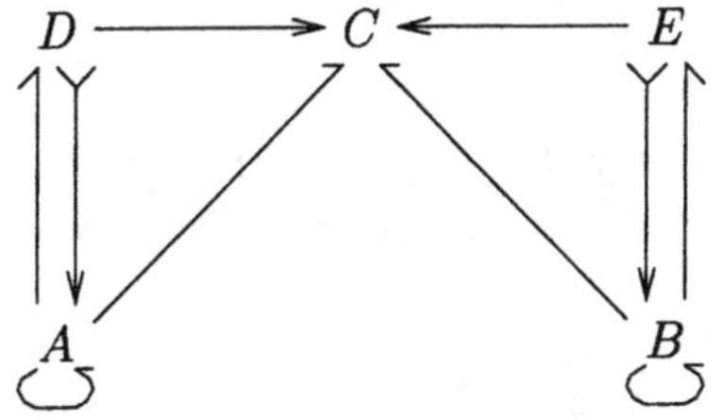

and, $A \rightharpoonup C \leftharpoondown B$ is a coproduct in $p\mathcal{K}$. Notice that $\mathcal{K}$ has no terminal object (C is terminal in $p\mathcal{K}$ but not in $\mathcal{K}$). In fact, for the property to fail it cannot have one because if $\mathcal{K}$ has terminal object then the inclusion functor $J : \mathcal{K} \to p\mathcal{K}$ creates colimits —see Proposition 5.2.4 (b).

In functor categories pullbacks can be computed pointwise and therefore the category of diagrams in $\mathcal{K}$ of type $\mathcal{G}$ comes equipped with a plenitude of pullbacks:

Proposition 5.3.5 Let $(\mathcal{K}, \mathcal{D})$ be a domain structure. Let $\mathcal{C}$ be the full-on-objects subcategory of $\mathcal{K}^{\mathcal{G}}$ of all cartesian and pointwise-admissible natural transformations. Then, $(\mathcal{K}^{\mathcal{G}}, \mathcal{C})$ is a domain structure and $p(\mathcal{K}^{\mathcal{G}}, \mathcal{C}) \cong p(\mathcal{K}, \mathcal{D})^{\mathcal{G}} \restriction | \mathcal{K}^{\mathcal{G}} |$.

PROOF: Clearly, every morphism in $\mathcal{C}$ is a mono in $\mathcal{K}^{\mathcal{G}}$. Moreover, $\mathcal{K}^{\mathcal{G}}$ has pullbacks of morphisms in $\mathcal{C}$ along arbitrary maps because pullbacks of admissible monos along arbitrary maps exist; and thus, for every $\varphi : \Xi \dot{\to} \Gamma$ in $\mathcal{K}^{\mathcal{G}}$ and $\mu : \Delta \dot{\rightarrowtail} \Gamma$ in $\mathcal{C}$, the

diagram

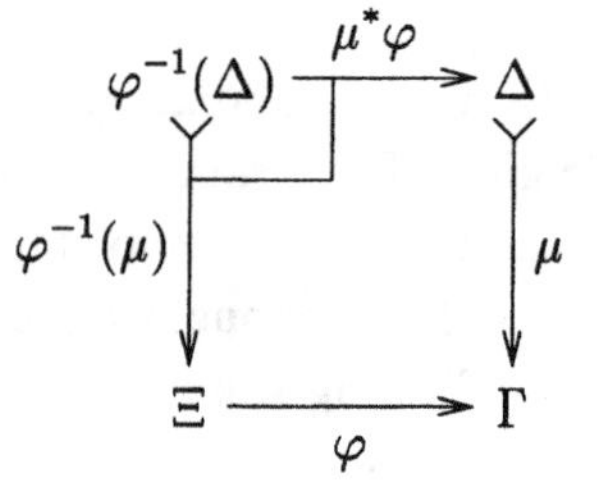

$$
\begin{array}{ccc}
\varphi^{-1}(\Delta) & \xrightarrow{\ \mu^*\varphi\ } & \Delta \\
\varphi^{-1}(\mu) \downarrow & & \downarrow \mu \\
\Xi & \xrightarrow[\ \varphi\ ]{} & \Gamma
\end{array}
$$

is a pullback in $\mathcal{K}^{\mathcal{G}}$ if and only if , for every $A \in |\,\mathcal{G}\,|$, the diagram

$$
\begin{array}{ccc}
\varphi^{-1}(\Delta)A & \xrightarrow{\ (\mu^*\varphi)_A\ } & \Delta A \\
\varphi^{-1}(\mu)_A \downarrow & & \downarrow \mu_A \\
\Xi A & \xrightarrow[\ \varphi_A\ ]{} & \Gamma A
\end{array}
$$

is a pullback in $\mathcal{K}$ and, for every $f : A \to B$ in $\mathcal{G}$, the map $\varphi^{-1}(\Delta)f$ is the unique mediating morphism (given by the universal property of pullbacks) making the diagram

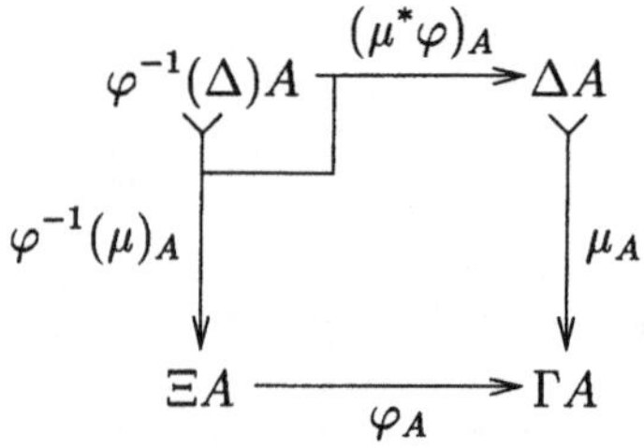

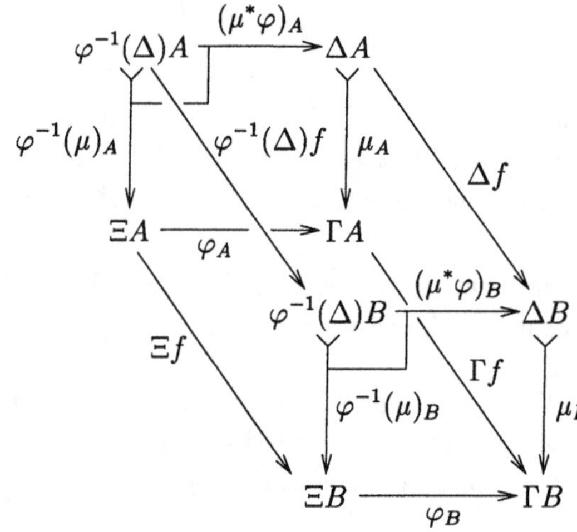

commute. Thus, $\varphi^{-1}(\mu)$ is pointwise-admissible; it is also cartesian because the right-hand face of the above diagram is a pullback and therefore so is the left-hand face. Hence, $\varphi^{-1}(\mu) \in \mathcal{C}$.

One half of the isomorphism $p(\mathcal{K}^{\mathcal{G}}, \mathcal{C}) \cong p(\mathcal{K}, \mathcal{D})^{\mathcal{G}} \restriction | \mathcal{K}^{\mathcal{G}} |$ is given by the mapping

$$[\mu, \varphi] : \Xi \rightharpoonup \Gamma \quad \mapsto \quad \{[\mu_A, \varphi_A] : \Xi A \rightharpoonup \Gamma A\}_{A \in |\mathcal{G}|} : \Xi \stackrel{.}{\rightharpoonup} \Gamma$$

which is shown to be well defined using that μ is cartesian and that φ is natural. The other half, assigns to a natural transformation $\{[\Delta A \stackrel{\mu_A}{\rightarrowtail} \Xi A, \Delta A \stackrel{\varphi_A}{\to} \Gamma A]\}_{A \in |\mathcal{G}|} : \Xi \stackrel{.}{\rightharpoonup} \Gamma$ the partial map $[\mu : \Delta \stackrel{.}{\rightarrowtail} \Xi, \varphi : \Delta \stackrel{.}{\to} \Gamma]$ where $\Delta : \mathcal{G} \to \mathcal{K}$ is the functor mapping an object A to ΔA and a morphism $f : A \to B$ to the unique Δf —guaranteed to exist by the naturality of $\{[\mu_A, \varphi_A]\}$— making the diagram

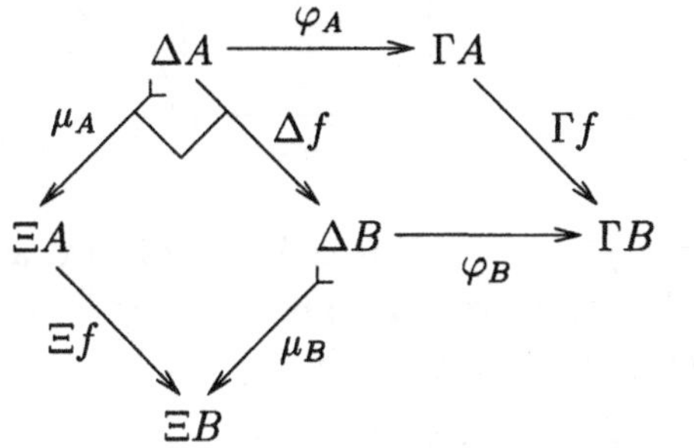

commute. Observe that, by construction, μ and φ are natural transformations, and that μ is cartesian and pointwise-admissible. □

Justified by the above proposition, *cartesian and pointwise-admissible* natural transformations will be called *admissible*. Note that, via the isomorphism of the above proposition, every admissible $\mu : \Delta \stackrel{.}{\rightarrowtail} \Gamma : \mathcal{G} \to \mathcal{K}$ induces a *partial inclusion* natural transformation $\mu^R : \Gamma \stackrel{.}{\rightharpoonup} \Delta : \mathcal{G} \to p\mathcal{K}$ given by ${\mu^R}_N = {\mu_N}^R$ for every $N \in | \mathcal{G} |$.

The next two lemmas provide the basis for characterising colimits of diagrams of total maps in categories of partial maps. The first one states that *colimits are stable* under pullbacks along admissible monos. The second one states that *admissibility is preserved* under colimits.

Lemma 5.3.6 Let $\gamma : \Gamma \stackrel{.}{\to} C : \mathcal{G} \to \mathcal{K}$ be colimiting in $p\mathcal{K}$. Then, for every admissible $m : D \rightarrowtail C$, the cone $m^*\gamma : \gamma^{-1}(D) \stackrel{.}{\to} D : \mathcal{G} \to \mathcal{K}$ is colimiting in $p\mathcal{K}$ and in $\mathcal{K}$.

PROOF: For every $\beta : \gamma^{-1}(D) \stackrel{.}{\rightharpoonup} B : \mathcal{G} \to p\mathcal{K}$ we have that $u : m^*\gamma \rightharpoonup \beta$ if and only if $u = v \circ m$ where v is the unique mediating morphism $\gamma \rightharpoonup \beta \circ \gamma^{-1}(m)^R$ because

($\Rightarrow$) $u \circ m^R : \gamma \rightharpoonup \beta \circ \gamma^{-1}(m)^R$ and therefore $u = u \circ m^R \circ m = v \circ m$.

($\Leftarrow$)

$$\begin{aligned} v \circ m \circ (m^*\gamma) &= v \circ \gamma \circ \gamma^{-1}(m) \\ &= \beta \circ \gamma^{-1}(m)^R \circ \gamma^{-1}(m) \\ &= \beta. \end{aligned}$$

Therefore, $m^*\gamma : \gamma^{-1}(D) \dot{\rightarrow} D$ is colimiting in $p\mathcal{K}$.

We now show that whenever β is pointwise-total, u is total. Let $v = [n, g]$, then $v : \gamma \rightharpoonup \beta \circ \gamma^{-1}(m)^R$ implies the existence of a unique $n^*\gamma$ such that

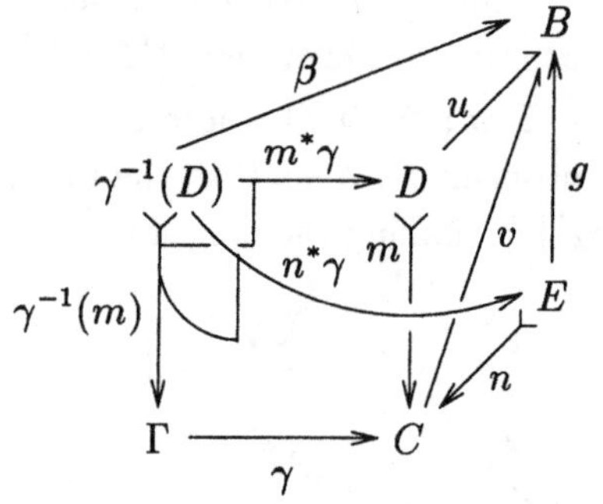

commutes. But then, $n^*\gamma : \gamma^{-1}(D) \dot{\rightarrow} E$ is colimiting in $p\mathcal{K}$ and therefore there is an isomorphism $i : m^*\gamma \cong n^*\gamma$. Moreover, since $n \circ i : m^*\gamma \rightarrowtail m \circ (m^*\gamma)$ it follows that $m = n \circ i$ and therefore $u = v \circ m = g \circ n^R \circ m = g \circ i$. □

As a corollary we improve Proposition 5.2.4 (a):

Corollary 5.3.7 The inclusion functor $J : \mathcal{K} \rightarrow p\mathcal{K}$ reflects colimits. □

Lemma 5.3.8 Let

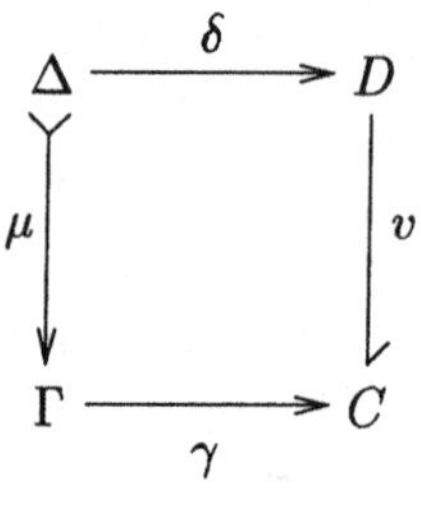

(5.8)

commute, where $\delta : \Delta \dot{\rightarrow} D : \mathcal{G} \rightarrow \mathcal{K}$ and $\gamma : \Gamma \dot{\rightarrow} C : \mathcal{G} \rightarrow \mathcal{K}$ are colimiting in $p\mathcal{K}$, $\mu : \Delta \dot{\rightarrowtail} \Gamma : \mathcal{G} \rightarrow \mathcal{K}$ is admissible, and v is the unique mediating morphism $\delta \rightharpoonup \gamma \circ \mu$.

Then, v is admissible and (5.8) is a pullback.

PROOF: Let $u = [m, f] : \gamma \rightharpoonup \delta \circ \mu^R$. Then, we have the situation

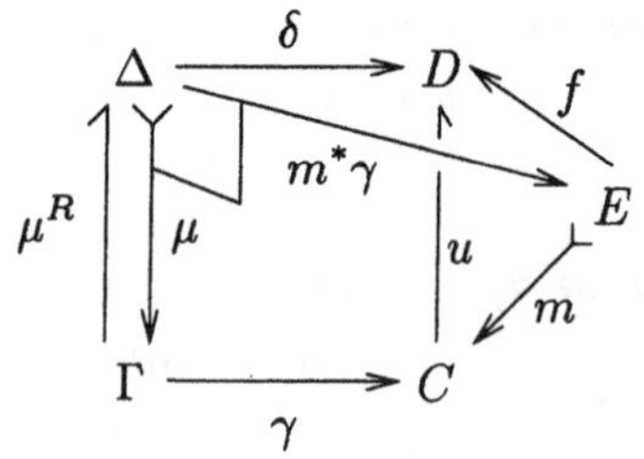

(5.9)

for a unique $m^*\gamma : \Delta \dot{\to} E$ which, by Lemma 5.3.6, is colimiting in $p\mathcal{K}$. Since $\delta : \Delta \dot{\to} D$ is also colimiting in $p\mathcal{K}$ and $f : m^*\gamma \to \delta$ it follows that f is an isomorphism and we are done, because $v = m \circ f^{-1} : \delta \rightarrowtail \gamma \circ \mu$ is admissible and the diagram (5.9) gives the required pullback. □

Theorem 5.3.9 (Plotkin) $p\mathcal{K}$ has colimits of diagrams in $\mathcal{K}$ of type $\mathcal{G}$ with pointwise-total colimiting cones if and only if

1. $\mathcal{K}$ has colimits of diagrams in $\mathcal{K}$ of type $\mathcal{G}$.
2. Whenever $\gamma : \Gamma \dot{\to} C : \mathcal{G} \to \mathcal{K}$ is colimiting in $\mathcal{K}$ and $m : D \rightarrowtail C$ is admissible then $m^*\gamma : \gamma^{-1}(D) \dot{\to} D : \mathcal{G} \to \mathcal{K}$ is colimiting in $\mathcal{K}$.
3. Whenever $\delta : \Delta \dot{\to} D : \mathcal{G} \to \mathcal{K}$ and $\gamma : \Gamma \dot{\to} C : \mathcal{G} \to \mathcal{K}$ are colimiting in $\mathcal{K}$, $\mu : \Delta \dot{\rightarrowtail} \Gamma : \mathcal{G} \to \mathcal{K}$ is admissible, and $m : \delta \to \gamma \circ \mu$ then m is admissible and

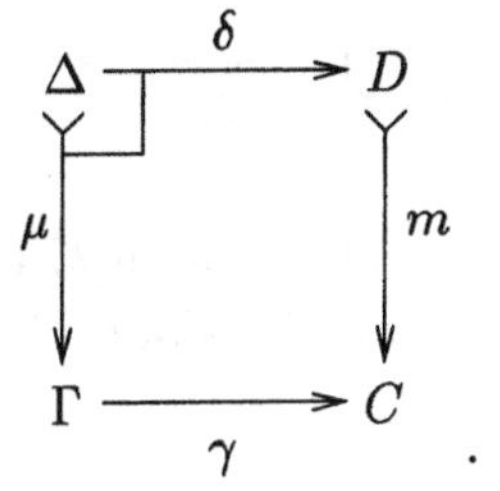

PROOF:
(⇒) (1) Follows from Corollary 5.3.7.
(2)–(3) Follow from Lemmas 5.3.6 and 5.3.8 observing that if $\Gamma : \mathcal{G} \to \mathcal{K}$ has colimit in $p\mathcal{K}$ and $\Gamma \dot{\to} C$ is colimiting in $\mathcal{K}$, then it is also colimiting in $p\mathcal{K}$.

(⇐) We show that if $\gamma : \Gamma \dot{\to} C : \mathcal{G} \to \mathcal{K}$ is colimiting in $\mathcal{K}$ then it is also colimiting in $p\mathcal{K}$.

Given $[\mu, \varphi] : \Gamma \dot{\rightharpoonup} A$, consider the diagram

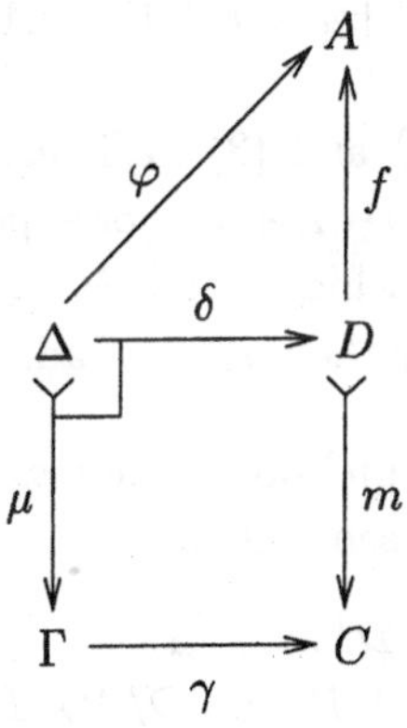

where $\delta : \Delta \dot{\rightarrow} D$ is colimiting in $\mathcal{K}$, and $f : \delta \rightarrow \varphi$ and $m : \delta \rightarrow \gamma \circ \mu$ are mediating morphisms. (By (3), m is admissible and makes the square a pullback). Then, we have that $[m, f] : \gamma \rightharpoonup [\mu, \varphi]$. To see that it is the unique such, suppose $[n, g] : \gamma \rightharpoonup [\mu, \varphi]$. Then there exists a unique $n^*\gamma$ such that

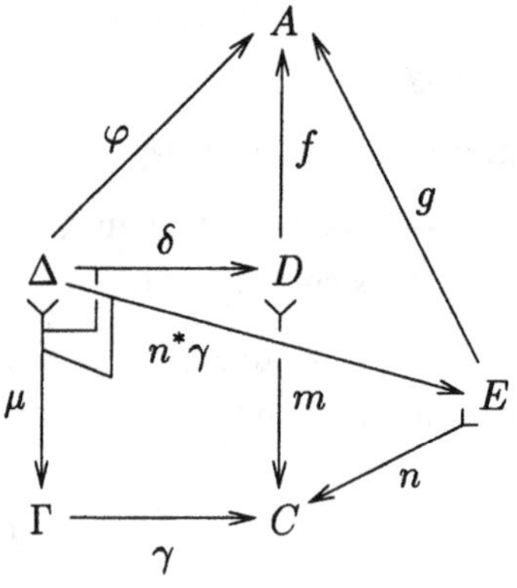

commutes. But, by (2), $n^*\gamma$ is colimiting in $\mathcal{K}$ and therefore there is an isomorphism $i : \delta \rightarrow n^*\gamma$. Moreover, since $n \circ i : \delta \rightarrow m \circ \delta$ and $g \circ i : \delta \rightarrow f \circ \delta$ we conclude that $[n, g] = [m, f]$. □

Corollary 5.3.10 If $\mathcal{K}$ has colimits of type $\mathcal{G}$ then $J : \mathcal{K} \rightarrow p\mathcal{K}$ preserves them if and only if (2) and (3) of Theorem 5.3.9 hold. □

It is time for applications. Assume that $p\mathcal{K}$ has binary coproducts and that $\mathcal{K}$ has terminal object (so that the coproduct injections are total).

Then, for $[m, f] : A \rightharpoonup C$ and $[n, g] : B \rightharpoonup C$, by Theorem 5.3.9, the unique mediating morphism $\llbracket [m, f], [n, g] \rrbracket$ equals $\big[m + n, \llbracket f, g \rrbracket\big] : A + B \rightharpoonup C$. And it follows that, for $[m, f] : A \rightharpoonup X$ and $[n, g] : B \rightharpoonup Y$,

$$[m, f] + [n, g] \quad = \quad [m + n, f + g] : A + B \rightharpoonup X + Y.$$

Moreover, putting statements (2) and (3) in Theorem 5.3.9 together, we have that to give an admissible subobject $[C \rightarrowtail A + B]$ corresponds to give a pair of admissible subobjects $([D \rightarrowtail A], [E \rightarrowtail B])$ for which $D + E \cong C$. Thus, the notion of admissibility of $A + B$ is determined *disjointly* by the notion of admissibility for A and for B.

Proposition 5.3.11 If $\mathcal{K}$ has terminal object and $p\mathcal{K}$ has finite coproducts then $\mathcal{D}$ is *extensive* (following [Law90]) in the sense that

$$\begin{aligned} \mathcal{D}/0 &\simeq \mathbf{1}, \\ \mathcal{D}/A + B &\simeq \mathcal{D}/A \times \mathcal{D}/B. \end{aligned}$$ □

It came as a nice surprise that under the mild assumption that maps $0 \to A$ are admissible, coproduct injections are to be admissible and coproducts are to be disjoint:

Proposition 5.3.12 If $\mathcal{K}$ has terminal object, $p\mathcal{K}$ has finite coproducts, and for every $A \in |\, p\mathcal{K}\,|$ the map $0 \to A$ is admissible then for every A_i $(i = 1, 2) \in |\, p\mathcal{K}\,|$, the coproduct injections $\amalg_i : A_i \to A_1 + A_2$ $(i = 1, 2)$ are admissible and $\amalg_1 \cap \amalg_2 = 0$.

PROOF: $A_1 \xrightarrow{\text{id}} A_1 \longleftarrow 0$ and $0 \longrightarrow A_2 \xleftarrow{\text{id}} A_2$ are coproducts and since

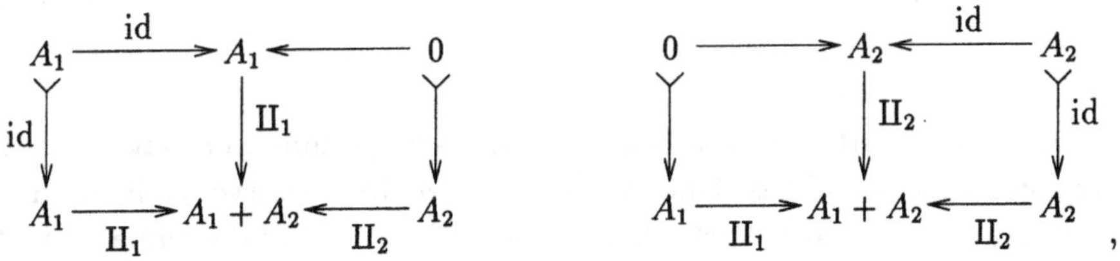

by Lemma 5.3.8, we conclude that $\amalg_i : A_i \to A_1 + A_2$ $(i = 1, 2)$ are admissible and that the above squares are pullbacks. In particular,

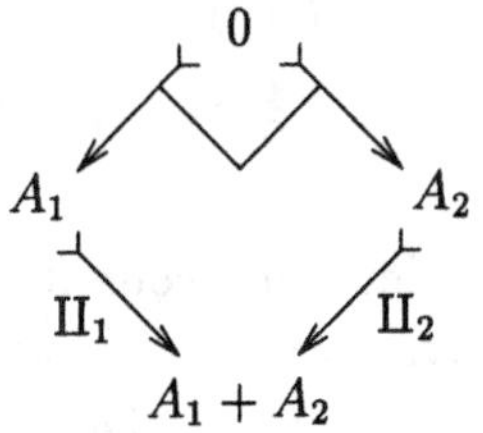

□

As a final application we show that, for order-enriched categories, the coproduct functor automatically enriches.

Proposition 5.3.13 Assume $\mathcal{K}$ has terminal object. Let $p\mathcal{K}$ be **Poset**-enriched (**Cpo**-enriched). If $\mathcal{K}$ has binary **Poset**-coproducts then binary coproducts in $p\mathcal{K}$ are **Poset**-coproducts (**Cpo**-coproducts).

PROOF: Consider the case when $p\mathcal{K}$ is **Poset**-enriched.

Let $[m, f] \sqsubseteq_i [m', f'] : A \rightharpoonup C$ and $[n, g] : B \rightharpoonup C$. Then, since

$$m + n \;=\; (m' \circ i) + n \;=\; (m' + n) \circ (i + \text{id})$$

and

$$[f, g] \;\sqsubseteq\; [f' \circ i, g] \;=\; [f', g] \circ (i + \text{id})$$

we conclude the monotonicity of $[\_, \_]$ in the first argument:

$$[[m, f], [n, g]] \;=\; [m + n, [f, g]] \;\sqsubseteq_{i+\text{id}}\; [m' + n, [f', g]] \;=\; [[m', f'], [n, g]] .$$

The monotonicity of $[\_,\_]$ in the second argument follows, because

$$\begin{aligned}
\big[[n,g],[m,f]\big] &= \big[[m,f],[n,g]\big] \circ [\amalg_2,\amalg_1] \\
&\sqsubseteq \big[[m',f'],[n,g]\big] \circ [\amalg_2,\amalg_1] \\
&= \big[[n,g],[m',f']\big].
\end{aligned}$$

Moreover, by Proposition 2.2.1, when $p\mathcal{K}$ is **Cpo**-enriched then so are the coproducts. □

When $p\mathcal{K}$ is partial cartesian closed all diagrams having colimit in $\mathcal{K}$ have colimit in $p\mathcal{K}$ simply because $J : \mathcal{K} \to p\mathcal{K}$ has right adjoint and therefore preserves colimits. Thus, for example, if $\mathcal{K}$ has binary coproducts then so does $p\mathcal{K}$. Further, by arguments analogous to those in cartesian closed categories, they interact with partial cartesian closure as expected; there are canonical natural isomorphisms,

$$\begin{aligned}
(A+B)\otimes C &\cong (A\otimes C)+(B\otimes C), \\
(A+B) \rightharpoonup C &\cong (A \rightharpoonup C)\otimes(B \rightharpoonup C).
\end{aligned}$$

We present another approach for calculating colimits that will allow us to infer the existence of the colimits needed for solving recursive type equations in $p\mathcal{K}$ from the existence of such colimits in $\mathcal{K}$ (see Proposition 5.4.4). The idea is to formalise the following argument: given a diagram, make it into a diagram in $\mathcal{K}$ by adjoining undefinedness, calculate its colimit in $\mathcal{K}$, and finally, *remove undefinedness* to obtain a colimit in $p\mathcal{K}$. Curiously, the last step cannot be formalised as it is and has to be reformulated as '*extract the defined part*'. Constructively, the process of removing undefinedness and the process of extracting definedness seem not to be the same, and proceeding in the second way forces us to restrict the analysis to diagrams in $\mathcal{K}$.

Theorem 5.3.14 Let $\mathcal{K}$ have terminal object and let $J \dashv L : p\mathcal{K} \to \mathcal{K}$. For every $\Gamma : \mathcal{G} \to \mathcal{K}$, if $L\Gamma$ has colimit in $\mathcal{K}$ then Γ has colimit in $p\mathcal{K}$.

PROOF: As Γ is a diagram in $\mathcal{K}$, we have a unique pointwise-total cone $\Gamma \dot{\to} 1$ which lifts to a cone $L(\Gamma \dot{\to} 1) : L\Gamma \dot{\to} L1$.

Now let $\gamma' : L\Gamma \dot{\to} C'$ be colimiting in $\mathcal{K}$, and let $(C' \to L1) : \gamma' \longrightarrow L(\Gamma \dot{\to} 1)$. Pulling back η_1 along $C' \to L1$, we end up in the situation

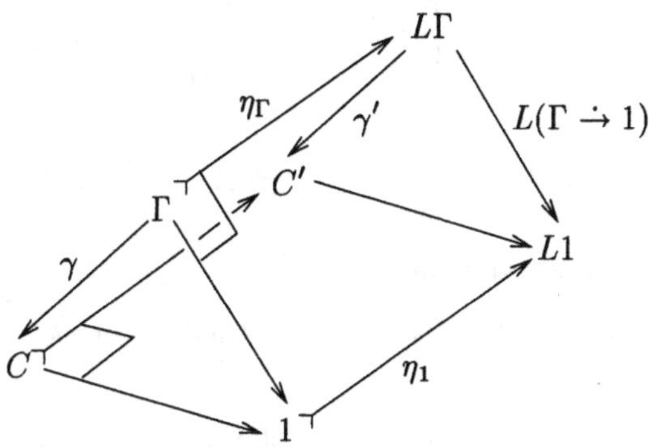

(5.10)

where $\gamma : \Gamma \dot{\to} C$ is the unique cone given by the universal property of pullbacks. (By the way, observe that $(C \rightarrowtail C')^R \circ \gamma' = \gamma \circ {\eta_\Gamma}^R$).

As $J : \mathcal{K} \to p\mathcal{K}$ preserves colimits, to show that γ is colimiting in $p\mathcal{K}$ it is enough to show that it is so in $\mathcal{K}$.

For a cone $\alpha : \Gamma \dot{\to} A$, the diagram (5.10) expands to

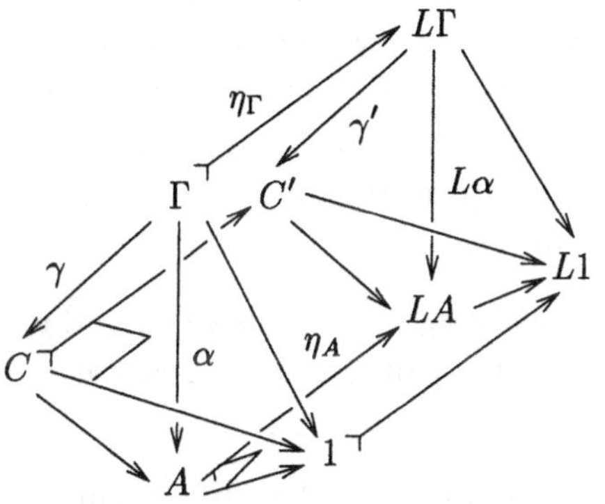

(5.11)

where $(C' \to LA) : \gamma' \to L\alpha$ and where $C \to A$ is the unique mediating morphism between the two specified pullbacks. Chasing diagram (5.11), we see that $\eta_A \circ (C \to A) \circ \gamma = \eta_A \circ \alpha$ and therefore $(C \to A) : \gamma \to \alpha$. It is the unique such, because for any $C \to A : \gamma \to \alpha$, chasing diagram (5.11) while keeping in mind that $(C \rightarrowtail C')^R \circ \gamma' = \gamma \circ {\eta_\Gamma}^R$ and that $\alpha \circ {\eta_\Gamma}^R = {\eta_A}^R \circ L\alpha$, the partial maps $[C \rightarrowtail C', C \to A]$ and ${\eta_A}^R \circ (C' \to LA)$ are seen to mediate between γ' and ${\eta_A}^R \circ L\alpha$ and, since γ' is colimiting in $p\mathcal{K}$, they are equal; making $C \to A$ be the unique map that appears in the pullback

$$\begin{array}{ccc} C & \longrightarrow & A \\ \downarrow & \lrcorner & \downarrow \eta_A \\ C' & \longrightarrow & LA \end{array} \quad .$$

□

Remark. A couple of comments on the proof:

1. The proof technique does not extend to diagrams Γ in $p\mathcal{K}$, as in general we only have a lax cone $\Gamma \overset{\cdot}{\underset{\leq}{\to}} 1$.
2. The proof does not show that L creates colimits, as we do not know whether the cones γ' and $L\gamma$ are isomorphic. In the next section, when considering ω-chains of embeddings in a **Cpo**-enriched setting this will turn out to be the case (see Theorem 5.4.7).

5.4 Colimits of ω-Chains of Embeddings

In this section we study the colimits needed to solve recursive type equations. In particular, we establish conditions under which the category of partial maps has colimits of ω-chains of embeddings provided that so does the category of total maps. First, we do it in the presence of the lifting functor as an application of Theorem 5.3.14; afterwards we do it for arbitrary categories of partial maps.

We recall the basic definitions:

Definition 5.4.1 In a **Poset**-category, $f \dashv g$ is an *adjoint pair* if $\mathrm{id} \leq g \circ f$ and $f \circ g \leq \mathrm{id}$. Further, whenever $g \circ f = \mathrm{id}$ the pair is called an *embedding-projection pair* (or simply, ep-pair). □

Following tradition, in an adjoint pair the first component is called the *left* adjoint whilst the second component is called the *right* adjoint. Since each of the adjoints uniquely determines the other one, the notations f^R, for the right adjoint of a left adjoint f, and g^L, for the left adjoint of a right adjoint g, are justified. In fact, for a **Poset**-category $\mathcal{C}$, defining $\mathcal{C}_L$ ($\mathcal{C}_R$) to be the subcategory of $\mathcal{C}$ of all left (right) adjoints, we have a duality of categories $(\_)^R : {\mathcal{C}_L}^{op} \cong \mathcal{C}_R : (\_)^L$. Further useful definitions are: $\mathcal{C}_A$ for the subcategory of $\mathcal{C}^{op} \times \mathcal{C}$ of all adjoint pairs, and $\mathcal{C}_E$ ($\mathcal{C}_P$) for the subcategory of $\mathcal{C}_L$ ($\mathcal{C}_R$) of all embeddings (projections). Clearly, the previous duality cuts down to a duality ${\mathcal{C}_E}^{op} \cong \mathcal{C}_P$.

Ep-pairs in a **Poset**-category of partial maps are such that an object A partially embeds into another one B if and only if A totally embeds into an admissible subobject of B.

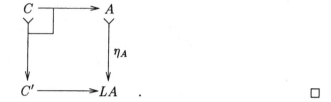

Proposition 5.4.2 Let $p\mathcal{K}$ be **Poset**-enriched. For every $A, B \in |\, p\mathcal{K}\,|$,

- $p\mathcal{K}_E(A,B) = \{n \circ f \mid f \in \mathcal{K}_E(A,D) \ \wedge\ n \in \mathcal{D}(D,B)$ for some $D \in |\,\mathcal{K}\,|\}$,
- $p\mathcal{K}_P(B,A) = \{[n,g] \mid n \in \mathcal{D}(D,B) \ \wedge\ g \in \mathcal{K}_P(D,A)$ for some $D \in |\,\mathcal{K}\,|\}$.

PROOF: We show that $[m,f] \dashv [n,g]$ is an ep-pair if and only if $g \in \mathcal{K}_P$ and $[m,f] = n \circ g^L$.

($\Rightarrow$) The equality $[n,g] \circ [m,f] = \mathrm{id}$ implies that m is an isomorphism and that there is a unique f' such that

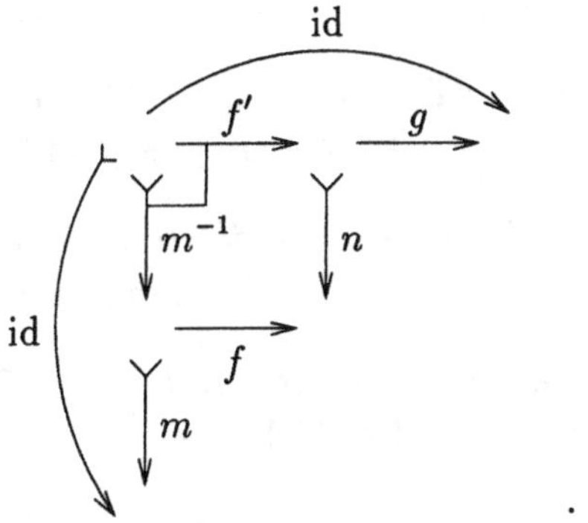

Then, $g \circ f' = \mathrm{id}$ and $[m,f] = n \circ f'$. Moreover, pre-composing with n at both sides of the inequality $(n \circ f') \circ (g \circ n^R) \sqsubseteq \mathrm{id}$ it follows that $n \circ f' \circ g \sqsubseteq n$, and since n is full we have that $f' \circ g \sqsubseteq \mathrm{id}$

($\Leftarrow$) Check the definition of ep-pair. □

Similarly we can prove:

Proposition 5.4.3 Let $p\mathcal{K}$ be **Poset**-enriched. For every $A, B \in |\, p\mathcal{K}\,|$,

- $p\mathcal{K}_L(A,B) = \{n \circ f \mid f \in \mathcal{K}_L(A,D) \ \wedge\ n \in \mathcal{D}(D,B)$ for some $D \in |\,\mathcal{K}\,|\}$,
- $p\mathcal{K}_R(B,A) = \{[n,g] \mid n \in \mathcal{D}(D,B) \ \wedge\ g \in \mathcal{K}_R(D,A)$ for some $D \in |\,\mathcal{K}\,|\}$. □

As a corollary to Theorem 5.3.14 we obtain:

Proposition 5.4.4 Let $\mathcal{K}$ have terminal object and let $J \dashv L : p\mathcal{K} \to \mathcal{K}$ in **Poset-CAT**. If $\mathcal{K}$ has colimits of ω-chains of embeddings then so does $p\mathcal{K}$. □

Remark. The lifting functor is required to be **Poset**-enriched so that ep-pairs are preserved (as they are adjoint pairs).

In the **Cpo**-enriched case, exploiting the limit/colimit coincidence, we strengthen the result by showing that the lifting functor creates colimits of ω-chains of embeddings.

We recall the order-theoretic characterisation of colimits of ω-chains of embeddings in **Cpo**-categories from which the limit/colimit coincidence follows:

Theorem 5.4.5 (Limit/Colimit Coincidence Theorem [SP82]**)** In a **Cpo**-category $\mathcal{C}$, for $\Gamma : \omega \to \mathcal{C}_E$ the following are equivalent:

1. $\gamma : \Gamma \dot{\to} C : \omega \to \mathcal{C}$ is colimiting in $\mathcal{C}$.
2. $\gamma : \Gamma \dot{\to} C : \omega \to \mathcal{C}_E$ and $\bigvee \gamma_n \circ (\gamma_n)^R = \mathrm{id}_C$.
3. $\gamma : \Gamma \dot{\to} C : \omega \to \mathcal{C}$ is **Cpo**-colimiting in $\mathcal{C}$.
4. $\gamma : \Gamma \dot{\to} C : \omega \to \mathcal{C}_E$ and $\gamma^R : C \dot{\to} \Gamma^R : \omega \to \mathcal{C}_P$ is limiting in $\mathcal{C}$.
5. $\gamma : \Gamma \dot{\to} C : \omega \to \mathcal{C}_E$ and $\gamma^R : C \dot{\to} \Gamma^R : \omega \to \mathcal{C}_P$ is **Cpo**-limiting in $\mathcal{C}$. □

The theorem below is essentially proved using Theorem 5.3.14, and the facts that colimits happen to be limits and that these are preserved by the lifting functor.

Definition 5.4.6 A functor $F : \mathcal{A} \to \mathcal{B}$ *pseudo-creates colimits* for a diagram Δ in $\mathcal{A}$ if whenever $F\Delta$ has colimit in $\mathcal{B}$ then Δ has colimit in $\mathcal{A}$ and F preserves it. □

Theorem 5.4.7 Let $\mathcal{K}$ have terminal object. If $J \dashv L : p\mathcal{K} \to \mathcal{K}$ in **Cpo-CAT** then L pseudo-creates colimits of ω-chains of embeddings.

PROOF: Given $\Gamma : \omega \to p\mathcal{K}_E$, if $\gamma' : L\Gamma \dot{\to} C'$ is colimiting in $\mathcal{K}$ then, by Theorem 5.3.14, we can construct $\gamma : \Gamma \dot{\to} C$ colimiting in $p\mathcal{K}$. Now, by the Limit/Colimit Coincidence Theorem, we have that $\gamma : \Gamma \dot{\to} C : \omega \to p\mathcal{K}_E$ and that $\gamma^R : C \dot{\to} \Gamma^R$ is limiting in $p\mathcal{K}$. Then, since L is a right adjoint, it preserves limits and therefore $L(\gamma^R) : LC \dot{\to} L(\Gamma^R)$ is limiting in $\mathcal{K}$. Moreover, as L is a **Poset**-functor, it preserves ep-pairs and hence $L(\gamma^R) = (L\gamma)^R$ and $L(\Gamma^R) = (L\Gamma)^R$. Thus, by the Limit/Colimit Coincidence Theorem, $L\gamma : L\Gamma \dot{\to} LC$ is colimiting in $\mathcal{K}$. □

In the general case (i.e., when the lifting functor is not assumed to exist), it is more convenient to work with limits of ω^{op}-chains of projections. The following two propositions will be essential when considering such limits.

Proposition 5.4.8 Let $p\mathcal{K}$ be **Poset**-enriched.

1. Projections in $\mathcal{K}$ are preserved by pulling-back along admissible monos.
2. For $g \in \mathcal{K}_P(B, A)$ and $n \in \mathcal{D}(D, A)$,

$$g^{-1}(n) \circ (n^* g)^L \circ (n^* g) \quad = \quad g^L \circ g \circ g^{-1}(n).$$

PROOF:

(1) Let $g \in \mathcal{K}_P$. Then $[g^{-1}(n), n^* g] = n^R \circ g$ is a projection in $p\mathcal{K}$ (with embedding $g^L \circ n$) and, by Proposition 5.4.2, $n^* g$ is an projection in $\mathcal{K}$.

(2) We calculate:

$$\begin{aligned} g^{-1}(n) \circ (n^*g)^L \circ (n^*g) &= ((n^*g) \circ g^{-1}(n)^R)^L \circ (n^*g) \\ &= (n^R \circ g)^L \circ (n^*g) \\ &= g^L \circ n \circ (n^*g) \\ &= g^L \circ g \circ g^{-1}(n). \end{aligned}$$ □

Proposition 5.4.9 Let $(\mathcal{K}, \mathcal{D})$ be a domain structure. Let $\pi : P \dot{\to} \Gamma : \omega^{op} \to \mathcal{K}$ be a cone and let $\mu : \Gamma' \dot{\rightarrowtail} \Gamma : \omega^{op} \to \mathcal{K}$ be admissible. Then, there exists a cone $\pi' : P' \dot{\to} \Gamma' : \omega^{op} \to \mathcal{K}$ and an admissible $m : P' \rightarrowtail P$ such that

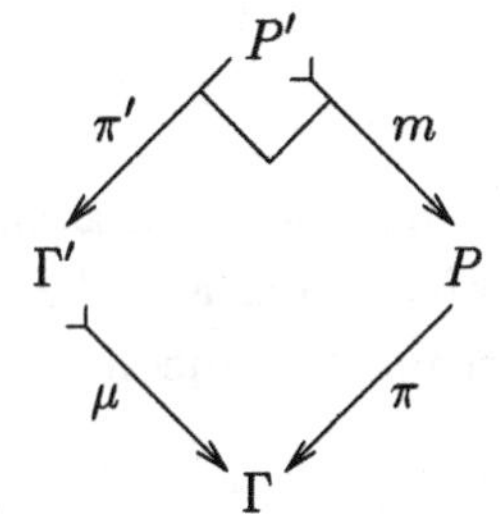

is a pullback in $\mathcal{K}^{\omega^{op}}$. And thus, π' is limiting whenever π is.

PROOF: Let

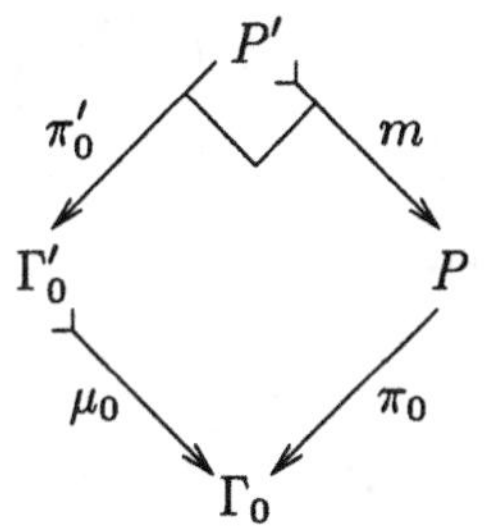

and for $k \in |\omega|$ define inductively ${\pi'}_{k+1}$ to be the unique morphism for which

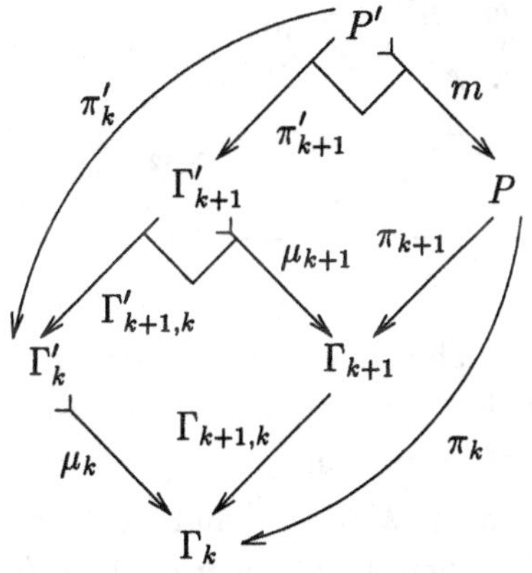

. □

Corollary 5.4.10 Let $(\mathcal{K},\mathcal{D})$ be a domain structure. For an admissible natural transformation $\mu : \Gamma' \dot{\rightarrowtail} \Gamma : \omega^{op} \to \mathcal{K}$, if $\pi : P \to \Gamma$ and $\pi' : P' \to \Gamma'$ are limiting then the unique $m : \mu \circ \pi' \to \pi$ is admissible and for every $k \in |\,\omega\,|$,

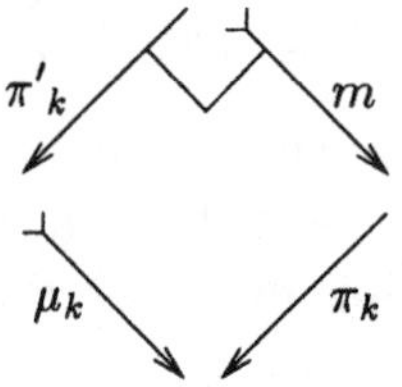

.
□

Theorem 5.4.11 Let $p\mathcal{K}$ be **Cpo**-enriched, and assume that $\mathcal{K}$ has limits of ω^{op}-chains of projections. If $\mathcal{D}$ has colimits of ω-chains and the inclusion functor $\mathcal{D} \to \mathcal{K}$ preserves them, then $p\mathcal{K}$ has limits of ω^{op}-chains of projections.

PROOF: Let $\langle [n_k, g_k] \rangle$ be an ω^{op}-chain of projections in $p\mathcal{K}$. For $j \in |\,\omega\,|$, define

$$g_k^{(j)} = \begin{cases} g_j & \text{if } k = 0 \\ n_{k-1}^{(j)}\,{}^*g_{k-1}^{(j+1)} & \text{if } k \geq 1 \end{cases} \qquad n_k^{(j)} \stackrel{def}{=} \begin{cases} n_j & \text{if } k = 0 \\ (g_{k-1}^{(j+1)})^{-1}(n_{k-1}^{(j)}) & \text{if } k \geq 1 \end{cases}$$

so that we are in the following situation

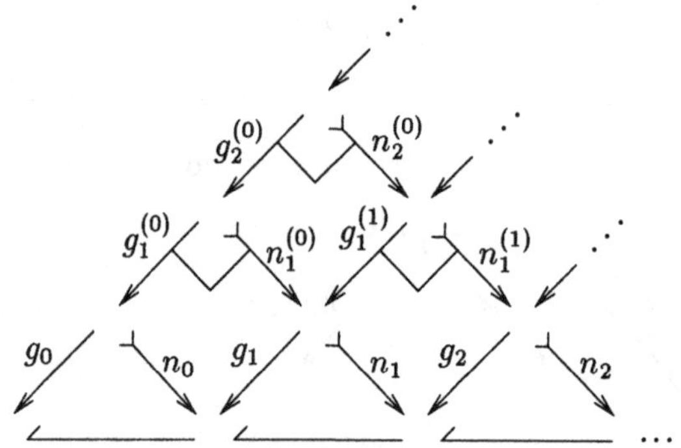

.

Let succ : $\omega \to \omega : k \mapsto k+1$. Then, by construction, $n^{(j)} : (g^{(j)}\,\mathrm{succ}) \dot{\rightarrowtail} g^{(j+1)}$ is admissible. And, since every g_k is a projection, by Proposition 5.4.8 (1), for every $j \in |\,\omega\,|$ the ω^{op}-chain $g^{(j)}$ consists of projections.

For every $j \in |\,\omega\,|$, let $\pi^{(j)}$ be a limit in $\mathcal{K}$ for $g^{(j)}$ and let m_j be the unique mediating morphism $n^{(j)} \circ (\pi^{(j)}\,\mathrm{succ}) \to \pi^{(j+1)}$. Then, by Corollary 5.4.10, $\langle m_j \rangle$ is an ω-chain in $\mathcal{D}$

and

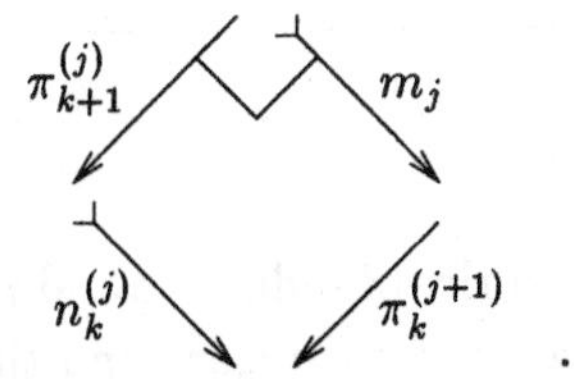

(5.12)

Letting μ be a colimit of $\langle m_j \rangle$ in $\mathcal{D}$ we will show that $\langle [\mu_k, \pi_0^{(k)}] \rangle$ is a limit of $\langle [n_k, g_k] \rangle$ in $p\mathcal{K}$.

Since $\pi_0^{(k)} \in \mathcal{K}_P$ and $\mu_k \in \mathcal{D}$ it follows that $[\mu_k, \pi_0^{(k)}] \in p\mathcal{K}_P$. Moreover, it is a cone because

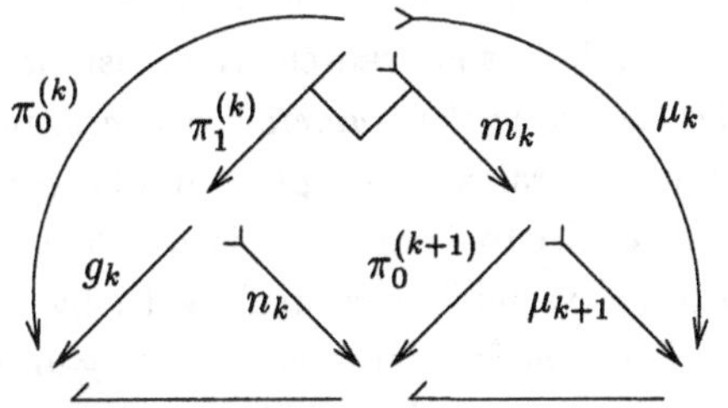

Finally, by the Limit/Colimit Coincidence Theorem, we need only check that $\bigsqcup [\mu_k, \pi_0^{(k)}]^L \circ [\mu_k, \pi_0^{(k)}] = \mathrm{id}$.

For $\phi_k = \mu_k \circ (\pi_0^{(k)})^L \circ \pi_0^{(k)}$ we have that $[\mu_k, \pi_0^{(k)}]^L \circ [\mu_k, \pi_0^{(k)}] = [\mu_k, \phi_k]$ and since $\mu_k \sqsubseteq_{m_k} \mu_{k+1}$, the inequality $[\mu_k, \phi_k] \sqsubseteq [\mu_{k+1}, \phi_{k+1}]$ is realised by m_k. Then, by Proposition 4.3.3 (1), $\bigsqcup [\mu_k, \pi_0^{(k)}]^L \circ [\mu_k, \pi_0^{(k)}] = \bigsqcup [\mu_k, \Phi_k]$ where $\Phi_k = \bigsqcup_{j \geq k} \phi_j \circ m_{k,j}$. But,

$$\begin{aligned}
\Phi_k &= \textstyle\bigsqcup_{j\geq k} \mu_j \circ (\pi_0^{(j)})^L \circ \pi_0^{(j)} \circ m_{k,j} \\
&= \textstyle\bigsqcup_{j\geq k} \mu_j \circ m_{k,j} \circ (\pi_{j-k}^{(j)})^L \circ \pi_{j-k}^{(j)} \quad \text{, using Proposition 5.4.8 (2) for diagram (5.12)} \\
&= \mu_k \circ \textstyle\bigsqcup_{j\geq 0} (\pi_j^{(k)})^L \circ \pi_j^{(k)} \\
&= \mu_k
\end{aligned}$$

and therefore, $\bigsqcup [\mu_k, \pi_0^{(k)}]^L \circ [\mu_k, \pi_0^{(k)}] = \bigsqcup [\mu_k, \mu_k]$. Now, using Lemma 4.3.4 and the argument in the proof of Proposition 4.3.7, we are done. □

Corollary 5.4.12 Let $(\mathcal{K}, \mathcal{D})$ be a uniform **Cpo**-domain-structure such that $p\mathcal{K}$ **Cpo**-enriches. If $\mathcal{K}$ has limits of ω^{op}-chains of projections and $\mathcal{D}$ has colimits of ω-chains then $p\mathcal{K}$ has limits of ω^{op}-chains of projections. □

6 Recursive Types

We thoroughly study the semantics of inductive and recursive types. Our point of view is that types constitute the objects of a category and that type constructors are ***bifunctors*** on the category of types. By a bifunctor on a category we mean a functor on two variables from the category to itself, contravariant in the first, covariant in the second.

First, following Peter Freyd, the stress is on the study of ***algebraically complete*** categories, i.e. those categories admitting all inductive types (in the sense that every endofunctor on them has an initial algebra —this is understood in a setting in which the phrase "every endofunctor" refers to a class of *enriched* endofunctors— see Definition 6.1.4). After observing that algebraic completeness guarantees the existence of parameterised initial algebras, we identify, under the name of *parameterised algebraically complete* categories, all those categories which are algebraically complete and such that every parameterised inductive type constructor gives rise to a parameterised inductive type (see Definition 6.1.7). Type constructors on several variables are dealt with by *Bekič's Lemma*, from which follow both the *Product Theorem* for Parameterised Algebraically Complete Categories (Theorem 6.1.14) and also the *dinaturality of* Fix (the functor delivering initial algebras).

Second, again following Peter Freyd, algebraic completeness is refined to *algebraic compactness* by imposing the axiom that, for every endofunctor, the inverse of an initial algebra is a final coalgebra. The compactness axiom is motivated with a simple argument showing that every bifunctor on an algebraically compact category admits a fixed-point. Further preliminary evidence for the suitability of algebraic compactness is that Bekič's Lemma (together with its corollaries) hold. More definite evidence is provided by the *fundamental property* of algebraically compact categories, viz. that every bifunctor on an algebraically compact category has a canonical and minimal fixed-point (Theorem 6.4.1), and by the fact that *recursive types reduce to inductive types* (see Section 6.5).

6.1 Algebraic Completeness

The category-theoretic solution of recursive type equations is based on the following, by now standard, assumptions:

1. Types constitute the objects of a category.
2. Type constructors are bifunctors on the category of types.

With this viewpoint, given a bifunctor, F, on a category, the *recursive* type $\mathrm{Fix}(F)$ is a *canonical* type which is a *fixed-point* of F; that is,

$$F(\mathrm{Fix}\,F, \mathrm{Fix}\,F) \;\cong\; \mathrm{Fix}\,F.$$

Intuitively, the isomorphism allows the *folding* and *unfolding* of the recursive type.

The concern of this section is the particular case in which the bifunctor reduces to an endofunctor yielding *inductive* types, $\mathrm{Fix}\,(F) = \mu X.FX$, satisfying

$$F(\mu X.FX) \;\cong\; \mu X.FX$$

and whose canonicity is due to a clear notion of *least fixed-point*, viz., an initial algebra. This is justified by the next lemma.

Definition 6.1.1 For a functor $F : \mathcal{A} \to \mathcal{A}$, the category of F-*algebras*, F-**Alg**, has objects (A, α) where $A \in |\,\mathcal{A}\,|$ and $\alpha : FA \to A$ in $\mathcal{A}$, and morphisms $h : (A, \alpha) \to (B, \beta)$ where $h : A \to B$ in $\mathcal{A}$ is such that

$$\begin{array}{ccc} FA & \xrightarrow{Fh} & FB \\ {\scriptstyle\alpha}\downarrow & & \downarrow{\scriptstyle\beta} \\ A & \xrightarrow[h]{} & B \end{array}$$

Composition and identities are as in $\mathcal{A}$. □

Lemma 6.1.2 (Lambek's Lemma [Lam68]**)** Initial algebras are fixed-points. □

Implicit in the proof of Lambek's Lemma there is:

Lemma 6.1.3 ([Fre91]) Endofunctors preserve their initial algebras. □

Categories admitting all inductive types are important and thus we proceed to study them. In [Fre91], Peter Freyd defined an *algebraically complete category* as one for which every endofunctor on it has an initial algebra. As he emphasised [Fre92], this should be understood in a 2-categorical setting, that is, a setting in which the phrase "every endofunctor" refers to an understood class of endofunctors. For us, such a 2-categorical setting will be determined by enrichment. Hence the following:

Definition 6.1.4 (c.f. [Fre91]) A $\mathcal{V}$-category $\mathcal{A}$ is $\mathcal{V}$-*algebraically complete* if for every $\mathcal{V}$-endofunctor F on $\mathcal{A}$, the underlying endofunctor F_0 on $\mathcal{A}_0$ has an initial algebra. □

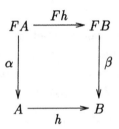

Remark. Another possible definition (more in the spirit of enriched category theory) would assume that $\mathcal{V}$ has equalisers and terminal object so that for every $\mathcal{V}$-functor $F : \mathcal{A} \to \mathcal{A}$ one can construct the $\mathcal{V}$-category F-**Alg** and require that this has a $\mathcal{V}$-initial object. We have not proceeded this way because the above definition suits our purposes without imposing any conditions on $\mathcal{V}$ and, further, because under some mild conditions (e.g., that $\mathcal{A}$ has cotensors with a strong generator in $\mathcal{V}_0$) both approaches are equivalent.

A non-trivial example of algebraic completeness is $\mathbf{Set}_\omega$, the category of countable sets and functions (see [AT90,Fre92]). Other examples are given in Section 6.6, whilst more familiar examples can be found among posets:

Proposition 6.1.5 ([Mar76]) A poset is algebraically complete if and only if it is chain-complete. □

A first basic property of algebraic completeness:

Proposition 6.1.6 ([Fre91]) If $\mathcal{A}$ is $\mathcal{V}$-algebraically complete then $\mathcal{A}_0$ has an initial object. □

An important consequence of algebraic completeness is that it guarantees the existence of *parameterised* initial algebras. Since, for a type constructor on $\mathcal{B}$ parameterised on $\mathcal{A}$, i.e. a functor $F : \mathcal{A} \times \mathcal{B} \to \mathcal{B}$, if $\mathcal{B}$ is algebraically complete then, for every $A \in |\mathcal{A}|$, there is an inductive type $\mu X.F(A, X)$ satisfying

$$F(A, \mu X.F(A, X)) \;\cong\; \mu X.F(A, X).$$

Moreover, parameterised inductive types can be extended to a type on $\mathcal{B}$ parameterised on $\mathcal{A}$ (i.e., a functor $\mathcal{A} \to \mathcal{B}$), mapping A to $\mu X.F(A, X)$ and denoted $F^\dagger$, which we now describe formally.

Let $\mathcal{V}$ be cartesian, and let $\mathcal{A}$ and $\mathcal{B}$ be $\mathcal{V}$-categories. Assume that $\mathcal{B}$ is $\mathcal{V}$-algebraically complete and let $F : \mathcal{A} \times \mathcal{B} \to \mathcal{B}$ be a $\mathcal{V}$-functor. As for every $A \in |\mathcal{A}|$ we have that $F(A, \_) : \mathcal{B} \to \mathcal{B}$ is a $\mathcal{V}$-functor, we can set $({F_0}^\dagger A, \iota_A^{F_0})$ to be an initial algebra for the endofunctor $F(A, \_)_0 = F_0(A, \_)$. To extend the action of ${F_0}^\dagger$ to morphisms, for every $f : X \to Y$ in $\mathcal{A}_0$, let ${F_0}^\dagger f : {F_0}^\dagger X \to {F_0}^\dagger Y$ be the unique morphism for which

$$\begin{array}{ccccc}
F(X, {F_0}^\dagger X) & & \xrightarrow{\;\iota_X^{F_0}\;} & & {F_0}^\dagger X \\
\Big\downarrow {\scriptstyle F(X, {F_0}^\dagger f)} & & & & \Big\downarrow {\scriptstyle {F_0}^\dagger f} \\
F(X, {F_0}^\dagger Y) & \xrightarrow[F(f, {F_0}^\dagger Y)]{} & F(Y, {F_0}^\dagger Y) & \xrightarrow[\iota_Y^{F_0}]{} & {F_0}^\dagger Y
\end{array}$$

or, equivalently,

$$\begin{array}{ccc} F(X, {F_0}^{\dagger}X) & \xrightarrow{\iota_X^{F_0}} & {F_0}^{\dagger}X \\ {\scriptstyle F(f, {F_0}^{\dagger}f)}\Big\downarrow & & \Big\downarrow{\scriptstyle {F_0}^{\dagger}f} \\ F(Y, {F_0}^{\dagger}Y) & \xrightarrow[\iota_Y^{F_0}]{} & {F_0}^{\dagger}Y \end{array} \qquad (6.1)$$

By the universal property of initial algebras, ${F_0}^{\dagger}$ is a functor $\mathcal{A}_0 \to \mathcal{B}_0$. Unfortunately it need not $\mathcal{V}$-enrich. To see this let $\mathcal{Z}$ be the **Poset**-category induced by the ordered monoid $Z = (\mathbb{Z}, \leq, 0, +)$ and consider the **Poset**-functor $F : \mathcal{Z} \times \mathcal{Z} \to \mathcal{Z} : (m, n) \mapsto m + 2n$. Every $i \in \mathbb{Z}$ is an initial algebra for the functor $F_0(Z, \_) : \mathcal{Z}_0 \to \mathcal{Z}_0 : n \mapsto 2n$ and since, for every $m \in \mathbb{Z}$,

$$\begin{array}{ccccc} F(Z, {F_0}^{\dagger}Z) & & \xrightarrow{\quad i \quad} & & {F_0}^{\dagger}Z \\ {\scriptstyle 2({F_0}^{\dagger}m) = F(0, {F_0}^{\dagger}m)}\Big\downarrow & & & & \Big\downarrow{\scriptstyle {F_0}^{\dagger}m} \iff {F_0}^{\dagger}m = -m \\ F(Z, {F_0}^{\dagger}Z) & \xrightarrow[F(m,0) = m]{} & F(Z, {F_0}^{\dagger}Z) & \xrightarrow[i]{} & {F_0}^{\dagger}Z \end{array}$$

it follows that ${F_0}^{\dagger} : \mathcal{Z} \to \mathcal{Z}$ does not **Poset**-enrich.

Thus the following definition is natural.

Definition 6.1.7 Let $\mathcal{V}$ be cartesian. A $\mathcal{V}$-category $\mathcal{B}$ is *parameterised $\mathcal{V}$-algebraically complete* if it is $\mathcal{V}$-algebraically complete and for every $\mathcal{V}$-functor $F : \mathcal{A} \times \mathcal{B} \to \mathcal{B}$ and every indexed family $\{\iota_A^{F_0} : F(A, {F_0}^{\dagger}A) \to {F_0}^{\dagger}A\}_{A \in |\mathcal{A}|}$ of initial $F_0(A, \_)$-algebras, the induced functor ${F_0}^{\dagger} : \mathcal{A}_0 \to \mathcal{B}_0$ $\mathcal{V}$-enriches.

A *parameterisation* on a parameterised $\mathcal{V}$-algebraically complete category $\mathcal{B}$ is a mapping associating every $\mathcal{V}$-functor $F : \mathcal{A} \times \mathcal{B} \to \mathcal{B}$ with a pair consisting of a $\mathcal{V}$-functor $F^{\dagger} : \mathcal{A} \to \mathcal{B}$ and an indexed family $\iota^{F_0} = \{\iota_A^{F_0} : F(A, F^{\dagger}A) \to F^{\dagger}A\}_{A \in |\mathcal{A}|}$ of initial $F_0(A, \_)$-algebras such that ${F^{\dagger}}_0 = {F_0}^{\dagger}$. □

Convention. From now on, in the situation of the above definition, the indexed family of initial algebras determining ${F_0}^{\dagger}$ will be left implicit. To avoid the axiom of choice we will assume that either our $\mathcal{V}$ has enough points (so that there is a unique $\mathcal{V}$-enrichment of ${F_0}^{\dagger}$) or that our parameterised $\mathcal{V}$-algebraically complete category comes equipped with a parameterisation. Moreover, when constructing new parameterised $\mathcal{V}$-algebraically complete categories from old ones we will be careful so that our constructions also apply to parameterisations.

Remark. It is possible to give a stronger definition of $\mathcal{V}$-algebraic completeness that implies the parameterised version; such a possibility will not be discussed here.

The fact that ι^{F_0} is a natural transformation $F_0 \circ \langle \mathrm{Id}_{\mathcal{A}_0}, {F_0}^\dagger \rangle \dot{\rightarrow} {F_0}^\dagger$, as (6.1) shows, motivates the following definition:

Definition 6.1.8 For a functor $F : \mathcal{A} \times \mathcal{B} \rightarrow \mathcal{B}$, the category of *parameterised F-algebras* is $F \circ \langle \mathrm{Id}_{\mathcal{A}}, \_ \rangle$-**Alg** where $F \circ \langle \mathrm{Id}_{\mathcal{A}}, \_ \rangle : \mathbf{CAT}(\mathcal{A}, \mathcal{B}) \rightarrow \mathbf{CAT}(\mathcal{A}, \mathcal{B})$. □

Remark. As expected, when $\mathcal{A} = \mathbf{1}$ in the above definition, algebras and parameterised algebras coincide.

Proposition 6.1.9 Let $\mathcal{V}$ be cartesian and let $F : \mathcal{A} \times \mathcal{B} \rightarrow \mathcal{B}$ be a $\mathcal{V}$-functor. If $\mathcal{B}$ is $\mathcal{V}$-algebraically complete then $({F_0}^\dagger, \iota^{F_0})$ is an initial parameterised F_0-algebra. □

As an application of this characterisation we have:

Proposition 6.1.10 Let $\mathcal{V}$ be cartesian, and let $\mathcal{A}$, $\mathcal{B}$ and $\mathcal{C}$ be $\mathcal{V}$-categories. Assume that $\mathcal{C}$ is $\mathcal{V}$-algebraically complete. Then, for $\mathcal{V}$-functors $F : \mathcal{B} \times \mathcal{C} \rightarrow \mathcal{C}$ and $G : \mathcal{A} \rightarrow \mathcal{B}$, there is a canonical natural isomorphism $\big(F \circ (G \times \mathrm{Id})\big)_0{}^\dagger \cong {F_0}^\dagger \circ G_0$.

Proof: Because $({F_0}^\dagger G_0, \iota^{F_0} G_0)$ is an initial parameterised $F_0 \circ (G_0 \times \mathrm{Id})$-algebra. □

The operation $(\_{}_0)^\dagger$ can be extended to act on natural transformations:

For cartesian $\mathcal{V}$, let $F, G : \mathcal{A} \times \mathcal{B} \rightarrow \mathcal{B}$ be $\mathcal{V}$-functors. Assume that $\mathcal{B}$ is $\mathcal{V}$-algebraically complete. For every $\eta : F \dot{\rightarrow} G : \mathcal{A} \times \mathcal{B} \rightarrow \mathcal{B}$, the components of the natural transformation $\eta^\dagger : {F_0}^\dagger \dot{\rightarrow} {G_0}^\dagger : \mathcal{A}_0 \rightarrow \mathcal{B}_0$ are defined as the unique morphisms such that

$$\begin{array}{ccccc}
F(A, {F_0}^\dagger A) & & \xrightarrow{\quad \iota^{F_0}_A \quad} & & {F_0}^\dagger A \\
\Big\downarrow {\scriptstyle F(A, \eta^\dagger_A)} & & & & \Big\downarrow {\scriptstyle \eta^\dagger_A} \\
F(A, {G_0}^\dagger A) & \xrightarrow[\eta_{(A, {G_0}^\dagger A)}]{} & G(A, {G_0}^\dagger A) & \xrightarrow[\iota^{G_0}_A]{} & {G_0}^\dagger A
\end{array}$$

Then, by construction, we have the following useful property:

Proposition 6.1.11 The operation $(\_)^\dagger$ preserves natural isomorphisms. In fact, if η is a natural isomorphism then $(\eta^\dagger)^{-1} = (\eta^{-1})^\dagger$. □

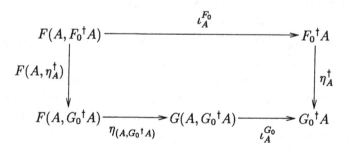

Proposition 6.1.12 Let $\mathcal{V}$ be a cartesian category with enough points. If $\mathcal{B}$ is parameterised $\mathcal{V}$-algebraically complete then, for every $\mathcal{V}$-category $\mathcal{A}$, the operation $(\_)^{\dagger}_{0} : \eta \mapsto \eta^{\dagger}$ is a functor $\mathcal{V}\text{-}\mathbf{CAT}(\mathcal{A} \times \mathcal{B}, \mathcal{B}) \to \mathcal{V}\text{-}\mathbf{CAT}(\mathcal{A}, \mathcal{B})$.

Moreover, whenever $\mathcal{V}$-**Cat** is 2-cartesian-closed, for a small $\mathcal{V}$-category $\mathcal{B}$, if the functor $\mathrm{Fix}\,(\_{}_0) : [\mathcal{B}, \mathcal{B}]_0 \to \mathcal{B}_0$ $\mathcal{V}$-enriches then, for every small $\mathcal{V}$-category $\mathcal{A}$, so does the functor $(\_)^{\dagger}_{0} : [\mathcal{A} \times \mathcal{B}, \mathcal{B}]_0 \to [\mathcal{A}, \mathcal{B}]_0$ (since it is the underlying functor of the unique $\mathcal{V}$-functor $(\_)^{\dagger}$ satisfying

$$\begin{array}{ccccc}
[\mathcal{A}, \mathcal{B}] \times \mathcal{A} & & \xrightarrow{\quad E \quad} & & \mathcal{B} \\
\uparrow {\scriptstyle (_)^{\dagger} \times \mathrm{Id}} & & & & \uparrow {\scriptstyle \mathrm{Fix}} \\
[\mathcal{A} \times \mathcal{B}, \mathcal{B}] \times \mathcal{A} & \xrightarrow[\Lambda \times \mathrm{Id}]{} & [\mathcal{A}, [\mathcal{B}, \mathcal{B}]] \times \mathcal{A} & \xrightarrow[E]{} & [\mathcal{B}, \mathcal{B}]
\end{array} \qquad (6.2)$$

where $\mathrm{Fix}_0 = \mathrm{Fix}\,(\_{}_0)$.) □

Defining $(\_)^{\dagger}$ as in (6.2) we have that $H_0{}^{\dagger} = \mathrm{Fix}\,(\_{}_0) \circ \Lambda(H)_0$ and that the *homogeneity* of the definition makes possible to strengthen Proposition 6.1.10 to an equality, since

$$\big(F \circ (G \times \mathrm{Id})\big)_0{}^{\dagger} = \mathrm{Fix}\,(\_{}_0) \circ \Lambda\big(F \circ (G \times \mathrm{Id})\big)_0 = \mathrm{Fix}\,(\_{}_0) \circ \Lambda(F)_0 \circ G_0 = F_0{}^{\dagger} \circ G_0. \quad (6.3)$$

Inductive types on several variables can be computed by a two step process as follows:

$$\begin{array}{l}
\mu(X,Y).\big(F(X,Y), G(X,Y)\big) \\
\quad \cong \quad (A, G^{\dagger}A) \;\text{ where } A = \mu X.F(X, G^{\dagger}X) \text{ and } G^{\dagger}X = \mu Y.G(X,Y).
\end{array}$$

The idea is that the system of equations

$$\left\{ \begin{array}{ll} X = F(X,Y) & \quad (1) \\ Y = G(X,Y) & \quad (2) \end{array} \right.$$

can be reduced to the system

$$\left\{ \begin{array}{l} X = F(X, G^{\dagger}X) \\ Y = G^{\dagger}X \end{array} \right.$$

and thus it can be solved by solving equation (1) with Y replaced by the parameterised solution of equation (2), and then calculating the solution of equation (2) with X replaced by the previously obtained inductive type.

The following can be found in [LS81] and [Fre92]:

Lemma 6.1.13 (Bekič's Lemma for Algebraically Complete Categories) Let $\mathcal{V}$ be cartesian, and let $\mathcal{A}$ and $\mathcal{B}$ be $\mathcal{V}$-categories. Assume that $\mathcal{B}$ is $\mathcal{V}$-algebraically complete. For a functor $F_0 : \mathcal{A}_0 \times \mathcal{B}_0 \to \mathcal{A}_0$ and a $\mathcal{V}$-functor $G : \mathcal{A} \times \mathcal{B} \to \mathcal{B}$, if (A, α) is an initial $F_0(\_, G_0^\dagger\_)$-algebra then $\big((A, G_0^\dagger A), (\alpha, \iota_A^{G_0})\big)$ is an initial $\langle F_0, G_0\rangle$-algebra. □

As a corollary we obtain the **Product Theorem for Parameterised Algebraically Complete Categories:**

Theorem 6.1.14 Let $\mathcal{V}$ be cartesian, and let $\mathcal{A}$ and $\mathcal{B}$ be $\mathcal{V}$-categories. If $\mathcal{A}$ and $\mathcal{B}$ are parameterised $\mathcal{V}$-algebraically complete then so is $\mathcal{A} \times \mathcal{B}$.

PROOF: Let $\mathcal{C}$ be a $\mathcal{V}$-category and let $F : \mathcal{C} \times \mathcal{A} \times \mathcal{B} \to \mathcal{A}$ and $G : \mathcal{C} \times \mathcal{A} \times \mathcal{B} \to \mathcal{B}$ be $\mathcal{V}$-functors.

For $C \in |\, \mathcal{C}_0 \,|$, since $G_0^\dagger(C, \_)$ is a parameterised initial $G_0(C, \_, =)$-algebra (as for every $A \in |\, \mathcal{A} \,|$, $G_0\big(C, A, G_0^\dagger(C, A)\big) \cong G_0^\dagger(C, A)$ is an initial $G_0(C, A, \_)$-algebra) we have that

$$G_0(C, \_, =)^\dagger \;\cong\; G_0^\dagger(C, \_);$$

moreover $\langle F_0(C, \_, =), G_0(C, \_, =)\rangle = \langle F, G\rangle_0(C, \_, =)$ and, by Bekič's Lemma, it follows that if (A, α) is an initial $F_0(C, \_, G_0^\dagger(C, \_))$-algebra then $\big((A, G_0^\dagger(C, A)), (\alpha, \iota_{(C,A)}^{G_0})\big)$ is an initial $\langle F, G\rangle_0(C, \_, =)$-algebra. Thus, $\langle F, G\rangle^\dagger$ is the $\mathcal{V}$-functor

$$\big\langle H^\dagger, G^\dagger \circ \langle \mathrm{Id}, H^\dagger\rangle\big\rangle : \mathcal{C} \to \mathcal{A} \times \mathcal{B}$$

where $H = F \circ \langle \mathrm{Id}, G^\dagger\rangle : \mathcal{C} \times \mathcal{A} \to \mathcal{A}$. □

A surprising consequence of Bekič's Lemma is *dinaturality* (cf. [Fre91]):

Proposition 6.1.15 Let $\mathcal{V}$ be cartesian and such that $\mathcal{V}$-**Cat** is 2-cartesian-closed. If $\mathcal{A}$ and $\mathcal{B}$ are $\mathcal{V}$-algebraically complete then, for every $\mathcal{V}$-functor $F : \mathcal{A} \to \mathcal{B}$,

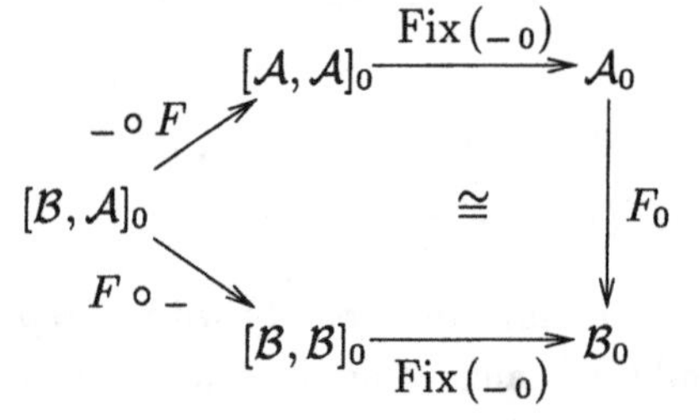

PROOF: Define $F' = F \circ \Pi_1 : \mathcal{A} \times \mathcal{B} \to \mathcal{B}$.

For a $\mathcal{V}$-functor $G : \mathcal{B} \to \mathcal{A}$, let $G' = G \circ \Pi_2 : \mathcal{A} \times \mathcal{B} \to \mathcal{A}$. By Bekič's Lemma, we have the canonical isomorphisms:

$$\begin{array}{ll} \mu(X,Y).(G_0Y, F_0X) & \\ \quad \cong & (A, {F_0'}^{\dagger}A) \text{ where } A = \mu X.G_0'(X, {F_0'}^{\dagger}X) = \mathrm{Fix}\,(G_0 \circ {F_0'}^{\dagger}), \\ \quad \cong & ({G_0'}^{\dagger}B, B) \text{ where } B = \mu Y.F_0'({G_0'}^{\dagger}Y, Y) = \mathrm{Fix}\,(F_0 \circ {G_0'}^{\dagger}). \end{array}$$

which induce the canonical isomorphisms:

$$\begin{array}{rcll} F(\mathrm{Fix}\,G_0F_0) & \cong & {F_0'}^{\dagger}A & \text{, because } {F_0'}^{\dagger} \cong F_0 \\ & \cong & B & \\ & \cong & \mathrm{Fix}\,(F_0G_0) & \text{, because } {G_0'}^{\dagger} \cong G_0. \end{array}$$

For $\eta : G \dot{\to} H : \mathcal{B} \to \mathcal{A}$ we have to show that

$$\begin{array}{ccc} F(\mathrm{Fix}\,G_0F_0) & \cong & \mathrm{Fix}\,(F_0G_0) \\ {\scriptstyle F(\mathrm{Fix}\,(\eta F_0))}\big\downarrow & & \big\downarrow{\scriptstyle \mathrm{Fix}\,(F_0\eta)} \\ F(\mathrm{Fix}\,H_0F_0) & \cong & \mathrm{Fix}\,(F_0H_0) \end{array} \qquad (6.4)$$

Recall that $\mathrm{Fix}\,(F_0\eta)$ is the unique such that

$$\begin{array}{ccccc} FG(\mathrm{Fix}\,F_0G_0) & & \xrightarrow{\quad \iota^{F_0G_0} \quad} & & \mathrm{Fix}\,(F_0G_0) \\ {\scriptstyle FG(\mathrm{Fix}\,(F_0\eta))}\big\downarrow & & & & \big\downarrow{\scriptstyle \mathrm{Fix}\,(F_0\eta)} \\ FG(\mathrm{Fix}\,F_0H_0) & \xrightarrow[F\eta_{\mathrm{Fix}\,(F_0H_0)}]{} & FH(\mathrm{Fix}\,F_0H_0) & \xrightarrow[\iota^{F_0H_0}]{} & \mathrm{Fix}\,(F_0H_0) \end{array} \qquad (6.5)$$

and that $\mathrm{Fix}\,(\eta F_0)$ is the unique such that

$$\begin{array}{ccccc} GF(\mathrm{Fix}\,G_0F_0) & & \xrightarrow{\quad \iota^{G_0F_0} \quad} & & \mathrm{Fix}\,(G_0F_0) \\ {\scriptstyle GF(\mathrm{Fix}\,(\eta F_0))}\big\downarrow & & & & \big\downarrow{\scriptstyle \mathrm{Fix}\,(\eta F_0)} \\ GF(\mathrm{Fix}\,H_0F_0) & \xrightarrow[\eta_{F(\mathrm{Fix}\,H_0F_0)}]{} & HF(\mathrm{Fix}\,H_0F_0) & \xrightarrow[\iota^{H_0F_0}]{} & \mathrm{Fix}\,(H_0F_0) \end{array} \qquad (6.6)$$

Applying F_0 to (6.6) and using the naturality of η we have

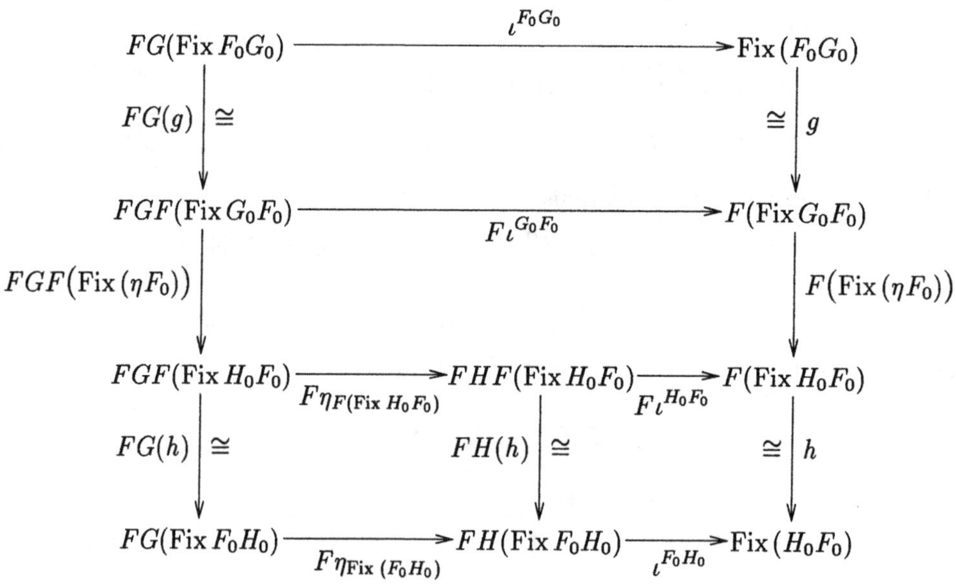

and, by the universal property of $\iota^{F_0 G_0}$ and (6.5), it follows that (6.4) is satisfied. $\qquad\square$

Yet another corollary of Bekič's Lemma:

Corollary 6.1.16 Let $\mathcal{V}$ be cartesian. For parameterised $\mathcal{V}$-algebraically complete categories $\mathcal{A}$ and $\mathcal{B}$, and $\mathcal{V}$-functors $F : \mathcal{A} \times \mathcal{B} \to \mathcal{A}$ and $G : \mathcal{A} \times \mathcal{B} \to \mathcal{B}$, if $\big((A, B), (\alpha, \beta)\big)$ is an initial $\langle F, G \rangle_0$-algebra then (A, α) is an initial $F_0(\_, B)$-algebra and (B, β) is an initial $G_0(A, \_)$-algebra.

PROOF: Let (X, χ) be an initial $F_0(\_, G_0^\dagger\_)$-algebra.

By Bekič's Lemma, there exists an isomorphism (u, v) such that

$$
\begin{array}{ccc}
F(X, G^\dagger X) & \xrightarrow{\;\chi\;} & X \\
{\scriptstyle F(u,v)}\downarrow & & \downarrow{\scriptstyle u} \\
F(A, B) & \xrightarrow[\;\alpha\;]{} & A
\end{array}
\qquad\qquad
\begin{array}{ccc}
G(X, G^\dagger X) & \xrightarrow{\;\iota_X^{G_0}\;} & G^\dagger X \\
{\scriptstyle G(u,v)}\downarrow & & \downarrow{\scriptstyle v} \\
G(A, B) & \xrightarrow[\;\beta\;]{} & B
\end{array}
$$

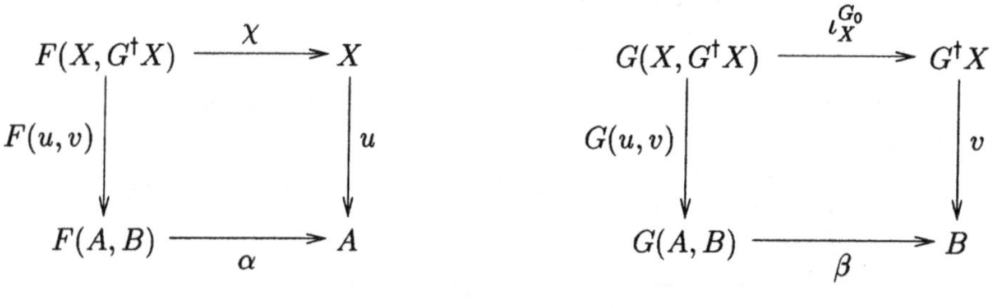

Then, $v \circ G^\dagger(u^{-1})$ is a $G_0(A, \_)$-algebra isomorphism $(G^\dagger A, \iota_A^{G_0}) \to (B, \beta)$. $\qquad\square$

6.2 Algebraic Compactness: Motivation

Given a bifunctor, F, on a category, $\mathcal{A}$, we seek a canonical type $\mathrm{Fix}\,(F)$ satisfying $F(\mathrm{Fix}\,F, \mathrm{Fix}\,F) \cong \mathrm{Fix}\,(F)$. We have already seen how to interpret such a recursive type when the bifunctor reduces to an endofunctor. Now, for a moment, suppose that it is known how to interpret recursive types when the bifunctor reduces to a *contravariant* endofunctor. That is, assume that for every contravariant endofunctor, G, on $\mathcal{A}$ there is a canonical $\mathrm{Fix}\,(G)$ satisfying

$$G(\mathrm{Fix}\,G) \;\cong\; \mathrm{Fix}\,(G). \tag{6.7}$$

Then, there is a candidate for $\mathrm{Fix}\,(F)$, viz., $\mathrm{Fix}\,(F^\dagger)$ because

$$\begin{aligned} F(\mathrm{Fix}\,F^\dagger, \mathrm{Fix}\,F^\dagger) &\cong F(\mathrm{Fix}\,F^\dagger, F^\dagger(\mathrm{Fix}\,F^\dagger)) \\ &\cong F^\dagger(\mathrm{Fix}\,F^\dagger) \\ &\cong \mathrm{Fix}\,(F^\dagger). \end{aligned}$$

Motivated by the above discussion we start the study of fixed-points for contravariant endofunctors. Observe that (6.7) implies $G^2(\mathrm{Fix}\,G) \cong G(\mathrm{Fix}\,G) \cong \mathrm{Fix}\,(G)$. Then, a natural choice for $\mathrm{Fix}\,(G)$ is $\mathrm{Fix}\,(G^2)$ and, in fact, this interpretation will turn out to be possible provided that $\mathcal{A}$ is sufficiently rich. To see this we first provide the analogue of Lemma 6.1.3 for contravariant endofunctors.

Lemma 6.2.1 Let G be a contravariant endofunctor. If G^2 has an initial algebra and a final coalgebra then G transforms initial G^2-algebras to final G^2-coalgebras and vice versa.

PROOF: Let (A, α) be an initial G^2-algebra and (Z, ζ) be a final G^2-coalgebra. By their universal properties the following two diagrams commute for unique f and g:

$$\begin{array}{ccc} G^2A & \xrightarrow{\alpha} & A \\ {\scriptstyle G^2 f}\downarrow & & \downarrow{\scriptstyle f} \\ G^2(GZ) & \xrightarrow[G\zeta]{} & GZ \end{array} \qquad\qquad \begin{array}{ccc} GA & \xrightarrow{G\alpha} & G^2(GA) \\ {\scriptstyle g}\downarrow & & \downarrow{\scriptstyle G^2 g} \\ Z & \xrightarrow[\zeta]{} & G^2 Z \end{array}$$

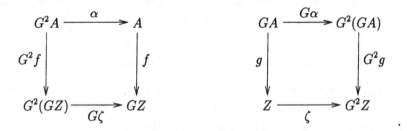

Applying G to the diagram on the right and gluing the resulting diagram with the one on the left, and proceeding dually, we get the following commuting diagrams:

$$
\begin{array}{ccc}
G^2A & \xrightarrow{\alpha} & A \\
{\scriptstyle G^2 f}\downarrow & & \downarrow{\scriptstyle f} \\
G^2(GZ) & \xrightarrow[G\zeta]{} & GZ \\
{\scriptstyle G^2(Gg)}\downarrow & & \downarrow{\scriptstyle Gg} \\
G^2(G^2A) & \xrightarrow[G^2\alpha]{} & G^2A
\end{array}
\qquad\qquad
\begin{array}{ccc}
G^2Z & \xrightarrow{G^2\zeta} & G^2(G^2Z) \\
{\scriptstyle Gf}\downarrow & & \downarrow{\scriptstyle G^2(Gf)} \\
GA & \xrightarrow{G\alpha} & G^2(GA) \\
{\scriptstyle g}\downarrow & & \downarrow{\scriptstyle G^2 g} \\
Z & \xrightarrow[\zeta]{} & G^2Z
\end{array}
.
$$

Then, by Lemma 6.1.3, $Gg \circ f$ and $g \circ Gf$ are both isomorphisms, and therefore so are $Gf \circ G^2g$ and $G^2f \circ Gg$. Thus, Gf and Gg have both right and left inverses and then so do f and g (as $Gg \circ f$ and $g \circ Gf$ are isomorphisms).

Notice, in passing, that since α is a G^2-algebra morphism $(G^2A, G^2\alpha) \to (A, \alpha)$ it follows that $\alpha^{-1} = Gg \circ f$. Similarly, $\zeta^{-1} = g \circ Gf$. □

By Lemma 6.2.1, for every contravariant endofunctor, G, on an algebraically bicomplete category it follows that

$$G(\mu X.G^2X) \;\cong\; \nu X.G^2X \quad\text{and}\quad G(\nu X.G^2X) \;\cong\; \mu X.G^2X.$$

So, if in addition, we have that

$$\mu X.G^2X \;\cong\; \nu X.G^2X \tag{6.8}$$

then G has a fixed-point as required.

The need for (6.8) motivates the following:

Definition 6.2.2 1. (c.f. [Fre91]) A $\mathcal{V}$-category is said to be *$\mathcal{V}$-algebraically compact* if it is $\mathcal{V}$-algebraically complete and the initial algebra of the underlying endofunctor of every $\mathcal{V}$-endofunctor on it is *free*, in the sense that its inverse is a final coalgebra.

2. For cartesian $\mathcal{V}$, a $\mathcal{V}$-category is *parameterised $\mathcal{V}$-algebraically compact* if it is $\mathcal{V}$-algebraically compact and parameterised $\mathcal{V}$-algebraically complete. □

Remark. In algebraically compact categories, initial algebras and final coalgebras are *canonically* isomorphic, in the sense that the unique algebra morphism from an initial algebra to the inverse of a final coalgebra is an isomorphism.

So far we have seen:

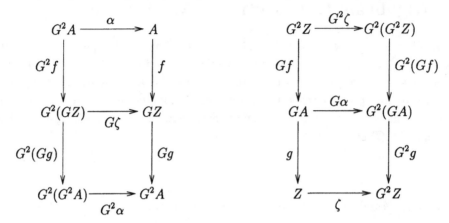

Proposition 6.2.3 Let $\mathcal{V}$ be cartesian. For every $\mathcal{V}$-bifunctor F on a parameterised $\mathcal{V}$-algebraically compact category, the bifunctor F_0 has a fixed-point, viz., $\mathrm{Fix}\,({F^{\dagger^2}}_0)$. □

The basic properties of algebraic completeness extend to compactness:

Proposition 6.2.4 ([Fre91]) If $\mathcal{A}$ is $\mathcal{V}$-algebraically compact then $\mathcal{A}_0$ has zero object. □

Hence there are no non-trivial examples of algebraically compact posets.

Lemma 6.2.5 (Bekič's Lemma for Alg. Compact Categories [Fre92]) Let $\mathcal{V}$ be cartesian, and let $\mathcal{A}$ and $\mathcal{B}$ be $\mathcal{V}$-categories. Assume that $\mathcal{B}$ is $\mathcal{V}$-algebraically compact. For a functor $F_0 : \mathcal{A}_0 \times \mathcal{B}_0 \to \mathcal{A}_0$ and a $\mathcal{V}$-functor $G : \mathcal{A} \times \mathcal{B} \to \mathcal{B}$, if (A, α) is a free $F_0(\_, G_0^\dagger\_)$-algebra then $\big((A, G_0^\dagger A), (\alpha, \iota_A^{G_0})\big)$ is a free $\langle F_0, G_0\rangle$-algebra. □

Again, as a corollary, we obtain the **Product Theorem for Parameterised Algebraically Compact Categories:**

Theorem 6.2.6 Let $\mathcal{V}$ be cartesian, and let $\mathcal{A}$ and $\mathcal{B}$ be $\mathcal{V}$-categories. If $\mathcal{A}$ and $\mathcal{B}$ are parameterised $\mathcal{V}$-algebraically compact then so is $\mathcal{A} \times \mathcal{B}$. □

Algebraic compactness is a *self-dual* property. Hence:

Corollary 6.2.7 Let $\mathcal{V}$ be cartesian.

1. If $\mathcal{A}$ is (parameterised) $\mathcal{V}$-algebraically compact then so is $\mathcal{A}^{op}$.
2. If $\mathcal{A}$ is parameterised $\mathcal{V}$-algebraically compact then so is $\mathcal{A}^{op} \times \mathcal{A}$. □

Although the above analysis motivates the introduction of algebraically compact categories by showing that they admit recursive types it neglects the issue of their canonicity. This is addressed below.

6.3 The Doubling Trick

The universal property of recursive types is better understood in the light of another approach to their interpretation. The idea is to *universally* reduce recursive types to inductive types. For this purpose, following a suggestion of John Power, we work with *involutory* categories (viz., those categories which are *self-dual via an involution*), and use the duality to transform bifunctors into endofunctors in a universal way. Then, the inductive type determined by the endofunctor should provide the required recursive type (see Section 6.4).

An abstraction of the category of involutory categories is given in the definition below. (For intuition think of $\mathcal{C}$ as being **CAT** and $(\_)^\circ$ as $(\_)^{op}$.)

Definition 6.3.1 Let $\mathcal{C}$ be a category and let $(\_)^\circ : \mathcal{C} \to \mathcal{C}$ be an involution (that is, $(\_)^\circ \circ (\_)^\circ = \mathrm{Id}_\mathcal{C}$). The category $\mathbf{Inv}(\mathcal{C}, (\_)^\circ)$ of *involutory* objects of $\mathcal{C}$ is defined to be the full subcategory of $(\_)^\circ$-**Alg** with $(\_)^\circ$-algebras (A, a) for which $a \circ a^\circ = \mathrm{id}_A$. □

Convention. In a category with binary products, if f is a morphism $X \to A_1 \times A_2$ then, for $i = 1, 2$, we write f_i for the composite $\pi_i \circ f : X \to A_i$.

Examples of involutory categories abound as for every locally small category $\mathcal{A}$, we have that $(\mathcal{A}^{op} \times \mathcal{A}, \langle \Pi_2, \Pi_1 \rangle)$ is an object of $\mathbf{Inv}(\mathbf{CAT}, (\_)^{op})$. In this case, morphisms $F : (\mathcal{A}^{op} \times \mathcal{A}, \langle \Pi_2, \Pi_1 \rangle) \to (\mathcal{B}^{op} \times \mathcal{B}, \langle \Pi_2, \Pi_1 \rangle)$ are functors $F : \mathcal{A}^{op} \times \mathcal{A} \to \mathcal{B}^{op} \times \mathcal{B}$ such that for every $f' \in \mathcal{A}^{op}$ and $f \in \mathcal{A}$, the equality $F_1(f', f) = F_2(f, f')$ holds. Motivated by this property, morphisms in $\mathbf{Inv}(\mathcal{C}, (\_)^\circ)$ are called *symmetric*.

Are there *cofree* involutory categories? Yes, as implied by

Proposition 6.3.2 If $\mathcal{C}$ has binary products then the forgetful functor $U : \mathbf{Inv}(\mathcal{C}, (\_)^\circ) \to \mathcal{C}$ is comonadic.

PROOF: We have that $U \dashv H : \mathcal{C} \to \mathbf{Inv}(\mathcal{C}, (\_)^\circ) : A \mapsto (A^\circ \times A, \langle {\pi_2}^\circ, {\pi_1}^\circ \rangle)$ with counit $\varepsilon_A = \pi_2 : A^\circ \times A \to A$, because for every $(B, b) \in |\, \mathbf{Inv}(\mathcal{C}, (\_)^\circ) \,|$ and $f : B \to A$ in $\mathcal{C}$,

$$
\begin{array}{c}
(A^\circ \times A, \langle {\pi_2}^\circ, {\pi_1}^\circ \rangle) \\
\Big\uparrow \exists !\, \check{f} = \langle f^\circ \circ b^\circ, f \rangle \\
(B, b)
\end{array}
\qquad \text{such that} \qquad
\begin{array}{ccc}
A^\circ \times A & \xrightarrow{\pi_2} & A \\
\check{f} \Big\uparrow & \nearrow_{f} & \\
B & &
\end{array}
\;.
$$

Let $\mathbb{H} : \mathcal{C} \to \mathcal{C}$ be the comonad determined by $U \dashv H$. The comparison functor from $\mathbf{Inv}(\mathcal{C}, (\_)^\circ)$ to the category of Eilenberg-Moore coalgebras $\mathcal{C}^{\mathbb{H}}$ sends (A, a) to $(A, \langle a^\circ, \mathrm{id} \rangle)$; its inverse maps (A, α) to $(A, {\alpha_1}^\circ)$. □

With the notation of the above proposition we have:

Proposition 6.3.3 If $\mathcal{C}$ is cartesian closed then so are the coKleisli category $\mathcal{C}_\mathbb{H}$ and $\mathbf{Inv}(\mathcal{C}, (\_)^\circ)$. Moreover, the comparison functor $\mathcal{C}_\mathbb{H} \to \mathbf{Inv}(\mathcal{C}, (\_)^\circ)$ preserves the cartesian closed structure.

PROOF: $\mathcal{C}_\mathbb{H}$ is cartesian closed because the coKleisli category of a cartesian closed category is cartesian closed.

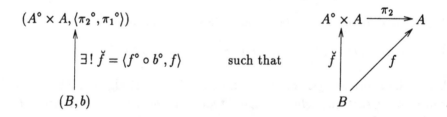

The cartesian closed structure of $\mathbf{Inv}(\mathcal{C}, (\_)^\circ)$ is as follows:

- Terminal object: $(1, 1^\circ \to 1)$.
- Binary products: $(A, a) \times (B, b) = (A \times B, (A \times B)^\circ \cong A^\circ \times B^\circ \xrightarrow{a \times b} A \times B)$.
- Exponentials: $(A, a)^{(B,b)} = (A^B, (A^B)^\circ \cong (A^\circ)^{B^\circ} \xrightarrow{a^{b^\circ}} A^B)$. □

Convention. We will write $\breve{A}$ and $(\_)^\S$ for $A^\circ \times A$ and $\langle {\pi_2}^\circ, {\pi_1}^\circ \rangle$ respectively. In addition, for every involutory object (B, b) and every $f : B \to A$, we will write $\breve{f}$ for $\langle f^\circ \circ b^\circ, f \rangle : (B, b) \to (\breve{A}, (\_)^\S)$.

The adjunction $U \dashv H$ of Proposition 6.3.2 provides a *universal* way to transform bifunctors into covariant endofunctors via the bijective correspondence:

$$\frac{\breve{\mathcal{A}} \xrightarrow{\;F\;} \mathcal{A}}{\breve{\mathcal{A}} \xrightarrow[\text{symmetric}]{\;\breve{F}\;} \breve{\mathcal{A}}}$$

The operation $(\_)\breve{}$ can be extended to contravariant endofunctors: for $G : \mathcal{A}^{op} \to \mathcal{A}$, we define $\breve{G}$ to be $(G \circ \Pi_1)\breve{} : \breve{\mathcal{A}} \to \breve{\mathcal{A}}$.

For simplicity, and because it suits our purposes, when defining $\mathbf{Inv}(\mathbf{CAT}, (\_)^{op})$ the 2-categorical structure of $\mathbf{CAT}$ was ignored. Nevertheless, *pseudo*-symmetric functors (i.e., symmetric up to isomorphism) will appear naturally (see Lemma 6.4.3) and hence it is necessary to relate them with symmetric functors. In particular, it happens that every pseudo-symmetric morphism into a cofree involutory object is isomorphic to a symmetric morphism.

Proposition 6.3.4 Let $\mathcal{C}$ be a 2-category with binary 2-products and let $(\_)^\circ$ be an involution on $\mathcal{C}_0$. For every $(B, b) \in |\, \mathbf{Inv}(\mathcal{C}_0, (\_)^\circ) \,|$ and $A \in |\, \mathcal{C}_0 \,|$, if

$$\begin{array}{ccc} B^\circ & \xrightarrow{\;f^\circ\;} & \breve{A}^\circ \\ {\scriptstyle b}\downarrow & \cong & \downarrow{\scriptstyle (\_)^\S} \\ B & \xrightarrow[\;f\;]{} & \breve{A} \end{array}$$

then $f \cong \breve{f_2} : (B, b) \to (\breve{A}, (\_)^\S)$.

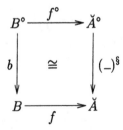

PROOF: Since

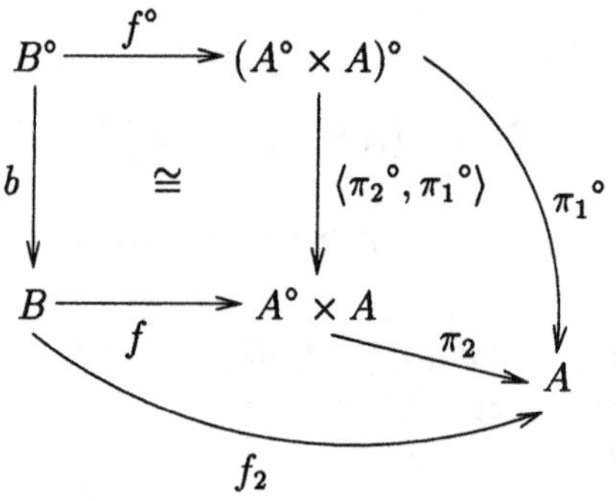

it follows that $f_2 \circ b \cong {f_1}^\circ$ and so $f = \langle f_1, f_2 \rangle \cong \langle (f_2 \circ b)^\circ, f_2 \rangle = \breve{f_2}$. □

6.4 Algebraic Compactness: Fundamental Property

As bifunctors $F : \breve{\mathcal{B}} \to \mathcal{B}$ correspond to symmetric endofunctors $\breve{F} : \breve{\mathcal{B}} \to \breve{\mathcal{B}}$, it is reasonable to expect to find $\mathrm{Fix}\,(F)$ from $\mathrm{Fix}\,(\breve{F})$. In this section we show that, provided that $\mathcal{B}$ is algebraically compact, this is possible. First, we outline why:

By Corollary 6.2.7 (2), $\breve{\mathcal{B}}$ is algebraically compact and therefore $\breve{F}$ has a free algebra $(\mathrm{Fix}\,\breve{F}, \iota^{\breve{F}})$. The coalgebra $\big((\mathrm{Fix}\,\breve{F})^{\S}, (\iota^{\breve{F}})^{\S}\big)$ is also free and the canonical isomorphism $\rho : \big((\mathrm{Fix}\,\breve{F})^{\S}, (\iota^{\breve{F}})^{\S}\big) \cong (\mathrm{Fix}\,\breve{F}, (\iota^{\breve{F}})^{-1})$ induces a free $\breve{F}$-algebra

$$\left\{ \begin{array}{lcl} F(\mathrm{Fix}\,F, \mathrm{Fix}\,F) & \xleftarrow{f^{-1}} & \mathrm{Fix}\,(F) \\ F(\mathrm{Fix}\,F, \mathrm{Fix}\,F) & \xrightarrow{f} & \mathrm{Fix}\,(F) \end{array} \right. \tag{6.9}$$

where

$$\mathrm{Fix}\,(F) = (\mathrm{Fix}\,\breve{F})_2$$

and

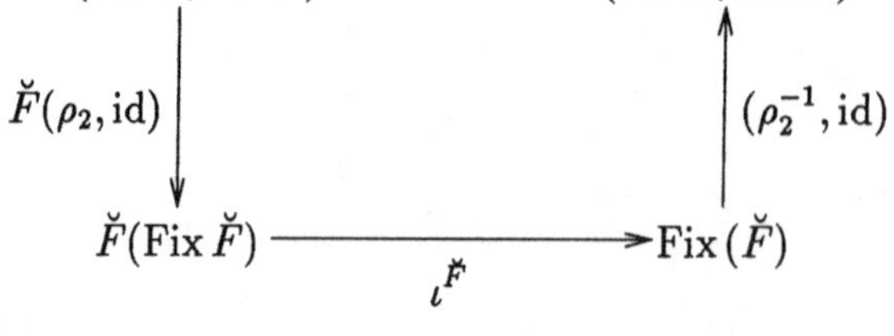

.

The freeness of (6.9) implies that it is *canonical* in that for every

$$(\beta' : B' \to F(B, B'), \beta : F(B', B) \to B)$$

there exists a unique $(u' : B' \to \mathrm{Fix}\,(F), u : \mathrm{Fix}\,(F) \to B)$ such that

$$\begin{array}{ccc} F(\mathrm{Fix}\,F, \mathrm{Fix}\,F) & \xleftarrow{f^{-1}} & \mathrm{Fix}\,(F) \\ {\scriptstyle F(u,u')}\uparrow & & \uparrow{\scriptstyle u'} \\ F(B, B') & \xleftarrow[\beta']{} & B' \end{array} \qquad \begin{array}{ccc} F(\mathrm{Fix}\,F, \mathrm{Fix}\,F) & \xrightarrow{f} & \mathrm{Fix}\,(F) \\ {\scriptstyle F(u',u)}\downarrow & & \downarrow{\scriptstyle u} \\ F(B', B) & \xrightarrow[\beta]{} & B \end{array} .$$

Moreover, $\mathrm{Fix}\,(F)$ is *minimal* in the sense that it is a *retract* of every fixed-point: for every $\beta : F(B, B) \cong B$ there exists a unique $\breve{F}$-algebra morphism $(u', u) : (f^{-1}, f) \to (\beta^{-1}, \beta)$ and, since

$$(u' \circ u, u' \circ u) = (f^{-1}, f) \xrightarrow{(u,u')} (\beta^{-1}, \beta) \xrightarrow{(u',u)} (f^{-1}, f)$$

it follows that $u' \circ u = \mathrm{id}$. That is, $\mathrm{Fix}\,(F)$ is a *retract* of B (with section u and retraction u'). Thus we conclude the **Fundamental Property of Algebraically Compact Categories** (slightly extending a previous result of Peter Freyd):

Theorem 6.4.1 Let $\mathcal{V}$ be cartesian. For every $\mathcal{V}$-bifunctor F on a parameterised $\mathcal{V}$-algebraically compact category, the bifunctor F_0 has a canonical and minimal fixed-point, viz., $(\mathrm{Fix}\,\breve{F}_0)_2$. □

The rest of the section justifies and generalises the above outline.

Convention. The duality associated to a involutory category $\mathcal{X}$ will be denoted $(\_)^x$, except when $\mathcal{X}$ is of the form $\breve{\mathcal{A}}$ where, following a previous convention, we use $(\_)^\S$. In addition, for cartesian $\mathcal{V}$, whenever a $\mathcal{V}$-functor $F : \mathcal{A} \to \mathcal{B}$ is said to be symmetric it is assumed that the $\mathcal{V}$-categories $\mathcal{A}$ and $\mathcal{B}$ are $\mathcal{V}$-involutory (i.e., self-dual via a $\mathcal{V}$-involution).

Moreover, a morphism f in $\mathcal{X}$ such that $f = f^x$ is called *symmetric*. We also call an object $X \in |\,\mathcal{X}\,|$ symmetric if id_X is too. For example, in $\breve{\mathcal{A}}$ the symmetric morphisms have the form (f, f) for some endomorphism f in $\mathcal{A}$ whilst the symmetric objects are those (A, A) for A in $\mathcal{A}$.

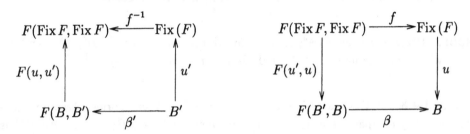

For symmetric endofunctors on an involutory category, the duality transforms initial algebras to final coalgebras. More generally,

Lemma 6.4.2 For a symmetric functor $F : \mathcal{A} \times \mathcal{B} \to \mathcal{B}$, if $\beta : F(A, B) \to B$ is an initial $F(A, \_)$-algebra then $\beta^b : B^b \to F(A^a, B^b)$ is a final $F(A^a, \_)$-coalgebra.

PROOF: Because x is an $F(A^a, \_)$-coalgebra morphism $(X, \chi) \to (B^b, \beta^b)$ if and only if $x = u^b$ where u is the unique $F(A, \_)$-algebra morphism $(B, \beta) \to (X^b, \chi^b)$. □

Lemma 6.4.3 Let $\mathcal{V}$ be cartesian, and let $\mathcal{A}$ and $\mathcal{B}$ be $\mathcal{V}$-categories. Assume that $\mathcal{B}$ is $\mathcal{V}$-algebraically compact. For a symmetric $\mathcal{V}$-functor $F : \mathcal{A} \times \mathcal{B} \to \mathcal{B}$, if $({F_0}^\dagger, \iota^{F_0})$ is an initial parameterised F_0-algebra then there exists a canonical natural isomorphism

$$\begin{CD}
\mathcal{A}_0^{op} @>({F_0}^\dagger)^{op}>> \mathcal{B}_0^{op} \\
@V(-)^aVV \overset{\rho}{\underset{\cong}{\Rightarrow}} @VV(-)^bV \\
\mathcal{A}_0 @>>{F_0}^\dagger> \mathcal{B}_0
\end{CD}$$

such that ρ_A is symmetric whenever A is.

PROOF: By Lemma 6.4.2, $(\iota_A^{F_0})^b$ is a final $F_0(A^a, \_)$-coalgebra and therefore the unique ρ_A in

$$\begin{CD}
({F_0}^\dagger A)^b @>(\iota_A^{F_0})^b>> \left(F(A, {F_0}^\dagger A)\right)^b = F(A^a, ({F_0}^\dagger A)^b) \\
@V\rho_AVV @VVF(A^a, \rho_A)V \\
{F_0}^\dagger(A^a) @>>(\iota_{A^a}^{F_0})^{-1}> F(A^a, {F_0}^\dagger(A^a))
\end{CD} \tag{6.10}$$

is an isomorphism.

To see that ρ is natural, let $f : X \to A$ in $\mathcal{A}_0$. Then, using the definitions we have that

$$
\begin{array}{ccc}
 & \xrightarrow{\iota^{F_0}_{A^a}} & \\[2mm]
F(\mathrm{id}, \rho_A^{-1}) = \left(F(\mathrm{id}, \rho_A)\right)^{-1} \Big\downarrow & & \Big\downarrow \rho_A^{-1} \\[4mm]
 & \xrightarrow{\left((\iota^{F_0}_A)^b\right)^{-1}} & \\[2mm]
F(f^a, (F_0^\dagger f)^b) = \left(F(f, F_0^\dagger f)\right)^b \Big\downarrow & & \Big\downarrow (F_0^\dagger f)^b \\[4mm]
 & \xrightarrow{\left((\iota^{F_0}_X)^b\right)^{-1}} & \\[2mm]
F(\mathrm{id}, \rho_A) \Big\downarrow & & \Big\downarrow \rho_X \\[4mm]
 & \xrightarrow{\iota^{F_0}_{X^a}} &
\end{array}
$$

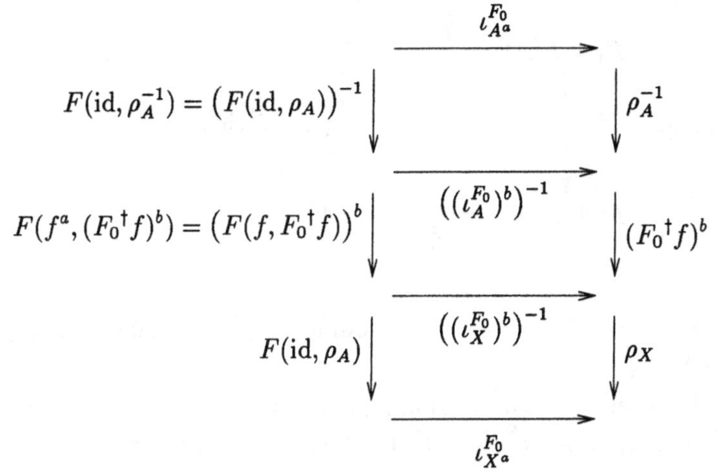

and hence $F_0^\dagger(f^a) = \rho_X \circ (F_0^\dagger f)^b \circ \rho_A^{-1}$.

Now assume A is symmetric, then applying $(\_)^b$ to (6.10) it follows that

$$
\begin{array}{ccc}
 & \xleftarrow{\;\iota^{F_0}_A = \iota^{F_0}_{A^a}\;} & \\[2mm]
\rho_A{}^b \Big\uparrow & & \Big\uparrow F(A, \rho_A{}^b) = F(A^a, \rho_A{}^b) \\[4mm]
 & \xleftarrow{\;\left((\iota^{F_0}_{A^a})^{-1}\right)^b = \left((\iota^{F_0}_A)^b\right)^{-1}\;} &
\end{array}
$$

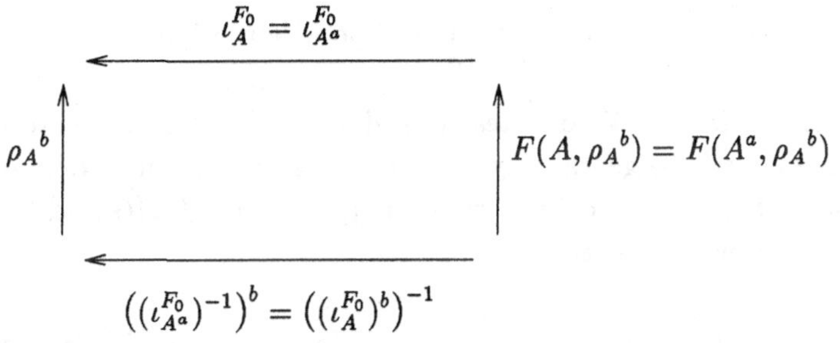

and therefore $\rho_A{}^b$ satisfies the same universal property as ρ_A. $\qquad\square$

The **Fundamental Property of Parameterised Algebraically Compact Categories:**

Theorem 6.4.4 Let $\mathcal{V}$ be cartesian, and let $\mathcal{A}$ and $\mathcal{B}$ be $\mathcal{V}$-categories. Assume that $\mathcal{B}$ is parameterised $\mathcal{V}$-algebraically compact. For a symmetric $\mathcal{V}$-functor $F : \mathcal{A} \times \breve{\mathcal{B}} \to \breve{\mathcal{B}}$, every initial parameterised F_0-algebra $(F_0^\dagger, \iota^{F_0})$ canonically induces an initial parameterised F_0-algebra $(F_0^\ddagger, \varphi^{F_0})$ such that $F^\ddagger$ is a symmetric $\mathcal{V}$-functor and $\varphi_A{}^\S = \varphi_A^{-1}$ for every symmetric A.

Proof: Following Proposition 6.3.4, define $F^{\ddagger} = (\Pi_2 \circ F^{\dagger})\check{}$. And let ${\varphi_A}^{F_0}$ be defined by

$$
\begin{array}{ccc}
F(A, F^{\ddagger}A) & \xrightarrow{\varphi_A^{F_0}} & F^{\ddagger}A \\
{\scriptstyle F(A,((\rho_A)_2,\mathrm{id}))}\downarrow & & \uparrow{\scriptstyle ((\rho_A)_2^{-1},\mathrm{id})} \\
F(A, F^{\dagger}A) & \xrightarrow[\iota_A^{F_0}]{} & F^{\dagger}A
\end{array}
.
$$

By construction, $F^{\ddagger}$ is a symmetric $\mathcal{V}$-functor. The parameterised F_0-algebra $(F_0^{\ddagger}, \varphi^{F_0})$ is initial because $\big((\rho_A)_2, \mathrm{id}\big) : \varphi_A^{F_0} \cong \iota_A^{F_0}$.

Now assume A symmetric. Then, by Lemma 6.4.3, ρ_A is symmetric. Say $\rho_A = (r_A, r_A)$. By (6.10) we have that $F\big(A, (r_A, r_A)\big) \circ (\iota_A^{F_0})^{\S} = (\iota_A^{F_0})^{-1} \circ (r_A, r_A)$, and therefore

$$
\begin{aligned}
{\varphi_A}^{\S} &= F\big(A, (\mathrm{id}, r_A)\big) \circ (\iota_A^{F_0})^{\S} \circ (\mathrm{id}, r_A^{-1}) \\
&= F\big(A, (r_A^{-1}, \mathrm{id})\big) \circ (\iota_A^{F_0})^{-1} \circ (r_A, \mathrm{id}) \\
&= {\varphi_A}^{-1}.
\end{aligned}
$$

□

The $(\_{}_0)^{\ddagger}$ operation allow us to refine Proposition 6.1.10:

Proposition 6.4.5 Let $\mathcal{V}$ be cartesian, and let $\mathcal{A}$, $\mathcal{B}$ and $\mathcal{C}$ be $\mathcal{V}$-categories. Assume that $\mathcal{C}$ is parameterised $\mathcal{V}$-algebraically compact. For symmetric $\mathcal{V}$-functors $F : \mathcal{B} \times \check{\mathcal{C}} \to \check{\mathcal{C}}$ and $G : \mathcal{A} \to \mathcal{B}$, the canonical natural isomorphism $\psi : \big(F \circ (G \times \mathrm{Id})\big)_0^{\ddagger} \cong F_0^{\ddagger} \circ G_0$ satisfies $\psi_A^{\S} = \psi_A^{-1}$ for every symmetric A.

Proof: Let A be symmetric and write H for $F \circ (G \times \mathrm{Id})$. By definition, ψ_A is the unique in

$$
\begin{array}{ccc}
F(GA, H^{\ddagger}A) & \xrightarrow{\varphi_A^{H_0}} & H^{\ddagger}A \\
{\scriptstyle F(GA,\psi_A)}\downarrow & & \downarrow{\scriptstyle \psi_A} \\
F(GA, F^{\ddagger}GA) & \xrightarrow[\varphi_{GA}^{F_0}]{} & F^{\ddagger}GA
\end{array}
. \tag{6.11}
$$

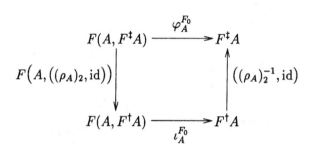

Applying $(\_)^{\S}$ and $(\_)^{-1}$ to (6.11) we obtain

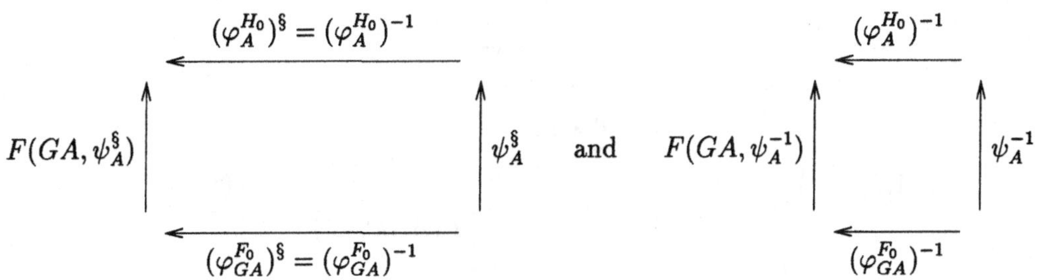

and therefore $\psi_A^{\S} = \psi_A^{-1}$. □

Proposition 6.4.6 Let $\mathcal{V}$ be cartesian, and let $\mathcal{A}$ and $\mathcal{B}$ be $\mathcal{V}$-categories. Assume that $\mathcal{B}$ is parameterised $\mathcal{V}$-algebraically compact. Let $F, G : \mathcal{A} \times \check{\mathcal{B}} \to \check{\mathcal{B}}$ be symmetric $\mathcal{V}$-functors and let $\eta : F \xrightarrow{\cdot} G$. Then,

1. $(\eta_A^{\ddagger})^{\S} = (\eta^{\S})_A^{\ddagger}$ for every symmetric A.

2. If η is an isomorphism such that $\eta_{(A,B)}^{\S} = \eta_{(A,B)}^{-1}$ for every symmetric (A, B) then $(\eta_A^{\ddagger})^{\S} = (\eta_A^{\ddagger})^{-1}$ for every symmetric A.

PROOF: Let $A \in |\mathcal{A}_0|$ be symmetric. Recall that by definition,

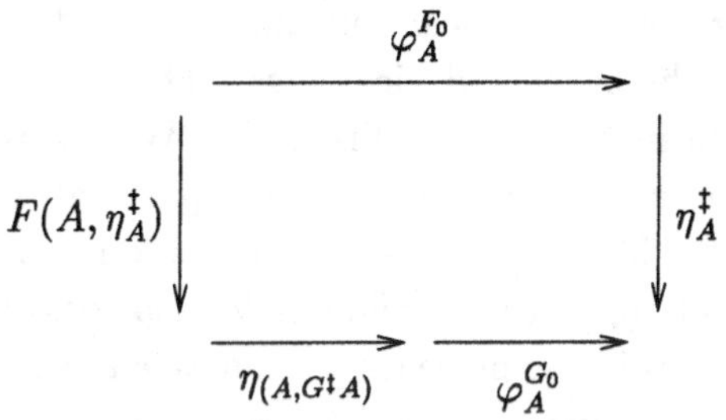

$$
\begin{array}{ccc}
 & \varphi_A^{F_0} & \\
 & \longrightarrow & \\
F(A, \eta_A^{\ddagger}) \downarrow & & \downarrow \eta_A^{\ddagger} \\
 & \eta_{(A, G^{\ddagger}A)} \quad \varphi_A^{G_0} & \\
 & \longrightarrow \quad \longrightarrow &
\end{array}
\qquad (6.12)
$$

(1) Applying $(\_)^{\S}$ to (6.12) and using the naturality of $\eta^{\S}$ we have

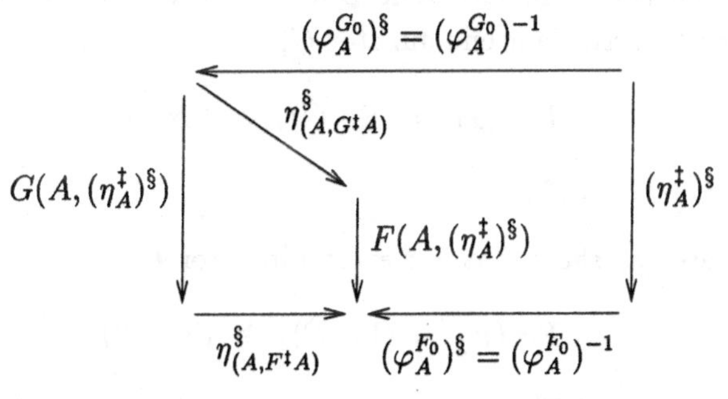

and thus $(\eta_A^{\ddagger})^{\S} = (\eta^{\S})_A^{\ddagger}$.

(2) Applying $(\_)^{-1}$ to (6.12) and using the naturality of η^{-1} we have

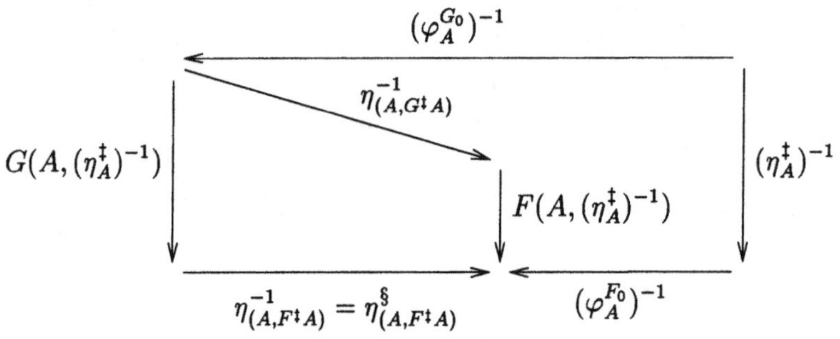

and thus $(\eta_A^\ddagger)^{-1} = (\eta^\S)_A^\ddagger = (\eta_A^\ddagger)^\S$. □

6.5 Recursive Types Reduce to Inductive Types

When $\mathcal{V}$ is cartesian, Propositions 6.2.3 and 6.4.1 provide two fixed-points for the underlying bifunctor of a $\mathcal{V}$-bifunctor F on a parameterised $\mathcal{V}$-algebraically compact category, viz., $\mathrm{Fix}\,(F^{\dagger 2}_{\ 0})$ and $(\mathrm{Fix}\,\breve{F}_0)_2$. The former was introduced for being a simple inductive type, the later for being canonical and minimal. In this section we show that one can be obtained from the other and vice versa. Thus reducing the recursive type $\mathrm{Fix}\,(F_0) = (\mathrm{Fix}\,\breve{F}_0)_2$ to the inductive type $\mathrm{Fix}\,(F^{\dagger 2}_{\ 0})$. We regard this result as a confirmation of the appropriateness of algebraically compact categories as a universe for interpreting recursive types. Moreover, because the reduction of recursive types to inductive types makes different approaches for finding fixed-points of bifunctors fit together and guarantees recursive types in the presence of inductive types, we henceforth propose that this be an indispensable requirement of a universe for interpreting recursive types.

To see that recursive types reduce to inductive types we proceed in two steps.

1. The case in which the bifunctor reduces to a contravariant endofunctor: we show that, for every contravariant endofunctor G,

$$\mathrm{Fix}\,(G) \;=\; (\mathrm{Fix}\,\breve{G})_2 \;\cong\; \mathrm{Fix}\,(G^2).$$

   That is, *endofunctors suffice*.

2. The general case: we show that, for every bifunctor F,

$$\mathrm{Fix}\,(F) \;=\; (\mathrm{Fix}\,\breve{F})_2 \;\cong\; \mathrm{Fix}\,(F^\dagger).$$

   That is, *one variable suffices*.

Proposition 6.5.1 For $G : \mathcal{A}^{op} \to \mathcal{A}$, the symmetric $\breve{G} : \breve{\mathcal{A}} \to \breve{\mathcal{A}}$ has an initial algebra if and only if $G^2 : \mathcal{A} \to \mathcal{A}$ has an initial algebra and a final coalgebra.

PROOF:

($\Rightarrow$) We show that

$$\text{if } \big((Z, A), (z, a)\big) \text{ is an initial } \breve{G}\text{-algebra then } (A, a \circ Gz) \text{ is an initial } G^2\text{-algebra.} \tag{6.13}$$

That G^2 has a final coalgebra follows by dualising (6.13) and by Lemma 6.4.2.

Let (X, x) be a G^2-algebra. Then $\big((GX, X), (\mathrm{id}_{GX}, x)\big)$ is a $\breve{G}$-algebra and, by initiality, the following diagrams commute

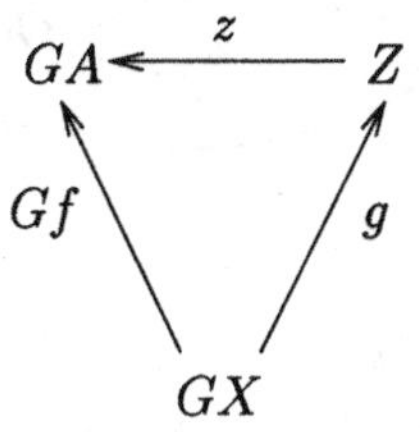

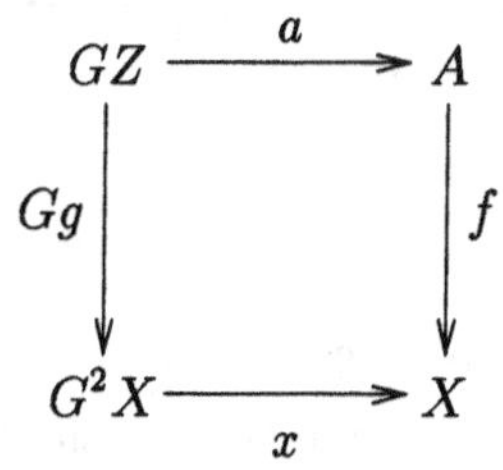

for unique g and f.

Applying G to the triangle and pasting we get

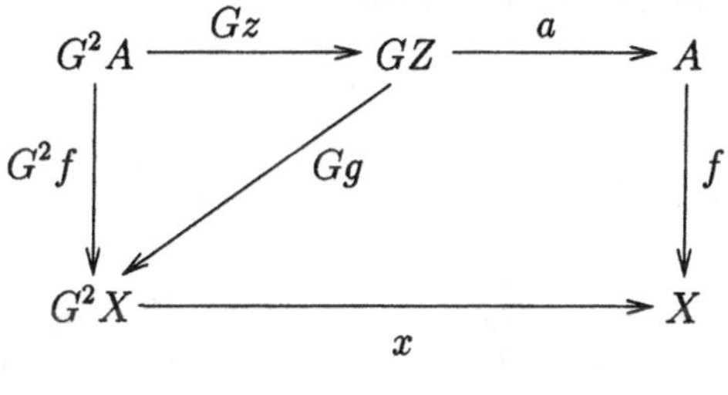

That is, f is a G^2-algebra morphism $(A, a \circ Gz) \to (X, x)$.

It is unique because for any other such, say u, we have that $(z^{-1} \circ Gu, u)$ is a $\breve{G}$-algebra morphism $\big((Z, A), (z, a)\big) \to \big((GX, X), (\mathrm{id}_{GX}, x)\big)$.

($\Leftarrow$) Let (A, α) be an initial G^2-algebra and let (Z, ζ) be a final G^2-coalgebra.

By Lemma 6.2.1, $(GZ, G\zeta)$ is an initial G^2-algebra, $(GA, G\alpha)$ is a final G^2-coalgebra and for $a : (GZ, G\zeta) \cong (A, \alpha)$ and $z : (Z, \zeta) \cong (GA, G\alpha)$ the equalities $\alpha = a \circ Gz$ and $\zeta = (Ga) \circ z$ hold.

We show that $\big((Z, A), (z, a)\big)$ is an initial $\breve{G}$-algebra.

Let (g, f) be a $\breve{G}$-algebra morphism $\big((Z, A), (z, a)\big) \to \big((Y, X), (y, x)\big)$. Then, f is a G^2-algebra morphism $(A, \alpha) \to (X, x \circ Gy)$ and g is a G^2-coalgebra morphism $(Y, (Gx) \circ y) \to (Z, \zeta)$. Thus uniqueness follows.

For existence note that by the universal properties of (A, α) and (Z, ζ) the following diagrams commute for unique f and g

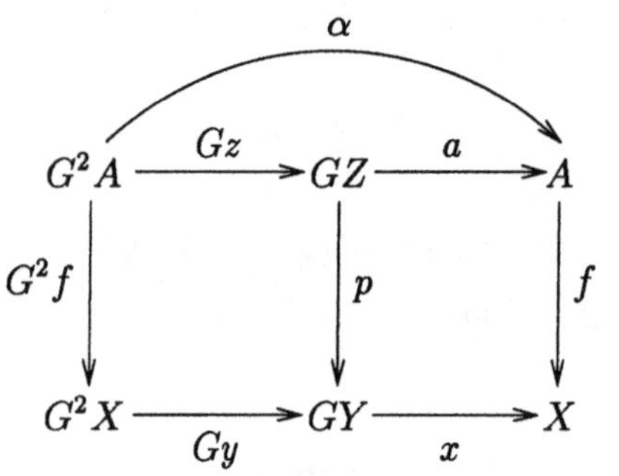

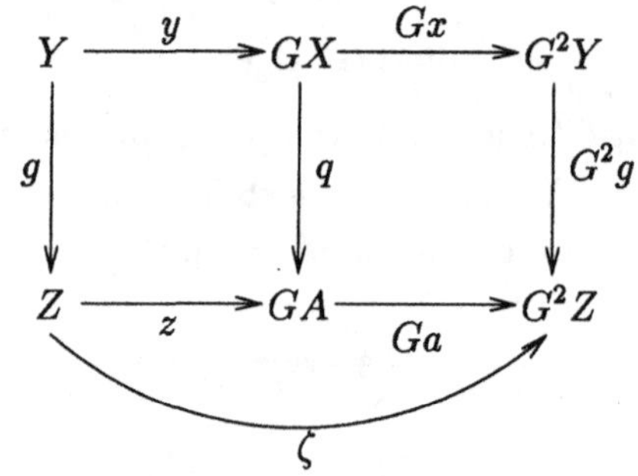

where $p = Gy \circ (G^2 f) \circ Gz^{-1}$ and $q = Ga^{-1} \circ (G^2 g) \circ Gx$.

On one hand, applying G to each of the above diagrams we get that Gg is the unique G^2-algebra morphism $(GZ, G\zeta) \to (GY, Gy \circ G^2 x)$ and that Gf is the unique G^2-coalgebra morphism $(GX, G^2 y \circ Gx) \to (GA, G\alpha)$.

On the other hand, applying G^2 to the right square in the left diagram and appending the left square, and proceeding dually we have,

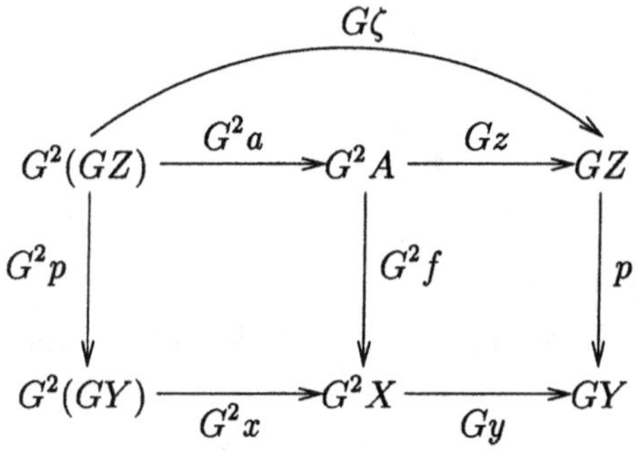

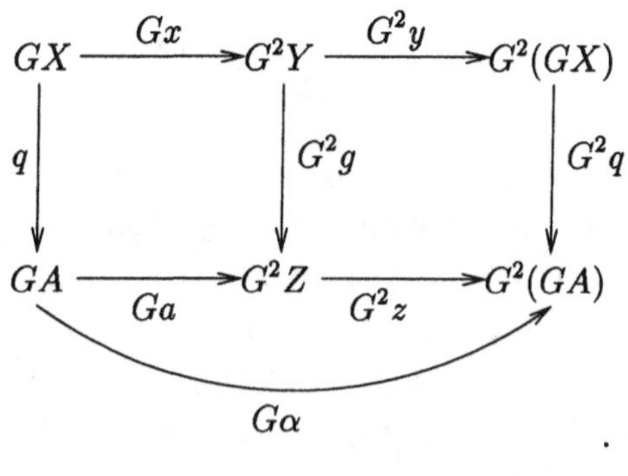

Therefore, $p = Gg$ and $q = Gf$. Thus implying that (g, f) is a $\breve{G}$-algebra morphism $((Z, A), (z, a)) \to ((Y, X), (y, x))$. $\square$

Corollary 6.5.2 (Endofunctors Suffice) Let $\mathcal{V}$ be cartesian and let $\mathcal{A}$ be parameterised $\mathcal{V}$-algebraically compact. For every contravariant $\mathcal{V}$-endofunctor G on $\mathcal{A}$, G_0^2 has free algebra and if (A, φ) is a free G_0^2-algebra then, writing a for the unique G_0^2-coalgebra morphism $(GA, G\varphi) \cong (A, \varphi^{-1})$, the $\breve{G}_0$-algebra $\big((A, A), (a^{-1}, a)\big)$ is free. □

Proposition 6.5.3 (One Variable Suffices) Let $\mathcal{V}$ be cartesian and let $\mathcal{A}$ be parameterised $\mathcal{V}$-algebraically compact. For every $\mathcal{V}$-bifunctor F on $\mathcal{A}$, ${F^\dagger}_0^2$ has free algebra and if (A, φ) is a free ${F^\dagger}_0^2$-algebra then, writing a for the unique ${F^\dagger}_0^2$-coalgebra morphism $(F^\dagger A, F^\dagger \varphi) \cong (A, \varphi^{-1})$ and α for $a \circ \iota_A^{F_0} \circ F(A, a^{-1})$, the $\breve{F}_0$-algebra $\big((A, A), (\alpha^{-1}, \alpha)\big)$ is free.

PROOF: Let $\big((Z, Z), (\zeta^{-1}, \zeta)\big)$ be a free $\breve{F}_0$-algebra.

If (u, v) is the unique $\breve{F}_0$-algebra morphism $\big((Z, Z), (\zeta^{-1}, \zeta)\big) \to \big((A, A), (\alpha^{-1}, \alpha)\big)$ then $(u \circ v, u \circ v)$ is an $\breve{F}_0$-algebra endomorphism on $\big((Z, Z), (\zeta^{-1}, \zeta)\big)$ and thus $u \circ v = \mathrm{id}_Z$.

If z is the unique $F_0(Z, \_)$-algebra morphism $(Z, \zeta) \to (F^\dagger Z, \iota_Z^{F_0})$ which, by Corollary 6.1.16, is an isomorphism then the following diagrams commute

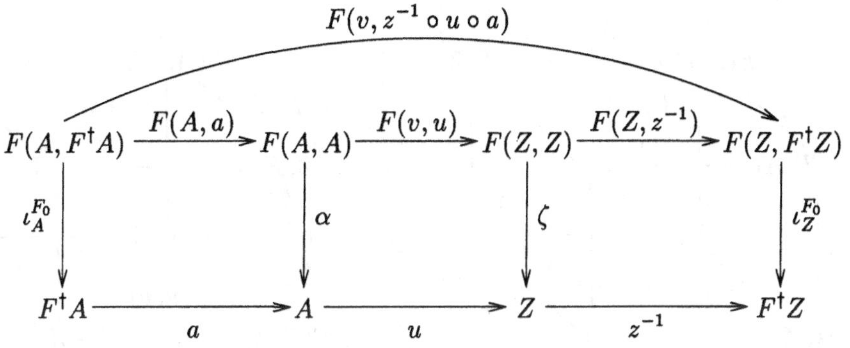

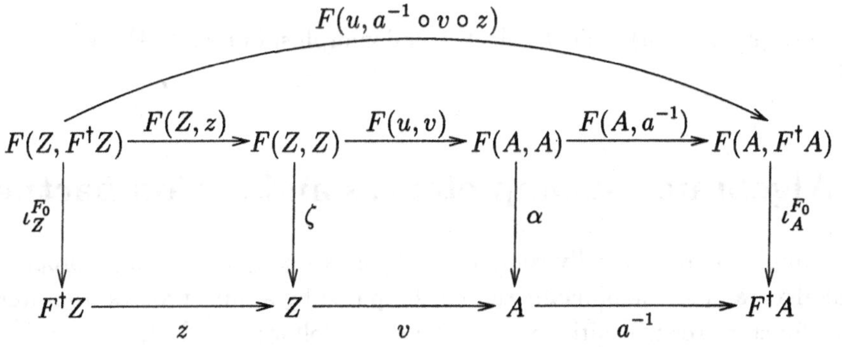

and it follows that $F^\dagger v = z^{-1} \circ u \circ a$ and $F^\dagger u = a^{-1} \circ v \circ z$. Then, $(v \circ u, v \circ u)$ is an $\breve{F^\dagger}_0$-algebra endomorphism on $\big((A, A), (\alpha^{-1}, \alpha)\big)$ which, by Corollary 6.5.2, is free and thus $v \circ u = \mathrm{id}_A$. □

Conversely:

Proposition 6.5.4 Let $\mathcal{V}$ be cartesian and let $\mathcal{A}$ be parameterised $\mathcal{V}$-algebraically compact. For every $\mathcal{V}$-bifunctor F on $\mathcal{A}$, $\breve{F}_0$ has free algebra and if $\big((A,A),(\alpha^{-1},\alpha)\big)$ is a free $\breve{F}_0$-algebra then, writing a for the unique $F_0(A,\_)$-algebra morphism $(F^\dagger A, \iota_A^{F_0}) \cong (A,\alpha)$, the ${F^{\dagger}}^{2}_{0}$-algebra $(A,(F^\dagger a)\circ a^{-1})$ is free.

PROOF: Recall that a is an isomorphism because, by Corollary 6.1.16, (A,α) is a free $F_0(A,\_)$-algebra.

By Proposition 6.5.1 ($\Rightarrow$) —see (6.13)— it is enough to show that $\big((A,A),(a^{-1},a)\big)$ is a free $\breve{F^\dagger}_0$-algebra.

Let $\big((Z,Z),(z^{-1},z)\big)$ be a free $\breve{F^\dagger}_0$-algebra.

If (u,v) is the unique $\breve{F^\dagger}_0$-algebra morphism $\big((Z,Z),(z^{-1},z)\big) \to \big((A,A),(a^{-1},a)\big)$ then $u\circ v = \mathrm{id}_Z$ because $(u\circ v, u\circ v)$ is an $\breve{F^\dagger}_0$-algebra endomorphism on $\big((Z,Z),(z^{-1},z)\big)$.

For $\zeta = z\circ \iota_Z^{F_0}\circ F(Z,z^{-1})$, the following two cubes commute

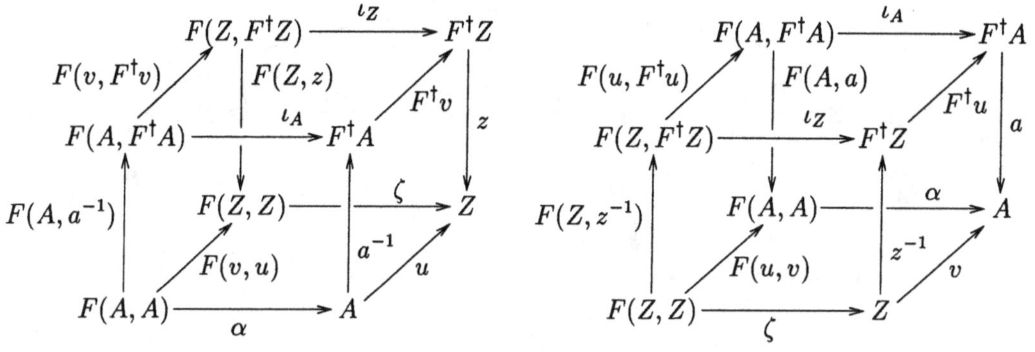

and therefore $(v\circ u, v\circ u)$ is an $\breve{F}_0$-algebra endomorphism on $\big((A,A),(\alpha^{-1},\alpha)\big)$. Thus, $v\circ u = \mathrm{id}_A$. □

6.6 Algebraic ω-Completeness and ω-Compactness

Various examples of algebraically complete categories satisfy the stronger property that the initial algebra of an endofunctor can be computed by a limit process from iterations of the endofunctor over the initial object. Hence the following definitions:

Definition 6.6.1 For an endofunctor F on a category with an initial object 0 we define its *standard ω-chain* Δ_F to be $\langle F^k(0), F^k(0\to F0)\rangle_{k\in|\omega|}$ and say that F is *initially ω-convergent* if Δ_F has colimit and F preserves it. □

Definition 6.6.2 (c.f. [Adá93]) A $\mathcal{V}$-category $\mathcal{A}$ is said to be $\mathcal{V}$*-algebraically* ω*-complete* if $\mathcal{A}_0$ has initial object and the underlying endofunctor of every $\mathcal{V}$-endofunctor on $\mathcal{A}$ is initially ω-convergent. □

A general result from [Adá93] yields that the following are algebraically ω-complete: $\mathbf{Pfn}_\omega$ (the category of countable sets and partial functions), $\mathbf{Rel}_\omega$ (the category of countable sets and relations), F-$\mathbf{Vec}_\omega$ (the category of countably dimensional vector spaces, for a countable field F, and linear functions) and $\mathbf{Well}_\omega$ (the category of countable well-ordered sets and join-preserving functions). Examples among posets are characterised by:

Proposition 6.6.3 ([Adá93]) A poset is algebraically ω-complete if and only if it has least element and every infinite chain has a unique upper bound. □

That $\mathcal{V}$-algebraic ω-completeness entails $\mathcal{V}$-algebraic completeness follows from the Basic Lemma.

Lemma 6.6.4 (Basic Lemma [SP82]) For an initially ω-convergent endofunctor F, if $\delta : \Delta_F \dot{\to} A$ is colimiting then, writing α for the unique $F\delta \cong (\delta\,\mathrm{succ}) : \Delta_F\,\mathrm{succ} \dot{\to} FA$ (where $\mathrm{succ} : \omega \to \omega : k \mapsto k+1$), the F-algebra (A, α) is initial. □

Corollary 6.6.5 $\mathcal{V}$-algebraic ω-completeness implies $\mathcal{V}$-algebraic completeness. □

The import of ω-completeness is that it provides most of the examples of algebraically complete categories. Unfortunately the concept is not useful for classifying categories for interpreting inductive types. For example, algebraically ω-complete posets are not even closed under binary products as $\omega + 1$ and $\mathbf{2}$ are algebraically ω-complete but $(\omega+1)\times\mathbf{2}$ is not, since the chain $\langle (k,0)\rangle_{k\in|\omega|}$ has two upper bounds, viz., $(\omega,0)$ and $(\omega,1)$.

Definition 6.6.6 (c.f. [Adá93]) A $\mathcal{V}$-category $\mathcal{A}$ is said to be $\mathcal{V}$*-algebraically* ω*-compact* if $\mathcal{A}_0$ has a zero object and the underlying endofunctor of every $\mathcal{V}$-endofunctor on $\mathcal{A}$ is ω*-convergent*, in the sense that it is initially and finally ω-convergent and the initial algebra induced by the colimit of its standard ω-chain is canonically isomorphic to the final coalgebra induced by the limit of its standard ω^{op}-chain. □

The paradigmatic example of ω-compactness is **pCpo** which, as will be shown, is **Cpo**-algebraically ω-compact (see Section 7.2). Two other examples are $\mathbf{Pin}_\omega$ (the category of countable sets and partial injections) and $\mathbf{Hil}_\omega$ (the category of countably dimensional Hilbert spaces and linear maps of norm at most 1) which, as shown in [Bar92], are algebraically ω-compact.

6.7 Algebraic Supercompleteness and Supercompactness

We conjecture that algebraic completeness and compactness are not closed under exponentiation and thus proceed to impose a *super* closure property on top of them which will guarantee closure under exponentiation while maintaining closure under finite products. In the compact case we further maintain closure under taking opposite categories.

Definition 6.7.1 Let $\mathcal{V}$ be cartesian and such that $\mathcal{V}$-**Cat** is 2-cartesian-closed. A $\mathcal{V}$-category $\mathcal{A}$ is said to be (parameterised) $\mathcal{V}$-algebraically (ω-)supercomplete (resp. (ω-)supercompact) if for every $\mathcal{V}$-category $\mathcal{B}$, the functor category $[\mathcal{B}, \mathcal{A}]$ is (parameterised) $\mathcal{V}$-algebraically (ω-)complete (resp. (ω-)compact). □

Examples do exist: **pCpo** is parameterised **Cpo**-algebraically ω-supercompact. The reasons being quite general and studied in Section 7.2 —see Theorem 7.3.12 (1).

The closure under binary products, exponentials and opposites is essentially due to the isomorphisms

$$\begin{aligned} [\mathcal{C}, \mathcal{A} \times \mathcal{B}] &\cong [\mathcal{C}, \mathcal{A}] \times [\mathcal{C}, \mathcal{B}], \\ [\mathcal{C}, [\mathcal{B}, \mathcal{A}]] &\cong [\mathcal{B} \times \mathcal{C}, \mathcal{A}], \text{ and} \\ [\mathcal{C}, \mathcal{A}^{op}] &\cong [\mathcal{C}^{op}, \mathcal{A}]^{op}. \end{aligned}$$

Proposition 6.7.2 Let $\mathcal{V}$ be cartesian and such that $\mathcal{V}$-**Cat** is 2-cartesian-closed.

1. **1** is parameterised $\mathcal{V}$-algebraically supercompact.
2. If $\mathcal{A}$ and $\mathcal{B}$ are parameterised $\mathcal{V}$-algebraically supercomplete (resp. supercompact) then so is $\mathcal{A} \times \mathcal{B}$.
3. If $\mathcal{A}$ is (parameterised) $\mathcal{V}$-algebraically supercomplete (resp. supercompact) and $\mathcal{B}$ is $\mathcal{V}$-algebraically supercomplete (resp. supercompact) then $[\mathcal{B}, \mathcal{A}]$ is (parameterised) $\mathcal{V}$-algebraically supercomplete (resp. supercompact).
4. If $\mathcal{A}$ is (parameterised) $\mathcal{V}$-algebraically supercompact then so is $\mathcal{A}^{op}$. □

7 Recursive Types in Cpo-Categories

We investigate **Cpo**-*algebraic completeness and compactness*. This is a particularly well behaved setting. For example, we show that **Cpo**-algebraic completeness and parameterised **Cpo**-algebraic completeness coincide; whilst, for $\mathbf{Cppo}_\perp$-categories, we further show the coincidence of **Cpo**-algebraic completeness and parameterised **Cpo**-algebraic compactness. As a by-product, we identify a *2-category of kinds*, called **Kind**, all of whose objects are parameterised **Cpo**-algebraically ω-compact categories. **Kind** is 2-cartesian-closed, op-closed, closed under the formation of categories of algebras and coalgebras with *lax homomorphisms*, and has a unique (up to isomorphism) *uniform fixed-point operator*. Thus, **Kind** is appropriate for interpreting type systems with kinds built by recursion from products, exponentials, algebras and coalgebras; but neither such a system nor its interpretation will be discussed here.

7.1 Cpo-Algebraic Completeness

Cpo-algebraic completeness is studied. First, we focus on those **Cpo**-categories for which the initial object *embeds* in every object of the category. The reason being that in this case the presence of colimits of ω-chains of embeddings guarantees algebraic ω-completeness which turns out to *coincide* with algebraic completeness. Further, an *equational* characterisation of initial algebras becomes available. Second, we explore categories of algebras and *lax homomorphisms* to finally show that algebraic completeness and parameterised algebraic completeness coincide.

Definition 7.1.1 In a **Poset**-category, an *e-initial* object is an initial object such that every morphism with it as source is an embedding. The dual notion is called a *p-terminal* object. An object which is both e-initial and p-terminal is called an *ep-zero*. □

In **Pposet** (the full subcategory of **Poset** of all pointed posets) the terminal object is p-terminal whilst in $\mathbf{Pposet}_\perp$ (the subcategory of **Pposet** of strict monotone functions) it is an ep-zero.

Lemma 7.1.2 In a **Poset**-category with initial object the following are equivalent:

1. The initial object is e-initial.

2. Every hom-poset has a least element and composition is right strict.

3. For every object X there exists $X \to 0$ such that for every object Y, the composite $X \to 0 \to Y$ is the least among all $X \to Y$.

4. For every object X there exists $X \to 0$ such that $(X \to 0 \to X) \leq \mathrm{id}_X$. □

Theorem 7.1.3 A **Cpo**-category with e-initial object and colimits of ω-chains of embeddings is **Cpo**-algebraically ω-complete.

PROOF: Let F be a **Cpo**-endofunctor on a **Cpo**-category with e-initial object and colimits of ω-chains of embeddings.

Since the initial object is e-initial and F preserves ep-pairs, the standard ω-chain Δ_F consists of embeddings and hence it has a colimit, say $\gamma : \Delta_F \dot{\to} C$. By the Limit/Colimit Coincidence Theorem, γ is a cone of embeddings and $\bigvee \gamma_n \circ (\gamma_n)^R = \mathrm{id}_C$. Thus, $F\gamma : F\Delta_F \dot{\to} FC$ is a cone of embeddings and since

$$\bigvee (F\gamma_n) \circ (F\gamma_n)^R = \bigvee F(\gamma_n \circ (\gamma_n)^R) = F(\bigvee \gamma_n \circ (\gamma_n)^R) = \mathrm{id}_{FC}$$

it follows, by the Limit/Colimit Coincidence Theorem, that $F\gamma$ is colimiting. Hence, F is initially ω-convergent. □

Example 7.1.4 Cppo has p-terminal object and limits of ω^{op}-chains of projections. Hence, it is **Cpo**-algebraically ω-cocomplete but it is not **Cpo**-algebraically compact (as it has no initial object). □

In the presence of an e-initial object, **Cpo**-algebraic completeness and **Cpo**-algebraic ω-completeness coincide:

Theorem 7.1.5 A **Cpo**-algebraically complete category with an e-initial object is **Cpo**-algebraically ω-complete.

PROOF: It is enough to show that the standard ω-chain of every **Cpo**-endofunctor has a colimit. This will be preserved, using the Limit/Colimit Coincidence Theorem, because **Cpo**-functors preserve embeddings and lubs of ω-chains.

Let F be a **Cpo**-endofunctor and let (A, α) be an initial F-algebra. The commuting diagram

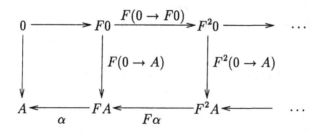

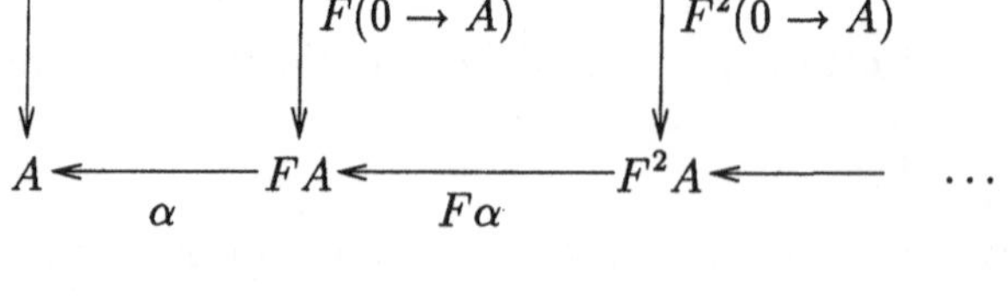

induces a cone of embeddings $\delta : \Delta_F \dot{\rightarrow} A$ defined by $\delta_0 = (0 \rightarrow A)$ and, for $k \in |\, \omega \,|$, by $\delta_{k+1} = \alpha \circ F\delta_k$. To see that it is colimiting we invoke the Limit/Colimit Coincidence Theorem and show that $\bigvee \delta_k \circ (\delta_k)^R$ is an F-algebra endomorphism on (A, α):

$$\begin{aligned}(\bigvee \delta_k \circ (\delta_k)^R) \circ \alpha &= \bigvee \delta_{k+1} \circ (\delta_{k+1})^R \circ \alpha \\ &= \bigvee \alpha \circ F(\delta_k) \circ F(\delta_k)^R \\ &= \alpha \circ F(\bigvee \delta_k \circ (\delta_k)^R).\end{aligned}$$

In passing notice that $\alpha : F\delta \cong (\delta\,\mathrm{succ})$ where $\mathrm{succ} : \omega \rightarrow \omega : k \mapsto k+1$. □

In the presence of an e-initial object, initial algebras of **Cpo**-endofunctors are characterised as those fixed-points whose least endomorphism is the identity.

Definition 7.1.6 ([Fre90]) Let $F : \mathcal{A} \rightarrow \mathcal{A}$ be a **Cpo**-functor. An *special F-invariant object* is a fixed-point $\alpha : FA \cong A$ such that id_A is the least F-algebra endomorphism on (A, α). □

Theorem 7.1.7 ([Fre90]) In a **Cppo**-category with right-strict composition, special invariant objects of **Cpo**-endofunctors are initial algebras.

PROOF: Let F be a **Cpo**-endofunctor on a **Cpo**-category $\mathcal{A}$ with e-initial object.

If (A, α) is an special F-invariant object then, writing fix for the least fixed-point operator in **Cppo**, we have that $\mathrm{fix}\,(\lambda x.\, \alpha \circ (Fx) \circ \alpha^{-1}) = \mathrm{id}_A$. Moreover, for every F-algebra (B, β), by the fixed-point property, $\mathrm{fix}\,(\lambda x.\, \beta \circ (Fx) \circ \alpha^{-1}) : (A, \alpha) \rightarrow (B, \beta)$. Finally, if $h : (A, \alpha) \rightarrow (B, \beta)$ then

$$\begin{array}{ccc} \mathcal{A}(A,A) & \xrightarrow{\lambda x.\, \alpha \circ (Fx) \circ \alpha^{-1}} & \mathcal{A}(A,A) \\ {\scriptstyle h \circ \_}\downarrow & & \downarrow{\scriptstyle h \circ \_} \\ \mathcal{A}(A,B) & \xrightarrow[\lambda x.\, \beta \circ (Fx) \circ \alpha^{-1}]{} & \mathcal{A}(A,B) \end{array}$$

and, by the uniformity of fix,

$$\mathrm{fix}\,(\lambda x.\, \beta \circ (Fx) \circ \alpha^{-1}) = h \circ \mathrm{fix}\,(\lambda x.\, \alpha \circ (Fx) \circ \alpha^{-1}) = h.$$ □

Aiming at establishing the equivalence between **Cpo**-algebraic completeness and parameterised **Cpo**-algebraic completeness we now start an excursion into categories of algebras and lax homomorphisms.

Definition 7.1.8 For a **Poset**-functor (**Cpo**-functor) $F : \mathcal{A} \to \mathcal{A}$, the **Poset**-category (**Cpo**-category) of *F-algebras* and *lax algebra morphisms*, F-$\mathbf{Alg}_{\leq}$, has objects (A, α) where $A \in |\mathcal{A}|$ and $\alpha : FA \to A$ in $\mathcal{A}$, and morphisms $h : (A,\alpha) \xrightarrow{\leq} (B,\beta)$ where $h : A \to B$ in $\mathcal{A}$ is such that

$$\begin{array}{ccc} FA & \xrightarrow{Fh} & FB \\ {\scriptstyle\alpha}\downarrow & \leq & \downarrow{\scriptstyle\beta} \\ A & \xrightarrow[h]{} & B \end{array} .$$

The hom-order, composition and identities are as in $\mathcal{A}$.

For a monad $\mathbb{T} : \mathcal{A} \to \mathcal{A}$ in **Poset-CAT** (**Cpo-CAT**), the **Poset**-category (**Cpo**-category) $\mathcal{A}^{\mathbb{T}}_{\leq}$ is the full subcategory of $\mathbb{T}$-$\mathbf{Alg}_{\leq}$ of Eilenberg-Moore algebras. □

Remark. In the **Cpo**-enriched case F-$\mathbf{Alg}_{\leq}$ and $\mathcal{A}^{\mathbb{T}}_{\leq}$ have hom-cpos because for every ω-chain $\langle f_k : (A,\alpha) \xrightarrow{\leq} (B,\beta)\rangle$,

$$(\forall k \in |\omega|.\ f_k \circ \alpha \leq \beta \circ F f_k) \ \Rightarrow\ (\bigvee f_k) \circ \alpha \ \leq\ \beta \circ \bigvee F(f_k) \ =\ \beta \circ F(\bigvee f_k).$$

Definition 7.1.9 An algebra of a **Poset**-endofunctor is *maximally initial* if it is initial and the unique algebra morphism to any other algebra is maximal among all lax algebra morphisms. □

Maximal initiality is relevant for it guarantees the monotonicity of the mapping which to an algebra associates the unique algebra morphism from the maximally-initial algebra into it.

Proposition 7.1.10 Initial algebras of **Cpo**-endofunctors are maximally initial.

PROOF: Let $F : \mathcal{A} \to \mathcal{A}$ be a **Cpo**-endofunctor. For an initial F-algebra (A,α) and a lax F-algebra morphism $h : (A,\alpha) \xrightarrow{\leq} (B,\beta)$ define $\Phi : \mathcal{A}(A,B) \to \mathcal{A}(A,B)$ as the continuous mapping $x \mapsto \beta \circ (Fx) \circ \alpha^{-1}$. Then, $\langle \Phi^k(h) \rangle$ is an ω-chain and

$$\begin{aligned} \bigvee \Phi^{k+1}(h) &= \bigvee \beta \circ F(\Phi^k h) \circ \alpha^{-1} \\ &= \beta \circ F\big(\bigvee \Phi^k(h)\big) \circ \alpha^{-1}. \end{aligned}$$

So $\bigvee \Phi^k(h)$ is an F-algebra morphism $(A,\alpha) \to (B,\beta)$ and also $h \leq \bigvee \Phi^k(h)$. □

Corollary 7.1.11 Let $F : \mathcal{A} \to \mathcal{A}$ be a **Cpo**-functor. If (A, α) is an initial F-algebra then, for every $B \in |\mathcal{A}|$, the mapping $\mathcal{A}(FB, B) \to \mathcal{A}(A, B)$ sending β to the unique $(A, \alpha) \to (B, \beta)$ is continuous.

PROOF: Let $u : \mathcal{A}(FB, B) \to \mathcal{A}(A, B)$ be the described mapping. If $\beta \leq \beta'$ then $u(\beta) : (A, \alpha) \overset{\to}{\leq} (B, \beta')$ and since, by Proposition 7.1.10, (A, α) is maximally initial it follows that $u(\beta) \leq u(\beta')$.

For an ω-chain $\langle \beta_k \rangle$ in $\mathcal{A}(FB, B)$, it follows that $\bigvee u(\beta_k) : (A, \alpha) \to (B, \bigvee \beta_k)$ and we are done. □

Theorem 7.1.12 **Cpo**-algebraic completeness (resp. compactness) implies parameterised **Cpo**-algebraic completeness (resp. compactness).

PROOF: Let $F : \mathcal{A} \times \mathcal{B} \to \mathcal{B}$ be a **Cpo**-functor. Assuming that $\mathcal{B}$ is **Cpo**-algebraically complete (compact) we show that $F^\dagger : \mathcal{A} \to \mathcal{B}$ is a **Cpo**-functor.

$F^\dagger$ is a **Cpo**-functor because $F^\dagger_{X,Y} : \mathcal{A}(X, Y) \to \mathcal{B}(F^\dagger X, F^\dagger Y)$ is the composition of the continuous mappings $\mathcal{A}(X, Y) \to \mathcal{B}(F(X, F^\dagger Y), F^\dagger Y)$ sending f to $\iota^F_Y \circ F(f, F^\dagger Y)$ and $\mathcal{B}(F(X, F^\dagger Y), F^\dagger Y) \to \mathcal{B}(F^\dagger X, F^\dagger Y)$ sending h to the unique $F(X, \_)$-algebra morphism $(F^\dagger X, \iota^F_X) \to (F^\dagger Y, h)$ —see Corollary 7.1.11. □

7.2 Cpo-Algebraic Compactness

In the vein of the previous section we study **Cpo**-algebraically compact categories with ep-zero. The result is that for **Cppo**$_\perp$-categories, completeness and compactness in their parameterised and ω forms all coincide (see Corollary 7.2.5).

Remark. When considering **Cppo**$_\perp$-enrichment (**Pposet**$_\perp$-enrichment), we take the monoidal structure on **Cppo**$_\perp$ (**Pposet**$_\perp$) to be the smash product for the tensor and the Sierpińsky space for the unit. Hence, to give a **Cppo**$_\perp$-enrichment (**Pposet**$_\perp$-enrichment) on a category is to give a **Cppo**-enrichment (**Pposet**-enrichment) in which composition is strict.

Frequently, explicit mention of ep-zeros is avoided because,

Proposition 7.2.1 A **Poset**-category has ep-zero if and only if it is **Pposet**$_\perp$-enriched and has an initial object. □

By Theorem 7.1.7 and its dual:

Theorem 7.2.2 ([Fre90]) In a **Cppo**$_\perp$-category, special invariant objects are free algebras. □

Moreover, because of the Limit/Colimit Coincidence Theorem, the above can be strengthened to:

Theorem 7.2.3 For a $\mathbf{Cppo}_\perp$-category, **Cpo**-algebraic completeness implies **Cpo**-algebraic ω-compactness.

PROOF: Let $\mathcal{A}$ be a $\mathbf{Cppo}_\perp$-category and let F be a **Cpo**-endofunctor on it.

By Theorem 7.1.5, if (A, α) is an initial F-algebra then the standard ω-chain has a colimiting cone of embeddings $\delta : \Delta_F \dot{\rightarrow} A$ for which $\alpha : F\delta \cong (\delta\,\mathrm{succ})$ where $\mathrm{succ} : \omega \rightarrow \omega : k \mapsto k+1$. Thus, $\alpha^{-1} : (\delta\,\mathrm{succ})^R \cong F(\delta^R)$ and since ${\Delta_F}^R$ is the standard ω^{op}-chain and, by the Limit/Colimit Coincidence Theorem, the cone $\delta^R : A \dot{\rightarrow} {\Delta_F}^R$ is limiting it follows, by the (dual of the) Basic Lemma, that (A, α^{-1}) is a final F-coalgebra. □

Corollary 7.2.4 A **Cpo**-category with ep-zero and colimits of ω-chains of embeddings is parameterised **Cpo**-algebraically ω-compact.

PROOF: By Theorems 7.1.3, 7.1.12 and 7.2.3. □

Corollary 7.2.5 For a $\mathbf{Cppo}_\perp$-category,

Cpo-alg. ω-completeness ⇛ **Cpo**-alg. completeness ≡ **Cpo**-alg. compactness ⇛ **Cpo**-alg. ω-compactness

parameterised **Cpo**-alg. completeness ⇛ **Cpo**-alg. completeness ≡ **Cpo**-alg. compactness ⇛ parameterised **Cpo**-alg. compactness □

7.3 Categories of Kinds

We introduce a 2-category of **Cpo**-algebraically compact categories, **Kind**, defined to contain categories in which the existence, preservation and coincidence of all colimits of standard ω-chains and limits of standard ω^{op}-chains is guaranteed.

Afterwards the closure properties of **Kind** are studied. In particular we show that it is 2-cartesian-closed and has a fixed-point operator characterised by a uniformity property, but much more holds (see Theorem 7.3.12).

7.3.1 PKind

For the sake of simplicity and generality we first concentrate on **Cpo**-algebraic cocompleteness. To guarantee the existence and preservation of limits of all standard ω^{op}-chains, we wish to group all those small **Cpo**-categories with p-terminal object and limits of ω^{op}-chains of projections in a 2-category (see Theorem 7.1.3).

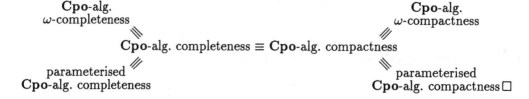

Definition 7.3.1 **PKind** is the 2-category of small **Cpo**-categories with p-terminal object and limits of ω^{op}-chains of projections, **Cpo**-functors and natural transformations. □

Corollary 7.3.2 1. Every category in **PKind** is parameterised **Cpo**-algebraically ω-cocomplete.

2. **PKind** is 2-cartesian.

PROOF:

(1) By Theorems 7.1.3 and 7.1.12.

(2) Because **1** is in **PKind** and, for $\mathcal{A}$, $\mathcal{B}$ in **PKind**, $\mathcal{A} \times \mathcal{B}$ has a p-terminal object and limits of ω^{op}-chains of projections given pointwise. □

PKind does not have exponentials, the reason being exclusively that the property of having a p-terminal object is not closed under exponentiation. For example, **Cppo** has a p-terminal object but $\mathbf{Cppo}^{\rightarrow}$ does not. For, if the terminal object $1 \to 1$ were to be p-terminal then, for every $A_0 \to A_1 \in |\, \mathbf{Cppo}^{\rightarrow} \,|$ it should happen that

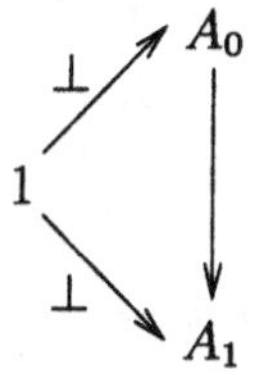

which is not always the case. Instead we have the weaker property

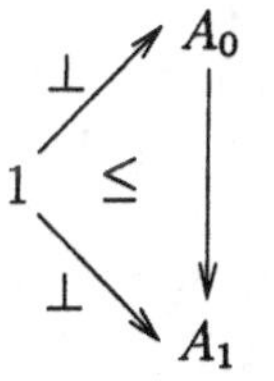

which we interpret as *lax* naturality (see page 22). Thus the following:

Definition 7.3.3 For small **Cpo**-categories $\mathcal{A}$ and $\mathcal{B}$, $[\mathcal{A}, \mathcal{B}]_{\leq}$ is the **Cpo**-category with the **Cpo**-functors $\mathcal{A} \to \mathcal{B}$ as the set of objects, and where the hom $[\mathcal{A}, \mathcal{B}]_{\leq}(F, G)$ is the cpo with underlying set $\mathrm{Nat}_{\leq}(F, G)$ of lax natural transformations $F \overset{\cdot}{\underset{\leq}{\to}} G$ ordered pointwise. □

For $\mathcal{A}$ in **Cpo-Cat** and $\mathcal{B}$ in **PKind**, it is easily verified that $[\mathcal{A}, \mathcal{B}]_{\leq}$ has p-terminal object, whilst —as we will see— the basic reason for which it has limits of ω^{op}-chains of projections is that projections are natural and that limits can be computed pointwise.

Lemma 7.3.4 Let $\mathcal{A}$ and $\mathcal{B}$ be **Cpo**-categories. Then, $\eta \in [\mathcal{A},\mathcal{B}]_{\leq}(F,G)$ is a projection if and only if $\eta : F \dot{\rightarrow} G$ and for every $A \in |\mathcal{A}|$, the component $\eta_A : FA \rightarrow GA$ is a projection in $\mathcal{B}$. □

Lemma 7.3.5 Let $\mathcal{A}$ and $\mathcal{B}$ be **Cpo**-categories and let $\Gamma : \mathcal{G} \rightarrow [\mathcal{A},\mathcal{B}]$. If for every $X \in |\mathcal{A}|$ the diagram $\Gamma_X : \mathcal{G} \rightarrow \mathcal{B} : e \mapsto (\Gamma e)_X$ has a **Cpo**-limit then so does the diagram $\Gamma : \mathcal{G} \rightarrow [\mathcal{A},\mathcal{B}] \rightarrow [\mathcal{A},\mathcal{B}]_{\leq}$

PROOF: Briefly, $\Gamma : \mathcal{G} \rightarrow [\mathcal{A},\mathcal{B}]$ has a **Cpo**-limit as it does pointwise, and the claim follows because they are preserved by $[\mathcal{A},\mathcal{B}] \rightarrow [\mathcal{A},\mathcal{B}]_{\leq}$.

In detail, for $X \in |\mathcal{A}|$ let $\pi^{(X)} : PX \dot{\rightarrow} \Gamma_X$ be **Cpo**-limiting. For every $f : X \rightarrow Y$ in $\mathcal{A}$ define $\Gamma_f : \Gamma_X \dot{\rightarrow} \Gamma_Y$ by $(\Gamma_f)_N = (\Gamma N)f$ for $N \in |\mathcal{G}|$ and let Pf be the unique mediating morphism $(\Gamma_f \circ \pi^{(X)}) \rightarrow \pi^{(Y)}$. This process defines a **Cpo**-functor $P : \mathcal{A} \rightarrow \mathcal{B}$, as each $\pi^{(X)}$ is **Cpo**-limiting, and a cone $\pi : P \dot{\rightarrow} \Gamma : \mathcal{G} \rightarrow [\mathcal{A},\mathcal{B}]$ where $(\pi_N)_X = \pi_N^{(X)}$ for $N \in |\mathcal{G}|$. We show that π is limiting in $[\mathcal{A},\mathcal{B}]_{\leq}$. Let $\gamma : Q \dot{\rightarrow} \Gamma : \mathcal{G} \rightarrow [\mathcal{A},\mathcal{B}]_{\leq}$ and for $X \in |\mathcal{A}|$ define $\gamma^{(X)} : QX \dot{\rightarrow} \Gamma_X$ by $\gamma_N^{(X)} = (\gamma_N)_X$ for $N \in |\mathcal{G}|$. If $\mu : \gamma \dot{\underset{\leq}{\rightarrow}} \pi$ then for every $X \in |\mathcal{A}|$ it follows that $\mu_X : \gamma^{(X)} \rightarrow \pi^{(X)}$, showing uniqueness. For existence, we need only verify that $\{\mu_X : \gamma^{(X)} \rightarrow \pi^{(X)}\} : Q \dot{\underset{\leq}{\rightarrow}} P$. For every $f : X \rightarrow Y$ in $\mathcal{A}$ since

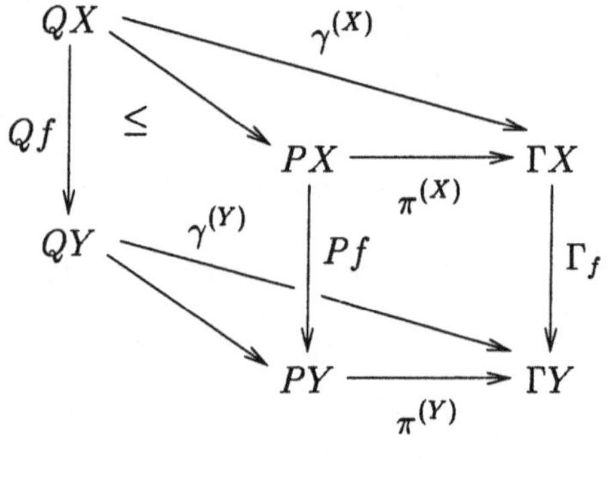

it follows that $\pi^{(Y)} \circ (\gamma^{(Y)} \rightarrow \pi^{(Y)}) \circ Qf \leq \pi^{(Y)} \circ (Pf) \circ (\gamma^{(X)} \rightarrow \pi^{(X)})$ and, as $\pi^{(Y)}$ is **Cpo**-limiting, we have $(\gamma^{(Y)} \rightarrow \pi^{(Y)}) \circ Qf \leq (Pf) \circ (\gamma^{(X)} \rightarrow \pi^{(X)})$ as desired. Finally, to conclude that π is **Cpo**-limiting, by Proposition 2.2.1, we need show that for every $\alpha, \beta : Q \dot{\underset{\leq}{\rightarrow}} P$ in $[\mathcal{A},\mathcal{B}]_{\leq}$,

$$\pi \circ \alpha \leq \pi \circ \beta \;\Rightarrow\; \alpha \leq \beta. \tag{7.1}$$

Assuming the antecedent of (7.1) we have that for every $N \in |\mathcal{G}|$ and every $X \in |\mathcal{A}|$,

$$\pi_N^{(X)} \circ \alpha_X \;=\; (\pi_N)_X \circ \alpha_X \;\leq\; (\pi_N)_X \circ \beta_X \;=\; \pi_N^{(X)} \circ \beta_X;$$

and hence, that for every $X \in |\mathcal{A}|$, $\pi^{(X)} \circ \alpha_X \leq \pi^{(X)} \circ \beta_X$. Thus, as $\pi^{(X)}$ is **Cpo**-limiting, it follows that $\alpha_X \leq \beta_X$ for every $X \in |\mathcal{A}|$ and so $\alpha \leq \beta$. □

Proposition 7.3.6 If $\mathcal{A}$ is in **Cpo-Cat** and $\mathcal{B}$ is in **PKind** then $[\mathcal{A},\mathcal{B}]_{\leq}$ is in **PKind**.

PROOF: The p-terminal object in $[\mathcal{A},\mathcal{B}]_{\leq}$ is the constantly 1 **Cpo**-functor and $[\mathcal{A},\mathcal{B}]_{\leq}$ has limits of ω^{op}-chains of projections by Lemma 7.3.5 using Lemma 7.3.4 and the Limit/Colimit Coincidence Theorem. □

Perhaps surprisingly, **PKind** is closed under the formation of categories of algebras and lax homomorphisms. Once again, for an endofunctor in **PKind**, it is easily verified that the category of algebras and lax homomorphisms has a p-terminal object; that it has limits of ω^{op}-chains of projections basically follows because projections are homomorphisms and the functor forgetting the algebra structure creates limits.

Lemma 7.3.7 Let F be a **Poset**-endofunctor on $\mathcal{A}$. Then $h : (A,\alpha) \xrightarrow{\leq} (B,\beta)$ is a projection in F-$\mathbf{Alg}_{\leq}$ if and only if $h : (A,\alpha) \to (B,\beta)$ and $h : A \to B$ is a projection in $\mathcal{A}$. □

Lemma 7.3.8 For a **Poset**-functor $F : \mathcal{A} \to \mathcal{A}$, the forgetful functor $U : F\text{-}\mathbf{Alg}_{\leq} \to \mathcal{A}$ creates **Poset**-limits of diagrams in F-**Alg**.

PROOF: Briefly because the forgetful functor F-**Alg** $\to \mathcal{A}$ creates **Poset**-limits and these are preserved by the inclusion functor F-**Alg** $\to F\text{-}\mathbf{Alg}_{\leq}$.

In detail, let $\Gamma : \mathcal{G} \to F\text{-}\mathbf{Alg}$ and let $\pi : A \dot{\to} U\Gamma : \mathcal{G} \to \mathcal{A}$ be a **Poset**-limit. The object mapping of Γ gives rise to a natural transformation $|\,\Gamma\,| : FU\Gamma \dot{\to} U\Gamma$ and thus there exists a unique $\alpha : |\,\Gamma\,| \circ F\pi \to \pi$. The cone $\pi : (A,\alpha) \dot{\to} \Gamma$ is **Poset**-limiting in $F\text{-}\mathbf{Alg}_{\leq}$ as should be clear after verifying that for $\rho : (B,\beta) \dot{\xrightarrow{\leq}} \Gamma$ the unique $h : \rho \to \pi$ is a lax F-algebra morphism $(\mathcal{B},\beta) \xrightarrow{\leq} (\mathcal{A},\alpha)$. This holds because chasing the diagram

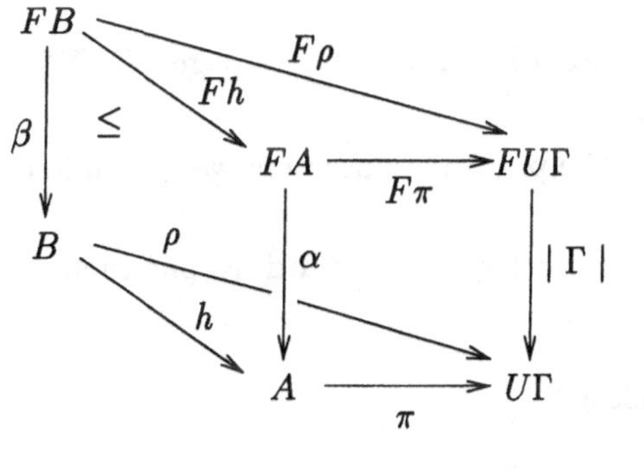

we have that $\pi \circ h \circ \beta \leq \pi \circ \alpha \circ Fh$ from which we conclude that $h \circ \beta \leq \alpha \circ Fh$. □

Corollary 7.3.9 For a monad $\mathbb{T} : \mathcal{A} \to \mathcal{A}$ in **Poset-CAT**, the forgetful functor $\mathcal{A}^{\mathbb{T}}_{\leq} \to \mathcal{A}$ creates **Poset**-limits of diagrams in $\mathcal{A}^{\mathbb{T}}$.

PROOF: Because the forgetful functors $\mathcal{A}^{\mathbb{T}} \to \mathcal{A}$ and $\mathbb{T}\text{-}\mathbf{Alg}_{\leq} \to \mathcal{A}$ create limits of diagrams in $\mathcal{A}^{\mathbb{T}}$, and $\mathcal{A}^{\mathbb{T}}_{\leq}$ is a full subcategory of $\mathbb{T}\text{-}\mathbf{Alg}_{\leq}$. □

Proposition 7.3.10 1. If $F : \mathcal{A} \to \mathcal{A}$ is in **PKind** then so is F-$\mathbf{Alg}_{\leq}$.

2. If $\mathbb{T} : \mathcal{A} \to \mathcal{A}$ is a monad in **PKind** then $\mathcal{A}^{\mathbb{T}}_{\leq}$ is in **PKind**.

PROOF:

(1) The p-terminal object is $F1 \to 1$ and F-$\mathbf{Alg}_{\leq}$ has limits of ω^{op}-chains of projections by Lemma 7.3.8 using Lemma 7.3.7 and the Limit/Colimit Coincidence Theorem.

(2) The p-terminal object, $T1 \to 1$, is an Eilenberg-Moore algebra and $\mathcal{A}^{\mathbb{T}}_{\leq}$ has limits of ω^{op}-chains of projections by Corollary 7.3.9 using Lemma 7.3.7 and the Limit/Colimit Coincidence Theorem. □

7.3.2 Kind

Kind is obtained by simply self dualising the property defining categories in **PKind**.

Definition 7.3.11 **Kind** is the 2-category of small **Cpo**-categories with ep-zero and colimits of ω-chains of embeddings, **Cpo**-functors and natural transformations. □

Remark. In [Bar92] it is observed that a non-empty $\mathbf{Pposet}_{\perp}$-category with colimits of ω-chains has ep-zero, viz., the colimit of $X \xrightarrow{\perp} X \xrightarrow{\perp} X \to \ldots$ for any object X. Unfortunately when restricting the ω-chains to embeddings, this does not hold. For example, the $\mathbf{Pposet}_{\perp}$-category induced by the ordered monoid $(\{\perp, \top\}, \vdash, \top, \wedge)$ has colimits of ω-chains of embeddings but does not have ep-zero.

Examples of categories in **Kind** are: $\boldsymbol{\omega}$**+1** (see page 37), **Pfn**, **Rel** (the category of sets and relations) and **pCpo**.

In virtue of the results of the previous subsection we conclude (1)–(5) below:

Theorem 7.3.12 1. Every category in **Kind** is parameterised **Cpo**-algebraically ω-supercompact.

2. **Kind** is 2-cartesian-closed.

3. If $\mathcal{A}$ is in **Kind** then so is $\mathcal{A}^{op}$.

4. If $F : \mathcal{A} \to \mathcal{A}$ is in **Kind** then so are F-$\mathbf{Alg}_{\leq}$ and F-$\mathbf{CoAlg}_{\geq}$ $(= (F^{op}\text{-}\mathbf{Alg}_{\leq})^{op})$.

5. If $\mathbb{T} : \mathcal{A} \to \mathcal{A}$ is a (co)monad in **Kind** then $\mathcal{A}^{\mathbb{T}}_{\leq}$ $(\mathcal{A}^{\mathbb{T}}_{\geq})$ is in **Kind**.

6. Fix is the unique (up to isomorphism) uniform fixed-point operator in **Kind**. That is, it is characterised by the uniformity property that for every zero-preserving

functor $V : \mathcal{B} \circ\!\!\rightarrow \mathcal{Y}$ in **Kind**,

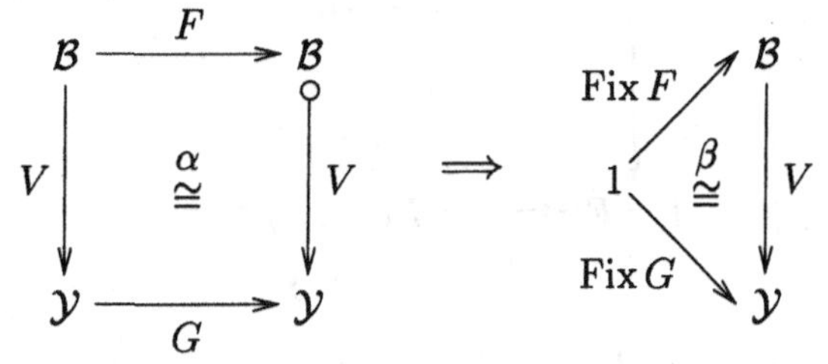

where $\beta : \iota^G \to (V\iota^F) \circ \alpha_{\mathrm{Fix}\,F}$.

PROOF: (6) Fix is uniform because

$V(\iota^F : F(\mathrm{Fix}\,F) \to \mathrm{Fix}\,F)$

$$\begin{array}{lll}
\cong & V(F(\mathrm{colim}\ \Delta_F) \to \mathrm{colim}\ \Delta_F) & ,\ \mathrm{Fix}\,F \cong \mathrm{colim}\ \Delta_F \\
= & VF(\mathrm{colim}\ \Delta_F) \to V(\mathrm{colim}\ \Delta_F) & \\
\cong & GV(\mathrm{colim}\ \Delta_F) \to V(\mathrm{colim}\ \Delta_F) & ,\ VF \cong GV \\
\cong & G(\mathrm{colim}\ V\Delta_F) \to \mathrm{colim}\ (V\Delta_F) & ,\ V \text{ preserves colimits of } \omega\text{-chains of embeddings} \\
\cong & G(\mathrm{colim}\ \Delta_G) \to \mathrm{colim}\ \Delta_G & ,\ V\Delta_F \cong \Delta_G \\
\cong & \iota^G : G(\mathrm{Fix}\,G) \to \mathrm{Fix}\,G. &
\end{array}$$

To see that it is the unique such we start with the universal property which gives $\boldsymbol{\omega}\mathbf{+1}$ its name:

Let $J : \omega + 1 \to \boldsymbol{\omega}\mathbf{+1}$ be the **Cpo**-functor sending $k \to l$ to $k : k \to l$. Then, every **Cpo**-functor $\Delta : \omega + 1 \to \mathcal{C}$ for which $\Delta \restriction \omega = (\omega \hookrightarrow \omega + 1 \xrightarrow{\Delta} \mathcal{C})$ is an ω-chain of embeddings and $\langle \Delta(n \to \omega) \rangle_{n \in |\omega|} : \Delta \restriction \omega \dot{\to} \Delta(\omega)$ is colimiting has *strict* Kan extension along J in **Cpo-Gpd**. That is, there exists a **Cpo**-functor Kan $\Delta : \boldsymbol{\omega}\mathbf{+1} \to \mathcal{C}$ such that $\Delta = (\mathrm{Kan}\ \Delta) \circ J$ and

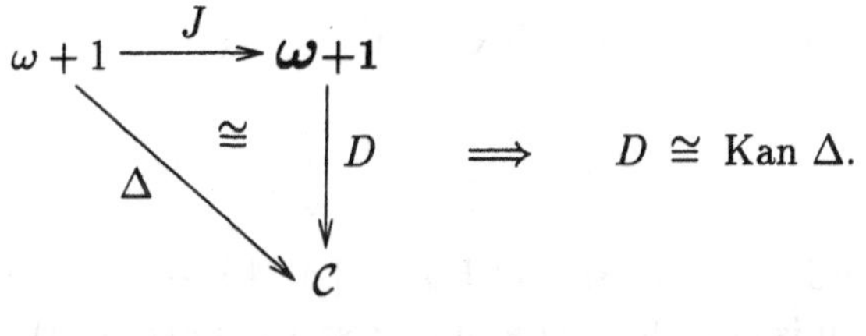

The crucial fact making the property hold is that $\boldsymbol{\omega}\mathbf{+1}$ is obtained from $\omega + 1$ by *freely* turning all its morphisms into embeddings.

Now, for $F : \mathcal{A} \to \mathcal{A}$ in **Kind** let $\Delta_F^\# : \omega + 1 \to \mathcal{A}$ be the diagram

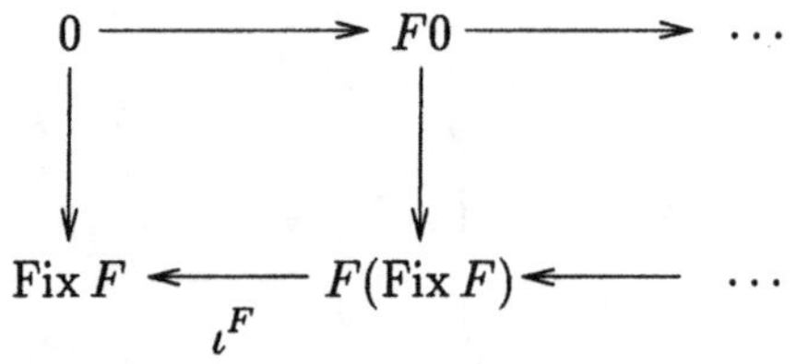

constructed in the proof of Theorem 7.1.5. Then we have that

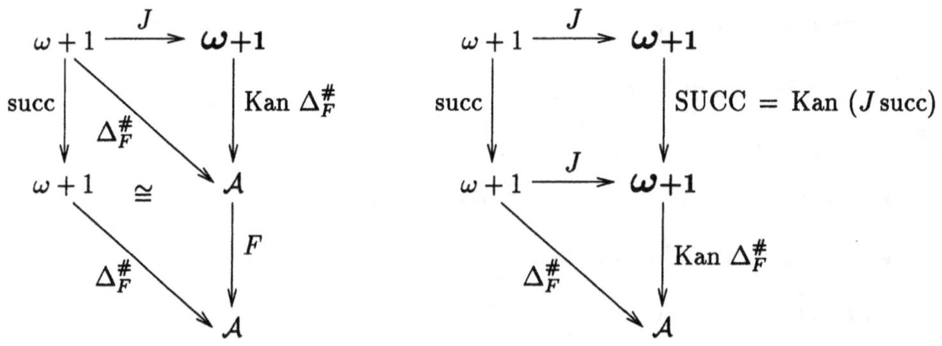

where $\mathrm{succ} : \omega + 1 \to \omega + 1$ sends $k \in |\,\omega\,|$ to $k + 1$ and ω to itself. Therefore

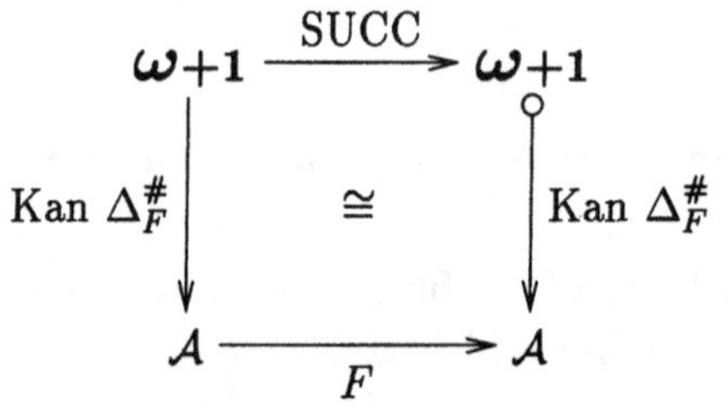

$$
\begin{array}{ccc}
\boldsymbol{\omega}\mathbf{+1} & \xrightarrow{\ \mathrm{SUCC}\ } & \boldsymbol{\omega}\mathbf{+1} \\
\mathrm{Kan}\ \Delta_F^\# \Big\downarrow & \cong & \Big\downarrow \mathrm{Kan}\ \Delta_F^\# \\
\mathcal{A} & \xrightarrow[\ F\ ]{} & \mathcal{A}
\end{array}
\qquad (7.2)
$$

And finally, if Y is a uniform fixed-point operator:

$$
\begin{aligned}
YF \ &\cong \ (\mathrm{Kan}\ \Delta_F^\#)(Y\ \mathrm{SUCC}) \quad , \text{applying the uniformity property to (7.2)} \\
&= \ (\mathrm{Kan}\ \Delta_F^\#)(\omega) \qquad\quad , Y\ \mathrm{SUCC} = \omega \\
&= \ \Delta_F^\#(\omega) \\
&= \ \mathrm{Fix}\,F.
\end{aligned}
$$
□

Remark. For $\mathcal{A}$ in **Kind**, the extension of Fix to $[\mathcal{A}, \mathcal{A}]_\leq \to \mathcal{A}$ is a locally continuous mapping, but in general it is not a functor as it only satisfies $\mathrm{Fix}\,(\eta \circ \mu) \leq (\mathrm{Fix}\,\eta) \circ (\mathrm{Fix}\,\mu)$.

Recalling that $(\_)^\dagger = \mathrm{Fix} \circ \Lambda(\_)$ we have:

Corollary 7.3.13 If $\mathcal{A}$ and $\mathcal{B}$ are in **Kind** then so is $(\_)^{\dagger} : [\mathcal{A} \times \mathcal{B}, \mathcal{B}] \to [\mathcal{A}, \mathcal{B}]$.

Moreover, it is *uniform* in the sense that

$$
\begin{array}{ccc}
\mathcal{A} \times \mathcal{B} \xrightarrow{\ F\ } \mathcal{B} & & \mathcal{A} \xrightarrow{\ F^{\dagger}\ } \mathcal{B} \\
\Big\downarrow{U \times V} \quad \cong^{\alpha} \quad \Big\downarrow{V} & \Longrightarrow & \Big\downarrow{U} \quad \cong^{\beta} \quad \Big\downarrow{V} \\
\mathcal{X} \times \mathcal{Y} \xrightarrow[\ G\ ]{} \mathcal{Y} & & \mathcal{X} \xrightarrow[\ G^{\dagger}\ ]{} \mathcal{Y}
\end{array}
$$

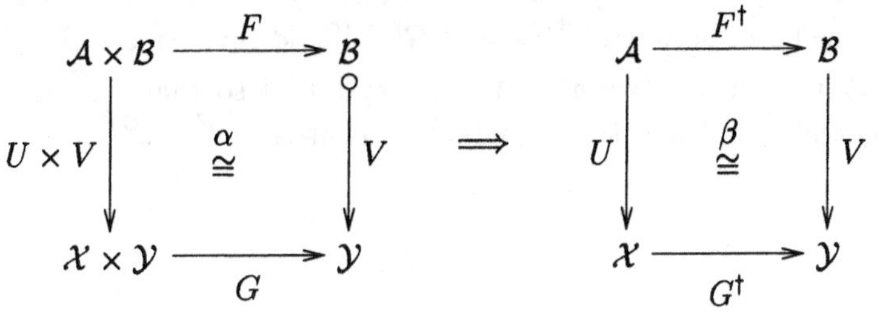

where $\beta_A : \iota^G_{UA} \to (V \iota^F_A) \circ \alpha_{(A, F^{\dagger}A)}$. $\qquad\qquad\square$

As the following proposition shows, sometimes the parameterised fixed-point operator can be constructed so as to satisfy a stronger *strict uniformity* property. (This will be needed in Section 9.2.)

Proposition 7.3.14 Let

$$
\begin{array}{ccc}
\mathcal{A} \times \mathcal{B} \xrightarrow{\ F\ } \mathcal{B} \\
\Big\downarrow{U \times V} \qquad\quad \Big\downarrow{V} \\
\mathcal{X} \times \mathcal{Y} \xrightarrow[\ G\ ]{} \mathcal{Y}
\end{array}
$$

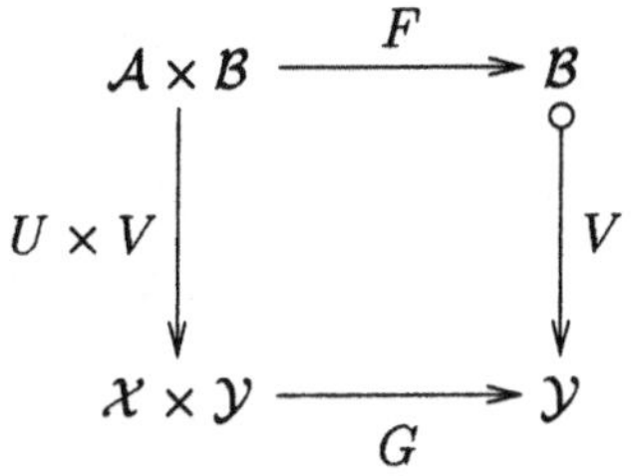

in **Kind**.

If V creates colimits of ω-chains of embeddings then for every initial parameterised G-algebra $(G^{\dagger}, \iota^G)$ there exists a unique initial parameterised F-algebra $(F^{\dagger}, \iota^F)$ such that

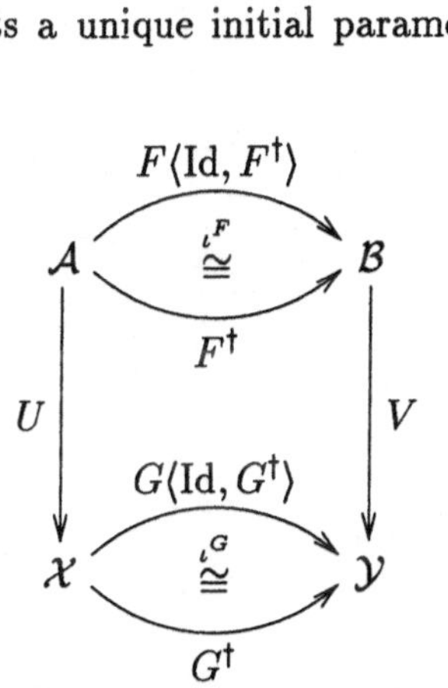

PROOF: For $A \in |\mathcal{A}|$, by Theorem 7.1.5, $G^{\dagger}UA = \operatorname{colim} \Delta_{G(UA,\_)}$ and since $V\Delta_{F(A,\_)} = \Delta_{G(UA,\_)}$ it follows that there exists a unique $F^{\dagger}A = \operatorname{colim} \Delta_{F(A,\_)}$ such that $VF^{\dagger}A = G^{\dagger}UA$. Also, for $f : A \to A'$ in $\mathcal{A}$, $F^{\dagger}f$ mediates between $F^{\dagger}A$ and $F^{\dagger}A'$ so that $VF^{\dagger}f$ mediates between $G^{\dagger}UA$ and $G^{\dagger}UA'$ and thus equals $G^{\dagger}Uf$.

Moreover, ι_A^F mediates between $F(A, F^{\dagger}A)$ and $F^{\dagger}A$ so that $V\iota_A^F$ mediates between $G(UA, G^{\dagger}UA)$ and $G^{\dagger}UA$ and thus equals ι_{UA}^G. That is, $V\iota^F = \iota^G U$. □

8 FPC

We present the metalanguage FPC [Plo85,Gun92] and study it as a programming language. First, a *call-by-value operational semantics* is provided. Second, *enriched categorical models* of FPC are defined and, on top of them, a *denotational semantics* is given. Finally, it is shown that **Poset**-models of FPC arising from **Poset**-domain-structures are *parametric* with respect to *representations* [Rey74,Rey83] and that, categorically, this corresponds to the lax naturality of the interpretation.

8.1 The Language

The metalanguage FPC is a type theory with sums, products, exponentials and recursive types based on the propositions-as-types paradigm [CF58,How80]. The grammar of FPC requires two syntax classes of variables: one called TypeVars for *type* variables and another called Vars for *expression* variables. The syntax of the language is given as follows:

$$
\begin{array}{rcl}
\mathtt{T} & \in & \text{TypeVars} \\
\tau \in \text{Types} & ::= & \mathtt{T} \mid \tau_1 + \tau_2 \mid \tau_1 \times \tau_2 \mid \tau_1 \rightharpoonup \tau_2 \mid \mu\mathtt{T}.\tau \\
\mathtt{x} & \in & \text{Vars} \\
e \in \text{Expressions} & ::= & \mathtt{x} \mid \mathtt{inl}_{\tau_1,\tau_2}(e) \mid \mathtt{inr}_{\tau_1,\tau_2}(e) \mid \mathtt{case}\ e\ \mathtt{of}\ \mathtt{inl}(\mathtt{x}_1).e_1\ \mathtt{or}\ \mathtt{inr}(\mathtt{x}_2).e_2 \mid \\
 & & \langle e_1, e_2\rangle \mid \mathtt{fst}(e) \mid \mathtt{snd}(e) \mid \lambda\mathtt{x}:\tau.e \mid e_1(e_2) \mid \mathtt{intro}_{\mu\mathtt{T}.\tau}(e) \mid \mathtt{elim}(e).
\end{array}
$$

As usual expressions are identified up to α-equivalence; $\mu\mathtt{T}.\tau$ binds $\mathtt{T}$ in τ, $\lambda\mathtt{x}:\tau.e$ binds $\mathtt{x}$ in e, and $\mathtt{case}\ e\ \mathtt{of}\ \mathtt{inl}(\mathtt{x}_1).e_1\ \mathtt{or}\ \mathtt{inr}(\mathtt{x}_2).e_2$ binds $\mathtt{x}_1$ in e_1 and $\mathtt{x}_2$ in e_2. The ordinary definitions of *free* variables, *bound* variables and *substitution* apply.

Remark. Despite that the tags on the expressions are essential for proving a *unique type* lemma (Lemma 8.1.1) we will usually drop them when they are clear from the context or unimportant.

The definition of the expressions is such that every type comes equipped with operators for *constructing* and for *destroying* expressions; these are, respectively,

$$\mathtt{inl}(\_)/\mathtt{inr}(\_)\ ,\ \langle\_,\_\rangle\ ,\ \lambda\mathtt{x}.\_\ ,\ \mathtt{intro}(\_)\ ,$$

and

$$\mathtt{case}\,\_\,\mathtt{of}\ \mathtt{inl}(\mathtt{x}_1).\_\ \mathtt{or}\ \mathtt{inr}(\mathtt{x}_2).\_\ ,\ \mathtt{fst}(\_)/\mathtt{snd}(\_)\ ,\ \_(\_)\ ,\ \mathtt{elim}(\_)\ .$$

This dichotomy corresponds, under the propositions-as-types paradigm, to the logical *introduction* and *elimination* rules (see the rules defining well-formed expressions on page 149).

The ability to define types recursively is a powerful tool. For example, it automatically provides a large supply of *basic* types. These are closed types (i.e., those with no free variables) specified by the grammar:

$$\begin{aligned} \sigma &::= \mathtt{T} \mid \sigma_1 + \sigma_2 \mid \sigma_1 \times \sigma_2 \mid \sigma_1 \rightharpoonup \sigma_2 \\ \beta \in \text{BasicTypes} &::= \sigma \mid \mu\mathtt{T}.\beta. \end{aligned}$$

The simplest basic type is $\mathtt{0} = \mu\mathtt{T}.\mathtt{T}$. From $\mathtt{0}$ we can construct $\mathtt{1} = \mathtt{0} \rightharpoonup \mathtt{0}$ and even more exciting types: $\mathtt{Nat} = \mu\mathtt{T}.\mathtt{1} + \mathtt{T}$, $\mathtt{NatList} = \mu\mathtt{T}.\mathtt{1} + (\mathtt{Nat} \times \mathtt{T})$, $\mathtt{Lambda} = \mu\mathtt{T}.\mathtt{Nat} + (\mathtt{T} \rightharpoonup \mathtt{T})$, etc. (see [Plo85,Gun92]).

A well-formed type consists of a list of distinct type variables and a type whose free type variables appear in the given list. Formally, we introduce type contexts and well-formed type contexts by the following grammar and rules:

$$\Theta \in \text{Type Contexts} ::= \langle\rangle \mid \langle \Theta, \mathtt{T} \rangle$$

$$\frac{}{\vdash \langle\rangle} \qquad\qquad \frac{\vdash \Theta}{\vdash \Theta, \mathtt{T}} \quad \mathtt{T} \notin \Theta$$

and define well-formed types to be those judgements $\Theta \vdash \tau$ derivable by the rules:

$$\boxed{\text{var}} \quad \frac{\vdash \Theta}{\Theta \vdash \Theta_i} \quad 1 \leq i \leq |\,\Theta\,|$$

$$\boxed{\star} \quad \frac{\Theta \vdash \tau_1 \qquad \Theta \vdash \tau_2}{\Theta \vdash \tau_1 \star \tau_2} \quad \text{where } \star \in \{+, \times, \rightharpoonup\}$$

$$\boxed{\mu} \quad \frac{\Theta, \mathtt{T} \vdash \tau}{\Theta \vdash \mu\mathtt{T}.\tau}$$

Remark. If $\Theta \vdash \tau$ is derivable then so is $\vdash \Theta$.

Although the type system of FPC does not have polymorphic types, the judgements $\Theta \vdash \tau$ allow *parameterisation*. For instance, one may think of $\mathtt{A} \vdash \mu\mathtt{T}.\mathtt{1} + (\mathtt{A} \times \mathtt{T})$ as the type of lists on $\mathtt{A}$.

Well-formed expression contexts are finite mappings assigning well-formed types to expression variables; they are defined by the following grammar and rules:

$$\Gamma \in \text{Expression Contexts} ::= \langle\rangle \mid \langle \Gamma, \mathbf{x} : \tau \rangle$$

$$\frac{\vdash \Theta}{\Theta \vdash \langle\rangle} \qquad\qquad \frac{\Theta \vdash \Gamma \quad \Theta \vdash \tau}{\Theta \vdash \Gamma, \mathbf{x} : \tau} \quad \mathbf{x} \notin \Gamma$$

Remark. If $\Theta \vdash \Gamma$ is derivable then, for every τ in Γ, so is $\Theta \vdash \tau$.

Well-formed expressions are defined to be those judgements $\Theta, \Gamma \vdash e : \tau$ derivable by the following rules

$$\boxed{\text{var}} \quad \frac{\Theta \vdash \Gamma}{\Theta, \Gamma \vdash \Gamma_i} \quad 1 \leq i \leq |\Gamma|$$

$$\boxed{+\text{Il}} \quad \frac{\Theta, \Gamma \vdash e : \tau_1 \qquad \Theta \vdash \tau_2}{\Theta, \Gamma \vdash \mathtt{inl}_{\tau_1,\tau_2}(e) : \tau_1 + \tau_2} \qquad \boxed{+\text{Ir}} \quad \frac{\Theta, \Gamma \vdash e : \tau_2 \qquad \Theta \vdash \tau_1}{\Theta, \Gamma \vdash \mathtt{inr}_{\tau_1,\tau_2}(e) : \tau_1 + \tau_2}$$

$$\boxed{+\text{E}} \quad \frac{\Theta, \Gamma \vdash e : \tau_1 + \tau_2 \qquad \Theta, \langle \Gamma, \mathbf{x}_1 : \tau_1 \rangle \vdash e_1 : \tau \qquad \Theta, \langle \Gamma, \mathbf{x}_2 : \tau_2 \rangle \vdash e_2 : \tau}{\Theta, \Gamma \vdash \mathtt{case}\ e\ \mathtt{of}\ \mathtt{inl}(\mathbf{x}_1).e_1\ \mathtt{or}\ \mathtt{inr}(\mathbf{x}_2).e_2 : \tau}$$

$$\boxed{\times\text{I}} \quad \frac{\Theta, \Gamma \vdash e_1 : \tau_1 \qquad \Theta, \Gamma \vdash e_2 : \tau_2}{\Theta, \Gamma \vdash \langle e_1, e_2 \rangle : \tau_1 \times \tau_2}$$

$$\boxed{\times\text{E}_1} \quad \frac{\Theta, \Gamma \vdash e : \tau_1 \times \tau_2}{\Theta, \Gamma \vdash \mathtt{fst}(e) : \tau_1} \qquad \boxed{\times\text{E}_2} \quad \frac{\Theta, \Gamma \vdash e : \tau_1 \times \tau_2}{\Theta, \Gamma \vdash \mathtt{snd}(e) : \tau_2}$$

$$\boxed{\rightharpoonup\text{I}} \quad \frac{\Theta, \langle \Gamma, \mathbf{x} : \tau_1 \rangle \vdash e : \tau_2}{\Theta, \Gamma \vdash \lambda \mathbf{x} : \tau_1 . e : \tau_1 \rightharpoonup \tau_2}$$

$$\boxed{\rightharpoonup\text{E}} \quad \frac{\Theta, \Gamma \vdash e : \tau_1 \rightharpoonup \tau_2 \qquad \Theta, \Gamma \vdash e_1 : \tau_1}{\Theta, \Gamma \vdash e(e_1) : \tau_2}$$

$$\boxed{\mu\text{I}} \quad \frac{\Theta, \Gamma \vdash e : \tau[\mathrm{T} \mapsto \mu\mathrm{T}.\tau]}{\Theta, \Gamma \vdash \mathtt{intro}_{\mu\mathrm{T}.\tau}(e) : \mu\mathrm{T}.\tau} \quad \mathrm{T} \notin \Theta$$

$$\boxed{\mu\text{E}} \quad \frac{\Theta, \Gamma \vdash e : \mu\mathrm{T}.\tau}{\Theta, \Gamma \vdash \mathtt{elim}(e) : \tau[\mathrm{T} \mapsto \mu\mathrm{T}.\tau]}$$

Remark. If $\Theta, \Gamma \vdash e : \tau$ is derivable then so are $\Theta \vdash \Gamma$ and $\Theta \vdash \tau$.

The operators $\mathtt{intro}(\_)$ and $\mathtt{elim}(\_)$ can be used to *implement self application*, and thus allow the coding of the paradoxical combinators. For example, the call-by-value fixed-point operator corresponds to the expression

$$\begin{aligned} Z_{\sigma,\tau} &\equiv \lambda \mathbf{f} : (\sigma \rightharpoonup \tau) \rightharpoonup \sigma \rightharpoonup \tau .\ V_{\sigma,\tau}(\mathtt{intro}\ V_{\sigma,\tau}) : && ((\sigma \rightharpoonup \tau) \rightharpoonup \sigma \rightharpoonup \tau) \rightharpoonup \sigma \rightharpoonup \tau \\ V_{\sigma,\tau} &\equiv \lambda \mathbf{x} : \mu\mathrm{T}.\mathrm{T} \rightharpoonup \sigma \rightharpoonup \tau .\ \lambda \mathbf{y} : \sigma .\ \mathbf{f}\ (\mathtt{elim}\ \mathbf{x}\ \mathbf{x})\ \mathbf{y} : && (\mu\mathrm{T}.\mathrm{T} \rightharpoonup \sigma \rightharpoonup \tau) \rightharpoonup \sigma \rightharpoonup \tau . \end{aligned}$$

(For the operational behaviour of Z see page 151.)

The typing discipline guarantees the following properties:

Lemma 8.1.1 (Unique Type) If $\Theta, \Gamma \vdash e : \tau$ and $\Theta, \Gamma \vdash e : \tau'$ are derivable then $\tau \equiv \tau'$. □

Lemma 8.1.2 (Substitution) If the judgements $\Theta, \langle \Gamma, \mathbf{x} : \tau' \rangle \vdash e : \tau$ and $\Theta, \Gamma \vdash e' : \tau'$ are derivable then so is $\Theta, \Gamma \vdash e[\mathbf{x} \mapsto e'] : \tau$. □

8.2 Operational Semantics

As it is now common practice after [Plo81], the operational semantics of expressions is given by a binary *evaluation* relation on expressions ($\leadsto$) defined by induction on the structure of expressions. The rules for *call-by-value* evaluation are:

$$\boxed{\text{var}} \quad \frac{}{\mathtt{x} \leadsto \mathtt{x}}$$

$$\boxed{+\text{Il}} \quad \frac{e \leadsto v}{\mathtt{inl}(e) \leadsto \mathtt{inl}(v)} \qquad \boxed{+\text{Ir}} \quad \frac{e \leadsto v}{\mathtt{inr}(e) \leadsto \mathtt{inr}(v)}$$

$$\boxed{+\text{El}} \quad \frac{e \leadsto \mathtt{inl}(v) \qquad e_1[\mathtt{x}_1 \mapsto v] \leadsto v'}{\mathtt{case}\ e\ \mathtt{of}\ \mathtt{inl}(\mathtt{x}_1).e_1\ \mathtt{or}\ \mathtt{inr}(\mathtt{x}_2).e_2 \leadsto v'}$$

$$\boxed{+\text{Er}} \quad \frac{e \leadsto \mathtt{inr}(v) \qquad e_2[\mathtt{x}_2 \mapsto v] \leadsto v'}{\mathtt{case}\ e\ \mathtt{of}\ \mathtt{inl}(\mathtt{x}_1).e_1\ \mathtt{or}\ \mathtt{inr}(\mathtt{x}_2).e_2 \leadsto v'}$$

$$\boxed{\times\text{I}} \quad \frac{e_1 \leadsto v_1 \qquad e_2 \leadsto v_2}{\langle e_1, e_2 \rangle \leadsto \langle v_1, v_2 \rangle}$$

$$\boxed{\times\text{E}_1} \quad \frac{e \leadsto \langle v_1, v_2 \rangle}{\mathtt{fst}(e) \leadsto v_1} \qquad \boxed{\times\text{E}_2} \quad \frac{e \leadsto \langle v_1, v_2 \rangle}{\mathtt{snd}(e) \leadsto v_2}$$

$$\boxed{\rightharpoonup\text{I}} \quad \frac{}{\lambda\mathtt{x}.e \leadsto \lambda\mathtt{x}.e}$$

$$\boxed{\rightharpoonup\text{E}} \quad \frac{e_1 \leadsto \lambda\mathtt{x}.e \qquad e_2 \leadsto v \qquad e[\mathtt{x} \mapsto v] \leadsto v'}{e_1(e_2) \leadsto v'}$$

$$\boxed{\mu\text{I}} \quad \frac{e \leadsto v}{\mathtt{intro}(e) \leadsto \mathtt{intro}(v)}$$

$$\boxed{\mu\text{E}} \quad \frac{e \leadsto \mathtt{intro}(v)}{\mathtt{elim}(e) \leadsto v}$$

The expressions v such that $v \leadsto v$, called ***values***, are characterised by the grammar,

$$v \in \text{Values} \quad ::= \quad \mathtt{x} \mid \mathtt{inl}_{\tau_1,\tau_2}(v) \mid \mathtt{inr}_{\tau_1,\tau_2}(v) \mid \langle v_1, v_2 \rangle \mid \lambda\mathtt{x} : \tau.\, e \mid \mathtt{intro}_{\mu\mathtt{T}.\tau}(v).$$

The notion of program:

Definition 8.2.1 A *program* p is an expression such that $\vdash p : \tau$ for some type τ. □

Program values are important for understanding the nature of types. For example, $\mathtt{0}$ and $\mathtt{1}$ are not exciting types but for different reasons: $\mathtt{0}$ has no program values, whilst $\mathtt{1}$ has, for example, the program value $\lambda\mathtt{x}.\mathtt{x}$.

An interesting program is the call-by-value fixed-point operator Z (see page 149); it evaluates as follows:

1. $Z \rightsquigarrow Z$.
2. For every value v,
$$Zv \quad \rightsquigarrow \quad \lambda \mathtt{y}.\, v\,\big(\mathtt{elim}(\mathtt{intro}V[\mathtt{f} \mapsto v])\,(\mathtt{intro}V[\mathtt{f} \mapsto v])\big)\,\mathtt{y}.$$
3. For every value v, the following rule is derivable:
$$\frac{Z(\lambda \mathtt{x}.\, e) \rightsquigarrow X \qquad e[\mathtt{x} \mapsto X]\, v \rightsquigarrow v'}{Z\,(\lambda \mathtt{x}.\, e)\, v \rightsquigarrow v'}\ .$$

Some properties of the evaluation relation are:

Proposition 8.2.2 $\rightsquigarrow$ is a partial computable function from Expressions to Values. □

Convention. We write $\Theta, \Gamma \vdash e \rightsquigarrow v : \tau$ to indicate that $\Theta, \Gamma \vdash e : \tau$ and that $e \rightsquigarrow v$. We also write $\Theta, \Gamma \vdash e\checkmark : \tau$ when $\Theta, \Gamma \vdash e \rightsquigarrow v : \tau$ for some value v.

Proposition 8.2.3 (Subject Reduction) If $\Theta, \Gamma \vdash e \rightsquigarrow v : \tau$ then $\Theta, \Gamma \vdash v : \tau$. □

8.3 Categorical Models

Essentially, the categorical structure needed to interpret FPC is a parameterised algebraically compact partial cartesian closed category with coproducts.

Definition 8.3.1 For cartesian $\mathcal{V}$, a *$\mathcal{V}$-model of FPC* is specified by

- a domain structure $(\mathcal{K}, \mathcal{D})$,
- a $\mathcal{V}$-category $\mathcal{L}$,
- $\mathcal{V}$-functors $\underline{+}, \underline{\otimes} : \mathcal{L} \times \mathcal{L} \to \mathcal{L}$ and $\underline{\rightharpoonup} : \mathcal{L}^{op} \times \mathcal{L} \to \mathcal{L}$, and
- mappings $(\_)^{\dagger}$ and $\iota^{(-)_0}$ associating every $\mathcal{V}$-functor $F : \mathcal{A} \times \mathcal{L} \to \mathcal{L}$ with a $\mathcal{V}$-functor $F^{\dagger} : \mathcal{A} \to \mathcal{L}$ and a natural transformation $\iota^{F_0} : F_0 \langle \mathrm{Id}, F_0^{\dagger} \rangle \stackrel{.}{\to} F_0^{\dagger}$

such that

- $p(\mathcal{K}, \mathcal{D}) \cong \mathcal{L}_0$,
- the underlying functors $+, \otimes : p\mathcal{K} \times p\mathcal{K} \to p\mathcal{K}$ and $\rightharpoonup : p\mathcal{K}^{op} \times p\mathcal{K} \to p\mathcal{K}$ of $\underline{+}, \underline{\otimes}$ and $\underline{\rightharpoonup}$ are, respectively, coproduct, partial product and partial exponential functors, and
- $\mathcal{L}$ is parameterised $\mathcal{V}$-algebraically compact with parameterisation $\big((\_)^{\dagger}, \iota^{(-)_0}\big)$. □

Remark. $p\mathcal{K}$ has zero object 0 (viz., a free $\mathrm{Id}_{p\mathcal{K}}$-algebra), $\mathcal{K}$ has terminal object $1 = 0 \rightharpoonup 0$ (see Proposition 5.3.2 (2)) and $J \cong \_ \otimes 1 : \mathcal{K} \to p\mathcal{K}$ has right adjoint.

8.4 Denotational Semantics

The interpretation of FPC in a categorical model is provided. Roughly speaking, well-formed types, $\Theta \vdash \tau$, are interpreted as symmetric functors $[\![\Theta \vdash \tau]\!] : \breve{p\mathcal{K}}^{|\Theta|} \to \breve{p\mathcal{K}}$ whilst well-formed expressions, $\Theta, \Gamma \vdash e : \tau$, are interpreted as indexed families of partial maps

$$\{[\![\Theta, \Gamma \vdash e : \tau]\!]_A : [\![\Theta \vdash \Gamma]\!]_2(A) \rightharpoonup [\![\Theta \vdash \tau]\!]_2(A)\}$$

where $A \in |\breve{p\mathcal{K}}|^{|\Theta|}$ is symmetric (that is, $A = ((X_1, X_1), \ldots, (X_{|\Theta|}, X_{|\Theta|}))$ for some $X \in |p\mathcal{K}|^{|\Theta|}$).

Throughout this section, we let $\mathcal{V}$ be cartesian and work with a fixed $\mathcal{V}$-model of FPC.

Interpretation of Types

Let us recall some notation and introduce more. We write $\breve{\mathcal{L}}$ for $\mathcal{L}^{op} \times \mathcal{L}$ and for a $\mathcal{V}$-functor $F : \breve{\mathcal{L}} \times \breve{\mathcal{L}} \to \mathcal{L}$ we write $\breve{F}$ for the symmetric $\mathcal{V}$-functor

$$\langle F \circ (\_)^{\S}, F\rangle : \breve{\mathcal{L}} \times \breve{\mathcal{L}} \to \breve{\mathcal{L}}$$

where $(\_)^{\S}$ is the $\mathcal{V}$-functor $\langle \Pi_2, \Pi_1\rangle \times \langle \Pi_2, \Pi_1\rangle : \breve{\mathcal{L}} \times \breve{\mathcal{L}} \to (\breve{\mathcal{L}} \times \breve{\mathcal{L}})^{op}$ (for details see Section 6.3).

Further, for a $\mathcal{V}$-functor $F : \mathcal{L} \times \mathcal{L} \to \mathcal{L}$ (resp. $F : \mathcal{L}^{op} \times \mathcal{L} \to \mathcal{L}$), the symmetric $\mathcal{V}$-functor $(F \circ (\Pi_2 \times \Pi_2))\breve{} : \breve{\mathcal{L}} \times \breve{\mathcal{L}} \to \breve{\mathcal{L}}$ (resp. $(F \circ (\Pi_1 \times \Pi_2))\breve{} : \breve{\mathcal{L}} \times \breve{\mathcal{L}} \to \breve{\mathcal{L}}$) is denoted $\breve{\breve{F}}$.

Definition 8.4.1 (Interpretation of Well-Formed Types) $\underline{[\![\Theta \vdash \tau]\!]} : \breve{\mathcal{L}}^{|\Theta|} \to \breve{\mathcal{L}}$.

- $\underline{[\![\Theta \vdash \Theta_i]\!]} = \Pi_i \qquad (1 \leq i \leq |\Theta|)$.

- $\underline{[\![\Theta \vdash \tau_1 \star \tau_2]\!]} = [\![\star]\!]\breve{\breve{}} \circ \langle \underline{[\![\Theta \vdash \tau_1]\!]}, \underline{[\![\Theta \vdash \tau_2]\!]}\rangle \qquad$ where $[\![\star]\!] = \begin{cases} \underline{+} & \text{, if } \star = + \\ \underline{\otimes} & \text{, if } \star = \times \\ \underline{\rightharpoonup} & \text{, if } \star = \rightharpoonup \end{cases}$.

- $\underline{[\![\Theta \vdash \mu \mathrm{T}.\tau]\!]} = [\![\Theta, \mathrm{T} \vdash \tau]\!]^{\ddagger}$. □

Remark. The parameterisation $(\_)^{\ddagger}$ on $\breve{\mathcal{L}}$ is the one induced, by Corollary 6.2.7 (2) and Theorem 6.4.4, from the given parameterisation on $\mathcal{L}$.

By construction and because of Theorem 6.4.4:

Proposition 8.4.2 $\underline{[\![\Theta \vdash \tau]\!]}$ is a symmetric $\mathcal{V}$-functor. □

Convention. Given a $\mathcal{V}$-functor $F : \mathcal{X} \to \mathcal{A}_1 \times \mathcal{A}_2$, for $i = 1, 2$, we write F_i for the composite $\Pi_i \circ F : \mathcal{X} \to \mathcal{A}_i$. And given $\eta : F \dot{\to} G : \mathcal{X} \to \mathcal{A}_1 \times \mathcal{A}_2$, for $i = 1, 2$, we write η_i for $\Pi_i \eta : F_i \dot{\to} G_i : \mathcal{X} \to \mathcal{A}_i$.

For $F : \mathcal{L} \times \mathcal{L} \to \mathcal{L}$, the equality $\Pi_i \circ \breve{F} = F \circ (\Pi_i \times \Pi_i)$ holds for $i = 1, 2$ and for $F : \mathcal{L}^{op} \times \mathcal{L} \to \mathcal{L}$, so do the equalities $\Pi_1 \circ \breve{F} = F \circ (\Pi_2 \times \Pi_1)$ and $\Pi_2 \circ \breve{F} = F \circ (\Pi_1 \times \Pi_2)$. Hence:

Proposition 8.4.3 For $i = 1, 2$,

$$\underline{[\![\Theta, \Gamma \vdash \tau_1 \star \tau_2]\!]}_i = [\![\star]\!] \circ \left\langle \underline{[\![\Theta, \Gamma \vdash \tau_1]\!]}_i, \underline{[\![\Theta, \Gamma \vdash \tau_2]\!]}_i \right\rangle \quad \text{where } \star \in \{+, \times\}.$$

Also,

$$\begin{aligned} \underline{[\![\Theta, \Gamma \vdash \tau_1 \rightharpoonup \tau_2]\!]}_1 &= \underline{\rightharpoonup} \circ \left\langle \underline{[\![\Theta, \Gamma \vdash \tau_1]\!]}_2, \underline{[\![\Theta, \Gamma \vdash \tau_2]\!]}_1 \right\rangle \\ \underline{[\![\Theta, \Gamma \vdash \tau_1 \rightharpoonup \tau_2]\!]}_2 &= \underline{\rightharpoonup} \circ \left\langle \underline{[\![\Theta, \Gamma \vdash \tau_1]\!]}_1, \underline{[\![\Theta, \Gamma \vdash \tau_2]\!]}_2 \right\rangle. \end{aligned}$$ □

Convention. To ease the notation, we will write $[\![\Theta \vdash \tau]\!]$ for the composite

$$p\breve{\mathcal{K}}^{|\Theta|} \cong \breve{\mathcal{L}_0}^{|\Theta|} \xrightarrow{\underline{[\![\Theta \vdash \tau]\!]}_0} \breve{\mathcal{L}_0} \cong p\breve{\mathcal{K}}_0.$$

The interpretation of types respects a substitution lemma (Lemma 8.4.4) establishing that the interpretation of the substitution of a type τ_2 for a variable T in a type τ_1 is *coherent* with the evaluation of the interpretation of the type τ_1 parameterised in T at the interpretation of the type τ_2. That is, evaluation is the semantic counterpart of syntactic substitution.

The substitution lemma is needed to interpret expressions. For example, we want

$$[\![\vdash \mathtt{elim}(e) : \tau[\mathrm{T} \mapsto \mu\mathrm{T}.\tau]]\!] : 1 \rightharpoonup [\![\vdash \tau[\mathrm{T} \mapsto \mu\mathrm{T}.\tau]]\!]_2 \tag{8.1}$$

to be obtained from $[\![\vdash e : \mu\mathrm{T}.\tau]\!] : 1 \rightharpoonup [\![\vdash \mu\mathrm{T}.\tau]\!]_2$ by *unfolding* the recursive type $\mu\mathrm{T}.\tau$; that is, by composing with the isomorphism $[\![\vdash \mu\mathrm{T}.\tau]\!]_2 \cong [\![\mathrm{T} \vdash \tau]\!]_2([\![\vdash \mu\mathrm{T}.\tau]\!])$. But then, to satisfy (8.1) we further need

$$[\![\vdash \tau[\mathrm{T} \mapsto \mu\mathrm{T}.\tau]]\!]_2 \cong [\![\mathrm{T} \vdash \tau]\!]_2([\![\vdash \mu\mathrm{T}.\tau]\!]).$$

Lemma 8.4.4 (Substitution Lemma) There exists a canonical natural isomorphism

$$\beta : \ [\![\Theta \vdash \tau_1[\mathrm{T} \mapsto \tau_2]]\!] \ \cong \ [\![\Theta, \mathrm{T} \vdash \tau_1]\!] \circ \langle \mathrm{Id}, [\![\Theta \vdash \tau_2]\!] \rangle$$

such that $\beta^{\S}_A = \beta^{-1}_A$ for every symmetric A.

PROOF: By induction on the derivation of τ_1 (see Appendix A). □

Remark. If $(\_)^{\dagger}_0$ is *homogeneous* (in the sense that for every symmetric $\mathcal{V}$-functors $F : \breve{\mathcal{L}}^{m+1} \to \breve{\mathcal{L}}$ and $G : \breve{\mathcal{L}}^n \to \breve{\mathcal{L}}^m$, $\big(F \circ (G \times \mathrm{Id})\big)^{\dagger}_0 = F^{\dagger}_0 \circ G_0$ —c.f. (6.3) on page 111— then so is $(\_)^{\ddagger}_0$; moreover, in this case, $\beta = \mathrm{id}$.

Interpretation of Expression Contexts

The interpretation of types is extended to expression contexts by taking the partial product of the interpretation of the types constituting the context. In particular, the empty context is interpreted as the terminal object in the category of total maps.

Definition 8.4.5 (Interpretation of Well-Formed Expression Contexts) $\underline{[\![\Theta \vdash \Gamma]\!]} : \breve{\mathcal{L}}^{|\Theta|} \to \breve{\mathcal{L}}$.

- $\underline{[\![\Theta \vdash \langle\rangle]\!]} = K(1,1)$.
- $\underline{[\![\Theta \vdash \Gamma, \mathbf{x} : \tau]\!]} = \breve{\underline{\otimes}} \circ \langle \underline{[\![\Theta \vdash \Gamma]\!]}, \underline{[\![\Theta \vdash \tau]\!]} \rangle$. □

The basic properties of the interpretation of types extend to the interpretation of expression contexts:

Proposition 8.4.6 1. $\underline{[\![\Theta \vdash \Gamma]\!]}$ is a symmetric $\mathcal{V}$-functor.

2. Let $\Gamma \equiv \mathbf{x}_1 : \tau_1, \ldots, \mathbf{x}_n : \tau_n$. Then, for $i = 1, 2$,

$$\begin{aligned} \underline{[\![\Theta \vdash \langle\rangle]\!]}_i &= K1, \\ \underline{[\![\Theta \vdash \Gamma, \mathbf{x} : \tau]\!]}_i &= \underline{\otimes} \circ \langle \underline{[\![\Theta \vdash \Gamma]\!]}_i, \underline{[\![\Theta \vdash \tau]\!]}_i \rangle. \end{aligned}$$ □

Interpretation of Expressions

The interpretation of expressions is defined in the standard way. Roughly speaking, variables correspond to projections, `inl`/`inr` to coproducts injections, `case` to coproduct selection, $\langle \_, \_ \rangle$ to partial pairing, `fst`/`snd` to projections, $\lambda\mathbf{x}.\_$ to currying, $\_(\_)$ to evaluation and `intro`/`elim` to folding/unfolding a recursive type. This is formalised in the definition below which should be understood in conjunction with Proposition 8.4.8.

Definition 8.4.7 (Interpretation of Well-Formed Expressions)

$$[\![\Theta,\Gamma \vdash e:\tau]\!] \quad = \quad \{[\![\Theta,\Gamma \vdash e:\tau]\!]_A \mid A \in |\, p\breve{\mathcal{K}}\, |^{|\Theta|} \text{ is symmetric}\}$$

is defined as follows:

- $[\![\Theta,\Gamma \vdash \Gamma_i]\!] = \pi_i \qquad (1 \le i \le |\, \Gamma \,|)$.
- $[\![\Theta,\Gamma \vdash \texttt{inl}(e):\tau_1+\tau_2]\!] = \amalg_1 \circ [\![\Theta,\Gamma \vdash e:\tau_1]\!]$.
- $[\![\Theta,\Gamma \vdash \texttt{inr}(e):\tau_1+\tau_2]\!] = \amalg_2 \circ [\![\Theta,\Gamma \vdash e:\tau_2]\!]$.
- $[\![\Theta,\Gamma \vdash \texttt{case}\ e\ \texttt{of}\ \texttt{inl}(\mathbf{x}_1).e_1\ \texttt{or}\ \texttt{inr}(\mathbf{x}_2).e_2:\tau]\!]$
  $= [[\![\Theta,\langle\Gamma,\mathbf{x}_1:\tau_1\rangle \vdash e_1:\tau]\!],[\![\Theta,\langle\Gamma,\mathbf{x}_2:\tau_2\rangle \vdash e_2:\tau]\!]] \circ \delta \circ \langle\!\langle \mathrm{id}, [\![\Theta,\Gamma \vdash e:\tau_1+\tau_2]\!]\rangle\!\rangle$
  where δ is the canonical natural isomorphism
  $[\![\Theta \vdash \Gamma]\!]_2 \otimes ([\![\Theta \vdash \tau_1]\!]_2 \dotplus [\![\Theta \vdash \tau_2]\!]_2) \cong ([\![\Theta \vdash \Gamma]\!]_2 \otimes [\![\Theta \vdash \tau_1]\!]_2) + ([\![\Theta \vdash \Gamma]\!]_2 \otimes [\![\Theta \vdash \tau_1]\!]_2)$.
- $[\![\Theta,\Gamma \vdash \langle e_1,e_2\rangle:\tau_1\times\tau_2]\!] = \langle\!\langle [\![\Theta,\Gamma \vdash e_1:\tau_1]\!],[\![\Theta,\Gamma \vdash e_2:\tau_2]\!]\rangle\!\rangle$.
- $[\![\Theta,\Gamma \vdash \texttt{fst}(e):\tau_1]\!] = \pi_1 \circ [\![\Theta,\Gamma \vdash e:\tau_1\times\tau_2]\!]$.
- $[\![\Theta,\Gamma \vdash \texttt{snd}(e):\tau_2]\!] = \pi_2 \circ [\![\Theta,\Gamma \vdash e:\tau_1\times\tau_2]\!]$.
- $[\![\Theta,\Gamma \vdash \lambda\mathbf{x}.e:\tau_1 \rightharpoonup \tau_2]\!] = p\lambda([\![\Theta,\langle\Gamma,\mathbf{x}:\tau_1\rangle \vdash e:\tau_2]\!])$.
- $[\![\Theta,\Gamma \vdash e(e_1):\tau_2]\!] = \varepsilon \circ \langle\!\langle [\![\Theta,\Gamma \vdash e:\tau_1 \rightharpoonup \tau_2]\!],[\![\Theta,\Gamma \vdash e_1:\tau_1]\!]\rangle\!\rangle$.
- $[\![\Theta,\Gamma \vdash \texttt{intro}(e):\mu\mathrm{T}.\tau]\!] = I \circ [\![\Theta,\Gamma \vdash e:\tau[\mathrm{T}\mapsto\mu\mathrm{T}.\tau]]\!]$ where $I = (\varphi^{[\![\Theta,\,\mathrm{T}\vdash\tau]\!]} \circ \beta)_2$.
- $[\![\Theta,\Gamma \vdash \texttt{elim}(e):\tau[\mathrm{T}\mapsto\mu\mathrm{T}.\tau]]\!] = E \circ [\![\Theta,\Gamma \vdash e:\mu\mathrm{T}.\tau]\!]$ where $E = (\varphi^{[\![\Theta,\,\mathrm{T}\vdash\tau]\!]} \circ \beta)_1$.

□

Remark. By Theorem 6.4.4 and Lemma 8.4.4, I and E above are mutual inverses.

The interpretation of expressions is well-defined:

Proposition 8.4.8 For every symmetric $A \in |\, p\breve{\mathcal{K}}\, |^{|\Theta|}$,

$$[\![\Theta,\Gamma \vdash e:\tau]\!]_A : [\![\Theta \vdash \Gamma]\!]_2(A) \rightharpoonup [\![\Theta \vdash \tau]\!]_2(A).$$

PROOF: By induction on the derivation of $\Theta,\Gamma \vdash e:\tau$.

- $\Theta,\Gamma \vdash \Gamma_i$ where $\Gamma \equiv \mathbf{x}_1:\tau_1,\ldots,\mathbf{x}_n:\tau_n$ and $1 \le i \le n$.

$$[\![\Theta,\Gamma \vdash \Gamma_i]\!]_A = \pi_i : [\![\Theta \vdash \tau_1]\!]_2(A) \otimes \ldots \otimes [\![\Theta \vdash \tau_n]\!]_2(A) \to [\![\Theta \vdash \tau_i]\!]_2(A)$$

Since

$$[\![\Theta \vdash \Gamma]\!]_2 = [\![\Theta \vdash \tau_1]\!]_2 \otimes \ldots \otimes [\![\Theta \vdash \tau_n]\!]_2$$

we are done.

- $\Theta, \Gamma \vdash \texttt{inl}(e) : \tau_1 + \tau_2$.
  By induction,
$$[\![\Theta, \Gamma \vdash e : \tau_1]\!]_A : [\![\Theta \vdash \Gamma]\!]_2(A) \rightharpoonup [\![\Theta \vdash \tau_1]\!]_2(A).$$
  Since
$$\amalg_1 : [\![\Theta \vdash \tau_1]\!]_2(A) \to [\![\Theta \vdash \tau_1]\!]_2(A) + [\![\Theta \vdash \tau_2]\!]_2(A)$$
  and
$$[\![\Theta \vdash \tau_1 + \tau_2]\!]_2 = [\![\Theta \vdash \tau_1]\!]_2 + [\![\Theta \vdash \tau_2]\!]_2$$
  we are done.
- $\Theta, \Gamma \vdash \texttt{inr}(e) : \tau_1 + \tau_2$. Analogous to the previous case.
- $\Theta, \Gamma \vdash \texttt{case}\ e\ \texttt{of}\ \texttt{inl}(\mathbf{x}_1).e_1\ \texttt{or}\ \texttt{inr}(\mathbf{x}_2).e_2 : \tau$.
  By induction,
$$[\![\Theta, \Gamma \vdash e : \tau_1 + \tau_2]\!]_A : [\![\Theta \vdash \Gamma]\!]_2(A) \rightharpoonup [\![\Theta \vdash \tau_1 + \tau_2]\!]_2(A)$$
  and, for $i = 1, 2$,
$$[\![\Theta, \langle \Gamma, \mathbf{x}_i : \tau_i \rangle \vdash e_i : \tau_i]\!]_A : [\![\Theta \vdash \Gamma, \mathbf{x}_i : \tau_i]\!]_2(A) \rightharpoonup [\![\Theta \vdash \tau]\!]_2(A).$$
  Since
$$[\![\Theta \vdash \tau_1 + \tau_2]\!]_2 = [\![\Theta \vdash \Gamma]\!]_2 + [\![\Theta \vdash \Gamma]\!]_2$$
  and
$$[\![\Theta \vdash \Gamma]\!]_2 \otimes [\![\Theta \vdash \tau_i]\!]_2 = [\![\Theta \vdash \Gamma, \mathbf{x}_i : \tau_i]\!]_2$$
  we are done.
- $\Theta, \Gamma \vdash \texttt{fst}(e) : \tau_1$.
  By induction,
$$[\![\Theta, \Gamma \vdash e : \tau_1 \times \tau_2]\!]_A : [\![\Theta \vdash \Gamma]\!]_2(A) \rightharpoonup [\![\Theta \vdash \tau_1 \times \tau_2]\!]_2(A).$$
  Since
$$[\![\Theta \vdash \tau_1 \times \tau_2]\!]_2 = [\![\Theta \vdash \tau_1]\!]_2 \otimes [\![\Theta \vdash \tau_2]\!]_2$$
  and
$$\pi_1 : [\![\Theta \vdash \tau_1]\!]_2(A) \otimes [\![\Theta \vdash \tau_2]\!]_2(A) \to [\![\Theta \vdash \tau_1]\!]_2(A)$$
  we are done.
- $\Theta, \Gamma \vdash \texttt{snd}(e) : \tau_2$. Analogous to the previous case.

- $\Theta, \Gamma \vdash \langle e_1, e_2 \rangle : \tau_1 \times \tau_2$.
  By induction, for $i = 1, 2$,

  $$[\![\Theta, \Gamma \vdash e_i : \tau_i]\!]_A : [\![\Theta \vdash \Gamma]\!]_2(A) \rightharpoonup [\![\Theta \vdash \tau_i]\!]_2(A).$$

  Since

  $$[\![\Theta \vdash \tau_1]\!]_2 \otimes [\![\Theta \vdash \tau_2]\!]_2 = [\![\Theta \vdash \tau_1 \times \tau_2]\!]_2$$

  we are done.

- $\Theta, \Gamma \vdash \lambda \mathbf{x}.e : \tau_1 \Rightarrow \tau_2$.
  By induction,

  $$[\![\Theta, \langle \Gamma, \mathbf{x}; \tau_1 \rangle \vdash e : \tau_2]\!]_A : [\![\Theta \vdash \Gamma, \mathbf{x} : \tau_1]\!]_2(A) \rightharpoonup [\![\Theta \vdash \tau_2]\!]_2(A).$$

  Since

  $$[\![\Theta \vdash \Gamma]\!]_2 \otimes [\![\Theta \vdash \tau_1]\!]_2 = [\![\Theta \vdash \Gamma, \mathbf{x} : \tau_1]\!]_2$$

  it follows that

  $$p\lambda([\![\Theta, \langle \Gamma, \mathbf{x}; \tau_1 \rangle \vdash e : \tau_2]\!]_A) : [\![\Theta \vdash \Gamma]\!]_2(A) \to [\![\Theta \vdash \tau_1]\!]_2(A) \Rightarrow [\![\Theta \vdash \tau_2]\!]_2(A).$$

  Finally

  $$[\![\Theta \vdash \tau_1]\!]_2(A) \Rightarrow [\![\Theta \vdash \tau_2]\!]_2(A) = [\![\Theta \vdash \tau_1]\!]_1(A) \Rightarrow [\![\Theta \vdash \tau_2]\!]_2(A) = [\![\Theta \vdash \tau_1 \Rightarrow \tau_2]\!]_2(A)$$

  and we are done.

- $\Theta, \Gamma \vdash e(e_1) : \tau_2$.
  By induction,

  $$[\![\Theta, \Gamma \vdash e : \tau_1 \Rightarrow \tau_2]\!]_A : [\![\Theta \vdash \Gamma]\!]_2(A) \rightharpoonup [\![\Theta \vdash \tau_1 \Rightarrow \tau_2]\!]_2(A)$$

  and

  $$[\![\Theta, \Gamma \vdash e_1 : \tau_1]\!]_A : [\![\Theta \vdash \Gamma]\!]_2(A) \rightharpoonup [\![\Theta \vdash \tau_1]\!]_2(A).$$

  Since

  $$[\![\Theta \vdash \tau_1 \Rightarrow \tau_2]\!]_2 = [\![\Theta \vdash \tau_1]\!]_1 \Rightarrow [\![\Theta \vdash \tau_2]\!]_2$$

  and

  $$[\![\Theta \vdash \tau_1]\!]_2(A) = [\![\Theta \vdash \tau_1]\!]_1(A)$$

  we are done.

- $\Theta, \Gamma \vdash \mathtt{intro}(e) : \mu\mathrm{T}.\tau$.
  By induction,

$$\llbracket \Theta, \Gamma \vdash e : \tau[\mathrm{T} \mapsto \mu\mathrm{T}.\tau] \rrbracket_A : \llbracket \Theta \vdash \Gamma \rrbracket_2(A) \rightharpoonup \llbracket \Theta \vdash \tau[\mathrm{T} \mapsto \mu\mathrm{T}.\tau] \rrbracket_2(A).$$

  Since

$$(\beta_A)_2 : \llbracket \Theta \vdash \tau[\mathrm{T} \mapsto \mu\mathrm{T}.\tau] \rrbracket_2(A) \cong \llbracket \Theta, \mathrm{T} \vdash \tau \rrbracket_2(A, \llbracket \Theta \vdash \mu\mathrm{T}.\tau \rrbracket A)$$

  and

$$(\varphi_A^{\llbracket \Theta,\, \mathrm{T} \vdash \tau \rrbracket})_2 : \llbracket \Theta, \mathrm{T} \vdash \tau \rrbracket_2(A, \llbracket \Theta, \mathrm{T} \vdash \tau \rrbracket^{\ddagger} A) \cong \llbracket \Theta, \mathrm{T} \vdash \tau \rrbracket_2^{\ddagger}(A)$$

  we are done.

- $\Theta, \Gamma \vdash \mathtt{elim}(e) : \tau[\mathrm{T} \mapsto \mu\mathrm{T}.\tau]$.
  By induction,

$$\llbracket \Theta, \Gamma \vdash e : \mu\mathrm{T}.\tau \rrbracket_A : \llbracket \Theta \vdash \Gamma \rrbracket_2(A) \rightharpoonup \llbracket \Theta \vdash \mu\mathrm{T}.\tau \rrbracket_2(A).$$

  Since

$$\llbracket \Theta \vdash \mu\mathrm{T}.\tau \rrbracket_2(A) = \llbracket \Theta, \mathrm{T} \vdash \tau \rrbracket_1^{\ddagger}(A),$$

$$(\varphi_A^{\llbracket \Theta,\, \mathrm{T} \vdash \tau \rrbracket})_1 : \llbracket \Theta, \mathrm{T} \vdash \tau \rrbracket_1^{\ddagger}(A) \cong \llbracket \Theta, \mathrm{T} \vdash \tau \rrbracket_1(A, \llbracket \Theta, \mathrm{T} \vdash \tau \rrbracket^{\ddagger} A),$$

$$(\beta_A)_1 : \llbracket \Theta, \mathrm{T} \vdash \tau \rrbracket_1(A, \llbracket \Theta \vdash \mu\mathrm{T}.\tau \rrbracket A) \cong \llbracket \Theta \vdash \tau[\mathrm{T} \mapsto \mu\mathrm{T}.\tau] \rrbracket_1(A)$$

  and

$$\llbracket \Theta \vdash \tau[\mathrm{T} \mapsto \mu\mathrm{T}.\tau] \rrbracket_1(A) = \llbracket \Theta \vdash \tau[\mathrm{T} \mapsto \mu\mathrm{T}.\tau] \rrbracket_2(A)$$

  we are done. □

8.5 Two Axiomatisations of Models

We impose axioms on domain structures so that their induced categories of partial maps are models of FPC. We will be concerned with two classes of models:

1. *Domain-theoretic models* (Subsection 8.5.1), corresponding to **Cpo**-domain-structures whose induced category of partial maps is a **Cpo**-model with respect to the approximation order and where algebraic compactness arises from the limit/colimit coincidence.

2. *Axiomatic $\mathcal{K}_*$-models* (Subsection 8.5.2), meaning models enriched over the full subcategory of the category of total maps of all those objects embodying undefinedness. (The approach taken here has been guided by the (more abstract) approach of [Sim92]).

8.5.1 Domain-Theoretic Models

Definition 8.5.1 A *domain-theoretic model of FPC* is specified by a uniform domain structure $(\mathcal{K}, \mathcal{D})$ and a **Cpo**-enrichment $\sqsubseteq$ for $\mathcal{K}$ satisfying:

AXIOM 1. $(\mathcal{K}, \sqsubseteq)$ has chosen binary **Poset**-coproducts.

AXIOM 2. $(\mathcal{K}, \sqsubseteq)$ has chosen binary **Poset**-products.

AXIOM 3. $(p\mathcal{K}, \precsim)$ is a **Poset**-category with chosen **Poset**-partial-exponentials.

AXIOM 4. $p\mathcal{K}$ has a chosen zero object.

AXIOM 5. $\mathcal{K}$ has chosen colimits of ω-chains of embeddings. □

Theorem 8.5.2 If $(\mathcal{K}, \mathcal{D}, \sqsubseteq)$ is a domain-theoretic model of FPC then $(p(\mathcal{K}, \mathcal{D}), \precsim)$ is a **Cpo**-model of FPC.

PROOF: Since, by Proposition 5.3.1 and Proposition 5.3.2 (2), $\mathcal{K}$ has terminal object it follows, by Axiom 3, that $J \dashv L : p\mathcal{K} \to \mathcal{K}$ is a **Poset**-adjunction.

Then, as $\mathcal{K}$ is **Cpo**-enriched, by Corollary 4.5.3, so is $p\mathcal{K}$.

Moreover, by Propositions 5.3.2 (1) and 5.3.3 the zero is an ep-zero and by Proposition 5.4.4 and Axiom 5, $p\mathcal{K}$ has colimits of ω-chains of embeddings. Hence, by Axiom 4 and Corollary 7.2.4, $p\mathcal{K}$ is parameterised **Cpo**-algebraically compact.

Finally, by Proposition 5.3.13, the binary coproduct functor is **Cpo**-enriched. By Proposition 5.1.3, using Corollary 5.2.5, the partial-product functor **Cpo**-enriches. And, since **Poset**-adjunctions between **Cpo**-categories are **Cpo**-adjunctions, it follows that the partial-exponential functor is **Cpo**-enriched. □

Example 8.5.3 For $\mathcal{W}$ a small **Cpo**-category, let $([\mathcal{W}, \mathbf{Cpo}], \sqsubseteq)$ be the **Cpo**-functor-category of **Cpo**-functors $\mathcal{W} \to \mathbf{Cpo}$ and natural transformations ordered pointwise, and let $\mathbf{\Sigma C}_{[\mathcal{W},\mathbf{Cpo}]}$ be the subcategory of $[\mathcal{W}, \mathbf{Cpo}]$ of all pointwise-admissible and cartesian natural transformations. Then, $([\mathcal{W}, \mathbf{Cpo}], \mathbf{\Sigma C}_{[\mathcal{W},\mathbf{Cpo}]}, \sqsubseteq)$ specifies a domain-theoretic model. □

8.5.2 Axiomatic $\mathcal{K}_*$-Models

Let $(\mathcal{K}, \mathcal{D})$ be a domain structure.

The first two axioms equip $p\mathcal{K}$ with the type constructors. In particular, we postulate the existence of a zero object which explicitly introduces undefinedness.

AXIOM 1. $\mathcal{K}$ has chosen binary coproducts $(+)$ and chosen binary products $(\times)$.

AXIOM 2. $p\mathcal{K}$ has a chosen zero object (0) and chosen partial exponentials $(\rightharpoonup)$.

Consequently, $\mathcal{K}$ has initial object (viz., 0), terminal object (viz., $1 = 0 \rightharpoonup 0$) and representation of partial maps (via $\eta, \varepsilon : J \dashv L : p\mathcal{K} \to \mathcal{K}$).

To state the rest of the axioms, those objects embodying undefinedness need to be identified. These have the characteristic feature that every partial map into them can be *completed* to a total map.

Definition 8.5.4 ([Ers73]) An object $A \in |\mathcal{K}|$ is said to be *complete* if for every $u : X \rightharpoonup A$ there exists $f : X \to A$ such that $u \subseteq f$. □

In the presence of lifting, complete objects are exactly those objects that are retracts of their lifting; the retraction being the way in which undefinedness is built-in the complete object.

Proposition 8.5.5 (c.f. [Mog88]) For $A, B \in |\mathcal{K}|$,

1. The following are equivalent:
   (a) A is complete.
   (b) A is a retract of LA in $\mathcal{K}$.
   (c) $\eta_A : A \rightarrowtail LA$ is a section in $\mathcal{K}$.
   (d) $\varepsilon_A \subseteq a$ for some total map $a : LA \to A$.
2. 1, LA and $A \rightharpoonup B$ are complete.
3. If A and B are complete then so is $A \times B$. □

Definition 8.5.6 Let $\mathcal{K}_*$ be the full subcategory of $\mathcal{K}$ of all complete objects. □

Remark. The above notation is adopted because complete objects have a *point that internalises undefinedness* (see Definition 8.5.9).

The previous proposition implies:

Corollary 8.5.7 $\mathcal{K}_*$ is cartesian. □

The third axiom states that, in a complete object, undefinedness is built-in in a unique way:

AXIOM 3. If A is a retract of LA in $\mathcal{K}$ via (η_A, f) and (η_A, g) then $f = g$.

Remark. Axiom 3 has been postulated on intuitive grounds and *not* for technical reasons. In fact, we could dispose of it provided that we endow complete objects with additional structure indicating the way in which undefinedness arises (i.e., considering Eilenberg-Moore algebras for the lifting monad).

Convention. For a complete object A, we will write ρ_A for the unique total map making A a retract of LA with section η_A.

Proposition 8.5.8 1. For $A \in |\mathcal{K}|$, $\rho_{LA} = L\varepsilon_A$.

2. For $A, B \in |\mathcal{K}|$, $\rho_{A \rightharpoonup B}$ is the transpose of

$$L(A \rightharpoonup B) \times A \stackrel{\varepsilon \otimes id}{\rightharpoonup} (A \rightharpoonup B) \times A \stackrel{\varepsilon}{\rightharpoonup} B.$$

3. For complete objects A and B,

$$\rho_{A \times B} = (L(A \times B) \stackrel{\langle L\pi_1, L\pi_2 \rangle}{\longrightarrow} LA \times LB \stackrel{\rho_A \times \rho_B}{\longrightarrow} A \times B). \qquad \square$$

Definition 8.5.9 The *least element* of a complete object A, is defined to be the total map $(1 \stackrel{\perp_A}{\longrightarrow} A) = (1 \to LA \stackrel{\rho_A}{\longrightarrow} A)$ where $1 \to LA$ represents the *zero map* $1 \rightharpoonup 0 \rightarrowtail A$. $\square$

Definition 8.5.10 A map between complete objects is *strict* if it preserves the least element. That is, $A \circ\!\!\rightarrow B$ if $(1 \stackrel{\perp}{\longrightarrow} A \to B) = (1 \stackrel{\perp}{\longrightarrow} B)$. $\square$

Examples of strict maps are: id_A, $A \to 1$ and ρ_A for every complete object A, Lu for every partial map u and the projections $\pi_i : A_1 \times A_2 \to A_i$ for $i = 1, 2$. Moreover, strict maps are closed under composition and pairing.

We write $\mathcal{K}_{*,\perp}$ for the subcategory of $\mathcal{K}_*$ of all complete objects and strict maps. From the above remarks, $\mathcal{K}_{*,\perp}$ is cartesian.

Let $\mathcal{L}$ be the $\mathcal{K}_*$-category with object-set $|\mathcal{K}|$, hom-objects $\mathcal{L}(A, B) = A \rightharpoonup B$, identities $j_A : 1 \to A \rightharpoonup A$ obtained as the transpose of

$$1 \times A \cong A \stackrel{\mathrm{id}}{\longrightarrow} A$$

and composition $M_{A,B,C} : (B \rightharpoonup C) \times (A \rightharpoonup B) \to A \rightharpoonup C$ obtained as the transpose of

$$((B \rightharpoonup C) \times (A \rightharpoonup B)) \times A \cong (B \rightharpoonup C) \times ((A \rightharpoonup B) \times A) \stackrel{\mathrm{id} \otimes \varepsilon}{\rightharpoonup} (B \rightharpoonup C) \times B \stackrel{\varepsilon}{\rightharpoonup} C.$$

Then, $\mathcal{L}_0 \cong p\mathcal{K}$.

Remark. Despite M being strict, $\mathcal{L}$ is not a $\mathcal{K}_{*,\perp}$-category because j_A fails to be strict.

The type constructors are $\mathcal{K}_*$-functors:

1. Let $\underline{+} : \mathcal{L} \times \mathcal{L} \to \mathcal{L}$ be the $\mathcal{K}_*$-functor sending (A, B) to $A + B$ and where $\underline{+}_{(A,B),(X,Y)} : (A \rightharpoonup X) \times (B \rightharpoonup Y) \to (A + B) \rightharpoonup (X + Y)$ is the transpose of

$$\begin{array}{ccc}
((A \rightharpoonup X) \times (B \rightharpoonup Y)) \times (A + B) & \longrightarrow & X + Y \\
\Big\downarrow \cong & & \Big\uparrow \varepsilon + \varepsilon \\
 & & ((A \rightharpoonup X) \times A) + ((B \rightharpoonup Y) \times B) \\
 & & \Big\uparrow \pi_1 + \pi_2 \\
\multicolumn{3}{c}{(((A \rightharpoonup X) \times A) \times (B \rightharpoonup Y)) + ((A \rightharpoonup X) \times ((B \rightharpoonup Y) \times B))}
\end{array} .$$

   Then, $\underline{+}_0 \cong + : p\mathcal{K} \times p\mathcal{K} \to p\mathcal{K}$.

2. Let $\underline{\otimes} : \mathcal{L} \times \mathcal{L} \to \mathcal{L}$ be the $\mathcal{K}_*$-functor sending (A, B) to $A \times B$ and where $\underline{\otimes}_{(A,B),(X,Y)} : (A \rightharpoonup X) \times (B \rightharpoonup Y) \to (A \times B) \rightharpoonup (X \times Y)$ is the transpose of

$$((A \rightharpoonup X) \times (B \rightharpoonup Y)) \times (A \times B) \cong ((A \rightharpoonup X) \times A) \times ((B \rightharpoonup Y) \times B) \overset{\varepsilon \otimes \varepsilon}{\rightharpoonup} X \times Y.$$

   Then, $\underline{\otimes}_0 \cong \otimes : p\mathcal{K} \times p\mathcal{K} \to p\mathcal{K}$.

3. Let $\underline{\rightharpoonup} : \mathcal{L}^{op} \times \mathcal{L} \to \mathcal{L}$ be the $\mathcal{K}_*$-functor sending (A, B) to $A \rightharpoonup B$ and where $\underline{\rightharpoonup}_{(A,B),(X,Y)} : (X \rightharpoonup A) \times (B \rightharpoonup Y) \to (A \rightharpoonup B) \rightharpoonup (X \rightharpoonup Y)$ is the transpose of

$$\begin{array}{ccc}
((X \rightharpoonup A) \times (B \rightharpoonup Y)) \times (A \rightharpoonup B) & \longrightarrow & X \rightharpoonup Y \\
\Big\downarrow \cong & & \Big\uparrow M \\
(B \rightharpoonup Y) \times ((A \rightharpoonup B) \times (X \rightharpoonup A)) & \xrightarrow[\mathrm{id} \times M]{} & (B \rightharpoonup Y) \times (X \rightharpoonup B)
\end{array} .$$

   Then, $\underline{\rightharpoonup}_0 \cong \rightharpoonup : p\mathcal{K}^{op} \times p\mathcal{K} \to p\mathcal{K}$.

Finally, AXIOM 4 postulates the existence of a suitable fixed-point operator in $\mathcal{K}_*$ which together with AXIOM 5 will guarantee the existence of all recursive types.

AXIOM 4. $\mathcal{K}_*$ has a uniform parameterised fixed-point operator.

That is, for every $f : A \times B \to B$ in $\mathcal{K}_*$ there exists $f^\dagger : A \to B$ such that

$$f \circ \langle \mathrm{id}, f^\dagger \rangle = f^\dagger$$

and,

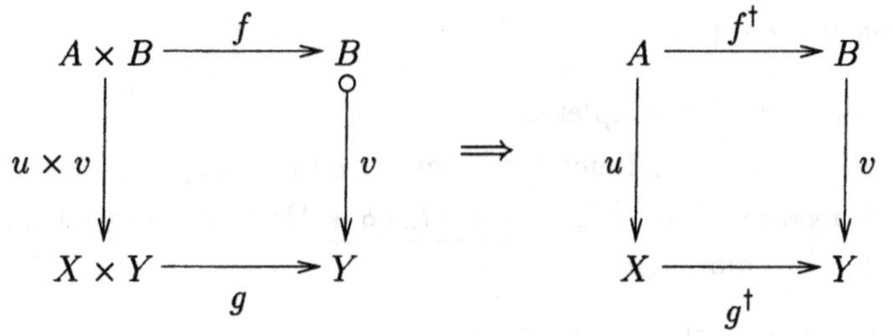

Let us pause to show an application of uniformity which will be needed later: for $f_i : A_i \times B_i \to B_i$ $(i = 1, 2)$ in $\mathcal{K}_*$, the commutativity of

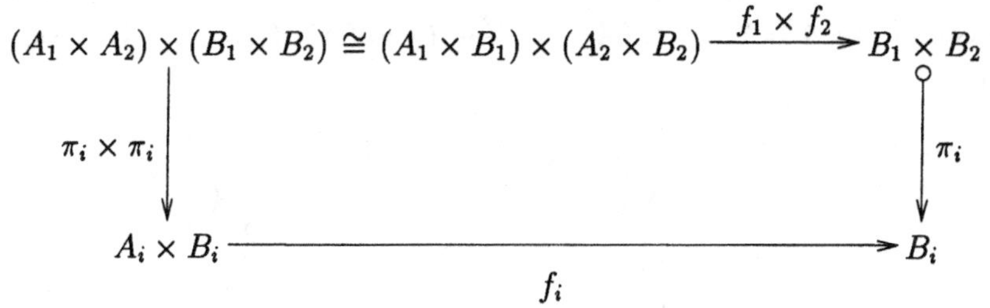

yields, by uniformity, $\pi_i \circ \big((f_1 \times f_2) \circ \cong\big)^\dagger = {f_i}^\dagger \circ \pi_i$. Thus,

$$\big((f_1 \times f_2) \circ \cong\big)^\dagger = {f_1}^\dagger \times {f_2}^\dagger. \tag{8.2}$$

Convention.

1. We set $\underline{(\ )} : p\mathcal{K} \cong \mathcal{L}_0 : \overline{(\ )}$.
2. Given a $\mathcal{K}_*$-functor $\underline{F} : \mathcal{A} \times \mathcal{L} \to \mathcal{L}$ we write F for the composite

$$\mathcal{A}_0 \times p\mathcal{K} \cong \mathcal{A}_0 \times \mathcal{L}_0 \xrightarrow{\underline{F}_0} \mathcal{L}_0 \cong p\mathcal{K}.$$

Moreover, given an $F(A, \_)$-algebra (B, β) and an $F(A', \_)$-coalgebra (C, γ), we write $\underline{\beta \circ F(\_, =) \circ \gamma} : \mathcal{A}(A', A) \times (C \rightharpoonup B) \to C \rightharpoonup B$ for the composite

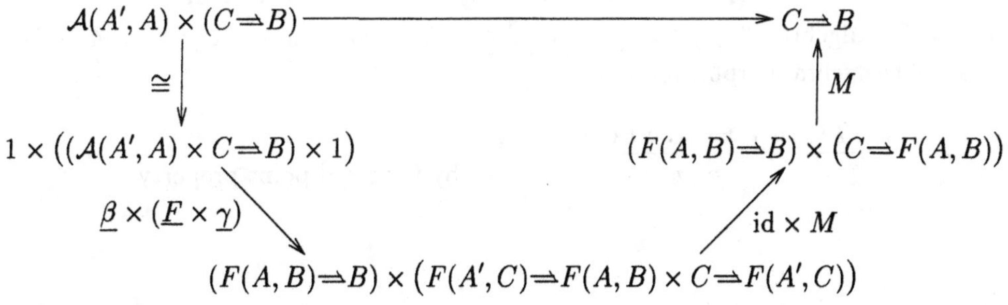

Axiom 5. Every $\mathcal{K}_*$-endofunctor on $\mathcal{L}$ has a chosen special invariant object.
That is, every $\mathcal{K}_*$-functor $\underline{F} : \mathcal{L} \to \mathcal{L}$ comes equipped with an F-invariant object $\alpha : FA \cong A$ such that $(\underline{\alpha \circ F(\_) \circ \alpha^{-1}})^\dagger = j_A : 1 \to A \rightharpoonup A$.

$\mathcal{L}$ admits recursive types:

1. $\mathcal{L}$ is $\mathcal{K}_*$-algebraically complete:
Let $\underline{F} : \mathcal{L} \to \mathcal{L}$ be a $\mathcal{K}_*$-functor and let (A, α) be an special F-invariant object.
For an F-algebra (B, β), if $\underline{u} = (\underline{\beta \circ F(\_) \circ \alpha^{-1}})^\dagger$ it follows that $u : (A, \alpha) \rightharpoonup (B, \beta)$ is an F-algebra morphism because

$$\begin{aligned} \underline{\beta \circ F(u) \circ \alpha^{-1}} &= \underline{\beta \circ F(\_) \circ \alpha^{-1}} \circ \underline{u} \\ &= \underline{u} \qquad \text{, by the fixed-point property.} \end{aligned}$$

Moreover, if $v : (A, \alpha) \rightharpoonup (B, \beta)$ is an F-algebra morphism then, writing $\underline{v \circ \_}$ for the composite $A \rightharpoonup A \cong 1 \times (A \rightharpoonup A) \xrightarrow{\underline{v} \times \mathrm{id}} (A \rightharpoonup B) \times (A \rightharpoonup A) \xrightarrow{M} A \rightharpoonup B$, we have that

$$\begin{array}{ccc} A \rightharpoonup A & \xrightarrow{\underline{\alpha \circ F(\_) \circ \alpha^{-1}}} & A \rightharpoonup A \\ {\scriptstyle \underline{v \circ \_}} \downarrow & & \downarrow {\scriptstyle \underline{v \circ \_}} \\ C \rightharpoonup A & \xrightarrow[\underline{\beta \circ F(\_) \circ \alpha^{-1}}]{} & C \rightharpoonup A \end{array}$$

and therefore

$$\begin{aligned} \underline{v} &= \underline{v \circ \_} \circ j_A \\ &= \underline{v \circ \_} \circ (\underline{\alpha \circ F(\_) \circ \alpha^{-1}})^\dagger \\ &= (\underline{\beta \circ F(\_) \circ \alpha^{-1}})^\dagger \qquad \text{, by uniformity.} \end{aligned}$$

2. $\mathcal{L}$ is $\mathcal{K}_*$-algebraically compact:
Let $\underline{F} : \mathcal{L} \to \mathcal{L}$ be a $\mathcal{K}_*$-functor and let (A, α) be an initial F-algebra.
For an F-coalgebra (C, γ), if $\underline{u} = (\underline{\alpha \circ F(\_) \circ \gamma})^\dagger$ it follows that $u : (C, \gamma) \rightharpoonup (A, \alpha^{-1})$ is an F-coalgebra morphism because

$$\begin{aligned} \underline{\alpha \circ F(u) \circ \gamma} &= \underline{\alpha \circ F(\_) \circ \gamma} \circ \underline{u} \\ &= \underline{u} \qquad \text{, by the fixed-point property.} \end{aligned}$$

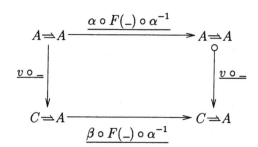

Moreover, if $v : (C, \gamma) \rightharpoonup (A, \alpha^{-1})$ is an F-coalgebra morphism then, writing $\underline{\_ \circ v}$ for the composite $A \rightleftharpoons A \cong (A \rightleftharpoons A) \times 1 \stackrel{\mathrm{id} \times \underline{v}}{\longrightarrow} (A \rightleftharpoons A) \times (C \rightleftharpoons A) \stackrel{M}{\longrightarrow} (C \rightleftharpoons A)$, we have that

$$\begin{array}{ccc} A \rightleftharpoons A & \xrightarrow{\underline{\alpha \circ F(\_) \circ \alpha^{-1}}} & A \rightleftharpoons A \\ {\scriptstyle \underline{\_ \circ v}} \downarrow & & \downarrow {\scriptstyle \underline{\_ \circ v}} \\ C \rightleftharpoons A & \xrightarrow[\underline{\alpha \circ F(\_) \circ \gamma}]{} & C \rightleftharpoons A \end{array}$$

and therefore

$$\begin{aligned} \underline{v} &= \underline{\_ \circ v} \circ j_A \\ &= \underline{\_ \circ v} \circ (\underline{\alpha \circ F(\_) \circ \alpha^{-1}})^{\dagger} \\ &= (\underline{\alpha \circ F(\_) \circ \gamma})^{\dagger} \qquad \text{, by uniformity.} \end{aligned}$$

3. $\mathcal{L}$ is parameterised $\mathcal{K}_*$-algebraically compact:
   Let $\underline{F} : \mathcal{A} \times \mathcal{L} \to \mathcal{L}$ be a $\mathcal{K}_*$-functor.
   For $A, B \in |\mathcal{A}|$, define

$$\Phi_{A,B} = \underline{\iota_B^F \circ F(\_,=) \circ (\iota_A^F)^{-1}} : \mathcal{A}(A, B) \times (F^{\dagger}A \rightleftharpoons F^{\dagger}B) \to F^{\dagger}A \rightleftharpoons F^{\dagger}B.$$

Then, for every $f : 1 \to \mathcal{A}(A, B)$,

$$\underline{\iota_B^F \circ F(f, \overline{\Phi^{\dagger} \circ f}) \circ (\iota_A^F)^{-1}} = \Phi \circ \langle f, \Phi^{\dagger} \circ f \rangle = \Phi^{\dagger} \circ f : 1 \to F^{\dagger}A \rightleftharpoons F^{\dagger}B$$

and therefore

$$\iota_B^F \circ F(f, \overline{\Phi^{\dagger} \circ f}) \circ (\iota_A^F)^{-1} = \overline{\Phi^{\dagger} \circ f} : F^{\dagger}A \rightharpoonup F^{\dagger}B.$$

Thus, $\overline{\Phi^{\dagger} \circ f} = F^{\dagger} f$.
In particular, $\overline{\Phi^{\dagger} \circ j_A} = F^{\dagger}(j_A) = \mathrm{id}_{F^{\dagger}A}$ and therefore $\Phi^{\dagger} \circ j_A = \underline{\mathrm{id}_{F^{\dagger}A}} = j_{F^{\dagger}A}$.

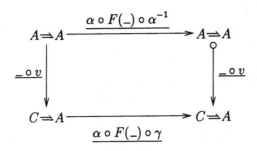

Moreover,

$$\begin{array}{ccc}
(\mathcal{A}(B,C) \times \mathcal{A}(A,B)) \times ((F^\dagger B \rightharpoonup F^\dagger C) \times (F^\dagger A \rightharpoonup F^\dagger B)) & \longrightarrow & (F^\dagger B \rightharpoonup F^\dagger C) \times (F^\dagger A \rightharpoonup F^\dagger B) \\
\cong \downarrow & & \uparrow \Phi \times \Phi \\
(\mathcal{A}(B,C) \times (F^\dagger B \rightharpoonup F^\dagger C)) \times (\mathcal{A}(A,B) \times (F^\dagger A \rightharpoonup F^\dagger B)) & & \\
M \times M \downarrow & & \downarrow M \\
\mathcal{A}(A,C) \times (F^\dagger A \rightharpoonup F^\dagger C) & \xrightarrow[\Phi]{} & F^\dagger A \rightharpoonup F^\dagger C
\end{array}$$

and, using (8.2), we have

$$\begin{array}{ccc}
\mathcal{A}(B,C) \times \mathcal{A}(A,B) & \xrightarrow{\Phi^\dagger \times \Phi^\dagger} & (F^\dagger B \rightharpoonup F^\dagger C) \times (F^\dagger A \rightharpoonup F^\dagger B) \\
M \downarrow & & \downarrow M \\
\mathcal{A}(A,C) & \xrightarrow[\Phi^\dagger]{} & F^\dagger A \rightharpoonup F^\dagger C
\end{array}$$

Hence, $\underline{F^\dagger} : \mathcal{A} \to \mathcal{L}$ defined as $\Phi^\dagger$ on hom-objects is a $\mathcal{K}_*$-functor such that $\underline{F^\dagger}_0 \cong F^\dagger : \mathcal{A}_0 \to p\mathcal{K}$.

Thus, we have proved:

Theorem 8.5.11 Let $(\mathcal{K}, \mathcal{D})$ be a domain structure satisfying AXIOMS 1–5. Then, $(\mathcal{K}, \mathcal{D})$, $\mathcal{L}$, $\underline{\pm}$, $\underline{\otimes}$, $\underline{\rightharpoonup}$ and $\underline{(\_)^\dagger}$ specify a $\mathcal{K}_*$-model of FPC. □

Example 8.5.12 $(\mathbf{Cpo}, \Sigma)$ satisfies AXIOMS 1–5. □

8.6 Poset-Models and Parametricity

Throughout this section, we consider a domain structure $(\mathcal{K}, \mathcal{D})$ together with a **Poset**-enrichment $\sqsubseteq$ for $\mathcal{K}$ such that $(p\mathcal{K}, \sqsubseteq)$ is a **Poset**-model of FPC and investigate the behaviour of expressions in it. We show that expressions are parametric with respect to representations (Definition 8.6.1) and that, categorically, this corresponds to the lax naturality of the interpretation.

Representations were introduced in [Rey74] as an initial formalisation of the notion of implementation. Here we generalise Reynolds' definition in two obvious ways: we state it in an arbitrary **Poset**-category (rather than in a category of domains) and we consider representations between morphisms (rather than between elements).

Definition 8.6.1 A *representation* between A and B is an indexed family of relations

$$\{(\![v]\!)_Z \subseteq p\mathcal{K}(Z, A) \times p\mathcal{K}(Z, B)\}_{Z \in |\, p\mathcal{K}\,|}$$

where $v \in p\mathcal{K}_R(A, B)$ and for every $a : Z \rightharpoonup A$ and $b : Z \rightharpoonup B$, $a \; (\![v]\!)_Z \; b \iff b \underset{\sim}{\sqsubset} v \circ a$. □

The motivation for parametricity (i.e., the property that the interpretation of an expression maps related environments to related values) is to guarantee *representation independence*. In our setting, this abstraction property is captured by lax naturality (Proposition 8.6.5). The following lemma suggests why.

Lemma 8.6.2 For $v_i \in p\mathcal{K}_R(A_i, B_i)$ $(i = 1, 2)$, $a : A_1 \rightharpoonup A_2$ and $b : B_1 \rightharpoonup B_2$, the following statements are equivalent:

1. For every $Z \in |\, p\mathcal{K}\,|$, $x : Z \rightharpoonup A_1$, $y : Z \rightharpoonup A_2$,

$$x \; (\![v_1]\!)_Z \; y \Rightarrow a \circ x \; (\![v_2]\!)_Z \; b \circ y.$$

2. For every $x : A_1 \rightharpoonup A_1$, $y : A_1 \rightharpoonup A_2$,

$$x \; (\![v_1]\!)_{A_1} \; y \Rightarrow a \circ x \; (\![v_2]\!)_{A_1} \; b \circ y.$$

3. $$\begin{array}{ccc} A_1 & \xrightarrow{\;a\;} & A_2 \\ {\scriptstyle v_1}\downarrow & \underset{\sim}{\sqsubset} & \downarrow{\scriptstyle v_2} \\ B_1 & \xrightarrow[\;b\;]{} & B_2 \end{array}$$ □

A neat aspect of our treatment is that the notion of representation on compound types is not imposed by definition but derived. This is done by characterising the representations of a compound type in terms of the representations of its constituent types. Pleasantly enough, representations of compound types turn out to be *logical* [Mit90].

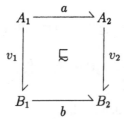

Proposition 8.6.3 For $i = 1, 2$, let $v_i \in p\mathcal{K}_R(A_i, B_i)$.

1. Let $a : A_1 \rightharpoonup A_2$ and $b : B_1 \rightharpoonup B_2$. Then,

$$p\lambda(a) \; (\![v_1 \overset{L}{\Rightarrow} v_2]\!) \; p\lambda(b)$$

$$\iff$$

$$\forall\, Z \in |\, p\mathcal{K} \,|, x : Z \rightharpoonup A_1, y : Z \rightharpoonup A_2.\; x \; (\![v_1]\!) \; y \Rightarrow a \circ x \; (\![v_2]\!) \; b \circ y.$$

2. Let $a : Z \rightharpoonup A_1 \otimes A_2$ and $b : Z \rightharpoonup B_1 \otimes B_2$. Then,

$$a \; (\![v_1 \otimes v_2]\!) \; b \iff \big(\pi_1 \circ a \; (\![v_1]\!) \; \pi_1 \circ b\big) \wedge \big(\pi_2 \circ a \; (\![v_2]\!) \; \pi_2 \circ b\big).$$

3. For $i = 1, 2$, if $a : Z \rightharpoonup A_i$ and $b : Z \rightharpoonup B_i$ then

$$\amalg_i \circ a \; (\![v_1 + v_2]\!) \; \amalg_i \circ b \iff a \; (\![v_i]\!) \; b.$$

PROOF:

(1) By Proposition 5.2.2 (3) and Lemma 8.6.2.

(2) ($\Rightarrow$) By Proposition 5.1.1 (2).

($\Leftarrow$) By monotonicity of $\langle\!\langle \_, = \rangle\!\rangle$ and Proposition 5.1.1 (5).

(3) ($\Rightarrow$) Because $\amalg_i$ is full (see Definition 4.2.2 (1)) as follows from the fact that $\amalg_i$ is an admissible mono (see Proposition 5.3.12) and that admissible monos are full (see Theorem 4.2.4).

($\Leftarrow$) By monotonicity of $\amalg_i \circ \_$. □

Before stating the correspondence between parametricity and lax naturality some definitions restricting the interpretation of types to representations are needed.

Definition 8.6.4 1. $[\![\Theta \vdash \tau]\!]_R : p\mathcal{K}_R^{|\Theta|} \to p\mathcal{K}$ is defined by

$$[\![\Theta \vdash \tau]\!]_R(v) \;=\; [\![\Theta \vdash \tau]\!]_2\big((v_1^L, v_1), \ldots, (v_{|\Theta|}^L, v_{|\Theta|})\big).$$

2. $[\![\Theta \vdash \tau]\!]_D : (p\mathcal{K}_R^{|\Theta|})\breve{\ } \to p\mathcal{K}$ is defined by

$$[\![\Theta \vdash \tau]\!]_D(v', v) \;=\; [\![\Theta \vdash \tau]\!]_2\big((v_1', v_1), \ldots, (v_{|\Theta|}', v_{|\Theta|})\big). \qquad \square$$

Convention. For $A \in p\mathcal{K}^{|\Theta|}$, $[\![\Theta, \Gamma \vdash e : \tau]\!]_A$ stands for $[\![\Theta, \Gamma \vdash e : \tau]\!]_{((A_1, A_1), \ldots, (A_{|\Theta|}, A_{|\Theta|}))}$.

Proposition 8.6.5 The following statements are equivalent:

1. For every $v \in p\mathcal{K}_R^{|\Theta|}(A, B)$,

   $\forall\, a \in p\mathcal{K}^{|\Theta|}(Z, A), b \in p\mathcal{K}^{|\Theta|}(Z, B).$

   $$a\ (\![[\![\Theta \vdash \Gamma]\!]_R(v)]\!)\ b \Longrightarrow [\![\Theta, \Gamma \vdash e : \tau]\!]_A \circ a\ (\![[\![\Theta \vdash \tau]\!]_R(v)]\!)\ [\![\Theta, \Gamma \vdash e : \tau]\!]_B \circ b.$$

2. $[\![\Theta, \Gamma \vdash e : \tau]\!] : [\![\Theta \vdash \Gamma]\!]_R \overset{\cdot}{\underset{\lesssim}{\to}} [\![\Theta \vdash \tau]\!]_R : p\mathcal{K}_R^{|\Theta|} \to p\mathcal{K}.$

3. $[\![\Theta, \Gamma \vdash e : \tau]\!] : [\![\Theta \vdash \Gamma]\!]_D \overset{\cdot\cdot}{\underset{\lesssim}{\to}} [\![\Theta \vdash \tau]\!]_D : (p\mathcal{K}_R^{|\Theta|})\breve{} \to p\mathcal{K}$. That is, for every $v \in p\mathcal{K}_R^{|\Theta|}(A, B)$,

$$\begin{array}{ccccc}
 & [\![\Theta \vdash \Gamma]\!]_D(A, A) & \xrightarrow{[\![\Theta, \Gamma \vdash e : \tau]\!]_A} & [\![\Theta \vdash \tau]\!]_D(A, A) & \\
{\scriptstyle [\![\Theta \vdash \Gamma]\!]_D(v, \mathrm{id})} \nearrow & & & & \searrow {\scriptstyle [\![\Theta \vdash \tau]\!]_D(\mathrm{id}, v)} \\
[\![\Theta \vdash \Gamma]\!]_D(B, A) & & \lesssim & & [\![\Theta \vdash \tau]\!]_D(A, B) \\
{\scriptstyle [\![\Theta \vdash \Gamma]\!]_D(\mathrm{id}, v)} \searrow & & & & \nearrow {\scriptstyle [\![\Theta \vdash \tau]\!]_D(v, \mathrm{id})} \\
 & [\![\Theta \vdash \Gamma]\!]_D(B, B) & \xrightarrow[{[\![\Theta, \Gamma \vdash e : \tau]\!]_B}]{} & [\![\Theta \vdash \tau]\!]_D(B, B) &
\end{array}$$

□

Finally,

Theorem 8.6.6 (Poset-Models are Parametric w.r.t. Representations)

$$[\![\Theta, \Gamma \vdash e : \tau]\!] : [\![\Theta \vdash \Gamma]\!]_R \overset{\cdot}{\underset{\lesssim}{\to}} [\![\Theta \vdash \tau]\!]_R : p\mathcal{K}_R^{|\Theta|} \to p\mathcal{K}.$$

PROOF: By induction on the derivation of $\Theta, \Gamma \vdash e : \tau$ (see Appendix B). □

9 Computational Soundness and Adequacy

The relationship between the operational notion of termination and the denotational notion of totality is examined. It is shown that in any model of FPC the interpretation of expressions is *computationally sound* (meaning that expressions whose evaluation terminates have total interpretations). Furthermore, for a wide class of domain-theoretic models this is strengthened by showing that they are also *computationally adequate* (in the sense that, the evaluation of a program terminates whenever its interpretation is total).

9.1 Soundness

The strategy for proving soundness is as usual: observe that values have total interpretations (Lemma 9.1.2) and that the interpretation of expressions is preserved under evaluation (Lemma 9.1.3). Both lemmas are proved by induction. The first one follows straightforwardly; the second one requires a substitution lemma for expressions (which is particularly interesting as it only holds when substituting expressions with *total* interpretation) and its proof is deferred to Appendix C.

Definition 9.1.1 A model of FPC is *computationally sound* if, for every $\vdash p : \tau$,

$$\vdash p\checkmark : \tau \text{ implies } [\![\vdash p : \tau]\!] \downarrow. \qquad \square$$

Lemma 9.1.2 In any model of FPC, $[\![\Theta, \Gamma \vdash v : \tau]\!] \downarrow$ for every value v.

PROOF: By induction on the structure of v. □

Lemma 9.1.3 In any model of FPC,

$$\text{if } \Theta, \Gamma \vdash e \leadsto v : \tau \text{ then } [\![\Theta, \Gamma \vdash e : \tau]\!] = [\![\Theta, \Gamma \vdash v : \tau]\!].$$

PROOF: By induction on the derivation of $e \leadsto v$ (see Appendix C). □

From the two previous lemmas:

Theorem 9.1.4 (Computational Soundness) In any model of FPC,

$$\text{if } \Theta, \Gamma \vdash e\checkmark : \tau \text{ then } [\![\Theta, \Gamma \vdash e : \tau]\!] \downarrow. \qquad \square$$

9.2 Adequacy

A model of FPC is computationally adequate when the operational notion of termination and the denotational notion of totality coincide. Formally,

Definition 9.2.1 A model of FPC is *computationally adequate* if, for every $\vdash p : \tau$,

$$[\![\vdash p : \tau]\!] \downarrow \text{ implies } \vdash p \checkmark : \tau. \qquad \square$$

The main mathematical effort of this section is to establish the computational adequacy of a wide class of domain-theoretic models (see Subsection 8.5.1).

Fix a $\mathcal{V}$-model of FPC. The first impulse to try to prove $[\![\vdash p : \tau]\!] \downarrow \Rightarrow \vdash p\checkmark : \tau$ is to proceed by induction on the structure of p. But this does not work. To see what goes wrong consider the case $p \equiv p_1(p_2)$. If $\varepsilon \circ \langle\!\langle [\![\vdash p_1 : \sigma \rightharpoonup \tau]\!], [\![\vdash p_2 : \sigma]\!] \rangle\!\rangle = [\![\vdash p_1(p_2) : \tau]\!]$ is total then so are $[\![\vdash p_1 : \sigma \rightharpoonup \tau]\!]$ and $[\![\vdash p_2 : \sigma]\!]$ and , by induction, there exist $\lambda \mathbf{x}.\, e$ and v such that $p_1 \rightsquigarrow \lambda \mathbf{x}.\, e$ and $p_2 \rightsquigarrow v$. But, there is no reason for which we can conclude that $e[\mathbf{x} \mapsto v]\checkmark$. The solution is to strengthen the induction hypothesis, roughly, to something like

$$[\![\vdash p : \tau]\!] \downarrow \;\Rightarrow\; \exists\, v.\, p \rightsquigarrow v \;\wedge\; [\![\vdash p : \tau]\!] \preceq_\tau v \qquad (9.1)$$

where $\{\, \preceq_\tau \subseteq \mathcal{K}(1, [\![\vdash \tau]\!]_2) \times \{v \in \text{Values} \mid\; \vdash v : \tau\}\}$ is a family of *formal-approximation* relations with enough closure properties to overcome the above and similar problems. The nature of the closure properties alluded is best illustrated with a couple of examples.

1. Consider the case $p \equiv p_1(p_2)$. If $[\![\vdash p_1 : \sigma \rightharpoonup \tau]\!]$ and $[\![\vdash p_2 : \sigma]\!]$ are total, by induction, there exist $\lambda \mathbf{x}.\, e$ and v such that $p_1 \rightsquigarrow \lambda \mathbf{x}.\, e \;\wedge\; [\![\vdash p_1 : \sigma \rightharpoonup \tau]\!] \preceq_{\sigma \rightharpoonup \tau} \lambda \mathbf{x}.\, e$ and $p_2 \rightsquigarrow v \;\wedge\; [\![\vdash p_2 : \sigma]\!] \preceq_\sigma v$. Thus, if we could built $\preceq_{\sigma \rightharpoonup \tau}$ and $\preceq_\sigma$ with the property that whenever $f \preceq_{\sigma \rightharpoonup \tau} \lambda \mathbf{x}.\, e$ and $x \preceq_\sigma v$ we have that

$$\varepsilon \circ \langle\!\langle f, x \rangle\!\rangle \downarrow \;\Rightarrow\; \exists\, v'.\, e[\mathbf{x} \mapsto v] \rightsquigarrow v' \;\wedge\; \varepsilon \circ \langle\!\langle f, x \rangle\!\rangle \preceq_\tau v' \qquad (9.2)$$

then, using that

$$\frac{e[\mathbf{x} \mapsto v] \rightsquigarrow v'}{p_1(p_2) \rightsquigarrow v'}$$

and putting $f = [\![\vdash p_1 : \sigma \rightharpoonup \tau]\!]$ and $x = [\![\vdash p_2 : \sigma]\!]$ in (9.2), we could conclude that

$$[\![\vdash p_1(p_2) : \tau]\!] \downarrow \;\Rightarrow\; \exists\, v'.\, p_1(p_2) \rightsquigarrow v' \;\wedge\; [\![\vdash p_1(p_2) : \tau]\!] \preceq_\tau v'.$$

2. Consider the case $p \equiv \mathtt{elim}(p')$. If $E \circ [\![\vdash p' : \mu \mathrm{T}.\, \tau']\!] = [\![\vdash \mathtt{elim}(p') : \tau'[\mathrm{T} \mapsto \mu \mathrm{T}.\tau']]\!]$ is total then so is $[\![\vdash p' : \mu \mathrm{T}.\, \tau']\!]$ and, by induction, there exists $\mathtt{intro}(v)$ such that $p' \rightsquigarrow \mathtt{intro}(v) \;\wedge\; [\![\vdash p' : \mu \mathrm{T}.\, \tau']\!] \preceq_{\mu \mathrm{T}.\tau'} \mathtt{intro}(v)$. Thus, if we could built $\preceq_{\mu \mathrm{T}.\tau'}$ and $\preceq_{\tau'[\mathrm{T} \mapsto \mu \mathrm{T}.\tau']}$ with the property that

$$x \preceq_{\mu \mathrm{T}.\tau'} \mathtt{intro}(v) \;\Rightarrow\; E \circ x \preceq_{\tau'[\mathrm{T} \mapsto \mu \mathrm{T}.\tau']} v \qquad (9.3)$$

then, using that

$$\frac{p' \rightsquigarrow \texttt{intro}(v)}{\texttt{elim}(p') \rightsquigarrow v}$$

and putting $x = [\![\vdash p' : \mu\mathrm{T}.\,\tau']\!]$ in (9.3), we could conclude that

$$[\![\vdash \texttt{elim}(p') : \tau'[\mathrm{T} \mapsto \mu\mathrm{T}.\tau']]\!] \downarrow \Rightarrow \exists\, v.\ \wedge \begin{array}{l} \texttt{elim}(p') \rightsquigarrow v \\ [\![\vdash \texttt{elim}(p') : \tau'[\mathrm{T} \mapsto \mu\mathrm{T}.\tau']]\!] \preceq_{\tau'[\mathrm{T} \mapsto \mu\mathrm{T}.\tau']} v. \end{array}$$

The reader is advised to consider the remaining cases and find out the other closure properties or to look at them in Corollary 9.2.17.

Remark. The actual induction hypothesis needed to carry out the proof is a suitable generalisation of (9.1) —see Lemma 9.2.18— to include expression contexts and expressions (as required, for example, to treat the case $p \equiv \lambda\mathbf{x}.\, e$).

Establishing the existence of the formal-approximation relations is a major task on which we now embark. Essentially the difficulty arises because they are defined recursively and one should guarantee that such a definition makes sense. But this is better discussed in the light of the following definitions:

For $\vdash \tau$, we define

$$\begin{aligned} \mathrm{Values}(\tau) &= \{v \in \mathrm{Values} \mid\ \vdash v : \tau\}, \\ \mathrm{Programs}(\tau) &= \{p \in \mathrm{Expressions} \mid\ \vdash p : \tau\} \end{aligned}$$

and, generalising from the formal-approximation relations, we set

$$|\,\mathcal{R}(\tau)\,| \;=\; \{(A, \preceq) \mid A \in |\,\mathcal{K}\,| \wedge \preceq \subseteq \mathcal{K}(1, A) \times \mathrm{Values}(\tau)\}.$$

Given $\preceq\ \subseteq \mathcal{K}(1, A) \times \mathrm{Values}(\tau)$, we define its extension to partial maps and programs, $\precsim\ \subseteq p\mathcal{K}(1, A) \times \mathrm{Programs}(\tau)$, by $u \precsim p \iff (u\downarrow\ \Rightarrow\ \exists v.\, p \rightsquigarrow v\ \wedge\ u \preceq v)$ —c.f. (9.1).

Now, in order to provide an equational description of the closure properties of $\preceq_{\sigma\star\tau}$ (for $\star \in \{+, \times, \rightharpoonup\}$) and to clarify the closure property of $\preceq_{\mu\mathrm{T}.\tau}$, the type constructors are *logically* extended to relations following Corollary 9.2.17.

Definition 9.2.2 For $\vdash \sigma$ and $\vdash \tau$,

1. Define $+_{\sigma,\tau} : |\mathcal{R}(\sigma)| \times |\mathcal{R}(\tau)| \to |\mathcal{R}(\sigma+\tau)|$ to be the function mapping $((A, \preceq_A), (B, \preceq_B))$ to $(A + B, \preceq_A + \preceq_B)$ where
$$x\ (\preceq_A + \preceq_B)\ \mathtt{inl}(v) \iff (\exists\, x'.\ x = \amalg_1 \circ x' \wedge x' \preceq_A v)$$
and
$$x\ (\preceq_A + \preceq_B)\ \mathtt{inr}(v) \iff (\exists\, x'.\ x = \amalg_2 \circ x' \wedge x' \preceq_B v).$$

2. Define $\otimes_{\sigma,\tau} : |\mathcal{R}(\sigma)| \times |\mathcal{R}(\tau)| \to |\mathcal{R}(\sigma \times \tau)|$ to be the function mapping $((A, \preceq_A), (B, \preceq_B))$ to $(A \otimes B, \preceq_A \otimes \preceq_B)$ where
$$x\ (\preceq_A \otimes \preceq_B)\ \langle v_1, v_2\rangle \iff (\pi_1 \circ x \preceq_A v_1) \wedge (\pi_2 \circ x \preceq_B v_2).$$

3. Define $\rightharpoonup_{\sigma,\tau} : |\mathcal{R}(\sigma)| \times |\mathcal{R}(\tau)| \to |\mathcal{R}(\sigma \rightharpoonup \tau)|$ to be the function mapping $((A, \preceq_A), (B, \preceq_B))$ to $(A \rightharpoonup B, \preceq_A \rightharpoonup \preceq_B)$ where
$$f\ (\preceq_A \rightharpoonup \preceq_B)\ \lambda\mathtt{x}.\, e \iff (x \preceq_A v \Rightarrow \varepsilon \circ \langle\!\langle f, x\rangle\!\rangle \precsim_B e[\mathtt{x} \mapsto v]). \qquad \square$$

Then, (1)–(3) in Corollary 9.2.17 below can be expressed as

$$\preceq_{\sigma\star\tau} \;=\; \preceq_\sigma [\![\star]\!] \preceq_\tau \qquad \text{where } [\![\star]\!] = \begin{cases} + & \text{, if } \star = + \\ \otimes & \text{, if } \star = \times \\ \rightharpoonup & \text{, if } \star = \rightharpoonup \end{cases}.$$

To see what happens with recursive types we look at an example. Recall that $\mathtt{Nat} \equiv \mu\mathrm{T}.1 + \mathrm{T}$ where $1 \equiv 0 \rightharpoonup 0$ and $0 \equiv \mu\mathrm{T}.\mathrm{T}$. Then, for $x \in \mathcal{K}(1, [\![\mathtt{Nat}]\!])$ and $v \in \mathrm{Values}(1 + \mathtt{Nat})$,

$$\begin{aligned} x \preceq_{\mathtt{Nat}} \mathtt{intro}(v) &\iff E \circ x \preceq_{1+\mathtt{Nat}} v \\ &\iff E \circ x\ (\preceq_1 + \preceq_{\mathtt{Nat}})\ v \end{aligned}$$

where $E : [\![\mathtt{Nat}]\!] \cong [\![1{+}\mathtt{Nat}]\!]$. Now, if for $\preceq\, \subseteq \mathcal{K}(1, [\![\tau[\mathrm{T} \mapsto \mu\mathrm{T}.\,\tau]]\!]) \times \mathrm{Values}(\tau[\mathrm{T} \mapsto \mu\mathrm{T}.\,\tau])$, we define $\mathbb{I} \preceq\ \subseteq \mathcal{K}(1, [\![\tau[\mathrm{T} \mapsto \mu\mathrm{T}.\,\tau]]\!]) \times \mathrm{Values}(\mu\mathrm{T}.\,\tau)$ by

$$x'\ (\mathbb{I} \preceq)\ \mathtt{intro}(v') \iff x' \preceq v';$$

we have that

$$x \preceq_{\mathtt{Nat}} \mathtt{intro}(v) \iff E \circ x\ \mathbb{I}(\preceq_1 + \preceq_{\mathtt{Nat}})\ \mathtt{intro}(v). \tag{9.4}$$

That is, intuitively,

$$E : \preceq_{\mathtt{Nat}} \;\cong\; \mathbb{I}(\preceq_1 + \preceq_{\mathtt{Nat}}). \tag{9.5}$$

And this is exactly where the difficulty in constructing $\preceq_{\mu\mathrm{T}.\tau}$ resides as we have to solve a recursive equation for relations! In the sequel, this will be done using the techniques of Section 7.3.

First we need to make $|\mathcal{R}(\tau)|$ into a category. But, what should a morphism $(A, \preceq_A) \rightharpoonup (B, \preceq_B)$ be? The answer is suggested by (9.4) and (9.5):

Definition 9.2.3 Given $\vdash \tau$, the category $\mathcal{R}(\tau)$ has objects $|\mathcal{R}(\tau)|$ and morphisms $u : (A, \preceq_A) \rightharpoonup (B, \preceq_B)$ where $u : A \rightharpoonup B$ is such that $x \preceq_A v \Rightarrow u \circ x \precsim_B v$. Composition and identities are as in $p\mathcal{K}$. □

We list some basic properties of the $\mathcal{R}(\tau)$'s:

1. For $u : (A, \preceq_A) \rightharpoonup (B, \preceq_B)$, $u' \precsim_A p \Rightarrow u \circ u' \precsim_B p$.

2. $\mathcal{R}(0) \cong p\mathcal{K}$.

3. $\mathcal{R}(\tau)$ has an initial object, viz. $(0, \emptyset)$, and the forgetful functor $U_\tau : \mathcal{R}(\tau) \to p\mathcal{K}$ preserves it.

4. $\mathbb{I}_{\mu T.\tau} : \mathcal{R}(\tau[T \mapsto \mu T.\tau]) \cong \mathcal{R}(\mu T.\tau) : \mathbb{E}_{\mu T.\tau}$ where

$$\mathbb{I}_{\mu T.\tau} : (A, \preceq) \mapsto (A, \mathbb{I}\preceq) \quad \text{with } x\,(\mathbb{I}\preceq)\,\mathtt{intro}(v) \iff x \preceq v$$

and

$$\mathbb{E}_{\mu T.\tau} : (A, \preceq) \mapsto (A, \mathbb{E}\preceq) \quad \text{with } x\,(\mathbb{E}\preceq)\,v \iff x \preceq \mathtt{intro}(v).$$

Proposition 9.2.4 For every $\vdash \tau$, $(0, \emptyset)$ is a zero object in $\mathcal{R}(\tau)$ if and only if $p\mathcal{K}$ is non-trivial.

PROOF:

($\Rightarrow$) If $(0, \emptyset)$ is a zero object in $\mathcal{R}(\mathtt{1})$ then the unique $1 \rightharpoonup 0$ is a morphism $(1, \{(\mathrm{id}_1, \lambda\mathtt{x} : \mathtt{0}.\,\mathtt{x})\}) \rightharpoonup (0, \emptyset)$ in $\mathcal{R}(\mathtt{1})$. Therefore we have that

$$(1 \rightharpoonup 0)\downarrow \;\Rightarrow\; \big((1 \rightharpoonup 0), \lambda\mathtt{x} : \mathtt{0}.\,\mathtt{x}\big) \in \emptyset$$

or equivalently, that

$$\neg\ (1 \rightharpoonup 0)\downarrow .$$

Hence, $1 \ncong 0$.

($\Leftarrow$) For $\vdash \tau$, let $(A, \preceq) \in |\mathcal{R}(\tau)|$. The unique $0 \to A$ in $p\mathcal{K}$ is a morphism $(0, \emptyset) \to (A, \preceq)$ and thus $(0, \emptyset)$ is initial in $\mathcal{R}(\tau)$. Moreover, if $p\mathcal{K}$ is non-trivial then the unique $1 \rightharpoonup 0$ in $p\mathcal{K}$ in not total and so the unique $A \rightharpoonup 0$ in $p\mathcal{K}$ is a morphism $(A, \preceq) \rightharpoonup (0, \emptyset)$; thus $(0, \emptyset)$ is terminal in $\mathcal{R}(\tau)$. □

Proposition 9.2.5 The functions $+_{\sigma,\tau}$, $\otimes_{\sigma,\tau}$ and $\mathrel{\underline{\rightharpoonup}}_{\sigma,\tau}$ extend to functors satisfying

$$\begin{array}{ccc} \mathcal{R}(\sigma) \times \mathcal{R}(\tau) & \xrightarrow{\star_{\sigma,\tau}} & \mathcal{R}(\sigma \star \tau) \\ \downarrow & & \downarrow \\ p\mathcal{K} \times p\mathcal{K} & \xrightarrow[\star]{} & p\mathcal{K} \end{array} \qquad \begin{array}{ccc} \mathcal{R}(\sigma)^{op} \times \mathcal{R}(\tau) & \xrightarrow{\mathrel{\underline{\rightharpoonup}}_{\sigma,\tau}} & \mathcal{R}(\sigma \mathrel{\underline{\rightharpoonup}} \tau) \\ \downarrow & & \downarrow \\ p\mathcal{K}^{op} \times p\mathcal{K} & \xrightarrow[\mathrel{\underline{\rightharpoonup}}]{} & p\mathcal{K} \end{array}$$

$(\star \in \{+, \otimes\})$

PROOF: We need to show that, for $u : (A, \preceq_A) \rightharpoonup (B, \preceq_B)$ and $u' : (A', \preceq_{A'}) \rightharpoonup (B', \preceq_{B'})$,

$$u \star u' : (A \star A', \preceq_A \star \preceq_{A'}) \rightharpoonup (B \star B', \preceq_B \star \preceq_{B'}) \qquad (\star \in \{+, \otimes\})$$

and

$$u \mathrel{\underline{\rightharpoonup}} u' : (B \mathrel{\underline{\rightharpoonup}} A', \preceq_B \mathrel{\underline{\rightharpoonup}} \preceq_{A'}) \rightharpoonup (A \mathrel{\underline{\rightharpoonup}} B', \preceq_A \mathrel{\underline{\rightharpoonup}} \preceq_{B'}).$$

We consider each case:

$+$: Assume that $x \ (\preceq_A + \preceq_{A'}) \ v$ and that $(u + u') \circ x \downarrow$. We have to show that $(u + u') \circ x \ (\preceq_B + \preceq_{B'}) \ v$. There are two cases:

- $v \equiv \mathtt{inl}(v_1)$: We need to find y such that $(u + u') \circ x = \amalg_1 \circ y$ and $y \preceq_B v_1$. By the first assumption, there exists x' such that $x = \amalg_1 \circ x'$ and $x' \preceq_A v_1$. Then, $u \circ x' \precsim_B v_1$, but since $\amalg_1 \circ u \circ x' = (u + u') \circ \amalg_1 \circ x' = (u + u') \circ x$ is total then so is $u \circ x'$ and hence $u \circ x' \preceq_B v_1$. Finally, take $y = u \circ x'$.
- $v \equiv \mathtt{inr}(v_2)$: analogous to the previous case.

$\otimes$: Assume that $x \ (\preceq_A \otimes \preceq_{A'}) \ \langle v_1, v_2 \rangle$. Writing $\preceq$ for $\preceq_B \otimes \preceq_{B'}$ we have to show that $(u \otimes u') \circ x \precsim \langle v_1, v_2 \rangle$.

By assumption, $\pi_1 \circ x \preceq_A v_1$ and $\pi_2 \circ x \preceq_{A'} v_2$. Then, $u \circ \pi_1 \circ x \precsim_B v_1$ and $u' \circ \pi_2 \circ x \precsim_{B'} v_2$ and hence $(u \otimes u') \circ x = \langle\!\langle u \circ \pi_1 \circ x, u \circ \pi_2 \circ x \rangle\!\rangle \precsim \langle v_1, v_2 \rangle$.

$\mathrel{\underline{\rightharpoonup}}$: Assume that $f \ (\preceq_B \mathrel{\underline{\rightharpoonup}} \preceq_{A'}) \ \lambda\mathbf{x}.e$. We have to show that $(u \mathrel{\underline{\rightharpoonup}} u') \circ f \downarrow$ and $x \preceq_A v$ imply $\varepsilon \circ \langle\!\langle (u \mathrel{\underline{\rightharpoonup}} u') \circ f, x \rangle\!\rangle \precsim_B e[\mathbf{x} \mapsto v]$.

Assume that $(u \mathrel{\underline{\rightharpoonup}} u') \circ f \downarrow$ and that $x \preceq_A v$. Then, $u \circ x \precsim_B v$ and, using the first assumption, it follows that $\varepsilon \circ \langle\!\langle f, u \circ x \rangle\!\rangle \precsim_{A'} e[\mathbf{x} \mapsto v]$. Hence,

$$\varepsilon \circ \langle\!\langle (u \mathrel{\underline{\rightharpoonup}} u') \circ f, x \rangle\!\rangle = u' \circ \varepsilon \circ \langle\!\langle f, u \circ x \rangle\!\rangle \precsim_{B'} e[\mathbf{x} \mapsto v]. \qquad \square$$

The type constructors on $p\mathcal{K}$ have been extended to the $\mathcal{R}(\tau)$'s but there are far too many relations in the $\mathcal{R}(\tau)$'s to be able to find recursive types for them. The way out is to find subcategories $p\mathcal{K}(\tau)$ of $\mathcal{R}(\tau)$ in which this is possible.

Precisely, we now assume that our fixed model of FPC is a **Cpo**-model and intend to construct the $p\mathcal{K}(\tau)$ with the following properties:

A1. $U_\tau : p\mathcal{K}(\tau) \to p\mathcal{K}$ is a **Cpo**-functor.

A2. $p\mathcal{K}(\tau)$ is parameterised **Cpo**-algebraically compact.

A3. For $\star = +, \otimes$ (resp. $\Rightarrow$), the functor $\star_{\sigma, \tau}$ cuts down to a **Cpo**-functor $p\mathcal{K}(\sigma) \times p\mathcal{K}(\tau) \to p\mathcal{K}(\sigma \star \tau)$ (resp. $p\mathcal{K}(\sigma)^{op} \times p\mathcal{K}(\tau) \to p\mathcal{K}(\sigma \Rightarrow \tau)$).

A4. $\mathbb{I}_{\mu T. \tau}$ cuts down to $p\mathcal{K}(\tau[T \mapsto \mu T. \tau]) \cong p\mathcal{K}(\mu T. \tau)$.

A5. [Strict Uniformity] For every pair of symmetric **Cpo**-functors F and G, if

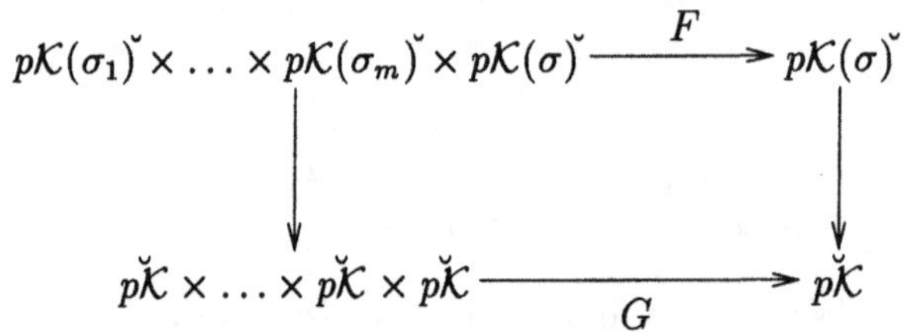

$$
\begin{array}{ccc}
p\mathcal{K}(\sigma_1)^{\vee} \times \ldots \times p\mathcal{K}(\sigma_m)^{\vee} \times p\mathcal{K}(\sigma)^{\vee} & \xrightarrow{\ F\ } & p\mathcal{K}(\sigma)^{\vee} \\
\big\downarrow & & \big\downarrow \\
p\check{\mathcal{K}} \times \ldots \times p\check{\mathcal{K}} \times p\check{\mathcal{K}} & \xrightarrow[\ G\ ]{} & p\check{\mathcal{K}}
\end{array}
\tag{9.6}
$$

then for every initial parameterised G-algebra $(G^\dagger, \iota^G)$ there exists an initial parameterised F-algebra $(F^\dagger, \iota^F)$ such that

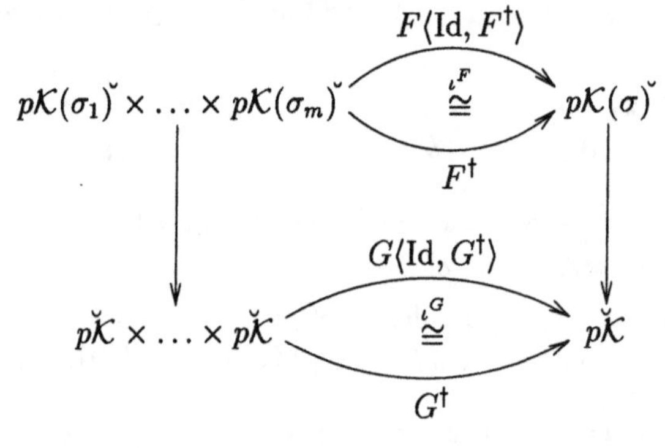

Before going into the construction of the $p\mathcal{K}(\tau)$'s we remark that the Strict Uniformity Property is stronger than it seems:

Proposition 9.2.6 Assume the Strict Uniformity Property. In the situation (9.6), for every initial parameterised G-algebra $(G^\dagger, \iota^G)$ there exists an initial parameterised F-algebra $(F^\dagger, \iota^F)$ such that

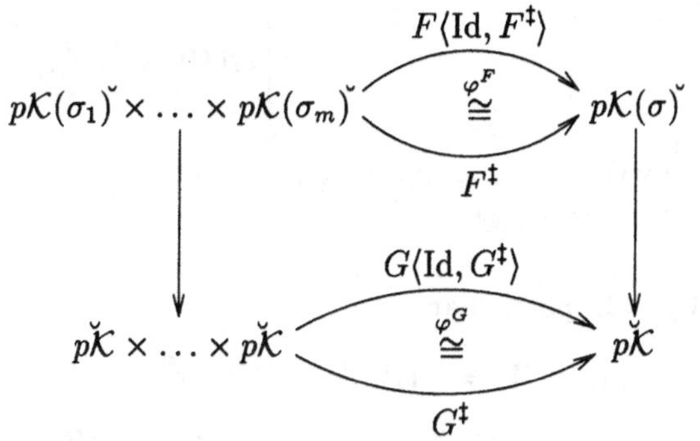

PROOF: Write W for $(U_{\sigma_1}{}^{op} \times U_{\sigma_1}) \times \ldots \times (U_{\sigma_m}{}^{op} \times U_{\sigma_m})$ and V for $U_\sigma{}^{op} \times U_\sigma$.
On the one hand,

$$\Pi_2 V F^\ddagger \;=\; U \Pi_2 F^\ddagger \;=\; U \Pi_2 F^\dagger \;=\; \Pi_2 G^\dagger W \;=\; \Pi_2 G^\ddagger W$$

and therefore $V F^\ddagger = G^\ddagger W$.
On the other hand, recall from pages 124 and 122 that

$$\varphi_X^F \;=\; \big((\rho_X^F)_2^{-1}, \mathrm{id}\big) \circ \iota_X^F \circ F\big(X, ((\rho_X^F)_2, \mathrm{id})\big) \tag{9.7}$$

where

$$
\begin{array}{ccc}
(F^\dagger X)^\S & \xrightarrow{\;(\iota_X^F)^\S\;} & F(X^\S, (F^\dagger X)^\S) \\[2pt]
{\scriptstyle \rho_X^F}\Big\downarrow & & \Big\downarrow {\scriptstyle F(X^\S, \rho_X^F)} \\[2pt]
F^\dagger(X^\S) & \xrightarrow{\;(\iota_{X^\S}^F)^{-1}\;} & F(X^\S, F^\dagger(X^\S))
\end{array}
$$

.

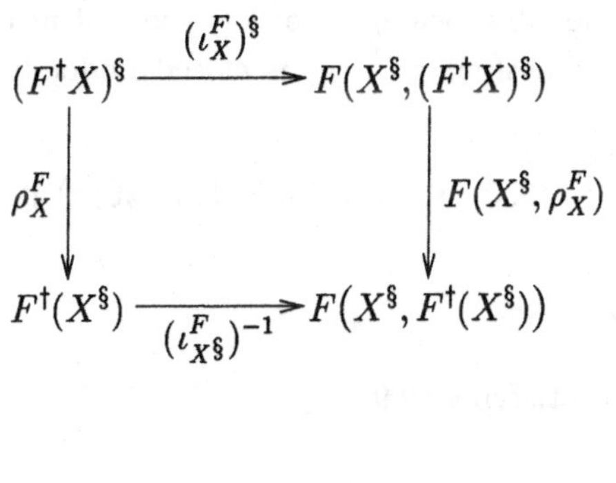

Then, applying V to the above diagram it follows that

$$\begin{array}{ccc}
(G^\dagger WX)^\S & \xrightarrow{(\iota^G_{WX})^\S} & G((WX)^\S, (G^\dagger WX)^\S) \\
{\scriptstyle V\rho^F_X}\Big\downarrow & & \Big\downarrow{\scriptstyle G((WX)^\S, V\rho^F_X)} \\
G^\dagger(WX)^\S & \xrightarrow[(\iota^G_{(WX)^\S})^{-1}]{} & G((WX)^\S, G^\dagger(WX)^\S)
\end{array}$$

and therefore $\rho^G W = V\rho^F$. In particular,

$$\Pi_2 \rho^G W \;=\; \Pi_2 V \rho^F \;=\; U\Pi_2\rho^F. \qquad (9.8)$$

And, applying V to (9.7) and using (9.8), the equality $V\varphi^F = \varphi^G W$ is easily verified. □

Further consequences of the Strict Uniformity Property, which will be used later, are given in Appendix D.

Returning to the definition of the $p\mathcal{K}(\tau)$'s we now show how it is shaped by Property (A1): if U_τ is a **Cpo**-functor then, for every ω-chain $\langle u_k : (A, \preceq_A) \rightharpoonup (B, \preceq_B)\rangle$ in $p\mathcal{K}(\tau)$, it should happen that $\bigsqcup_{p\mathcal{K}} u_k \;=\; \bigsqcup_{p\mathcal{K}(\tau)} u_k : (A, \preceq_A) \rightharpoonup (B, \preceq_B)$. How this could be guaranteed is shown by the following chain of implications: if $x \preceq_A v$ then

$\bigsqcup u_k \circ x \downarrow$

$\Rightarrow \exists\, l.\, \forall k \geq l.\; u_k \circ x \downarrow$, assuming that

$\mathcal{K}(1, A)$ *is inaccessible by lubs of* ω*-chains in* $p\mathcal{K}(1, A)$ (9.9)

$\Rightarrow \exists\, l.\, \forall k \geq l.\; u_k \circ x \preceq_B v$, because $u_k : (A, \preceq_A) \rightharpoonup (B, \preceq_B)$

$\Rightarrow \bigsqcup u_k \circ x \preceq_B v$, assuming that

${\preceq_B}^{-1}(v)$ *is closed under lubs of* ω*-chains in* $p\mathcal{K}(1, B)$. (9.10)

How to cut down the relations in the $\mathcal{R}(\tau)$'s is then dictated by (9.10):

Definition 9.2.7 Let $p\mathcal{K}(\tau)$ be the full subcategory of $\mathcal{R}(\tau)$ consisting of all those objects $(A, \preceq)$ such that for every $v \in \text{Values}(\tau)$, $\preceq^{-1}(v)$ is closed under lubs of ω-chains in $p\mathcal{K}(1, A)$. □

Proposition 9.2.8 For every $\vdash \tau$, $(0, \emptyset)$ is a zero object in $p\mathcal{K}(\tau)$ if and only if $p\mathcal{K}$ is non-trivial.

PROOF: As in Proposition 9.2.4. □

We identify those **Cpo**-models satisfying (9.9):

Definition 9.2.9 A **Cpo**-model of FPC is ***absolute*** if for every $A \in |\mathcal{K}|$, $\mathcal{K}(1, A)$ is inaccessible by lubs of ω-chains in $p\mathcal{K}(1, A)$. □

Proposition 9.2.10 In an absolute **Cpo**-model of FPC, for every $(A, \preceq) \in |p\mathcal{K}(\tau)|$ and $p \in \text{Programs}(\tau)$, $\precsim^{-1}(p)$ is closed under lubs of ω-chains in $p\mathcal{K}(1, A)$.

PROOF: Let $\langle u_k \rangle$ be an ω-chain in $p\mathcal{K}(1, A)$ such that $u_k \precsim p$. If $\bigsqcup u_k \downarrow$ there exists l such that $u_l \downarrow$. Then, for every $k \geq l$, $u_k \downarrow$ and thus there exists v_k such that $p \leadsto v_k$ and $u_k \preceq v_k$. Since $\leadsto$ is functional, there exists v such that $p \leadsto v$ and $u_k \preceq v$. But then $\bigsqcup u_k \preceq v$ and thus $\bigsqcup u_k \precsim p$. □

In domain-theoretic models of FPC (see Definition 8.5.1) absoluteness has a simple characterisation:

Proposition 9.2.11 A domain-theoretic model of FPC is absolute if and only if $[\text{id}_1]$ is inaccessible by lubs of ω-chains in $\mathcal{D}(1)$. □

Remark. Equivalently, the above could have been stated as: the $\mathcal{D}$-classifier $t : 1 \rightarrowtail \Sigma$ is inaccessible by lubs of ω-chains in $\mathcal{K}(1, \Sigma)$. (This motivates the terminology as, in absolute domain-theoretic models of FPC, ***computable truth is absolute*** in that the only way to approximate it is to have it.)

Example 9.2.12 For a small **Cpo**-category $\mathcal{W}$, the domain-theoretic model $([\mathcal{W}, \mathbf{Cpo}], \Sigma\mathbf{C}_{[\mathcal{W},\mathbf{Cpo}]})$ is absolute if and only if $\mathcal{W}$ has a finite number of connected components. □

From now on, and till the end of the section, let our fixed **Cpo**-model of FPC be an absolute non-trivial domain-theoretic one. Then, as follows from the previous analysis, $p\mathcal{K}(\tau)$ with the order inherited from $p\mathcal{K}$ is **Cpo**-enriched and U_τ is a **Cpo**-functor, but even better:

Proposition 9.2.13 Properties (A1)–(A5) hold.

PROOF: Property (A1) holds by construction of $p\mathcal{K}(\tau)$.

Property (A2) holds, as follows from Corollary 7.2.4, because $p\mathcal{K}(\tau)$ has ep-zero, (viz. $(0, \emptyset)$); $p\mathcal{K}$ has colimits of ω-chains of embeddings; and

$$U_\tau : p\mathcal{K}(\tau) \to p\mathcal{K} \text{ creates colimits of } \omega\text{-chains of embeddings} \tag{9.11}$$

as we now show. Given an ω-chain of embeddings $\langle (A_k, \precsim_k), f_k \rangle$ in $p\mathcal{K}(\tau)$ and a colimit $\phi : \langle A_k, f_k \rangle \dot{\to} A$ in $p\mathcal{K}$, by the Limit/Colimit Coincidence Theorem, it is enough to endow A with a relation $\preceq \subseteq \mathcal{K}(1, A) \times \text{Values}(\tau)$ such that

$$(A, \preceq) \in |\, p\mathcal{K}(\tau)\, |, \tag{9.12}$$
$$\phi_k : (A_k, \precsim_k) \to (A, \preceq), \quad \text{and} \tag{9.13}$$
$$\phi_k{}^R : (A, \preceq) \rightharpoonup (A_k, \precsim_k). \tag{9.14}$$

In fact (9.12)–(9.14) determine $\preceq$ as, by (9.14), we should have that $x \preceq v \;\Rightarrow\; \phi_k{}^R \circ x \precsim_k v$; whilst

$$\begin{aligned} &\phi_k{}^R \circ x \precsim_k v \\ &\quad\Rightarrow\;\; \phi_k \circ \phi_k{}^R \circ x \precsim v && \text{, by (9.13)} \\ &\quad\Rightarrow\;\; x = \bigsqcup \phi_k \circ \phi_k{}^R \circ x \precsim v && \text{, by (9.12) using Proposition 9.2.10} \\ &&& \quad\text{and the Limit/Colimit Coincidence Theorem} \\ &\quad\Rightarrow\;\; x \preceq v. \end{aligned}$$

Thus, we define

$$x \preceq v \iff \forall k \in |\, \omega\, |.\ \phi_k{}^R \circ x \precsim_k v$$

and check that (9.12)–(9.14) are satisfied. First, for every ω-chain $\langle x_l \rangle$ in $\mathcal{K}(1, A)$ such that $x_l \preceq v$ we have that $\phi_k{}^R \circ x_l \precsim_k v$ and therefore $\phi_k{}^R \circ \bigsqcup x_l = \bigsqcup_l \phi_k{}^R \circ x_l \precsim_k v$. That is, $\bigsqcup x_l \preceq v$ and thus $(A, \preceq) \in |\, p\mathcal{K}(\tau)\, |$. Second, $\phi_k : (A_k, \precsim_k) \to (A, \preceq)$ if and only if $x \precsim_k v \;\Rightarrow\; \forall l \in |\, \omega\, |.\ \phi_l{}^R \circ \phi_k \circ x \precsim_l v$. And assuming that $x \precsim_k v$, for $l \leq k$ we have that $\phi_l{}^R \circ \phi_k \circ x = f_{l,k}{}^R \circ x$ (using $\phi_l{}^R = f_{l,k}{}^R \circ \phi_k{}^R$) and since $f_{l,k}{}^R : (A_k, \precsim_k) \rightharpoonup (A_l, \precsim_l)$ it follows that $f_{l,k}{}^R \circ x \precsim_l v$; whilst, for $l \geq k$ we have that $\phi_l{}^R \circ \phi_k \circ x = f_{k,l} \circ x$ (using $\phi_k = \phi_l \circ f_{k,l}$) and since $f_{k,l} : (A_k, \precsim_k) \to (A_l, \precsim_l)$ it follows that $f_{k,l} \circ x \precsim_l v$. Third, $\phi_k{}^R : (A, \preceq) \rightharpoonup (A_k, \precsim_k)$ by definition.

Property (A3) holds because for every $(A, \preceq_A) \in |\, p\mathcal{K}(\sigma)\,|$ and $(B, \preceq_B) \in |\, p\mathcal{K}(\tau)\,|$,

$$(A \star B, \preceq_A \star \preceq_B) \in |\, p\mathcal{K}(\sigma \star \tau)\,| \qquad (\star \in \{+, \otimes, \rightharpoonup\}).$$

We consider each case:

$+$: Let $\langle x_k \rangle$ be an ω-chain in $\mathcal{K}(1, A + B)$ such that $x_k\ (\preceq_A + \preceq_B)\ v$. There are two cases:

- $v \equiv \mathtt{inl}(v_1)$: Then, for $k \in |\,\omega\,|$, there exists x'_k such that $x_k = \amalg_1 \circ x'_k$ and $x'_k \preceq_A v_1$. As $\amalg_1$ is full (by Proposition 5.3.12 and Theorem 4.2.4), $\langle x'_k \rangle$ is an ω-chain in $\mathcal{K}(1, A)$. Moreover, $\bigsqcup x_k = \amalg_1 \circ \bigsqcup x'_k$ and $\bigsqcup x'_k \preceq_A v_1$. That is, $\bigsqcup x_k\ (\preceq_A + \preceq_B)\ \mathtt{inl}(v_1)$.
- $v \equiv \mathtt{inr}(v_2)$: analogous to the previous case.

$\otimes$: Let $\langle x_k \rangle$ be an ω-chain in $\mathcal{K}(1, A \otimes B)$ such that $x_k\ (\preceq_A \otimes \preceq_B)\ \langle v_1, v_2 \rangle$. Then, for $k \in |\,\omega\,|$, $\pi_1 \circ x_k \preceq_A v_1$ and $\pi_2 \circ x_k \preceq_B v_2$. Thus $\pi_1 \circ \bigsqcup x_k = \bigsqcup \pi_1 \circ x_k \preceq_A v_1$ and $\pi_2 \circ \bigsqcup x_k = \bigsqcup \pi_2 \circ x_k \preceq_B v_2$. That is, $\bigsqcup x_k\ (\preceq_A \otimes \preceq_B)\ \langle v_1, v_2 \rangle$.

$\rightharpoonup$: Let $\langle f_k \rangle$ be an ω-chain in $\mathcal{K}(1, A \rightharpoonup B)$ such that $f_k\ (\preceq_A \rightharpoonup \preceq_B)\ \lambda\mathbf{x}.e$. Assuming that $x \preceq_A v$, for $k \in |\,\omega\,|$, $\varepsilon \circ \langle\!\langle f_k, x \rangle\!\rangle \precsim_B e[\mathbf{x} \mapsto v]$ and therefore, by Proposition 9.2.10, $\varepsilon \circ \langle\!\langle \bigsqcup f_k, x \rangle\!\rangle = \bigsqcup \varepsilon \circ \langle\!\langle f_k, v \rangle\!\rangle \precsim_B e[\mathbf{x} \mapsto v]$. That is, $\bigsqcup f_k\ (\preceq_A \rightharpoonup \preceq_B)\ \lambda\mathbf{x}.e$.

Property (A4) holds because

$$(\mathbb{I} \preceq)^{-1}(\mathtt{intro}(v)) = \preceq^{-1}(v) \quad \text{and} \quad (\mathbb{E} \preceq)^{-1}(v) = \preceq^{-1}(\mathtt{intro}(v)).$$

Finally, the Strict Uniformity Property holds by Proposition 7.3.14 (which is applicable because $U_\tau{}^{op} \times U_\tau$ preserves the zero object and creates colimits of ω-chains of embeddings as so does U_τ —see (9.11)). □

Now that Properties (A1)–(A5) are known to hold, the formal-approximation relations are constructed by providing a *non-standard* interpretation of types in the $p\mathcal{K}(\tau)$'s (Proposition 9.2.14) which extends the interpretation of types (Definition 8.4.1) respecting the folding/unfolding of recursive types (Corollary 9.2.15) and the substitution of types (Lemma 9.2.16).

Convention. Given $\Theta \equiv \mathrm{T}_1, \ldots, \mathrm{T}_m$ and $\vdash \sigma_i$ $(1 \le i \le m)$ we write $\vec{\sigma}$ for $\sigma_1, \ldots, \sigma_m$ and $[\Theta \mapsto \vec{\sigma}]$ for $[\mathrm{T}_1 \mapsto \sigma_1, \ldots, \mathrm{T}_m \mapsto \sigma_m]$.

Proposition 9.2.14 There exists an interpretation

$$\llparenthesis \Theta \vdash \tau \rrparenthesis(\vec{\sigma}) : p\mathcal{K}(\sigma_1)^{\vee} \times \ldots \times p\mathcal{K}(\sigma_{|\Theta|})^{\vee} \to p\mathcal{K}(\tau[\Theta \mapsto \vec{\sigma}])^{\vee}.$$

such that $\llparenthesis \Theta \vdash \tau \rrparenthesis(\vec{\sigma})$ is a symmetric **Cpo**-functor and

$$\begin{array}{ccc} p\mathcal{K}(\sigma_1)^{\vee} \times \ldots \times p\mathcal{K}(\sigma_{|\Theta|})^{\vee} & \xrightarrow{\llparenthesis \Theta \vdash \tau \rrparenthesis(\vec{\sigma})} & p\mathcal{K}(\tau[\Theta \mapsto \vec{\sigma}])^{\vee} \\ \downarrow & & \downarrow \\ p\check{\mathcal{K}} \times \ldots \times p\check{\mathcal{K}} & \xrightarrow[\llbracket \Theta \vdash \tau \rrbracket]{} & p\check{\mathcal{K}} \end{array}.$$

PROOF: By induction on the derivation of τ.
Write m for $|\Theta|$.

- $\tau \equiv \Theta_i$ $(1 \le i \le m)$: Define $\llparenthesis \Theta \vdash \Theta_i \rrparenthesis(\vec{\sigma}) = \Pi_i$.

- $\tau \equiv \tau_1 \star \tau_2$ where $\star \in \{+, \times, \rightharpoonup\}$:
  Define $\llparenthesis \Theta \vdash \tau_1 \star \tau_2 \rrparenthesis(\vec{\sigma}) = \llparenthesis \star_{\tau_1[\Theta \mapsto \vec{\sigma}], \tau_2[\Theta \mapsto \vec{\sigma}]} \rrparenthesis^{\vee} \circ \langle \llparenthesis \Theta \vdash \tau_1 \rrparenthesis(\vec{\sigma}), \llparenthesis \Theta \vdash \tau_2 \rrparenthesis(\vec{\sigma}) \rangle$
  where $\llparenthesis \star_{\sigma,\tau} \rrparenthesis = \begin{cases} +_{\sigma,\tau} & , \text{if } \star = + \\ \otimes_{\sigma,\tau} & , \text{if } \star = \times \\ \rightharpoonup_{\sigma,\tau} & , \text{if } \star = \rightharpoonup \end{cases}$.
  By induction, $\llparenthesis \Theta \vdash \tau_i \rrparenthesis(\vec{\sigma})$ $(i = 1, 2)$ are symmetric **Cpo**-functors and therefore so is $\llparenthesis \Theta \vdash \tau_1 \star \tau_2 \rrparenthesis(\vec{\sigma})$.
  Moreover,

$$\begin{array}{ccc} p\mathcal{K}(\sigma_1)^{\vee} \times \ldots \times p\mathcal{K}(\sigma_m)^{\vee} & \xrightarrow{\langle \llparenthesis \Theta \vdash \tau_1 \rrparenthesis(\vec{\sigma}), \llparenthesis \Theta \vdash \tau_2 \rrparenthesis(\vec{\sigma}) \rangle} & p\mathcal{K}(\tau_1[\Theta \mapsto \vec{\sigma}])^{\vee} \times p\mathcal{K}(\tau_2[\Theta \mapsto \vec{\sigma}])^{\vee} \\ \downarrow & & \downarrow \\ p\check{\mathcal{K}} \times \ldots \times p\check{\mathcal{K}} & \xrightarrow[\langle \llbracket \Theta \vdash \tau_1 \rrbracket, \llbracket \Theta \vdash \tau_2 \rrbracket \rangle]{} & p\check{\mathcal{K}} \times p\check{\mathcal{K}} \end{array}$$

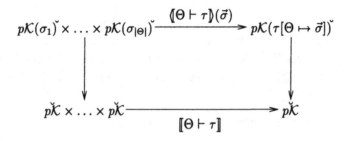

and since it follows from Proposition 9.2.5 and Property (A3) that

$$\begin{array}{ccc} p\mathcal{K}(\tau_1[\Theta \mapsto \vec{\sigma}])\breve{} \times p\mathcal{K}(\tau_2[\Theta \mapsto \vec{\sigma}])\breve{} & \xrightarrow{\langle\!|\star_{\tau_1[\Theta\mapsto\vec{\sigma}],\tau_2[\Theta\mapsto\vec{\sigma}]}|\!\rangle\breve{}\breve{}} & p\mathcal{K}(\tau_1[\Theta \mapsto \vec{\sigma}] \star \tau_2[\Theta \mapsto \vec{\sigma}])\breve{} \\ \downarrow & & \downarrow \\ p\breve{\mathcal{K}} \times p\breve{\mathcal{K}} & \xrightarrow[\llbracket\star\rrbracket\breve{}]{} & p\breve{\mathcal{K}} \end{array} \tag{9.15}$$

we are done.

- $\tau \equiv \mu\mathrm{T}.\,\tau'$:
  By induction, $\langle\!|\Theta, \mathrm{T} \vdash \tau'|\!\rangle(\vec{\sigma}, \mu\mathrm{T}.\,\tau'[\Theta \mapsto \vec{\sigma}])$ is a symmetric **Cpo**-functor and, writing τ'' for $\tau'[\Theta \mapsto \vec{\sigma}, \mathrm{T} \mapsto \mu\mathrm{T}.\tau'[\Theta \mapsto \vec{\sigma}]] \equiv \tau'[\mathrm{T} \mapsto \mu\mathrm{T}.\,\tau'][\Theta \mapsto \vec{\sigma}]$, we have that

$$\begin{array}{ccc} p\mathcal{K}(\sigma_1)\breve{} \times \ldots \times p\mathcal{K}(\sigma_m)\breve{} \times p\mathcal{K}(\mu\mathrm{T}.\,\tau'[\Theta \mapsto \vec{\sigma}])\breve{} & \xrightarrow{\langle\!|\Theta, \mathrm{T} \vdash \tau'|\!\rangle(\vec{\sigma}, \mu\mathrm{T}.\,\tau'[\Theta \mapsto \vec{\sigma}])} & p\mathcal{K}(\tau'')\breve{} \\ \downarrow & & \downarrow \\ p\breve{\mathcal{K}} \times \ldots \times p\breve{\mathcal{K}} \times p\breve{\mathcal{K}} & \xrightarrow[\llbracket\Theta, \mathrm{T} \vdash \tau'\rrbracket]{} & p\breve{\mathcal{K}} \end{array}$$

commutes.
Therefore, also

$$\begin{array}{ccccc} p\mathcal{K}(\sigma_1)\breve{} \times \ldots \times p\mathcal{K}(\sigma_m)\breve{} \times p\mathcal{K}(\mu\mathrm{T}.\,\tau'[\Theta \mapsto \vec{\sigma}])\breve{} & & \xrightarrow{F} & & p\mathcal{K}(\mu\mathrm{T}.\,\tau'[\Theta \mapsto \vec{\sigma}])\breve{} \\ & \searrow^{\langle\!|\Theta, \mathrm{T} \vdash \tau'|\!\rangle(\vec{\sigma}, \mu\mathrm{T}.\,\tau'[\Theta \mapsto \vec{\sigma}])} & & \nearrow_{\mathbb{I}^{op} \times \mathbb{I}} & \\ \downarrow & & p\mathcal{K}(\tau'')\breve{} & & \downarrow \\ & & & \searrow & \\ p\breve{\mathcal{K}} \times \ldots \times p\breve{\mathcal{K}} \times p\breve{\mathcal{K}} & & \xrightarrow[\llbracket\Theta, \mathrm{T} \vdash \tau'\rrbracket]{} & & p\breve{\mathcal{K}} \end{array}$$

commutes (where F is a symmetric **Cpo**-functor) and, by the Strict Uniformity

Property and Proposition 9.2.6, there exists $F^{\dagger}$ such that

$$\begin{array}{ccc}
p\mathcal{K}(\sigma_1)^{\vee} \times \ldots \times p\mathcal{K}(\sigma_m)^{\vee} & \xrightarrow{\quad F^{\ddagger} \quad} & p\mathcal{K}(\mu\mathrm{T}.\,\tau'[\Theta \mapsto \vec{\sigma}])^{\vee} \\
\big\downarrow & & \big\downarrow \\
p\check{\mathcal{K}} \times \ldots \times p\check{\mathcal{K}} & \xrightarrow[\llbracket \Theta, \mathrm{T} \vdash \tau' \rrbracket^{\ddagger} = \llbracket \Theta \vdash \mu\mathrm{T}.\,\tau' \rrbracket]{} & p\check{\mathcal{K}}
\end{array} .$$

Defining $\llbracket \Theta \vdash \mu\mathrm{T}.\tau' \rrbracket(\vec{\sigma}) = F^{\ddagger}$ we are done. □

Inspecting the last case in the above proof and using Proposition 9.2.6 we have:

Corollary 9.2.15 For $F = (\mathbb{I}^{op} \times \mathbb{I}) \circ \langle\!\vert \Theta, \mathrm{T} \vdash \tau \vert\!\rangle(\vec{\sigma}, \mu\mathrm{T}.\,\tau[\Theta \mapsto \vec{\sigma}])$,

$$\begin{array}{ccc}
p\mathcal{K}(\sigma_1)^{\vee} \times \ldots \times p\mathcal{K}(\sigma_{|\Theta|})^{\vee} & \overset{F\langle \mathrm{Id}, \langle\!\vert \Theta \vdash \mu\mathrm{T}.\,\tau \vert\!\rangle(\vec{\sigma}) \rangle}{\underset{\langle\!\vert \Theta \vdash \mu\mathrm{T}.\,\tau \vert\!\rangle(\vec{\sigma})}{\overset{\longrightarrow}{\underset{\longrightarrow}{\cong}}}} & p\mathcal{K}(\mu\mathrm{T}.\,\tau[\Theta \mapsto \vec{\sigma}])^{\vee} \\
\big\downarrow & & \big\downarrow \\
p\check{\mathcal{K}} \times \ldots \times p\check{\mathcal{K}} & \overset{\llbracket \Theta, \mathrm{T} \vdash \tau \rrbracket \langle \mathrm{Id}, \llbracket \Theta \vdash \mu\mathrm{T}.\,\tau \rrbracket \rangle}{\underset{\llbracket \Theta \vdash \mu\mathrm{T}.\,\tau \rrbracket}{\overset{\longrightarrow}{\underset{\longrightarrow}{\cong^{\varphi}}}}} & p\check{\mathcal{K}}
\end{array} .$$

□

Lemma 9.2.16 (Substitution Lemma) There exists a canonical natural isomorphism

$$\langle\!\vert \Theta \vdash \tau_1[\mathrm{T} \mapsto \tau_2] \vert\!\rangle(\vec{\sigma}) \;\cong\; \langle\!\vert \Theta, \mathrm{T} \vdash \tau_1 \vert\!\rangle(\vec{\sigma}, \tau_2[\Theta \mapsto \vec{\sigma}]) \circ \langle \mathrm{Id}, \langle\!\vert \Theta \vdash \tau_2 \vert\!\rangle(\vec{\sigma}) \rangle$$

satisfying

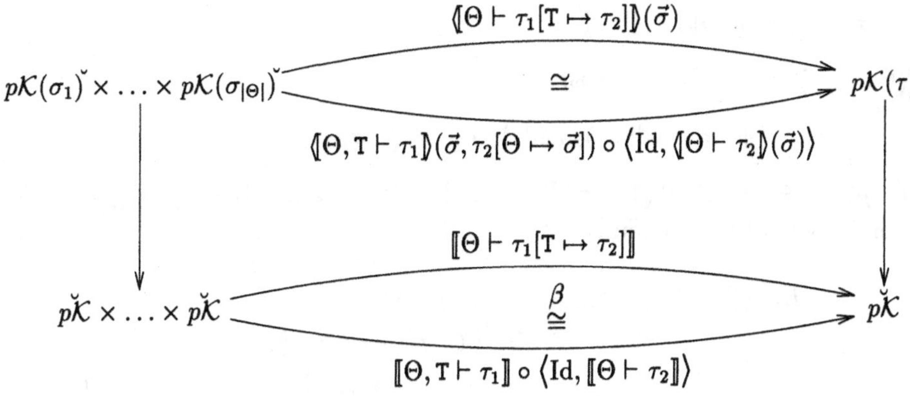

where $\tau \equiv \tau_1[\Theta \mapsto \vec{\sigma}, \mathrm{T} \mapsto \tau_2[\Theta \mapsto \vec{\sigma}]] \equiv \tau_1[\mathrm{T} \mapsto \tau_2][\Theta \mapsto \vec{\sigma}]$ and β is given by Lemma 8.4.4.

PROOF: By induction on the derivation of τ_1 (along the lines of the proof of Lemma 8.4.4 —see Appendix A— suitably generalising the permutation and contraction lemmas) using (9.15), and Propositions 9.2.6, D.0.1 and D.0.2.

The details are left to the reader. □

From the non-standard interpretation of types, the formal-approximation relations are easily extracted:

Corollary 9.2.17 There exists a family of relations $\{\preceq_\tau \subseteq \mathcal{K}(1, [\![\vdash \tau]\!]_2) \times \mathrm{Values}(\tau)\}$ such that

1. • $x \preceq_{\sigma+\tau} \mathtt{inl}(v) \iff \exists\, x'.\, x = \amalg_1 \circ x' \wedge x' \preceq_\sigma v.$

   • $x \preceq_{\sigma+\tau} \mathtt{inr}(v) \iff \exists\, x'.\, x = \amalg_2 \circ x' \wedge x' \preceq_\tau v.$

2. $x \preceq_{\sigma\times\tau} \langle v_1, v_2 \rangle \iff (\pi_1 \circ x \preceq_\sigma v_1) \wedge (\pi_2 \circ x \preceq_\tau v_2).$

3. $f \preceq_{\sigma \rightharpoonup \tau} \lambda \mathbf{x}.\, e \iff (x \preceq_\sigma v \Rightarrow \varepsilon \circ \langle\!\langle f, x \rangle\!\rangle \precsim_\tau e[\mathbf{x} \mapsto v]).$

4. $x \preceq_{\mu\mathrm{T}.\tau} \mathtt{intro}(v) \iff E \circ x \preceq_{\tau[\mathrm{T} \mapsto \mu\mathrm{T}.\tau]} v.$

PROOF: By Proposition 9.2.14, $(\!|\vdash \tau|\!)_2$ is of the form $([\![\vdash \tau]\!]_2, \preceq_\tau)$.

The family $\{\preceq_\tau\}$ has the above properties because

1. $(\!|\vdash \sigma + \tau|\!)_2 = (\!|\vdash \sigma|\!)_2 + (\!|\vdash \tau|\!)_2$.
2. $(\!|\vdash \sigma \times \tau|\!)_2 = (\!|\vdash \sigma|\!)_2 \otimes (\!|\vdash \tau|\!)_2$.
3. $(\!|\vdash \sigma \Rightarrow \tau|\!)_2 = (\!|\vdash \sigma|\!)_1 \Rightarrow (\!|\vdash \tau|\!)_2$ and $(\!|\vdash \sigma|\!)_1 = (\!|\vdash \sigma|\!)_2$.
4. $(\!|\vdash \mu\mathrm{T}.\,\tau|\!) \cong (\mathbb{I}^{op} \times \mathbb{I})\big((\!|\mathrm{T} \vdash \tau|\!)(\!|\vdash \mu\mathrm{T}.\,\tau|\!)\big) \cong (\mathbb{I}^{op} \times \mathbb{I})(\!|\vdash \tau[\mathrm{T} \mapsto \mu\mathrm{T}.\,\tau]|\!)$ so that, by Corollary 9.2.15 and Lemma 9.2.16,

$$\begin{aligned} E : ([\![\vdash \mu\mathrm{T}.\,\tau]\!]_2, \preceq_{\mu\mathrm{T}.\,\tau}) &= (\!|\vdash \mu\mathrm{T}.\,\tau|\!)_2 \\ &\cong \mathbb{I}\,(\!|\vdash \tau[\mathrm{T} \mapsto \mu\mathrm{T}.\,\tau]|\!)_2 \\ &= ([\![\vdash \tau[\mathrm{T} \mapsto \mu\mathrm{T}.\tau]]\!]_2, \mathbb{I} \preceq_{\tau[\mathrm{T} \mapsto \mu\mathrm{T}.\,\tau]}) : I \end{aligned}$$

and hence

$$\begin{aligned} & x \preceq_{\mu\mathrm{T}.\tau} \mathtt{intro}(v) \\ & \quad \Rightarrow\ E \circ x\ (\mathbb{I} \preceq_{\tau[\mathrm{T} \mapsto \mu\mathrm{T}.\tau]})\ \mathtt{intro}(v) \\ & \quad \Rightarrow\ E \circ x \preceq_{\tau[\mathrm{T} \mapsto \mu\mathrm{T}.\tau]} v \\ & \qquad\quad \Rightarrow\ E \circ x\ (\mathbb{I} \preceq_{\tau[\mathrm{T} \mapsto \mu\mathrm{T}.\tau]})\ \mathtt{intro}(v) \\ & \qquad\quad \Rightarrow\ x = I \circ E \circ x \preceq_{\mu\mathrm{T}.\tau} \mathtt{intro}(v). \end{aligned}$$

□

The main lemma, where the induction hinted at the beginning of the subsection takes place, follows:

Lemma 9.2.18 For $\Gamma \equiv \mathbf{x}_1 : \tau_1, \ldots, \mathbf{x}_n : \tau_n$,

if $x_i \preceq_{\tau_i} v_i$ $(1 \le i \le n)$ then $[\![\Gamma \vdash e : \tau]\!] \circ \langle\!\langle x_1, \ldots, x_n \rangle\!\rangle \precsim_\tau e[\mathbf{x}_1 \mapsto v_1, \ldots, \mathbf{x}_n \mapsto v_n]$.

PROOF: By induction on the structure of e.

Write x for $\langle\!\langle x_1, \ldots, x_n \rangle\!\rangle$ and $[\vec{\mathbf{x}} \mapsto \vec{v}]$ for $[\mathbf{x}_1 \mapsto v_1, \ldots, \mathbf{x}_n \mapsto v_n]$.

- $e \equiv \mathbf{x}_i$ $(1 \le i \le n)$:

$$[\![\Gamma \vdash \mathbf{x}_i : \tau_i]\!] \circ x = \pi_i \circ x = x_i \preceq_{\tau_i} v_i \quad \text{and} \quad \mathbf{x}_i[\vec{\mathbf{x}} \mapsto \vec{v}] \equiv v_i \rightsquigarrow v_i.$$

- $e \equiv \mathtt{inl}(e')$:
Assume that $[\![\Gamma \vdash \mathtt{inl}(e') : \tau' + \tau'']\!] \circ x \downarrow$.
Then, since $[\![\Gamma \vdash \mathtt{inl}(e') : \tau' + \tau'']\!] \circ x = \amalg_1 \circ [\![\Gamma \vdash e' : \tau']\!] \circ x$ it follows that $[\![\Gamma \vdash e' : \tau']\!] \circ x \downarrow$ and, by induction, there exists v' such that $e'[\vec{\mathbf{x}} \mapsto \vec{v}] \rightsquigarrow v'$ and $[\![\Gamma \vdash e' : \tau']\!] \circ x \preceq_{\tau'} v'$.

Therefore,

$$\mathtt{inl}(e')[\vec{\mathbf{x}} \mapsto \vec{v}] \equiv \mathtt{inl}(e'[\vec{\mathbf{x}} \mapsto \vec{v}]) \rightsquigarrow \mathtt{inl}(v')$$

and

$$\amalg_1 \circ [\![\Gamma \vdash e' : \tau']\!] \circ x \preceq_{\tau'+\tau''} \mathtt{inl}(v').$$

- $e \equiv \mathtt{inr}(e'')$: analogous to the previous case.
- $e \equiv \mathtt{case}\ e_0\ \mathtt{of}\ \mathtt{inl}(\mathtt{y}_1).e_1\ \mathtt{or}\ \mathtt{inr}(\mathtt{y}_2).e_2$:
  Assume that $[\![\Gamma \vdash \mathtt{case}\ e_0\ \mathtt{of}\ \mathtt{inl}(\mathtt{y}_1).e_1\ \mathtt{or}\ \mathtt{inr}(\mathtt{y}_2).e_2 : \tau]\!] \circ x \downarrow$.
  Then, since

$$\begin{aligned} &[\![\Gamma \vdash \mathtt{case}\ e_0\ \mathtt{of}\ \mathtt{inl}(\mathtt{y}_1).e_1\ \mathtt{or}\ \mathtt{inr}(\mathtt{y}_2).e_2 : \tau]\!] \circ x \\ &\quad = \big[[\![\Gamma, \mathtt{y}_1 : \tau' \vdash e_1 : \tau]\!], [\![\Gamma, \mathtt{y}_2 : \tau'' \vdash e_2 : \tau]\!]\big] \circ \delta \circ \langle\!\langle x, [\![\Gamma \vdash e_0 : \tau' + \tau'']\!] \circ x \rangle\!\rangle \end{aligned}$$

  it follows that $[\![\Gamma \vdash e_0 : \tau' + \tau'']\!] \circ x \downarrow$ and, by induction, there exists v' such that $e_0[\vec{\mathbf{x}} \mapsto \vec{v}] \rightsquigarrow v'$ and $[\![\Gamma \vdash e_0 : \tau' + \tau'']\!] \circ x \preceq_{\tau'+\tau''} v'$.
  There are two subcases:

  - $v' \equiv \mathtt{inl}(v_1')$:
    Then, $e_0[\vec{\mathbf{x}} \mapsto \vec{v}] \rightsquigarrow \mathtt{inl}(v_1')$ and $[\![\Gamma \vdash e_0 : \tau' + \tau'']\!] \circ x \preceq_{\tau'+\tau''} \mathtt{inl}(v_1')$. Thus there exists y such that $[\![\Gamma \vdash e_0 : \tau' + \tau'']\!] \circ x = \amalg_1 \circ y$ and $y \preceq_{\tau'} v_1'$.
    Then, since

$$\begin{aligned} &[\![\Gamma \vdash \mathtt{case}\ e_0\ \mathtt{of}\ \mathtt{inl}(\mathtt{y}_1).e_1\ \mathtt{or}\ \mathtt{inr}(\mathtt{y}_2).e_2 : \tau]\!] \circ x \\ &\quad = \big[[\![\Gamma, \mathtt{y}_1 : \tau' \vdash e_1 : \tau]\!], [\![\Gamma, \mathtt{y}_2 : \tau'' \vdash e_2 : \tau]\!]\big] \circ \delta \circ \langle\!\langle x, \amalg_1 \circ y \rangle\!\rangle \\ &\quad = [\![\Gamma, \mathtt{y}_1 : \tau' \vdash e_1 : \tau]\!] \circ \langle\!\langle x, y \rangle\!\rangle \end{aligned}$$

    it follows that $[\![\Gamma, \mathtt{y}_1 : \tau' \vdash e_1 : \tau]\!] \circ \langle\!\langle x, y \rangle\!\rangle \downarrow$ and, by induction, there exists v'' such that $e_1[\vec{\mathbf{x}} \mapsto \vec{v}, \mathtt{y}_1 \mapsto v_1'] \rightsquigarrow v''$ and $[\![\Gamma, \mathtt{y}_1 : \tau' \vdash e_1 : \tau]\!] \circ \langle\!\langle x, y \rangle\!\rangle \preceq_\tau v''$.
    Therefore,

$$e[\vec{\mathbf{x}} \mapsto \vec{v}] \rightsquigarrow v''$$

    and

$$[\![\Gamma \vdash e : \tau]\!] \circ x \preceq_\tau v''.$$

  - $v' \equiv \mathtt{inr}(v_2')$: analogous to the previous subcase.

- $e \equiv \mathtt{fst}(e')$:
  Assume that $[\![\Gamma \vdash \mathtt{fst}(e') : \tau]\!] \circ x \downarrow$.
  Then, since $[\![\Gamma \vdash \mathtt{fst}(e') : \tau]\!] \circ x = \pi_1 \circ [\![\Gamma \vdash e' : \tau \times \sigma]\!] \circ x$ it follows that $[\![\Gamma \vdash e' : \tau \times \sigma]\!] \circ x \downarrow$ and, by induction, there exists $\langle v_1', v_2' \rangle$ such that $e'[\vec{\mathbf{x}} \mapsto \vec{v}] \rightsquigarrow \langle v_1', v_2' \rangle$ and $[\![\Gamma \vdash e' : \tau \times \sigma]\!] \circ x \preceq_{\tau\times\sigma} \langle v_1', v_2' \rangle$.

Therefore,

$$\mathtt{fst}(e')[\vec{\mathbf{x}} \mapsto \vec{v}] \equiv \mathtt{fst}(e'[\vec{\mathbf{x}} \mapsto \vec{v}]) \leadsto v_1'$$

and

$$\pi_1 \circ [\![\Gamma \vdash e' : \tau \times \sigma]\!] \circ x \preceq_\tau v_1'.$$

- $e \equiv \mathbf{snd}(e')$: analogous to the previous case.
- $e \equiv \langle e_1, e_2 \rangle$:
  Assume that $[\![\Gamma \vdash \langle e_1, e_2\rangle : \sigma_1 \times \sigma_2]\!] \circ x \downarrow$.
  Then, since $[\![\Gamma \vdash \langle e_1, e_2\rangle : \sigma_1 \times \sigma_2]\!] \circ x = \langle\!\langle [\![\Gamma \vdash e_1 : \sigma_1]\!] \circ x, [\![\Gamma \vdash e_2 : \sigma_2]\!] \circ x \rangle\!\rangle$, for $i = 1, 2$, it follows that $[\![\Gamma \vdash e_i : \sigma_i]\!] \circ x \downarrow$ and, by induction, there exists v_i' such that $e_i[\vec{\mathbf{x}} \mapsto \vec{v}] \leadsto v_i'$ and $\pi_i \circ [\![\Gamma \vdash \langle e_1, e_2\rangle : \sigma_1 \times \sigma_2]\!] \circ x = [\![\Gamma \vdash e_i : \sigma_i]\!] \circ x \preceq_{\sigma_i} v_i'$.
  Therefore

  $$\langle e_1, e_2\rangle[\vec{\mathbf{x}} \mapsto \vec{v}] \equiv \langle e_1[\vec{\mathbf{x}} \mapsto \vec{v}], e_2[\vec{\mathbf{x}} \mapsto \vec{v}]\rangle \leadsto \langle v_1', v_2'\rangle$$

  and

  $$[\![\Gamma \vdash \langle e_1, e_2\rangle : \sigma_1 \times \sigma_2]\!] \circ x \preceq_{\sigma_1 \times \sigma_2} \langle v_1', v_2'\rangle.$$

- $e \equiv \lambda \mathbf{y}.\, e'$:
  Then,

  $$(\lambda \mathbf{y}.\, e')[\vec{\mathbf{x}} \mapsto \vec{v}] \equiv \lambda \mathbf{y}.\, e'[\vec{\mathbf{x}} \mapsto \vec{v}] \leadsto \lambda \mathbf{y}.\, e'[\vec{\mathbf{x}} \mapsto \vec{v}]$$

  and

  $$[\![\Gamma \vdash \lambda \mathbf{y}.\, e' : \sigma_1 \rightharpoonup \sigma_2]\!] \circ x \preceq_{\sigma_1 \rightharpoonup \sigma_2} \lambda \mathbf{y}.\, e'[\vec{\mathbf{x}} \mapsto \vec{v}]$$

  because if $y \preceq_{\sigma_1} v'$ then

  $$\begin{aligned} &\varepsilon \circ \langle\!\langle [\![\Gamma \vdash \lambda \mathbf{y}.\, e' : \sigma_1 \rightharpoonup \sigma_2]\!] \circ x, y \rangle\!\rangle \\ &\quad = \quad \varepsilon \circ (p\lambda([\![\Gamma, \mathbf{y} : \sigma_1 \vdash e' : \sigma_2]\!]) \otimes \mathrm{id}) \circ \langle\!\langle x, y\rangle\!\rangle \\ &\quad = \quad [\![\Gamma, \mathbf{y} : \sigma_1 \vdash e' : \sigma_2]\!] \circ \langle\!\langle x, y\rangle\!\rangle \\ &\quad \precsim_{\sigma_2} \quad e'[\vec{\mathbf{x}} \mapsto \vec{v}, \mathbf{y} \mapsto v'] \qquad\qquad \text{by induction.} \end{aligned}$$

- $e \equiv e_1(e_2)$:
  Assume that $[\![\Gamma \vdash e_1(e_2) : \tau]\!] \circ x \downarrow$.
  Since $[\![\Gamma \vdash e_1(e_2) : \tau]\!] \circ x = \varepsilon \circ \langle\!\langle [\![\Gamma \vdash e_1 : \sigma \rightharpoonup \tau]\!] \circ x, [\![\Gamma \vdash e_2 : \sigma]\!] \circ x \rangle\!\rangle$ it follows that $[\![\Gamma \vdash e_1 : \sigma \rightharpoonup \tau]\!] \circ x \downarrow$ and $[\![\Gamma \vdash e_2 : \sigma]\!] \circ x \downarrow$. Thus, by induction, there exist $\lambda \mathbf{y}.\, e'$ and v' such that $e_1[\vec{\mathbf{x}} \mapsto \vec{v}] \leadsto \lambda \mathbf{y}.\, e' \ \wedge\ [\![\Gamma \vdash e_1 : \sigma \rightharpoonup \tau]\!] \circ x \preceq_{\sigma \rightharpoonup \tau} \lambda \mathbf{y}.\, e'$ and $e_2[\vec{\mathbf{x}} \mapsto \vec{v}] \leadsto v' \ \wedge\ [\![\Gamma \vdash e_2 : \sigma]\!] \circ x \preceq_\sigma v'$.

Then,

$$\begin{aligned}
&[\![\Gamma \vdash e_1(e_2) : \tau]\!] \circ x \\
&\quad = \quad \varepsilon \circ \langle\!\langle [\![\Gamma \vdash e_1 : \sigma \Rightarrow \tau]\!] \circ x, [\![\Gamma \vdash e_2 : \sigma]\!] \circ x \rangle\!\rangle \\
&\quad \precsim_\tau \quad e'[\mathtt{y} \mapsto v']
\end{aligned}$$

Therefore, as $[\![\Gamma \vdash e_1(e_2) : \tau]\!] \circ x \downarrow$, there exists v'' such that $e'[\mathtt{y} \mapsto v'] \rightsquigarrow v''$ and

$$[\![\Gamma \vdash e_1(e_2) : \tau]\!] \circ x \preceq_\tau v''.$$

Also,

$$e_1(e_2)[\vec{\mathtt{x}} \mapsto \vec{v}] \equiv e_1[\vec{\mathtt{x}} \mapsto \vec{v}](e_2[\vec{\mathtt{x}} \mapsto \vec{v}]) \rightsquigarrow v''.$$

- $e \equiv \mathtt{intro}(e')$:
  Assume that $[\![\Gamma \vdash \mathtt{intro}(e') : \mu\mathrm{T}.\,\tau']\!] \circ x \downarrow$.
  Then, since $[\![\Gamma \vdash \mathtt{intro}(e') : \mu\mathrm{T}.\,\tau']\!] \circ x = I \circ [\![\Gamma \vdash e' : \tau'[\mathrm{T} \mapsto \mu\mathrm{T}.\,\tau']]\!] \circ x$ it follows that $[\![\Gamma \vdash e' : \tau'[\mathrm{T} \mapsto \mu\mathrm{T}.\,\tau']]\!] \circ x \downarrow$ and, by induction, there exists v' such that $e'[\vec{\mathtt{x}} \mapsto \vec{v}] \rightsquigarrow v'$ and $[\![\Gamma \vdash e' : \tau'[\mathrm{T} \mapsto \mu\mathrm{T}.\,\tau']]\!] \circ x \preceq_{\tau'[\mathrm{T} \mapsto \mu\mathrm{T}.\,\tau']} v'$.
  Therefore,

  $$\mathtt{intro}(e')[\vec{\mathtt{x}} \mapsto \vec{v}] \equiv \mathtt{intro}(e'[\vec{\mathtt{x}} \mapsto \vec{v}]) \rightsquigarrow \mathtt{intro}(v')$$

  and

  $$I \circ [\![\Gamma \vdash e' : \tau'[\mathrm{T} \mapsto \mu\mathrm{T}.\,\tau']]\!] \circ x \preceq_{\mu\mathrm{T}.\,\tau'} \mathtt{intro}(v').$$

- $e \equiv \mathtt{elim}(e')$:
  Assume that $[\![\Gamma \vdash \mathtt{elim}(e') : \tau'[\mathrm{T} \mapsto \mu\mathrm{T}.\,\tau']]\!] \circ x \downarrow$.
  Then, since $[\![\Gamma \vdash \mathtt{elim}(e') : \tau'[\mathrm{T} \mapsto \mu\mathrm{T}.\,\tau']]\!] \circ x = E \circ [\![\Gamma \vdash e' : \mu\mathrm{T}.\,\tau']\!] \circ x$ it follows that $[\![\Gamma \vdash e' : \mu\mathrm{T}.\,\tau']\!] \circ x \downarrow$ and, by induction, there exists $\mathtt{intro}(v')$ such that $e'[\vec{\mathtt{x}} \mapsto \vec{v}] \rightsquigarrow \mathtt{intro}(v')$ and $[\![\Gamma \vdash e' : \mu\mathrm{T}.\,\tau']\!] \circ x \preceq_{\mu\mathrm{T}.\,\tau'} \mathtt{intro}(v')$.
  Therefore,

  $$\mathtt{elim}(e')[\vec{\mathtt{x}} \mapsto \vec{v}] \equiv \mathtt{elim}(e'[\vec{\mathtt{x}} \mapsto \vec{v}]) \rightsquigarrow v'$$

  and

  $$E \circ [\![\Gamma \vdash e' : \mu\mathrm{T}.\,\tau']\!] \circ x \preceq_{\tau'[\mathrm{T} \mapsto \mu\mathrm{T}.\,\tau']} v'. \qquad \square$$

Finally:

Theorem 9.2.19 (Computational Adequacy) Every absolute non-trivial domain-theoretic model of FPC is computationally adequate.

PROOF: Because, by Lemma 9.2.18, $[\![\vdash p : \tau]\!] \precsim_\tau p$. □

Remark. Properties (A1)–(A5), which play a fundamental organisational role in our proof of computational adequacy, provide sufficient conditions for establishing such a result for arbitrary $\mathcal{V}$-models. In fact, it is implicit in our analysis that:

> A $\mathcal{V}$-model of FPC for which there are $\mathcal{V}$-categories $\mathcal{L}(\tau)$, such that $\mathcal{L}(\tau)_0 \cong p\mathcal{K}(\tau)$, satisfying Properties (A1)–(A5) where '**Cpo**' is replaced by '$\mathcal{V}$' and '**Cpo**-functor' by 'functor that $\mathcal{V}$-enriches', is computationally adequate.

Remark. Using (A3), domain structures with a **Cpo**-category of total maps satisfying the axioms (DTM1)–(DTM4) and absoluteness, and equipped with structure for interpreting natural numbers and booleans can be shown to be computationally adequate for call-by-value PCF with sums and products (c.f. [BCL85]).

Corollary 9.2.20 For every non-empty small **Cpo**-category $\mathcal{W}$, the domain-theoretic model specified by $([\mathcal{W}, \mathbf{Cpo}], \Sigma\mathbf{C}_{[\mathcal{W},\mathbf{Cpo}]})$ is computationally adequate. □

Remark. Thus there are computationally-adequate *non*-absolute domain-theoretic models.

10 Summary and Further Research

We have initiated an abstract approach to domain theory as needed for the denotational semantics of deterministic programming languages. To provide an explicit semantic treatment of non-termination, we decided to make partiality the core of our theory. Thus, we focussed on categories of partial maps. We have studied the representability of partial maps and shown its equivalence with classifiability. We have observed that, once partiality is taken as primitive, a notion of approximation may be derived. In fact, two notions of approximations based on testing and observing partial maps have been considered and shown to coincide. Further we have characterised when the approximation relation between partial maps is domain-theoretic in the (technical) sense that the category of partial maps **Cpo**-enriches with respect to it.

Concerning the semantics of type constructors in categories of partial maps we have: presented a characterisation of colimits of diagrams of total maps due to Gordon Plotkin; studied order-enriched partial cartesian closure; and provided conditions to guarantee the existence of the limits needed to solve recursive type equations. Concerning the semantics of recursive types we have: made Peter Freyd's notion of algebraic compactness the central concept; motivated the compactness axiom; established the fundamental property of parameterised algebraically compact categories (slightly extending a previous result of Peter Freyd); and shown that in algebraically compact categories recursive types reduce to inductive types. Special attention has been paid to **Cpo**-algebraic compactness, leading to the identification of a 2-category of kinds with very strong closure properties.

As an application of the theory developed, enriched categorical models of the metalanguage FPC have been defined and two abstract classes of models, including domain-theoretic models, have been axiomatised. Further, the metalanguage FPC was considered as a programming language with a call-by-value operational semantics and a denotational semantics (defined on top of a categorical model). It was observed that the interpretation of FPC expressions in **Poset**-models arising from **Poset**-domain-structures is representation-independent. The denotational semantics was shown to be computationally sound for the operational semantics and, more strikingly, a computational adequacy result for an axiomatisation of absolute non-trivial domain-theoretic models was proved.

The main conclusion drawn from our investigation is, thus, that axiomatic domain theory is not a dream but a possibility. But much work remains to be done as we now indicate.

10.1 Towards Axiomatic Domain Theory

We have not tried to axiomatise categories of partial maps and partial products. We plan to do it in a way for which there is a representation theorem along the following lines:

> Every axiomatised **Cpo**-category of partial maps $\mathcal{C}$ is equivalent to one of the form $(p(\mathcal{C}_t, \mathcal{D}), \sqsubseteq)$ where $\mathcal{C}_t$ is the subcategory of total maps in $\mathcal{C}$.

so that our current approach will transfer to the new one. We wonder whether such a representation theorem is available for bicategories of partial maps (see Definition 5.1.6 and Proposition 5.1.7) but, if not, we hope that the thorough study of categories of partial maps done will lead us to a natural axiomatisation.

Concerning recursive types we have obtained algebraic compactness (from the Limit/Colimit Coincidence Theorem) by stating closure under ep-zero objects and colimits of ω-chains of embeddings as axioms. Recently, in [Wag94], the category of complete internal preorders (cipos) in a sheaf topos over a suitable Heyting algebra has been shown to be closed under colimits of ω-chains of retractions. This result unifies previously known ones as, depending on the choice of the complete Heyting algebra, the cipos externally appear as cpos or generalised metric spaces. We would like to see whether our approach based on **Cpo**-enrichment generalises to cipo-enrichment. If so, this might suggest new (hopefully non-order-theoretic) examples. But even if not, we might hope to approach the old question of representability of categories of domains from this viewpoint. It might well happen that the structure required of cipo-models of FPC (or some appealing notion of cipo-categories of domains) forces the complete Heyting algebra over which the cipos are taken to be such that, externally, the cipos are some kind of complete partial order; thus making order-enrichment the only alternative.

10.2 Algebraic Completeness and Compactness

There are some (we believe, interesting and hard) questions which remain open:

1. We have exhibited a **Poset**-functor with a parameterised initial algebra which does not enrich. However a counterexample for

   $$\mathcal{V}\text{-algebraic completeness implies parameterised } \mathcal{V}\text{-algebraic completeness} \quad (10.1)$$

   is still missing. In fact, we conjecture that (10.1) does not hold in general and plan to investigate conditions under which it does.

2. We conjecture that algebraically complete categories are not closed under exponentiation.

3. We wonder which closure properties (apart from closure under initial object) are forced on a category by algebraic completeness. In particular, are **Cpo**-algebraically complete categories with e-initial object closed under colimits of ω-chains of embeddings?

For the sake of generality and to encompass more applications (e.g., the extensional pers of [FMRS92] where algebraic compactness holds for all *realisable* functors) we would like to investigate completeness and compactness in a 2-categorical setting. As it turns out the basic definitions can be easily stated. First, in a 2-cartesian-category $\mathcal{C}$, the category of algebras for an arrow $F : A \to A$ is defined as the *inserter* [Kel89] of the pair (F, Id_A). That is, a datum

$$\begin{array}{ccc} F\text{-}\mathbf{Alg} & \xrightarrow{\;p\;} & A \\ {\scriptstyle p}\downarrow & \overset{\sigma}{\Longrightarrow} & \downarrow{\scriptstyle \mathrm{Id}_A} \\ A & \xrightarrow[\;F\;]{} & A \end{array}$$

with the universal property that for every other datum

$$\begin{array}{ccc} X & \xrightarrow{\;q\;} & A \\ {\scriptstyle q}\downarrow & \overset{\tau}{\Longrightarrow} & \downarrow{\scriptstyle \mathrm{Id}_A} \\ A & \xrightarrow[\;F\;]{} & A \end{array}$$

there exists a unique $u : X \to F\text{-}\mathbf{Alg}$ such that

$$u \circ p = q : X \to A \quad \text{and} \quad u\sigma = \tau : F \circ q \Rightarrow q : X \to A.$$

Then, initial F-algebras are defined as initial objects in $\mathcal{C}(1, F\text{-}\mathbf{Alg})$. And thus, the notions of algebraic completeness and compactness can be introduced.

10.3 Computational Adequacy

We conjecture that the computational adequacy result of Chapter 9 could also be proved assuming Properties (A1)–(A4) on page 176 and replacing the Strict Uniformity Property by the following (categorically more appealing) Uniformity Property:

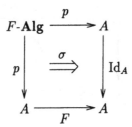

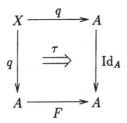

A5′. [Uniformity] For every pair of symmetric **Cpo**-functors F and G, if

$$\begin{array}{ccc} p\mathcal{K}(\sigma_1)^{\smile} \times \ldots \times p\mathcal{K}(\sigma_m)^{\smile} \times p\mathcal{K}(\sigma)^{\smile} & \xrightarrow{\quad F \quad} & p\mathcal{K}(\sigma)^{\smile} \\ {\scriptstyle W \times V}\big\downarrow & \overset{\alpha}{\cong} & \big\downarrow{\scriptstyle V} \\ p\breve{\mathcal{K}} \times \ldots \times p\breve{\mathcal{K}} \times p\breve{\mathcal{K}} & \xrightarrow[\quad G \quad]{} & p\breve{\mathcal{K}} \end{array}$$

then

$$\begin{array}{ccc} p\mathcal{K}(\sigma_1)^{\smile} \times \ldots \times p\mathcal{K}(\sigma_m)^{\smile} & \xrightarrow{\quad F^{\dagger} \quad} & p\mathcal{K}(\sigma)^{\smile} \\ {\scriptstyle W}\big\downarrow & \overset{\alpha'}{\cong} & \big\downarrow{\scriptstyle V} \\ p\breve{\mathcal{K}} \times \ldots \times p\breve{\mathcal{K}} & \xrightarrow[\quad G^{\dagger} \quad]{} & p\breve{\mathcal{K}} \end{array}$$

where $\alpha'_X : \iota^G_{WX} \to (V\iota^F_X) \circ \alpha_{(X,F^{\dagger}X)}$.

In fact, as we now show, we can go a long way towards a proof. First, we define the non-standard interpretation of types:

Definition 10.3.1 For $\vdash \sigma_i$ $(1 \leq i \leq |\,\Theta\,|)$,

$$\llparenthesis \Theta \vdash \tau \rrparenthesis(\vec{\sigma}) : p\mathcal{K}(\sigma_1)^{\smile} \times \ldots \times p\mathcal{K}(\sigma_{|\Theta|})^{\smile} \to p\mathcal{K}(\tau[\Theta \mapsto \vec{\sigma}])^{\smile}.$$

- $\llparenthesis \Theta \vdash \Theta_i \rrparenthesis(\vec{\sigma}) = \Pi_i \qquad (1 \leq i \leq |\,\Theta\,|)$.
- For $\star \in \{+, \times, \rightharpoonup\}$,
$$\llparenthesis \Theta \vdash \tau_1 \star \tau_2 \rrparenthesis(\vec{\sigma}) = \llparenthesis \star_{\tau_1[\Theta \mapsto \vec{\sigma}], \tau_2[\Theta \mapsto \vec{\sigma}]} \rrparenthesis^{\smile} \circ \langle \llparenthesis \Theta \vdash \tau_1 \rrparenthesis(\vec{\sigma}), \llparenthesis \Theta \vdash \tau_2 \rrparenthesis(\vec{\sigma}) \rangle.$$
- $\llparenthesis \Theta \vdash \mu \mathrm{T}.\, \tau \rrparenthesis(\vec{\sigma}) = \big((\mathbb{I}_{\mu \mathrm{T}.\, \tau[\Theta \mapsto \vec{\sigma}]}{}^{op} \times \mathbb{I}_{\mu \mathrm{T}.\, \tau[\Theta \mapsto \vec{\sigma}]}) \circ \llparenthesis \Theta, \mathrm{T} \vdash \tau \rrparenthesis(\vec{\sigma}, \mu \mathrm{T}.\, \tau[\Theta \mapsto \vec{\sigma}]) \big)^{\ddagger}$. □

Second, we observe that, by construction, the non-standard interpretation of types has the following properties:

Proposition 10.3.2 $\llparenthesis \Theta \vdash \tau \rrparenthesis(\vec{\sigma})$ is a symmetric **Cpo**-functor. □

Lemma 10.3.3 (Substitution Lemma) There exists a canonical natural isomorphism

$$\beta : \; \llparenthesis \Theta \vdash \tau_1[\mathrm{T} \mapsto \tau_2] \rrparenthesis(\vec{\sigma}) \;\cong\; \llparenthesis \Theta, \mathrm{T} \vdash \tau_1 \rrparenthesis(\vec{\sigma}, \tau_2[\Theta \mapsto \vec{\sigma}]) \circ \langle \mathrm{Id}, \llparenthesis \Theta \vdash \tau_2 \rrparenthesis(\vec{\sigma}) \rangle$$

such that $\beta^{\S}_X = \beta^{-1}_X$ for every symmetric X. □

Then, writing $⦇\vdash \tau⦈_2 = (⟪⦇\tau⦈⟫, \ll_\tau)$, it follows that the family of relations $\{\ll_\tau \subseteq \mathcal{K}(1, ⟪⦇\tau⦈⟫) \times \mathrm{Values}(\tau)\}$ satisfies:

$$\ll_{\sigma\star\tau} \;=\; \ll_\sigma ⦇\star_{\sigma,\tau}⦈ \ll_\tau \qquad (\star \in \{+, \times, \rightharpoonup\})$$

and

$$E : \ll_{\mu\mathtt{T}.\tau} \;\cong\; \mathbb{I} \ll_{\tau[\mathtt{T} \mapsto \mu\mathtt{T}.\tau]}$$

where E is the unfolding induced by the *non-standard* interpretation.

Third, we relate the non-standard and standard interpretations of types and try to define the formal-approximation relations by transferring the above properties.

Proposition 10.3.4 There exists a canonical natural isomorphism

$$\begin{array}{ccc}
p\mathcal{K}(\sigma_1)\check{} \times \ldots \times p\mathcal{K}(\sigma_m)\check{} & \xrightarrow{⦇\Theta \vdash \tau⦈(\vec{\sigma})} & p\mathcal{K}(\tau[\Theta \mapsto \vec{\sigma}])\check{} \\
\downarrow & \kappa^{\vec{\sigma}}_{\Theta\vdash\tau} \; \cong & \downarrow \\
p\check{\mathcal{K}} \times \ldots \times p\check{\mathcal{K}} & \xrightarrow[\llbracket\Theta \vdash \tau\rrbracket]{} & p\check{\mathcal{K}}
\end{array}$$

such that $\kappa_X^{\S} = \kappa_X^{-1}$ for every symmetric X. □

Definition 10.3.5 For $\vdash \tau$, define $\preceq_\tau \subseteq \mathcal{K}(1, \llbracket\vdash \tau\rrbracket_2) \times \mathrm{Values}(\tau)$ by

$$x \preceq_\tau v \iff \kappa_2 \circ x \ll_\tau v. \qquad \square$$

It follows that $\preceq_{\sigma\star\tau} = \preceq_\sigma ⦇\star_{\sigma,\tau}⦈ \preceq_\tau$ $(\star \in \{+, \times, \rightharpoonup\})$ but, unfortunately,

$$E : \preceq_{\mu\mathtt{T}.\tau} \;\cong\; \mathbb{I} \preceq_{\tau[\mathtt{T} \mapsto \mu\mathtt{T}.\tau]} \tag{10.2}$$

is not easy to establish. To appreciate the problem observe that

$$x \preceq_{\mu\mathtt{T}.\tau} \mathtt{intro}(v) \iff \kappa_2 \circ x \ll_{\mu\mathtt{T}.\tau} \mathtt{intro}(v) \iff E \circ \kappa_2 \circ x \ll_{\tau[\mathtt{T} \mapsto \mu\mathtt{T}.\tau]} v$$

and

$$E \circ x \preceq_{\tau[\mathtt{T} \mapsto \mu\mathtt{T}.\tau]} v \iff \kappa_2 \circ E \circ x \ll_{\tau[\mathtt{T} \mapsto \mu\mathtt{T}.\tau]} v.$$

Thus, to satisfy (10.2) we need

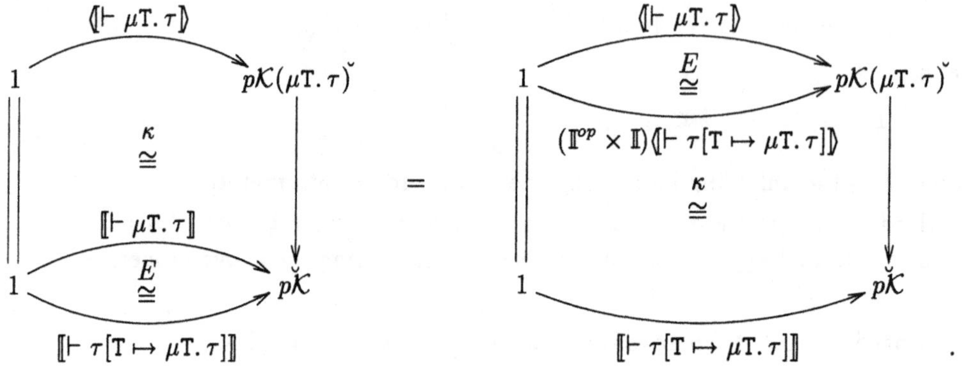

We can even go further and note that, by the construction of κ, the above equality is implied by the following

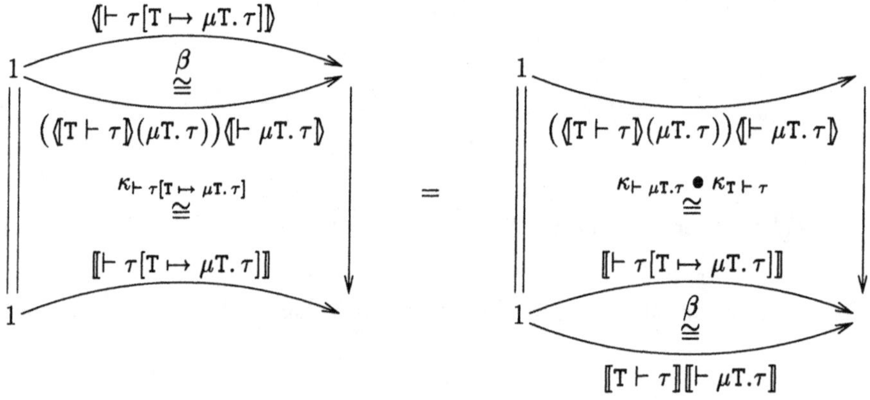
(10.3)

where $\kappa_{\vdash\, \mu \mathrm{T}.\, \tau} \bullet \kappa_{\mathrm{T} \,\vdash\, \tau}$ is the composite

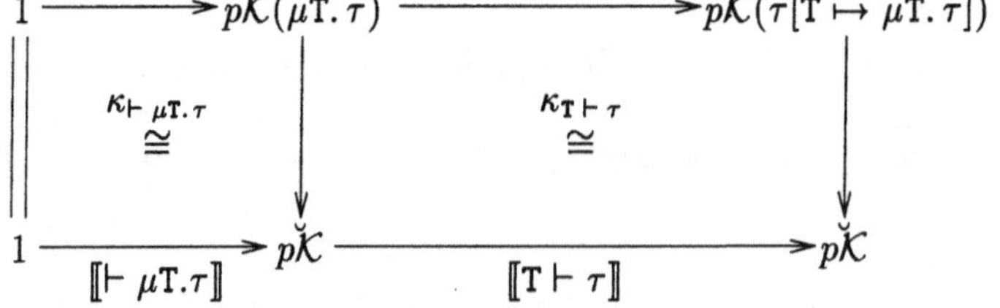

At this point, we generalise (10.3) obtaining:

Conjecture 10.3.6

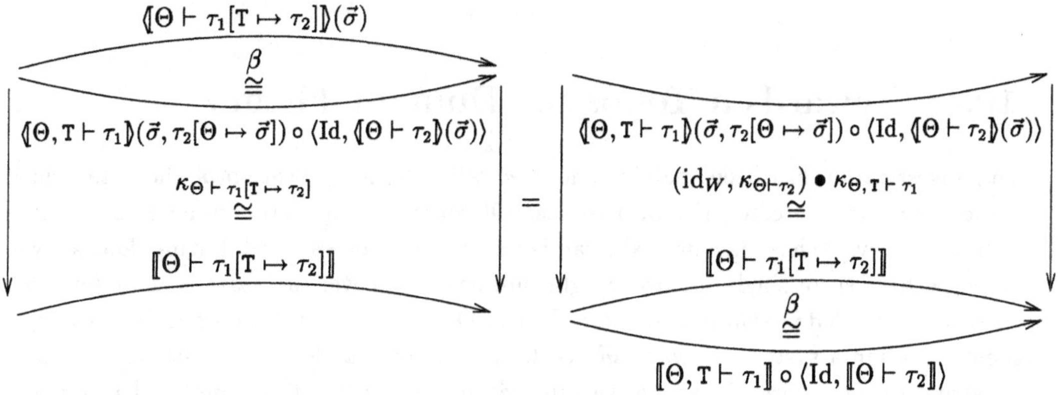

where $(\mathrm{id}_W, \kappa_{\Theta \vdash \tau_2}) \bullet \kappa_{\Theta, \mathrm{T} \vdash \tau_1}$ is the composite

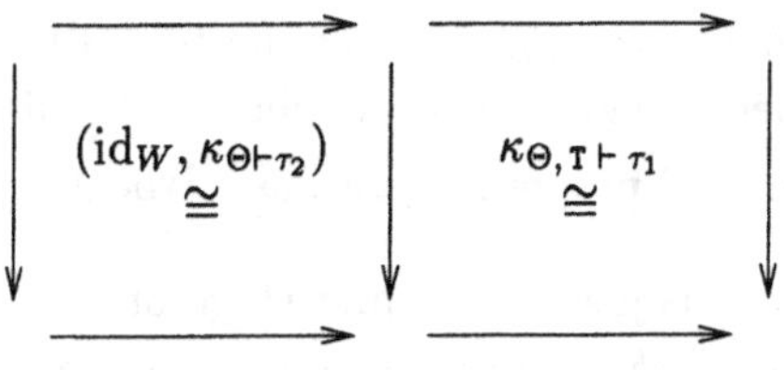

. □

Attempting to prove the conjecture by induction on the derivation of τ_1 is the natural step. It is possible to re-establish the induction hypothesis in the cases $\tau_1 \equiv \Theta_i$ and $\tau_1 \equiv \tau' \star \tau''$ ($\star \in \{+, \times, \rightharpoonup\}$). The last case, $\tau_1 \equiv \mu \mathrm{T}'.\,\tau$, involves such an unbearable number of canonical isomorphisms that we feel that a new technique is necessary.

The above problem is more general than it seems and concerns the *relation between interpretations of FPC*. A slightly simplified version of the general question behind it is:

> Given a model of FPC and two interpretations $\mathcal{I}[\![\_]\!]$ and $\mathcal{J}[\![\_]\!]$ on it, there exists a canonical natural isomorphism $i : \mathcal{I}[\![\Theta \vdash \tau]\!] \cong \mathcal{J}[\![\Theta \vdash \tau]\!] : j$, but are the interpretations of expressions essentially the same, in the sense that the equality
>
> $$i_2 \circ \mathcal{I}[\![\Theta, \Gamma \vdash e : \tau]\!] \;=\; \mathcal{J}[\![\Theta, \Gamma \vdash e : \tau]\!] \circ j_2 \qquad (10.4)$$
>
> holds?

In the absence of recursive types (10.4) can be established with no difficulty, but the general case seems a delicate *coherence* problem.

Of course, another question that we expect to consider is the adequacy of $\mathcal{K}_*$-models of FPC (see Subsection 8.5.2). To this end, we plan to extend the relational properties of domains of [Pit93a] to $\mathcal{K}_*$-models and prove the existence of the formal approximation relations using the technique proposed therein.

10.4 Towards a Topos for Domain Theory

Our investigation has been mainly concerned with the identification of the categorical structure present in categories of domains. Of course, as we were aiming at axiomatic domain theory, we have favoured abstraction over concreteness. And, having done so, we have (perhaps surprisingly) gained insight into how to recover the *naive view of domains as sets* as intended in synthetic domain theory. Our main motivation for such a development is to find a systematic way *tailored to the domains under consideration* to obtain constructive set theories in which we can reason about types (domains) and programs (partial maps between domains). As a by-product, we expect that this model-theoretic approach will help in formalising program logics (e.g., in the spirit of LCF [Sco69] with partial elements [Sco79] and reasoning principles for recursive types [Pit93a]) that account for the computational phenomenon being modelled by the domains under consideration.

An investigation of the kind proposed here was advocated by Dana Scott in [Sco80]:

> "The functor category is just a very first stage of the investigation: in topos theory the categories of *sheaves* result from putting a kind of modal operator into the logic, and making a reinterpretation of the logical connectives and quantifiers. The passage from $\mathcal{S}^{\mathcal{C}^{op}}$ is one of finding c.c.c. as cartesian closed subcategories of the functor category. There are many of them and many still contain $\mathcal{C}$ as a cartesian closed subcategory. So, there is much to look for, and — I am sure — much left to be discovered of definite logical interest."

After we proved Theorem 4.3.9, Gordon Plotkin envisaged the possibility of embedding a small category $\mathcal{K}$ (of a given **Cpo**-domain-structure $(\mathcal{K}, \mathcal{D})$ for which $p\mathcal{K}$ **Cpo**-enriches with respect to $\sqsubseteq$) in a sheaf topos. The idea is to exploit the fact that $\mathcal{D}$ is locally a cpo to specify *chain-open* covers:

Definition 10.4.1 (Plotkin) Let $(\mathcal{K}, \mathcal{D})$ be a domain structure. For every $D \in |\mathcal{K}|$, let $K_{\text{chain-open}}(D)$ be the set of all those countable chains $\{m_k : D_k \rightarrowtail D \text{ in } \mathcal{D}\}$ such that $\bigsqcup [m_k]$ in $\mathcal{D}(D)$ exists and equals $[\mathrm{id}_D]$. □

Our terminology on sheaves is as in Sections III.2 and III.4 of [LM92] except for the following:

Definition 10.4.2 A basis for a (Grothendieck) topology on a category $\mathcal{C}$ is a function K which assigns to each object C a collection $K(C)$ consisting of families of morphisms with codomain C such that

1. if $f : C' \to C$ is an isomorphism then $\{f : C' \to C\} \in K(C)$;
2. if $\{f_i : C_i \to C \mid i \in I\} \in K(C)$ then, for every $g : Z \to C$ in $\mathcal{C}$ and $i \in I$, the diagram $Z \xrightarrow{g} C \xleftarrow{f_i} C_i$ has pullback and $\{g^* f_i \to Z \mid i \in I\} \in K(Z)$;
3. if $\{f_i : C_i \to C \mid i \in I\} \in K(C)$ and, for every $i \in I$, $\{g_{ij} : Z_{ij} \to C_i \mid j \in I_i\} \in K(C_i)$ then $\{f_i \circ g_{ij} : Z_{ij} \to C \mid i \in I, j \in I_i\} \in K(C)$. □

We would like $K_{\text{chain-open}}$ to be a basis for a subcanonical topology on $\mathcal{K}$. The next two propositions determine when this is possible. In particular, Proposition 10.4.4 exhibits the essence of uniform domain structures.

Proposition 10.4.3 $K_{\text{chain-open}}$ is a basis for a topology on $\mathcal{K}$ if and only if pulling-back admissible monos along total maps is a continuous operation. □

Proposition 10.4.4 Assume that $K_{\text{chain-open}}$ is a basis for a topology on $\mathcal{K}$, and let $J_{\text{chain-open}}$ be the topology generated by $K_{\text{chain-open}}$. Then, the following statements are equivalent

1. $J_{\text{chain-open}}$ is subcanonical.
2. $(\mathcal{K}, \mathcal{D})$ is uniform (Definition 4.3.5).
3. The representable presheaves $p\mathcal{K}^{op} \to \mathbf{Set}$ satisfy the sheaf condition with respect to every cover in $K_{\text{chain-open}}$. □

Then, when $(\mathcal{K}, \mathcal{D})$ is a uniform **Cpo**-domain-structure such that $p\mathcal{K}$ **Cpo**-enriches with respect to $\sqsubseteq$ we have that $K_{\text{chain-open}}$ is a basis for a subcanonical topology. Thus, every small $\mathcal{K}$ embeds, by Yoneda, into the (Grothendieck) topos $\text{Sh}(\mathcal{K}, J_{\text{chain-open}})$. For one example, take $\mathcal{K}$ to be **SFP** (the category of bifinite domains and continuous functions) and $\mathcal{D}(D)$ to be the collection of Scott-open subsets of D.

One can even imagine to tighten the above toposes so that the structure of domain-theoretic models of FPC is preserved by the Yoneda embedding. The preservation of partial cartesian closure is immediate whilst to preserve binary coproducts we plan to consider the sheaf topos whose topology is determined by both chain-open and *binary-coproduct* covers (Definition 10.4.5).

Definition 10.4.5 Let $(\mathcal{K}, \mathcal{D})$ be a domain structure. For every object $D \in |\mathcal{K}|$, let $K_+(D) = \{f, g \in \mathcal{K} \mid A \xrightarrow{f} D \xleftarrow{g} B \text{ is a coproduct in } p\mathcal{K}\}$. □

The appropriateness of these toposes as a constructive set theory for domain theory is under investigation; results in this direction will be reported elsewhere.

10.5 Reasoning about Recursive Types

In a series of papers, Pitts [Pit92,Pit93b,Pit93a] has studied *proof principles* for reasoning about recursively defined domains derived from the initiality/finality property given by the compactness axiom. In particular, [Pit93a] establishes a mixed induction/coinduction property of *abstract* relations on recursive domains in $\mathbf{Cppo}_\perp$, shows how it specialises to well-known principles, and presents various applications. This work is carried over in $\mathbf{Cppo}_\perp$ ($\cong$ **pCpo**) but we believe it generalises to the axiomatic $\mathcal{K}_*$-models of Section 8.5. Such an investigation is left as future work.

A *coinduction principle* available for our domain-theoretic models can be found in [Fio93a] (see also [RT93,Rut93]). There, ordered categorical bisimulations are defined, and from a strong-extensionality theorem stating that the inequality relation on the final coalgebra of a **Cpo**-endofunctor is maximal among all bisimulations, the following proof principle is derived:

> For a **Cpo**-endofunctor, if R is an ordered categorical bisimulation on the final coalgebra U, and u and u' are elements of U for which $u\ R\ u'$, then $u \leq u'$.

The relation between the above two approaches is still unclear.

10.6 Non-determinism

In our study of partiality, the lifting monad arose when discussing the representability of partial maps. Non-determinism seems to arise in the same way (intuitively because partiality is a restricted form of non-determinism —viz., when at most one output is possible). We plan to study whether this can be stated precisely and, if so, we will try to transfer our approach to that setting. We expect that there will be things to adjust but hope that our abstract categorical setting is modular enough to allow the reusability of part of the theory developed.

Another possible way to incorporate non-determinism in our abstract setting is by emphasising the view of admissible monos as observable properties (in the vein of [Abr87] and [Rob87]). For example, consider domain structures $(\mathcal{K}, \mathcal{D})$ for which

1. $\mathcal{K}$ has binary products, and
2. the mapping $\mathcal{D}$ determines a binary-product preserving functor $\mathcal{K} \to \mathbf{Loc}$ where **Loc** is the category of locales.

Generalising from the characterisation of maximal units for the lifting monad (see Definition 4.5.5, Proposition 4.5.6 and the discussion after it), we could describe the powerdomain of an object by modal operators (see [Rob87]) on its locale of admissible monos. Then, an abstract powerdomain construction, internalising the powerdomain construction on locales, might be given by the data:

PD 1. a monad $(P, \eta, \mu) : \mathcal{K} \to \mathcal{K}$,

PD 2. a natural transformation $\sqcup : \times \circ \langle P, P \rangle \dot{\to} P$ making P a semilattice, and

PD 3. natural transformations $\Box^P, \Diamond^P : \mathcal{D}P \dot{\to} \mathcal{D}P$

subject to the conditions:

PC 1. that, for every $A \in |\mathcal{K}|$, $(\mathcal{D}(PA), \Box^P_A, \Diamond^P_A)$ is a powerlocale,

PC 2. that, writing $(VL, \Box^V_L, \Diamond^V_L)$ for the free powerlocale on a locale L, the unique natural transformation $\iota : (V\mathcal{D}(A), \Box^V_{\mathcal{D}A}, \Diamond^V_{\mathcal{D}A}) \dot{\to} (\mathcal{D}(PA), \Box^P_A, \Diamond^P_A)$ making the following diagram commute

$$\begin{array}{ccc} \mathcal{D} & \xrightarrow{\{-\}} & V\mathcal{D} \\ & \searrow^{\mathcal{D}\eta} & \downarrow{\iota} \\ & & \mathcal{D}P \end{array}$$

is an isomorphism,

PC 3. that $\mathcal{D}\mu = (\mathcal{D}PP \cong VV\mathcal{D} \xrightarrow{\bigcup} V\mathcal{D} \cong \mathcal{D}P)$, and

PC 4. that $\mathcal{D}\sqcup = (\mathcal{D}(P \times P) \cong \mathcal{D}P \times \mathcal{D}P \cong V\mathcal{D} \times V\mathcal{D} \xrightarrow{\cup} V\mathcal{D} \cong \mathcal{D}P)$.

Remark. Note that, by (PD 3) and (PC 1), the mapping $A \mapsto (\mathcal{D}(PA), \Box^P_A, \Diamond^P_A)$ determines a functor $\mathcal{K} \to$ **PowerLoc** where **PowerLoc** denotes the category of powerlocales.

This approach might provide connections with axiomatic semantics and program logics [Abr87,Rob87,Zha91] and open the possibility of establishing adequacy results by means of methods based on formal neighbourhoods [ML83,Abr90].

10.7 Polymorphism

We have not treated polymorphic languages. It would be interesting to axiomatise domain-theoretic models of polymorphism [CGW89] and see whether the representation-independence and adequacy results (Theorems 8.6.6 and 9.2.19) can be extended to that setting.

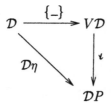

A Lemma 8.4.4

A substitution lemma for types in FPC is proved. As usual, permutation and contraction lemmas are needed and thus these are also proved.

Remark. The proofs do intensive and implicit use of Theorem 6.4.4 and Propositions 6.4.5 and 6.4.6.

Lemma A.0.1 (Permutation Lemma) Let $| \Theta | = m$ and $| \Theta' | = m'$. There exists a canonical natural isomorphism

$$\sigma : [\![\Theta, \mathrm{T}, \mathrm{T}', \Theta' \vdash \tau]\!] \cong [\![\Theta, \mathrm{T}', \mathrm{T}, \Theta' \vdash \tau]\!] \circ \langle \Pi_1, \ldots, \Pi_m, \Pi_{m+2}, \Pi_{m+1}, \Pi_{m+3}, \ldots, \Pi_{m+m'+2} \rangle$$

such that $\sigma_A^{\S} = \sigma_A^{-1}$ for every $A = A^{\S}$.

PROOF: By induction on the derivation of τ.

Write Π for $\langle \Pi_1, \ldots, \Pi_m, \Pi_{m+2}, \Pi_{m+1}, \Pi_{m+3}, \ldots, \Pi_{m+m'+2} \rangle$.

- $\tau \equiv \Theta_i$ $(1 \leq i \leq m)$:

$$[\![\Theta, \mathrm{T}, \mathrm{T}', \Theta' \vdash \Theta_i]\!] = \Pi_i = \Pi_i \circ \Pi = [\![\Theta, \mathrm{T}', \mathrm{T}, \Theta' \vdash \Theta_i]\!] \circ \Pi.$$

- $\tau \equiv \mathrm{T}$:

$$[\![\Theta, \mathrm{T}, \mathrm{T}', \Theta' \vdash \Theta_i]\!] = \Pi_{m+1} = \Pi_{m+2} \circ \Pi = [\![\Theta, \mathrm{T}', \mathrm{T}, \Theta' \vdash \Theta_i]\!] \circ \Pi.$$

- $\tau \equiv \mathrm{T}'$:

$$[\![\Theta, \mathrm{T}, \mathrm{T}', \Theta' \vdash \Theta_i]\!] = \Pi_{m+2} = \Pi_{m+1} \circ \Pi = [\![\Theta, \mathrm{T}', \mathrm{T}, \Theta' \vdash \Theta_i]\!] \circ \Pi.$$

- $\tau \equiv \Theta'_i$ $(1 \leq i \leq m')$:

$$[\![\Theta, \mathrm{T}, \mathrm{T}', \Theta' \vdash \Theta_i]\!] = \Pi_{i+m+2} = \Pi_{i+m+2} \circ \Pi = [\![\Theta, \mathrm{T}', \mathrm{T}, \Theta' \vdash \Theta_i]\!] \circ \Pi.$$

- $\tau \equiv \tau_1 \star \tau_2$ where $\star \in \{+, \times, \rightharpoonup\}$:

$$\begin{aligned}
[\![\Theta, \mathrm{T}, \mathrm{T}', \Theta' \vdash \tau_1 \star \tau_2]\!] &= [\![\star]\!]^{\smile} \circ \langle [\![\Theta, \mathrm{T}, \mathrm{T}', \Theta' \vdash \tau_1]\!], [\![\Theta, \mathrm{T}, \mathrm{T}', \Theta' \vdash \tau_2]\!] \rangle \\
&\cong [\![\star]\!]^{\smile} \circ \langle [\![\Theta, \mathrm{T}', \mathrm{T}, \Theta' \vdash \tau_1]\!] \circ \Pi, [\![\Theta, \mathrm{T}', \mathrm{T}, \Theta' \vdash \tau_2]\!] \circ \Pi \rangle \\
&= [\![\star]\!]^{\smile} \circ \langle [\![\Theta, \mathrm{T}', \mathrm{T}, \Theta' \vdash \tau_1]\!], [\![\Theta, \mathrm{T}', \mathrm{T}, \Theta' \vdash \tau_2]\!] \rangle \circ \Pi \\
&= [\![\Theta, \mathrm{T}', \mathrm{T}, \Theta' \vdash \tau_1 \star \tau_2]\!] \circ \Pi.
\end{aligned}$$

- $\tau \equiv \mu \mathrm{T}''.\tau'$:

$$\begin{aligned}
[\![\Theta, \mathrm{T}, \mathrm{T}', \Theta' \vdash \mu \mathrm{T}''.\tau']\!] &= [\![\Theta, \mathrm{T}, \mathrm{T}', \Theta', \mathrm{T}'' \vdash \tau']\!]^{\ddagger} \\
&\cong \left([\![\Theta, \mathrm{T}', \mathrm{T}, \Theta', \mathrm{T}'' \vdash \tau']\!] \circ (\Pi \times \mathrm{Id})\right)^{\ddagger} \\
&\cong [\![\Theta, \mathrm{T}', \mathrm{T}, \Theta', \mathrm{T}'' \vdash \tau']\!]^{\ddagger} \circ \Pi \\
&= [\![\Theta, \mathrm{T}', \mathrm{T}, \Theta' \vdash \mu \mathrm{T}''.\tau']\!] \circ \Pi.
\end{aligned}$$

□

Lemma A.0.2 (Contraction Lemma) Let $|\,\Theta\,| = m$ and $|\,\Theta'\,| = m'$. There exists a canonical natural isomorphism

$$\gamma : \; [\![\Theta, \mathrm{T}, \Theta' \vdash \tau]\!] \;\cong\; [\![\Theta, \Theta' \vdash \tau]\!] \circ \langle \Pi_1, \ldots, \Pi_m, \Pi_{m+2}, \ldots, \Pi_{m+m'+1} \rangle$$

such that $\gamma_A^{\S} = \gamma_A^{-1}$ for every $A = A^{\S}$.

PROOF: By induction on the derivation of τ.

Write Π for $\langle \Pi_1, \ldots, \Pi_m, \Pi_{m+2}, \ldots, \Pi_{m+m'+1} \rangle$

- $\tau \equiv \Theta_i$ $(1 \le i \le m)$:

$$[\![\Theta, \mathrm{T}, \Theta' \vdash \Theta_i]\!] = \Pi_i = \Pi_i \circ \Pi = [\![\Theta, \Theta' \vdash \Theta_i]\!] \circ \Pi.$$

- $\tau \equiv \Theta'_i$ $(1 \le i \le m')$:

$$[\![\Theta, \mathrm{T}, \Theta' \vdash \Theta'_i]\!] = \Pi_{i+m+1} = \Pi_{i+m} \circ \Pi = [\![\Theta, \Theta' \vdash \Theta'_i]\!] \circ \Pi.$$

- $\tau \equiv \tau_1 \star \tau_2$ where $\star \in \{+, \times, \rightharpoonup\}$:

$$\begin{aligned}
[\![\Theta, \mathrm{T}, \Theta' \vdash \tau_1 \star \tau_2]\!] &= [\![\star]\!]^{\smile} \circ \langle [\![\Theta, \mathrm{T}, \Theta' \vdash \tau_1]\!], [\![\Theta, \mathrm{T}, \Theta' \vdash \tau_2]\!] \rangle \\
&\cong [\![\star]\!]^{\smile} \circ \langle [\![\Theta, \Theta' \vdash \tau_1]\!] \circ \Pi, [\![\Theta, \Theta' \vdash \tau_2]\!] \circ \Pi \rangle \\
&= [\![\star]\!]^{\smile} \circ \langle [\![\Theta, \Theta' \vdash \tau_1]\!], [\![\Theta, \Theta' \vdash \tau_2]\!] \rangle \circ \Pi \\
&= [\![\Theta, \Theta' \vdash \tau_1 \star \tau_2]\!] \circ \Pi.
\end{aligned}$$

- $\tau \equiv \mu \mathrm{T}'.\tau'$:

$$\begin{aligned}
[\![\Theta, \mathrm{T}, \Theta' \vdash \mu \mathrm{T}'.\tau']\!] &= [\![\Theta, \mathrm{T}, \Theta', \mathrm{T}' \vdash \tau']\!]^{\ddagger} \\
&\cong \left([\![\Theta, \Theta', \mathrm{T}' \vdash \tau']\!] \circ (\Pi \times \mathrm{Id})\right)^{\ddagger} \\
&\cong [\![\Theta, \Theta', \mathrm{T}' \vdash \tau']\!]^{\ddagger} \circ \Pi \\
&= [\![\Theta, \Theta' \vdash \mu \mathrm{T}'.\tau']\!] \circ \Pi.
\end{aligned}$$

□

Lemma 8.4.4 (Substitution Lemma) There exists a canonical natural isomorphism

$$\beta: \ [\![\Theta \vdash \tau_1[\mathrm{T} \mapsto \tau_2]]\!] \ \cong \ [\![\Theta, \mathrm{T} \vdash \tau_1]\!] \circ \langle \mathrm{Id}, [\![\Theta \vdash \tau_2]\!] \rangle$$

such that $\beta_A^{\S} = \beta_A^{-1}$ for every $A = A^{\S}$.

PROOF: By induction on the derivation of τ_1.

Write m for $\mid \Theta \mid$.

- $\tau_1 \equiv \Theta_i \ (1 \leq i \leq m)$:

$$\begin{aligned} [\![\Theta \vdash \Theta_i[\mathrm{T} \mapsto \tau_2]]\!] &= [\![\Theta \vdash \Theta_i]\!] = \Pi_i = \Pi_i \circ \langle \Pi_1, \ldots, \Pi_m, [\![\Theta \vdash \tau_2]\!] \rangle \\ &= [\![\Theta, \mathrm{T} \vdash \Theta_i]\!] \circ \langle \mathrm{Id}, [\![\Theta \vdash \tau_2]\!] \rangle. \end{aligned}$$

- $\tau \equiv \mathrm{T}$:

$$[\![\Theta \vdash \mathrm{T}[\mathrm{T} \mapsto \tau_2]]\!] = [\![\Theta \vdash \tau_2]\!] = \Pi_{m+1} \circ \langle \mathrm{Id}, [\![\Theta \vdash \tau_2]\!] \rangle = [\![\Theta, \mathrm{T} \vdash \mathrm{T}]\!] \circ \langle \mathrm{Id}, [\![\Theta \vdash \tau_2]\!] \rangle.$$

- $\tau_1 \equiv \tau \star \tau'$ where $\star \in \{+, \times, \rightharpoonup\}$:

$$\begin{aligned} & [\![\Theta \vdash (\tau \star \tau')[\mathrm{T} \mapsto \tau_2]]\!] \\ &= [\![\Theta \vdash \tau[\mathrm{T} \mapsto \tau_2] \star \tau'[\mathrm{T} \mapsto \tau_2]]\!] \\ &= [\![\star]\!]^{\smile} \circ \langle [\![\Theta \vdash \tau[\mathrm{T} \mapsto \tau_2]]\!], [\![\Theta \vdash \tau'[\mathrm{T} \mapsto \tau_2]]\!] \rangle \\ &\cong [\![\star]\!]^{\smile} \circ \langle [\![\Theta, \mathrm{T} \vdash \tau]\!] \circ \langle \mathrm{Id}, [\![\Theta, \vdash \tau_2]\!] \rangle, [\![\Theta, \mathrm{T} \vdash \tau']\!] \circ \langle \mathrm{Id}, [\![\Theta, \vdash \tau_2]\!] \rangle \rangle \\ &= [\![\star]\!]^{\smile} \circ \langle [\![\Theta, \mathrm{T} \vdash \tau]\!], [\![\Theta, \mathrm{T} \vdash \tau']\!] \rangle \circ \langle \mathrm{Id}, [\![\Theta, \vdash \tau_2]\!] \rangle \\ &= [\![\Theta, \mathrm{T} \vdash \tau \star \tau']\!] \circ \langle \mathrm{Id}, [\![\Theta, \vdash \tau_2]\!] \rangle. \end{aligned}$$

- $\tau_1 \equiv \mu \mathrm{T}'.\tau$:

$$\begin{aligned} [\![\Theta \vdash (\mu \mathrm{T}'.\tau)[\mathrm{T} \mapsto \tau_2]]\!] &= [\![\Theta \vdash \mu \mathrm{T}'.\tau[\mathrm{T} \mapsto \tau_2]]\!] \\ &= [\![\Theta, \mathrm{T}' \vdash \tau[\mathrm{T} \mapsto \tau_2]]\!]^{\ddagger} \\ &\cong ([\![\Theta, \mathrm{T}', \mathrm{T} \vdash \tau]\!] \circ \langle \mathrm{Id}, [\![\Theta, \mathrm{T}' \vdash \tau_2]\!] \rangle)^{\ddagger} \end{aligned}$$

$$\begin{aligned} & [\![\Theta, \mathrm{T}', \mathrm{T} \vdash \tau]\!] \circ \langle \mathrm{Id}, [\![\Theta, \mathrm{T}' \vdash \tau_2]\!] \rangle \\ &\cong [\![\Theta, \mathrm{T}, \mathrm{T}' \vdash \tau]\!] \circ \langle \Pi_1, \ldots, \Pi_m, \Pi_{m+2}, \Pi_{m+1} \rangle \circ \langle \mathrm{Id}, [\![\Theta, \mathrm{T}' \vdash \tau_2]\!] \rangle \\ &= [\![\Theta, \mathrm{T}, \mathrm{T}' \vdash \tau]\!] \circ \langle \mathrm{Id}, [\![\Theta, \mathrm{T}' \vdash \tau_2]\!], \Pi_{m+1} \rangle \\ &\cong [\![\Theta, \mathrm{T}, \mathrm{T}' \vdash \tau]\!] \circ \langle \mathrm{Id}, [\![\Theta \vdash \tau_2]\!] \circ \langle \Pi_1, \ldots, \Pi_m \rangle, \Pi_{m+1} \rangle \\ &= [\![\Theta, \mathrm{T}, \mathrm{T}' \vdash \tau]\!] \circ (\langle \mathrm{Id}, [\![\Theta \vdash \tau_2]\!] \rangle \times \mathrm{Id}) \end{aligned}$$

$$\begin{aligned} [\![\Theta \vdash (\mu \mathrm{T}'.\tau)[\mathrm{T} \mapsto \tau_2]]\!] &\cong [\![\Theta, \mathrm{T}, \mathrm{T}' \vdash \tau]\!]^{\ddagger} \circ \langle \mathrm{Id}, [\![\Theta \vdash \tau_2]\!] \rangle \\ &= [\![\Theta, \mathrm{T} \vdash \mu \mathrm{T}'.\tau]\!] \circ \langle \mathrm{Id}, [\![\Theta \vdash \tau_2]\!] \rangle. \end{aligned}$$

□

B Theorem 8.6.6

Theorem 8.6.6 (Poset-Models are Parametric w.r.t. Representations)

$$[\![\Theta,\Gamma \vdash e : \tau]\!] : [\![\Theta \vdash \Gamma]\!]_R \overset{\cdot}{\underset{\lesssim}{\to}} [\![\Theta \vdash \tau]\!]_R : p\mathcal{K}_R^{|\Theta|} \to p\mathcal{K}.$$

PROOF: By induction on the derivation of $\Theta, \Gamma \vdash e : \tau$.

- $\Theta, \Gamma \vdash \Gamma_i$ where $\Gamma \equiv \mathbf{x}_1 : \tau_1, \ldots, \mathbf{x}_n : \tau_n$:

  $$\begin{array}{ll} \Pi_i \circ [\![\Theta \vdash \Gamma]\!]_R(v) & \\ \quad = \Pi_i \circ \big([\![\Theta \vdash \tau_1]\!]_R(v) \otimes \ldots \otimes [\![\Theta \vdash \tau_n]\!]_R(v)\big) & \\ \quad \sqsubseteq\!\!\!\sim\ [\![\Theta \vdash \tau_i]\!]_R(v) \circ \Pi_i & \text{, by Proposition 5.1.1 (2).} \end{array}$$

- $\Theta, \Gamma \vdash \texttt{inl}(e) : \tau_1 + \tau_2$:

  By induction,

$$\begin{array}{ccc} [\![\Theta \vdash \Gamma]\!]_R(A) & \xrightarrow{[\![\Theta,\Gamma \vdash e : \tau_1]\!]_A} & [\![\Theta \vdash \tau_1]\!]_R(A) \\ {\scriptstyle [\![\Theta \vdash \Gamma]\!]_R(v)}\downarrow & \lesssim & \downarrow{\scriptstyle [\![\Theta \vdash \tau_1]\!]_R(v)} \\ [\![\Theta \vdash \Gamma]\!]_R(B) & \xrightarrow[{[\![\Theta,\Gamma \vdash e : \tau_1]\!]_B}]{} & [\![\Theta \vdash \tau_1]\!]_R(B) \end{array} .$$

  Also,

$$\begin{array}{ccc} [\![\Theta \vdash \tau_1]\!]_R(A) & \xrightarrow{\Pi_1} & [\![\Theta \vdash \tau_1]\!]_R(A) + [\![\Theta \vdash \tau_2]\!]_R(A) = [\![\Theta \vdash \tau_1 + \tau_2]\!]_R(A) \\ {\scriptstyle [\![\Theta \vdash \tau_1]\!]_R(v)}\downarrow & & \downarrow{\scriptstyle [\![\Theta \vdash \tau_1]\!]_R(v) + [\![\Theta \vdash \tau_2]\!]_R(v) = [\![\Theta \vdash \tau_1 + \tau_2]\!]_R(v)} \\ [\![\Theta \vdash \tau_1]\!]_R(B) & \xrightarrow[\Pi_1]{} & [\![\Theta \vdash \tau_1]\!]_R(B) + [\![\Theta \vdash \tau_2]\!]_R(B) = [\![\Theta \vdash \tau_1 + \tau_2]\!]_R(B) \end{array} .$$

  Then, gluing the above two diagrams it follows that $[\![\Theta, \Gamma \vdash \texttt{inl}(e) : \tau_1 + \tau_2]\!]$ satisfies the corresponding diagram.

- $\Theta, \Gamma \vdash \texttt{inr}(e) : \tau_1 + \tau_2$: analogous to the previous case.

- $\Theta, \Gamma \vdash \texttt{case}\ e\ \texttt{of}\ \texttt{inl}(\texttt{x}_1).e_1\ \texttt{or}\ \texttt{inr}(\texttt{x}_2).e_2 : \tau$:
  Let $G = [\![\Theta \vdash \Gamma]\!]_R$, $T = [\![\Theta \vdash \tau]\!]_R$, and $T^{(i)} = [\![\Theta \vdash \tau_i]\!]_R$ $(i = 1, 2)$.
  By induction,

$$
\begin{array}{ccc}
G(A) & \xrightarrow{\ a = [\![\Theta, \Gamma \vdash e : \tau_1 + \tau_2]\!]_A\ } & T^{(1)}(A) + T^{(2)}(A) \\
{\scriptstyle G(v)}\downarrow & \sqsubseteq & \downarrow{\scriptstyle T^{(1)}(v) + T^{(2)}(v)} \\
G(B) & \xrightarrow[\ b = [\![\Theta, \Gamma \vdash e : \tau_1 + \tau_2]\!]_B\ ]{} & T^{(1)}(B) + T^{(2)}(B)
\end{array}
$$

and, for $i = 1, 2$,

$$
\begin{array}{ccc}
G(A) + T^{(i)}(A) & \xrightarrow{\ a_i = [\![\Theta, \Gamma \vdash e_i : \tau_i]\!]_A\ } & T(A) \\
{\scriptstyle G(v) + T^{(i)}(v)}\downarrow & \sqsubseteq & \downarrow{\scriptstyle T(v)} \\
G(B) + T^{(i)}(B) & \xrightarrow[\ b_i = [\![\Theta, \Gamma \vdash e_i : \tau_i]\!]_B\ ]{} & T(B)
\end{array}
\quad .
$$

Then,

$$
\begin{array}{ccc}
 & \xrightarrow{\qquad G(v) \qquad} & \\
{\scriptstyle \langle\!\langle \mathrm{id}, a \rangle\!\rangle}\downarrow & \sqsupseteq & \downarrow{\scriptstyle \langle\!\langle \mathrm{id}, b \rangle\!\rangle} \\
 & \xrightarrow[\ G(v) \otimes (T^{(1)}(v) + T^{(2)}(v))\ ]{} & \\
{\scriptstyle \delta_A}\downarrow\cong & & \cong\downarrow{\scriptstyle \delta_B} \\
 & \xrightarrow[\ (G(v) \otimes T^{(1)}(v)) + (G(v) \otimes T^{(2)}(v))\ ]{} & \\
{\scriptstyle [a_1, a_2]}\downarrow & \sqsupseteq & \downarrow{\scriptstyle [b_1, b_2]} \\
 & \xrightarrow[\qquad T(v) \qquad]{} &
\end{array}
$$

because

$$
\begin{array}{lll}
\langle\!\langle \mathrm{id}, b\rangle\!\rangle \circ G(v) & & \\
\quad = & \langle\!\langle G(v), b \circ G(v)\rangle\!\rangle & \text{, by Proposition 5.1.1 (5)} \\
\quad \underset{\sim}{\sqsubset} & \langle\!\langle G(v), \left(T^{(1)}(v) + T^{(2)}(v)\right) \circ a\rangle\!\rangle & \text{, as } \langle\!\langle -, = \rangle\!\rangle \text{ is monotone} \\
\quad = & \left(G(v) \otimes \left(T^{(1)}(v) + T^{(2)}(v)\right)\right) \circ \langle\!\langle \mathrm{id}, a\rangle\!\rangle &
\end{array}
$$

and

$$
\begin{array}{lll}
[b_1, b_2] \circ \left(\left(G(v) \otimes T^{(1)}(v)\right) + \left(G(v) \otimes T^{(2)}(v)\right)\right) & & \\
\quad = & [b_1 \circ \left(G(v) + T^{(1)}(v)\right), b_2 \circ \left(G(v) + T^{(2)}(v)\right)] & \\
\quad \underset{\sim}{\sqsubset} & [T(v) \circ a_1, T(v) \circ a_2] & \text{, as } [\, -, = \,] \text{ is monotone} \\
\quad = & T(v) \circ [a_1, a_2]. &
\end{array}
$$

- $\Theta, \Gamma \vdash \mathtt{fst}(e) : \tau_1$:
  By induction,

$$
\begin{array}{ccc}
[\![\Theta \vdash \Gamma]\!]_R(A) & \xrightarrow{[\![\Theta, \Gamma \vdash e : \tau_1 \times \tau_2]\!]_A} & [\![\Theta \vdash \tau_1 \times \tau_2]\!]_R(A) \\
{\scriptstyle [\![\Theta \vdash \Gamma]\!]_R(v)} \downarrow & \underset{\sim}{\sqsubset} & \downarrow {\scriptstyle [\![\Theta \vdash \tau_1 \times \tau_2]\!]_R(v)} \\
[\![\Theta \vdash \Gamma]\!]_R(B) & \xrightarrow[{[\![\Theta, \Gamma \vdash e : \tau_1 \times \tau_2]\!]_B}]{} & [\![\Theta \vdash \tau_1 \times \tau_2]\!]_R(B)
\end{array}
.
$$

Also,

$$
\begin{array}{ccc}
[\![\Theta \vdash \tau_1 \times \tau_2]\!]_R(A) & \xrightarrow{\pi_1} & [\![\Theta \vdash \tau_1]\!]_R(A) \\
{\scriptstyle [\![\Theta \vdash \tau_1 \times \tau_2]\!]_R(v)} \downarrow & \underset{\sim}{\sqsubset} & \downarrow {\scriptstyle [\![\Theta \vdash \tau_1]\!]_R(v)} \\
[\![\Theta \vdash \tau_1 \times \tau_2]\!]_R(B) & \xrightarrow[\pi_1]{} & [\![\Theta \vdash \tau_1]\!]_R(B)
\end{array}
$$

because

$$\begin{aligned}
&\pi_1 \circ [\![\Theta \vdash \tau_1 \times \tau_2]\!]_R(v) \\
&\quad = \pi_1 \circ \big([\![\Theta \vdash \tau_1]\!]_R(v) \otimes [\![\Theta \vdash \tau_2]\!]_R(v)\big) \\
&\quad \precsim [\![\Theta \vdash \tau_1]\!]_R(v) \circ \pi_1 \qquad\qquad \text{, by Proposition 5.1.1 (2).}
\end{aligned}$$

Gluing the above two diagrams it follows that $[\![\Theta, \Gamma \vdash \mathtt{fst}(e) : \tau_1]\!]$ satisfies the corresponding diagram.

- $\Theta, \Gamma \vdash \mathtt{snd}(e) : \tau_2$: analogous to the previous case.

- $\Theta, \Gamma \vdash \langle e_1, e_2 \rangle : \tau_1 \times \tau_2$:
  By induction, for $i = 1, 2$,

$$\begin{array}{ccc}
[\![\Theta \vdash \Gamma]\!]_R(A) & \xrightarrow{\;a_i = [\![\Theta, \Gamma \vdash e_i : \tau_i]\!]_A\;} & [\![\Theta \vdash \tau_i]\!]_R(A) \\
{\scriptstyle [\![\Theta \vdash \Gamma]\!]_R(v)}\big\downarrow & \precsim & \big\downarrow{\scriptstyle [\![\Theta \vdash \tau_i]\!]_R(v)} \\
[\![\Theta \vdash \Gamma]\!]_R(B) & \xrightarrow[\;b_i = [\![\Theta, \Gamma \vdash e_i : \tau_i]\!]_B\;]{} & [\![\Theta \vdash \tau_i]\!]_R(B)
\end{array} \quad .$$

Then,

$$\begin{aligned}
&[\![\Theta, \Gamma \vdash \langle e_1, e_2 \rangle : \tau_1 \times \tau_2]\!]_B \circ [\![\Theta \vdash \Gamma]\!]_R(v) \\
&\quad = \langle\!\langle b_1, b_2 \rangle\!\rangle \circ [\![\Theta \vdash \Gamma]\!]_R(v) \\
&\quad = \langle\!\langle b_1 \circ [\![\Theta \vdash \Gamma]\!]_R(v), b_2 \circ [\![\Theta \vdash \Gamma]\!]_R(v) \rangle\!\rangle \\
&\quad \precsim \langle\!\langle [\![\Theta \vdash \tau_1]\!]_R(v) \circ a_1, [\![\Theta \vdash \tau_2]\!]_R(v) \circ a_2 \rangle\!\rangle \qquad \text{, as } \langle\!\langle -, = \rangle\!\rangle \text{ is monotone} \\
&\quad = \big([\![\Theta \vdash \tau_1]\!]_R(v) \otimes [\![\Theta \vdash \tau_2]\!]_R(v)\big) \circ \langle\!\langle a_1, a_2 \rangle\!\rangle \\
&\quad = [\![\Theta \vdash \tau_1 \times \tau_2]\!]_R(v) \circ [\![\Theta, \Gamma \vdash \langle e_1, e_2 \rangle : \tau_1 \times \tau_2]\!]_A.
\end{aligned}$$

- $\Theta, \Gamma \vdash \lambda \mathbf{x}.e : \tau_1 \rightharpoonup \tau_2$:
  Let $G = [\![\Theta \vdash \Gamma]\!]_R$, $T = [\![\Theta \vdash \tau_1 \rightharpoonup \tau_2]\!]$, and $T^{(i)} = [\![\Theta \vdash \tau_i]\!]$ $(i = 1, 2)$.
  By induction,

$$\begin{array}{ccc}
G(A) \otimes T_R^{(1)}(A) & \xrightarrow{a = [\![\Theta, \langle \Gamma, \mathbf{x} : \tau_1 \rangle \vdash e : \tau_2]\!]_A} & T_R^{(2)}(A) \\
{\scriptstyle G(v) \otimes T_R^{(1)}(v)} \downarrow & \lesssim & \downarrow {\scriptstyle T_R^{(2)}(v)} \\
G(B) \otimes T_R^{(1)}(B) & \xrightarrow[b = [\![\Theta, \langle \Gamma, \mathbf{x} : \tau_1 \rangle \vdash e : \tau_2]\!]_B]{} & T_R^{(2)}(B)
\end{array} .$$

Then, by Proposition 5.2.2 (3), and the calculation

$$\begin{array}{rcll}
\left(T_R^{(1)}(v)\right)^L & = & T_2^{(1)}\left(\left((v_1^L, v_1), \ldots, (v_m^L, v_m)\right)^L\right) & \text{, because } T_2^{(1)} \text{ is a } \mathbf{Poset}\text{-functor} \\
& = & T_2^{(1)}\left((v_1, v_1^L), \ldots, (v_m, v_m^L)\right) & \\
& = & T_1^{(1)}\left((v_1^L, v_1), \ldots, (v_m^L, v_m)\right) & \text{, because } T^{(1)} \text{ is symmetric} \\
& = & T_1^{(1)}(v) &
\end{array}$$

it follows that

$$\begin{array}{ccc}
G(A) & \xrightarrow{p\lambda(a)} & T_R^{(1)}(A) \rightharpoonup T_R^{(2)}(A) \\
{\scriptstyle G(v)} \downarrow & \lesssim & \downarrow {\scriptstyle \left(T_R^{(1)}(v)\right)^L \rightharpoonup T_R^{(2)}(v) = T_1^{(1)}(v) \rightharpoonup T_2^{(2)}(v) = T_R(v)} \\
G(B) & \xrightarrow[p\lambda(b)]{} & T_R^{(1)}(B) \rightharpoonup T_R^{(2)}(B)
\end{array} .$$

- $\Theta, \Gamma \vdash e(e_1) : \tau_2$:
  Let $G = [\![\Theta \vdash \Gamma]\!]_R$, $T = [\![\Theta \vdash \tau_1 \rightharpoonup \tau_2]\!]_R$, and $T^{(i)} = [\![\Theta \vdash \tau_i]\!]_R$ $(i = 1, 2)$.
  By induction,

$$
\begin{array}{ccc}
G(A) & \xrightarrow{a = [\![\Theta, \Gamma \vdash e : \tau_1 \rightharpoonup \tau_2]\!]_A} & T(A) \\
{\scriptstyle G(v)} \downarrow & \underset{\sim}{\sqsubset} & \downarrow {\scriptstyle T(v) = (T^{(1)}(v))^L \rightharpoonup T^{(2)}(v)} \\
G(B) & \xrightarrow[b = [\![\Theta, \Gamma \vdash e : \tau_1 \rightharpoonup \tau_2]\!]_B]{} & T(B)
\end{array}
$$

and

$$
\begin{array}{ccc}
G(A) & \xrightarrow{a_1 = [\![\Theta, \Gamma \vdash e_1]\!]_A} & T^{(1)}(A) \\
{\scriptstyle G(v)} \downarrow & \underset{\sim}{\sqsubset} & \downarrow {\scriptstyle T^{(1)}(v)} \\
G(B) & \xrightarrow[b_1 = [\![\Theta, \Gamma \vdash e_1]\!]_B]{} & T^{(1)}(B)
\end{array}
.
$$

Then, by Proposition 5.1.1 (5) and the monotonicity of $\langle\!\langle -, = \rangle\!\rangle$,

$$
\begin{array}{ccc}
G(A) & \xrightarrow{\langle\!\langle a, a_1 \rangle\!\rangle} & (T^{(1)}(A) \rightharpoonup T^{(2)}(A)) \otimes T^{(1)}(A) \\
{\scriptstyle G(v)} \downarrow & \underset{\sim}{\sqsubset} & \downarrow {\scriptstyle ((T^{(1)}(v))^L \rightharpoonup T^{(2)}(v)) \otimes T^{(1)}(v)} \\
G(B) & \xrightarrow[\langle\!\langle b, b_1 \rangle\!\rangle]{} & (T^{(1)}(B) \rightharpoonup T^{(2)}(B)) \otimes T^{(1)}(B)
\end{array}
.
$$

Finally, by Proposition 5.2.2 (2), $[\![\Theta, \Gamma \vdash e(e_1) : \tau_2]\!]$ satisfies the corresponding diagram.

- $\Theta, \Gamma \vdash \texttt{intro}(e) : \mu\mathrm{T}.\tau$:
  By induction,

$$\begin{array}{ccc}
[\![\Theta \vdash \Gamma]\!]_R(A) & \xrightarrow{[\![\Theta, \Gamma \vdash e : \tau[\mathrm{T} \mapsto \mu\mathrm{T}.\tau]]\!]_A} & [\![\Theta \vdash \tau[\mathrm{T} \mapsto \mu\mathrm{T}.\tau]]\!]_R(A) \\
{\scriptstyle [\![\Theta \vdash \Gamma]\!]_R(v)} \downarrow & \sqsubseteq & \downarrow {\scriptstyle [\![\Theta \vdash \tau[\mathrm{T} \mapsto \mu\mathrm{T}.\tau]]\!]_R(v)} \\
[\![\Theta \vdash \Gamma]\!]_R(B) & \xrightarrow[{[\![\Theta, \Gamma \vdash e : \tau[\mathrm{T} \mapsto \mu\mathrm{T}.\tau]]\!]_B}]{} & [\![\Theta \vdash \tau[\mathrm{T} \mapsto \mu\mathrm{T}.\tau]]\!]_R(B)
\end{array}$$

  And since, by naturality,

$$\begin{array}{ccc}
[\![\Theta \vdash \tau[\mathrm{T} \mapsto \mu\mathrm{T}.\tau]]\!]_R(A) & \xrightarrow[\cong]{I_A} & [\![\Theta \vdash \mu\mathrm{T}.\tau]\!]_R(A) \\
{\scriptstyle [\![\Theta \vdash \tau[\mathrm{T} \mapsto \mu\mathrm{T}.\tau]]\!]_R(v)} \downarrow & & \downarrow {\scriptstyle [\![\Theta \vdash \mu\mathrm{T}.\tau]\!]_R(v)} \\
[\![\Theta \vdash \tau[\mathrm{T} \mapsto \mu\mathrm{T}.\tau]]\!]_R(B) & \xrightarrow[I_B]{\cong} & [\![\Theta \vdash \mu\mathrm{T}.\tau]\!]_R(B)
\end{array}$$

  it follows that $[\![\Theta, \Gamma \vdash \texttt{intro}(e) : \mu\mathrm{T}.\tau]\!]$ satisfies the corresponding diagram.
- $\Theta, \Gamma \vdash \texttt{elim}(e) : \tau[\mathrm{T} \mapsto \mu\mathrm{T}.\tau]$: analogous to the previous case. □

C Lemma 9.1.3

We prove that the interpretation of expressions is preserved under evaluation. To do this, a substitution lemma (together with permutation and contraction lemmas) for expressions is needed and thus these are also proved.

Lemma C.0.1 (Permutation Lemma) In any model of FPC,

$$\begin{aligned}&[\![\Theta, \langle\Gamma, \mathbf{x}:\tau, \mathbf{x}':\tau', \Gamma'\rangle \vdash e:\tau'']\!] \\ &\quad = [\![\Theta, \langle\Gamma, \mathbf{x}':\tau', \mathbf{x}:\tau, \Gamma'\rangle \vdash e:\tau'']\!] \circ \langle\!\langle \pi_1, \ldots, \pi_n, \pi_{n+2}, \pi_{n+1}, \pi_{n+3}, \ldots, \pi_{n+n'+2}\rangle\!\rangle\end{aligned}$$

where $|\Gamma| = n$ and $|\Gamma'| = n'$.

PROOF: By induction on the structure of e.

Write π for $\langle\!\langle \pi_1, \ldots, \pi_n, \pi_{n+2}, \pi_{n+1}, \pi_{n+3}, \ldots, \pi_{n+n'+2}\rangle\!\rangle$.

- $e \equiv \mathbf{x}_i$ $(1 \le i \le n)$:

$$\begin{aligned}[\![\Theta, \langle\Gamma, \mathbf{x}:\tau, \mathbf{x}':\tau', \Gamma'\rangle \vdash \mathbf{x}_i:\tau_i]\!] &= \pi_i = \pi_i \circ \pi \\ &= [\![\Theta, \langle\Gamma, \mathbf{x}':\tau', \mathbf{x}:\tau, \Gamma'\rangle \vdash \mathbf{x}_i:\tau_i]\!] \circ \pi.\end{aligned}$$

- $e \equiv \mathbf{x}$:

$$\begin{aligned}[\![\Theta, \langle\Gamma, \mathbf{x}:\tau, \mathbf{x}':\tau', \Gamma'\rangle \vdash \mathbf{x}:\tau]\!] &= \pi_{n+1} = \pi_{n+2} \circ \pi \\ &= [\![\Theta, \langle\Gamma, \mathbf{x}':\tau', \mathbf{x}:\tau, \Gamma'\rangle \vdash \mathbf{x}:\tau]\!] \circ \pi.\end{aligned}$$

- $e \equiv \mathbf{x}'$:

$$\begin{aligned}[\![\Theta, \langle\Gamma, \mathbf{x}:\tau, \mathbf{x}':\tau', \Gamma'\rangle \vdash \mathbf{x}':\tau']\!] &= \pi_{n+2} = \pi_{n+1} \circ \pi \\ &= [\![\Theta, \langle\Gamma, \mathbf{x}':\tau', \mathbf{x}:\tau, \Gamma'\rangle \vdash \mathbf{x}':\tau']\!] \circ \pi.\end{aligned}$$

- $e \equiv \mathbf{x}'_i$ $(1 \le i \le n')$:

$$\begin{aligned}[\![\Theta, \langle\Gamma, \mathbf{x}:\tau, \mathbf{x}':\tau', \Gamma'\rangle \vdash \mathbf{x}'_i:\tau'_i]\!] &= \pi_{n+i+2} = \pi_{n+i+2} \circ \pi \\ &= [\![\Theta, \langle\Gamma, \mathbf{x}':\tau', \mathbf{x}:\tau, \Gamma'\rangle \vdash \mathbf{x}'_i:\tau'_i]\!] \circ \pi.\end{aligned}$$

- $e \equiv \mathtt{inl}(e_1)$:

$$\begin{aligned}&[\![\Theta, \langle\Gamma, \mathbf{x}:\tau, \mathbf{x}':\tau', \Gamma'\rangle \vdash \mathtt{inl}(e_1):\tau_1+\tau_2]\!] \\ &\quad = \amalg_1 \circ [\![\Theta, \langle\Gamma, \mathbf{x}:\tau, \mathbf{x}':\tau', \Gamma'\rangle \vdash e_1:\tau_1]\!] \\ &\quad = \amalg_1 \circ [\![\Theta, \langle\Gamma, \mathbf{x}':\tau', \mathbf{x}:\tau, \Gamma'\rangle \vdash e_1:\tau_1]\!] \circ \pi \\ &\quad = [\![\Theta, \langle\Gamma, \mathbf{x}':\tau', \mathbf{x}:\tau, \Gamma'\rangle \vdash \mathtt{inl}(e_1):\tau_1+\tau_2]\!] \circ \pi.\end{aligned}$$

- $e \equiv \mathtt{inr}(e_2)$: analogous to the previous case.

- $e \equiv \texttt{case}\ e_0\ \texttt{of}\ \texttt{inl}(\mathbf{x}_1).e_1\ \texttt{or}\ \texttt{inr}(\mathbf{x}_2).e_2$:

$$
\begin{aligned}
&[\![\Theta, \langle\Gamma, \mathbf{x}:\tau, \mathbf{x}':\tau', \Gamma'\rangle \vdash \texttt{case}\ e_0\ \texttt{of}\ \texttt{inl}(\mathbf{x}_1).e_1\ \texttt{or}\ \texttt{inr}(\mathbf{x}_2).e_2 : \tau'']\!]\\
&\quad = \big[[\![\Theta, \langle\Gamma, \mathbf{x}:\tau, \mathbf{x}':\tau', \Gamma', \mathbf{x}_1:\tau_1\rangle \vdash e_1 : \tau'']\!], [\![\Theta, \langle\Gamma, \mathbf{x}:\tau, \mathbf{x}':\tau', \Gamma', \mathbf{x}_2:\tau_2\rangle \vdash e_2 : \tau'']\!]\big]\\
&\qquad \circ \delta \circ \langle\!\langle \mathrm{id}, [\![\Theta, \langle\Gamma, \mathbf{x}:\tau, \mathbf{x}':\tau', \Gamma'\rangle \vdash e_0 : \tau_1 + \tau_2]\!]\rangle\!\rangle\\
&\quad = \big[u_1 \circ (\pi \otimes \mathrm{id}_{[\![\tau_1]\!]}), u_2 \circ (\pi \otimes \mathrm{id}_{[\![\tau_2]\!]})\big] \circ \delta \circ \langle\!\langle \mathrm{id}, u_0 \circ \pi\rangle\!\rangle\\
&\qquad\qquad\qquad , \text{writing } u_0 \text{ for } [\![\Theta, \langle\Gamma, \mathbf{x}':\tau', \mathbf{x}:\tau, \Gamma'\rangle \vdash e_0 : \tau_1 + \tau_2]\!] \text{ and}\\
&\qquad\qquad\qquad u_i\ (i = 1,2) \text{ for } [\![\Theta, \langle\Gamma, \mathbf{x}':\tau', \mathbf{x}:\tau, \Gamma', \mathbf{x}_i:\tau_i\rangle \vdash e_i : \tau'']\!]\\
&\quad = [u_1, u_2] \circ \big((\pi \otimes \mathrm{id}_{[\![\tau_1]\!]}) + (\pi \otimes \mathrm{id}_{[\![\tau_2]\!]})\big) \circ \delta \circ \langle\!\langle \mathrm{id}, u_0 \circ \pi\rangle\!\rangle\\
&\quad = [u_1, u_2] \circ \delta \circ (\pi \otimes \mathrm{id}_{[\![\tau_1]\!]+[\![\tau_2]\!]}) \circ \langle\!\langle \mathrm{id}, u_0 \circ \pi\rangle\!\rangle\\
&\qquad\qquad\qquad , \text{by naturality of } \delta\\
&\quad = [u_1, u_2] \circ \delta \circ \langle\!\langle \pi, u_0 \circ \pi\rangle\!\rangle\\
&\quad = [u_1, u_2] \circ \delta \circ \langle\!\langle \mathrm{id}, u_0\rangle\!\rangle \circ \pi\\
&\quad = [\![\Theta, \langle\Gamma, \mathbf{x}':\tau', \mathbf{x}:\tau, \Gamma'\rangle \vdash \texttt{case}\ e_0\ \texttt{of}\ \texttt{inl}(\mathbf{x}_1).e_1\ \texttt{or}\ \texttt{inr}(\mathbf{x}_2).e_2 : \tau'']\!] \circ \pi.
\end{aligned}
$$

- $e \equiv \langle e_1, e_2\rangle$:

$$
\begin{aligned}
&[\![\Theta, \langle\Gamma, \mathbf{x}:\tau, \mathbf{x}':\tau', \Gamma'\rangle \vdash \langle e_1, e_2\rangle : \tau_1 \times \tau_2]\!]\\
&\quad = \langle\!\langle [\![\Theta, \langle\Gamma, \mathbf{x}:\tau, \mathbf{x}':\tau', \Gamma'\rangle \vdash e_1 : \tau_1]\!], [\![\Theta, \langle\Gamma, \mathbf{x}:\tau, \mathbf{x}':\tau', \Gamma'\rangle \vdash e_2 : \tau_2]\!]\rangle\!\rangle\\
&\quad = \langle\!\langle [\![\Theta, \langle\Gamma, \mathbf{x}':\tau', \mathbf{x}:\tau, \Gamma'\rangle \vdash e_1 : \tau_1]\!] \circ \pi, [\![\Theta, \langle\Gamma, \mathbf{x}':\tau', \mathbf{x}:\tau, \Gamma'\rangle \vdash e_2 : \tau_2]\!] \circ \pi\rangle\!\rangle\\
&\quad = \langle\!\langle [\![\Theta, \langle\Gamma, \mathbf{x}':\tau', \mathbf{x}:\tau, \Gamma'\rangle \vdash e_1 : \tau_1]\!], [\![\Theta, \langle\Gamma, \mathbf{x}':\tau', \mathbf{x}:\tau, \Gamma'\rangle \vdash e_2 : \tau_2]\!]\rangle\!\rangle \circ \pi\\
&\quad = [\![\Theta, \langle\Gamma, \mathbf{x}':\tau', \mathbf{x}:\tau, \Gamma'\rangle \vdash \langle e_1, e_2\rangle : \tau_1 \times \tau_2]\!] \circ \pi.
\end{aligned}
$$

- $e \equiv \texttt{fst}(e')$:

$$
\begin{aligned}
&[\![\Theta, \langle\Gamma, \mathbf{x}:\tau, \mathbf{x}':\tau', \Gamma'\rangle \vdash \texttt{fst}(e') : \tau_1]\!]\\
&\quad = \pi_1 \circ [\![\Theta, \langle\Gamma, \mathbf{x}:\tau, \mathbf{x}':\tau', \Gamma'\rangle \vdash e' : \tau_1 \times \tau_2]\!]\\
&\quad = \pi_1 \circ [\![\Theta, \langle\Gamma, \mathbf{x}':\tau', \mathbf{x}:\tau, \Gamma'\rangle \vdash e' : \tau_1 \times \tau_2]\!] \circ \pi\\
&\quad = [\![\Theta, \langle\Gamma, \mathbf{x}':\tau', \mathbf{x}:\tau, \Gamma'\rangle \vdash \texttt{fst}(e') : \tau_1]\!] \circ \pi.
\end{aligned}
$$

- $e \equiv \texttt{snd}(e')$: analogous to the previous case.

- $e \equiv \lambda\mathbf{x}''.\, e'$:

$$
\begin{aligned}
&[\![\Theta, \langle\Gamma, \mathbf{x}:\tau, \mathbf{x}':\tau', \Gamma'\rangle \vdash \lambda\mathbf{x}''.\, e' : \tau_1 \rightharpoonup \tau_2]\!]\\
&\quad = p\lambda\big([\![\Theta, \langle\Gamma, \mathbf{x}:\tau, \mathbf{x}':\tau', \Gamma', \mathbf{x}'':\tau_1\rangle \vdash e' : \tau_2]\!]\big)\\
&\quad = p\lambda\big([\![\Theta, \langle\Gamma, \mathbf{x}':\tau', \mathbf{x}:\tau, \Gamma', \mathbf{x}'':\tau_1\rangle \vdash e' : \tau_2]\!] \circ (\pi \otimes \mathrm{id})\big)\\
&\quad = p\lambda\big([\![\Theta, \langle\Gamma, \mathbf{x}':\tau', \mathbf{x}:\tau, \Gamma', \mathbf{x}'':\tau_1\rangle \vdash e' : \tau_2]\!]\big) \circ \pi \qquad , \text{because } \pi\downarrow\\
&\quad = [\![\Theta, \langle\Gamma, \mathbf{x}':\tau', \mathbf{x}:\tau, \Gamma'\rangle \vdash \lambda\mathbf{x}''.\, e' : \tau_1 \rightharpoonup \tau_2]\!] \circ \pi.
\end{aligned}
$$

- $e \equiv e_1(e_2)$:

$$\begin{aligned}
&[\![\Theta, \langle\Gamma, \mathbf{x} : \tau, \mathbf{x}' : \tau', \Gamma'\rangle \vdash e_1(e_2) : \tau'']\!] \\
&= \varepsilon \circ \langle\!\langle [\![\Theta, \langle\Gamma, \mathbf{x} : \tau, \mathbf{x}' : \tau', \Gamma'\rangle \vdash e_1 : \tau_2 \rightharpoonup \tau'']\!], [\![\Theta, \langle\Gamma, \mathbf{x} : \tau, \mathbf{x}' : \tau', \Gamma'\rangle \vdash e_2 : \tau_2]\!] \rangle\!\rangle \\
&= \varepsilon \circ \\
&\quad \langle\!\langle [\![\Theta, \langle\Gamma, \mathbf{x}' : \tau', \mathbf{x} : \tau, \Gamma'\rangle \vdash e_1 : \tau_2 \rightharpoonup \tau'']\!] \circ \pi, [\![\Theta, \langle\Gamma, \mathbf{x}' : \tau', \mathbf{x} : \tau, \Gamma'\rangle \vdash e_2 : \tau_2]\!] \circ \pi \rangle\!\rangle \\
&= \varepsilon \circ \langle\!\langle [\![\Theta, \langle\Gamma, \mathbf{x}' : \tau', \mathbf{x} : \tau, \Gamma'\rangle \vdash e_1 : \tau_2 \rightharpoonup \tau'']\!], [\![\Theta, \langle\Gamma, \mathbf{x}' : \tau', \mathbf{x} : \tau, \Gamma'\rangle \vdash e_2 : \tau_2]\!] \rangle\!\rangle \circ \pi \\
&= [\![\Theta, \langle\Gamma, \mathbf{x}' : \tau', \mathbf{x} : \tau, \Gamma'\rangle \vdash e_1(e_2) : \tau'']\!] \circ \pi.
\end{aligned}$$

- $e \equiv \mathtt{intro}(e')$:

$$\begin{aligned}
&[\![\Theta, \langle\Gamma, \mathbf{x} : \tau, \mathbf{x}' : \tau', \Gamma'\rangle \vdash \mathtt{intro}(e') : \mu\mathrm{T}.\,\tau_1]\!] \\
&= I \circ [\![\Theta, \langle\Gamma, \mathbf{x} : \tau, \mathbf{x}' : \tau', \Gamma'\rangle \vdash e' : \tau_1[\mathrm{T} \mapsto \mu\mathrm{T}.\,\tau_1]]\!] \\
&= I \circ [\![\Theta, \langle\Gamma, \mathbf{x}' : \tau', \mathbf{x} : \tau, \Gamma'\rangle \vdash e' : \tau_1[\mathrm{T} \mapsto \mu\mathrm{T}.\,\tau_1]]\!] \circ \pi \\
&= [\![\Theta, \langle\Gamma, \mathbf{x}' : \tau', \mathbf{x} : \tau, \Gamma'\rangle \vdash \mathtt{intro}(e') : \mu\mathrm{T}.\,\tau_1]\!] \circ \pi.
\end{aligned}$$

- $e \equiv \mathtt{elim}(e')$:

$$\begin{aligned}
&[\![\Theta, \langle\Gamma, \mathbf{x} : \tau, \mathbf{x}' : \tau', \Gamma'\rangle \vdash \mathtt{elim}(e') : \tau_1[\mathrm{T} \mapsto \mu\mathrm{T}.\,\tau_1]]\!] \\
&= E \circ [\![\Theta, \langle\Gamma, \mathbf{x} : \tau, \mathbf{x}' : \tau', \Gamma'\rangle \vdash e' : \mu\mathrm{T}.\,\tau_1]\!] \\
&= E \circ [\![\Theta, \langle\Gamma, \mathbf{x}' : \tau', \mathbf{x} : \tau, \Gamma'\rangle \vdash e' : \mu\mathrm{T}.\,\tau_1]\!] \circ \pi \\
&= [\![\Theta, \langle\Gamma, \mathbf{x}' : \tau', \mathbf{x} : \tau, \Gamma'\rangle \vdash \mathtt{elim}(e') : \tau_1[\mathrm{T} \mapsto \mu\mathrm{T}.\,\tau_1]]\!] \circ \pi. \qquad \square
\end{aligned}$$

Lemma C.0.2 (Contraction Lemma) In any model of FPC,

$$[\![\Theta, \langle\Gamma, \mathbf{x} : \tau', \Gamma'\rangle \vdash e : \tau]\!] = [\![\Theta, \langle\Gamma, \Gamma'\rangle \vdash e : \tau]\!] \circ \langle\!\langle \pi_1, \ldots, \pi_n, \pi_{n+2}, \ldots, \pi_{n+n'+1} \rangle\!\rangle$$

where $|\,\Gamma\,| = n$ and $|\,\Gamma'\,| = n'$.

PROOF: By induction on the structure of e.

Write π for $\langle\!\langle \pi_1, \ldots, \pi_n, \pi_{n+2}, \ldots, \pi_{n+n'+1} \rangle\!\rangle$.

- $e \equiv \mathbf{x}_i$ $(1 \leq i \leq n)$:

$$[\![\Theta, \langle\Gamma, \mathbf{x} : \tau', \Gamma'\rangle \vdash \mathbf{x}_i : \tau_i]\!] = \pi_i = \pi_i \circ \pi = [\![\Theta, \langle\Gamma, \Gamma'\rangle \vdash \mathbf{x}_i : \tau_i]\!] \circ \pi.$$

- $e \equiv \mathbf{x}'_i$ $(1 \leq i \leq n')$:

$$[\![\Theta, \langle\Gamma, \mathbf{x} : \tau, \Gamma'\rangle \vdash \mathbf{x}'_i : \tau'_i]\!] = \pi_{n+i+1} = \pi_{n+i} \circ \pi = [\![\Theta, \langle\Gamma, \Gamma'\rangle \vdash \mathbf{x}'_i : \tau'_i]\!] \circ \pi.$$

- $e \equiv \mathtt{inl}(e_1)$:

$$\begin{aligned}
[\![\Theta, \langle\Gamma, \mathbf{x} : \tau', \Gamma'\rangle \vdash \mathtt{inl}(e_1) : \tau_1 + \tau_2]\!] &= \amalg_1 \circ [\![\Theta, \langle\Gamma, \mathbf{x} : \tau', \Gamma'\rangle \vdash e_1 : \tau_1]\!] \\
&= \amalg_1 \circ [\![\Theta, \langle\Gamma, \Gamma'\rangle \vdash e_1 : \tau_1]\!] \circ \pi \\
&= [\![\Theta, \langle\Gamma, \Gamma'\rangle \vdash \mathtt{inl}(e_1) : \tau_1 + \tau_2]\!] \circ \pi.
\end{aligned}$$

- $e \equiv \mathtt{inr}(e_2)$: analogous to the previous case.

- $e \equiv \texttt{case}\ e_0\ \texttt{of}\ \texttt{inl}(\mathbf{x}_1).e_1\ \texttt{or}\ \texttt{inr}(\mathbf{x}_2).e_2$:

$$
\begin{aligned}
&[\![\Theta, \langle\Gamma, \mathbf{x}:\tau', \Gamma'\rangle \vdash \texttt{case}\ e_0\ \texttt{of}\ \texttt{inl}(\mathbf{x}_1).e_1\ \texttt{or}\ \texttt{inr}(\mathbf{x}_2).e_2 : \tau]\!]\\
&\quad= \big[[\![\Theta, \langle\Gamma, \mathbf{x}:\tau', \Gamma', \mathbf{x}_1:\tau_1\rangle \vdash e_1:\tau]\!], [\![\Theta, \langle\Gamma, \mathbf{x}:\tau', \Gamma', \mathbf{x}_2:\tau_2\rangle \vdash e_2:\tau]\!]\big]\\
&\qquad\circ\, \delta \circ \langle\!\langle \mathrm{id}, [\![\Theta, \langle\Gamma, \mathbf{x}:\tau', \Gamma'\rangle \vdash e_0 : \tau_1+\tau_2]\!]\rangle\!\rangle\\
&\quad= \big[u_1 \circ (\pi \otimes \mathrm{id}_{[\![\tau_1]\!]}), u_2 \circ (\pi \otimes \mathrm{id}_{[\![\tau_2]\!]})\big] \circ \delta \circ \langle\!\langle \mathrm{id}, u_0 \circ \pi\rangle\!\rangle\\
&\qquad\qquad\text{, writing } u_0 \text{ for } [\![\Theta, \langle\Gamma, \Gamma'\rangle \vdash e_0 : \tau_1+\tau_2]\!] \text{ and}\\
&\qquad\qquad u_i\ (i=1,2) \text{ for } [\![\Theta, \langle\Gamma, \Gamma', \mathbf{x}_i:\tau_i\rangle \vdash e_i:\tau]\!]\\
&\quad= [u_1, u_2] \circ \delta \circ \langle\!\langle \mathrm{id}, u_0\rangle\!\rangle \circ \pi\\
&\quad= [\![\Theta, \langle\Gamma, \Gamma'\rangle \vdash \texttt{case}\ e_0\ \texttt{of}\ \texttt{inl}(\mathbf{x}_1).e_1\ \texttt{or}\ \texttt{inr}(\mathbf{x}_2).e_2 : \tau]\!] \circ \pi.
\end{aligned}
$$

- $e \equiv \langle e_1, e_2\rangle$:

$$
\begin{aligned}
&[\![\Theta, \langle\Gamma, \mathbf{x}:\tau', \Gamma'\rangle \vdash \langle e_1, e_2\rangle : \tau_1 \times \tau_2]\!]\\
&\quad= \langle\!\langle [\![\Theta, \langle\Gamma, \mathbf{x}:\tau', \Gamma'\rangle \vdash e_1:\tau_1]\!], [\![\Theta, \langle\Gamma, \mathbf{x}:\tau', \Gamma'\rangle \vdash e_2:\tau_2]\!]\rangle\!\rangle\\
&\quad= \langle\!\langle [\![\Theta, \langle\Gamma, \Gamma'\rangle \vdash e_1:\tau_1]\!] \circ \pi, [\![\Theta, \langle\Gamma, \Gamma'\rangle \vdash e_2:\tau_2]\!] \circ \pi\rangle\!\rangle\\
&\quad= [\![\Theta, \langle\Gamma, \Gamma'\rangle \vdash \langle e_1, e_2\rangle : \tau_1 \times \tau_2]\!] \circ \pi.
\end{aligned}
$$

- $e \equiv \texttt{fst}(e')$:

$$
\begin{aligned}
[\![\Theta, \langle\Gamma, \mathbf{x}:\tau', \Gamma'\rangle \vdash \texttt{fst}(e'):\tau]\!] &= \pi_1 \circ [\![\Theta, \langle\Gamma, \mathbf{x}:\tau', \Gamma'\rangle \vdash e' : \tau \times \tau_2]\!]\\
&= \pi_1 \circ [\![\Theta, \langle\Gamma, \Gamma'\rangle \vdash e' : \tau \times \tau_2]\!] \circ \pi\\
&= [\![\Theta, \langle\Gamma, \Gamma'\rangle \vdash \texttt{fst}(e'):\tau]\!] \circ \pi.
\end{aligned}
$$

- $e \equiv \texttt{snd}(e')$: analogous to the previous case.
- $e \equiv \lambda\mathbf{x}'.\, e'$:

$$
\begin{aligned}
[\![\Theta, \langle\Gamma, \mathbf{x}:\tau', \Gamma'\rangle \vdash \lambda\mathbf{x}'.\, e' : \tau_1 \Rightarrow \tau_2]\!] &= p\lambda([\![\Theta, \langle\Gamma, \mathbf{x}:\tau', \Gamma', \mathbf{x}':\tau_1\rangle \vdash e':\tau_2]\!])\\
&= p\lambda\big([\![\Theta, \langle\Gamma, \Gamma', \mathbf{x}':\tau_1\rangle \vdash e':\tau_2]\!] \circ (\pi \otimes \mathrm{id})\big)\\
&= [\![\Theta, \langle\Gamma, \Gamma'\rangle \vdash \lambda\mathbf{x}'.\, e' : \tau_1 \Rightarrow \tau_2]\!] \circ \pi.
\end{aligned}
$$

- $e \equiv e_1(e_2)$:

$$
\begin{aligned}
&[\![\Theta, \langle\Gamma, \mathbf{x}:\tau', \Gamma'\rangle \vdash e_1(e_2):\tau]\!]\\
&\quad= \varepsilon \circ \langle\!\langle [\![\Theta, \langle\Gamma, \mathbf{x}:\tau', \Gamma'\rangle \vdash e_1:\tau'' \Rightarrow \tau]\!], [\![\Theta, \langle\Gamma, \mathbf{x}:\tau', \Gamma'\rangle \vdash e_2:\tau'']\!]\rangle\!\rangle\\
&\quad= \varepsilon \circ \langle\!\langle [\![\Theta, \langle\Gamma, \Gamma'\rangle \vdash e_1:\tau'' \Rightarrow \tau]\!] \circ \pi, [\![\Theta, \langle\Gamma, \Gamma'\rangle \vdash e_2:\tau'']\!] \circ \pi\rangle\!\rangle\\
&\quad= [\![\Theta, \langle\Gamma, \Gamma'\rangle \vdash e_1(e_2):\tau]\!] \circ \pi.
\end{aligned}
$$

- $e \equiv \mathtt{intro}(e')$:

$$\begin{aligned}
&[\![\Theta, \langle\Gamma, \mathbf{x} : \tau', \Gamma'\rangle \vdash \mathtt{intro}(e') : \mu T.\, \tau'']\!] \\
&\quad = I \circ [\![\Theta, \langle\Gamma, \mathbf{x} : \tau', \Gamma'\rangle \vdash e' : \tau''[T \mapsto \mu T.\, \tau'']]\!] \\
&\quad = I \circ [\![\Theta, \langle\Gamma, \Gamma'\rangle \vdash e' : \tau''[T \mapsto \mu T.\, \tau'']]\!] \circ \pi \\
&\quad = [\![\Theta, \langle\Gamma, \Gamma'\rangle \vdash \mathtt{intro}(e') : \mu T.\, \tau'']\!] \circ \pi.
\end{aligned}$$

- $e \equiv \mathtt{elim}(e')$:

$$\begin{aligned}
&[\![\Theta, \langle\Gamma, \mathbf{x} : \tau', \Gamma'\rangle \vdash \mathtt{elim}(e') : \tau''[T \mapsto \mu T.\, \tau'']]\!] \\
&\quad = E \circ [\![\Theta, \langle\Gamma, \mathbf{x} : \tau', \Gamma'\rangle \vdash e' : \mu T.\, \tau'']\!] \\
&\quad = E \circ [\![\Theta, \langle\Gamma, \Gamma'\rangle \vdash e' : \mu T.\, \tau'']\!] \circ \pi \\
&\quad = [\![\Theta, \langle\Gamma, \Gamma'\rangle \vdash \mathtt{elim}(e') : \tau''[T \mapsto \mu T.\, \tau'']]\!] \circ \pi. \qquad \square
\end{aligned}$$

Lemma C.0.3 (Substitution Lemma) In any model of FPC, if $[\![\Theta, \Gamma \vdash e' : \tau']\!] \downarrow$ then $[\![\Theta, \Gamma \vdash e[\mathbf{x} \mapsto e'] : \tau]\!] = [\![\Theta, \langle\Gamma, \mathbf{x} : \tau'\rangle \vdash e : \tau]\!] \circ \langle\!\langle \mathrm{id}, [\![\Theta, \Gamma \vdash e' : \tau']\!]\rangle\!\rangle$.

PROOF: By induction on the structure of e.

- $e \equiv \mathbf{x}_i$ $(1 \leq i \leq |\,\Gamma\,|)$:

$$\begin{aligned}
[\![\Theta, \Gamma \vdash \mathbf{x}_i[\mathbf{x} \mapsto e'] : \tau_i]\!] &= \pi_i = \pi_i \circ \langle\!\langle \mathrm{id}, [\![\Theta, \Gamma \vdash e' : \tau']\!]\rangle\!\rangle \\
&= [\![\Theta, \langle\Gamma, \mathbf{x} : \tau'\rangle \vdash \mathbf{x}_i : \tau_i]\!] \circ \langle\!\langle \mathrm{id}, [\![\Theta, \Gamma \vdash e' : \tau']\!]\rangle\!\rangle.
\end{aligned}$$

- $e \equiv \mathbf{x}$:

$$\begin{aligned}
[\![\Theta, \Gamma \vdash \mathbf{x}[\mathbf{x} \mapsto e'] : \tau']\!] &= [\![\Theta, \Gamma \vdash e' : \tau']\!] \\
&= [\![\Theta, \langle\Gamma, \mathbf{x} : \tau'\rangle \vdash \mathbf{x} : \tau']\!] \circ \langle\!\langle \mathrm{id}, [\![\Theta, \Gamma \vdash e' : \tau']\!]\rangle\!\rangle.
\end{aligned}$$

- $e \equiv \mathtt{inl}(e_1)$:

$$\begin{aligned}
&[\![\Theta, \Gamma \vdash \mathtt{inl}(e_1)[\mathbf{x} \mapsto e'] : \tau_1 + \tau_2]\!] \\
&\quad = [\![\Theta, \Gamma \vdash \mathtt{inl}(e_1[\mathbf{x} \mapsto e']) : \tau_1 + \tau_2]\!] \\
&\quad = \amalg_1 \circ [\![\Theta, \Gamma \vdash e_1[\mathbf{x} \mapsto e'] : \tau_1]\!] \\
&\quad = \amalg_1 \circ [\![\Theta, \langle\Gamma, \mathbf{x} : \tau'\rangle \vdash e_1 : \tau_1]\!] \circ \langle\!\langle \mathrm{id}, [\![\Theta, \Gamma \vdash e' : \tau']\!]\rangle\!\rangle \\
&\quad = [\![\Theta, \langle\Gamma, \mathbf{x} : \tau'\rangle \vdash \mathtt{inl}(e_1) : \tau_1 + \tau_2]\!] \circ \langle\!\langle \mathrm{id}, [\![\Theta, \Gamma \vdash e' : \tau']\!]\rangle\!\rangle.
\end{aligned}$$

- $e \equiv \mathtt{inr}(e_2)$: analogous to the previous case.

- $\mathtt{case}\ e_0\ \mathtt{of}\ \mathtt{inl}(\mathbf{x}_1).e_1\ \mathtt{or}\ \mathtt{inr}(\mathbf{x}_2).e_2$:

$$
\begin{aligned}
&[\![\Theta,\Gamma \vdash (\mathtt{case}\ e_0\ \mathtt{of}\ \mathtt{inl}(\mathbf{x}_1).e_1\ \mathtt{or}\ \mathtt{inr}(\mathbf{x}_2).e_2)[\mathbf{x} \mapsto e'] : \tau]\!]\\
&\quad= [\![\Theta,\Gamma \vdash \mathtt{case}\ e_0[\mathbf{x} \mapsto e']\ \mathtt{of}\ \mathtt{inl}(\mathbf{x}_1).e_1[\mathbf{x} \mapsto e']\ \mathtt{or}\ \mathtt{inr}(\mathbf{x}_2).e_2[\mathbf{x} \mapsto e'] : \tau]\!]\\
&\quad= \big[[\![\Theta,\langle\Gamma,\mathbf{x}_1:\tau_1\rangle \vdash e_1[\mathbf{x} \mapsto e'] : \tau]\!], [\![\Theta,\langle\Gamma,\mathbf{x}_2:\tau_2\rangle \vdash e_2[\mathbf{x} \mapsto e'] : \tau]\!]\big]\\
&\qquad \circ \delta \circ \big\langle\!\big\langle \mathrm{id}, [\![\Theta,\Gamma \vdash e_0[\mathbf{x} \mapsto e'] : \tau_1+\tau_2]\!]\big\rangle\!\big\rangle\\
&\quad= \big[v_1 \circ \langle\!\langle \mathrm{id}, [\![\Theta,\langle\Gamma,\mathbf{x}_1:\tau_1\rangle \vdash e' : \tau']\!]\rangle\!\rangle, v_2 \circ \langle\!\langle \mathrm{id}, [\![\Theta,\langle\Gamma,\mathbf{x}_2:\tau_2\rangle \vdash e' : \tau']\!]\rangle\!\rangle\big]\\
&\qquad \circ \delta \circ \big\langle\!\big\langle \mathrm{id}, u_0 \circ \langle\!\langle \mathrm{id}, [\![\Theta,\Gamma \vdash e' : \tau']\!]\rangle\!\rangle\big\rangle\!\big\rangle \qquad \text{(C.1)}
\end{aligned}
$$

, writing u_0 for $[\![\Theta,\langle\Gamma,\mathbf{x}:\tau'\rangle \vdash e_0 : \tau_1+\tau_2]\!]$ and v_i $(i=1,2)$ for $[\![\Theta,\langle\Gamma,\mathbf{x}_i:\tau_i,\mathbf{x}:\tau'\rangle \vdash e_i : \tau]\!]$.

By the permutation lemma, for $u_i = [\![\Theta,\langle\Gamma,\mathbf{x}:\tau',\mathbf{x}_i:\tau_i\rangle \vdash e_i : \tau]\!]$ $(i=1,2)$,

$$v_i \;=\; u_i \circ \langle\!\langle \pi_1,\ldots,\pi_n,\pi_{n+2},\pi_{n+1}\rangle\!\rangle$$

and, by the contraction lemma,

$$[\![\Theta,\langle\Gamma,\mathbf{x}_i:\tau_i\rangle \vdash e' : \tau']\!] \;=\; [\![\Theta,\Gamma \vdash e' : \tau']\!] \circ \langle\!\langle \pi_1,\ldots,\pi_n\rangle\!\rangle.$$

Hence, for $i = 1, 2$,

$$
\begin{aligned}
&v_i \circ \big\langle\!\big\langle \mathrm{id}, [\![\Theta,\langle\Gamma,\mathbf{x}_i:\tau_i\rangle \vdash e' : \tau']\!]\big\rangle\!\big\rangle\\
&\quad= u_i \circ \langle\!\langle \pi_1,\ldots,\pi_n,\pi_{n+2},\pi_{n+1}\rangle\!\rangle \circ \big\langle\!\big\langle \mathrm{id}, [\![\Theta,\Gamma \vdash e' : \tau']\!] \circ \langle\!\langle \pi_1,\ldots,\pi_n\rangle\!\rangle\big\rangle\!\big\rangle\\
&\quad= u_i \circ \langle\!\langle \pi_1,\ldots,\pi_n, [\![\Theta,\Gamma \vdash e' : \tau']\!] \circ \langle\!\langle \pi_1,\ldots,\pi_n\rangle\!\rangle, \pi_{n+1}\rangle\!\rangle\\
&\quad= u_i \circ \big(\big\langle\!\big\langle \mathrm{id}, [\![\Theta,\Gamma \vdash e' : \tau']\!]\big\rangle\!\big\rangle \otimes \mathrm{id}_{[\![\tau_i]\!]}\big). \qquad \text{(C.2)}
\end{aligned}
$$

Finally, from (C.1) and (C.2),

$$
\begin{aligned}
&[\![\Theta,\Gamma \vdash (\mathtt{case}\ e_0\ \mathtt{of}\ \mathtt{inl}(\mathbf{x}_1).e_1\ \mathtt{or}\ \mathtt{inr}(\mathbf{x}_2).e_2)[\mathbf{x} \mapsto e'] : \tau]\!]\\
&\quad= \big[u_1 \circ \big(\big\langle\!\big\langle \mathrm{id}, [\![\Theta,\Gamma \vdash e' : \tau']\!]\big\rangle\!\big\rangle \otimes \mathrm{id}_{[\![\tau_1]\!]}\big), u_2 \circ \big(\big\langle\!\big\langle \mathrm{id}, [\![\Theta,\Gamma \vdash e' : \tau']\!]\big\rangle\!\big\rangle \otimes \mathrm{id}_{[\![\tau_2]\!]}\big)\big]\\
&\qquad \circ \delta \circ \big\langle\!\big\langle \mathrm{id}, u_0 \circ \big\langle\!\big\langle \mathrm{id}, [\![\Theta,\Gamma \vdash e' : \tau']\!]\big\rangle\!\big\rangle\big\rangle\!\big\rangle\\
&\quad= [u_1,u_2] \circ \delta \circ \langle\!\langle \mathrm{id}, u_0\rangle\!\rangle \circ \big\langle\!\big\langle \mathrm{id}, [\![\Theta,\Gamma \vdash e' : \tau']\!]\big\rangle\!\big\rangle\\
&\quad= [\![\Theta,\langle\Gamma,\mathbf{x}:\tau'\rangle \vdash \mathtt{case}\ e_0\ \mathtt{of}\ \mathtt{inl}(\mathbf{x}_1).e_1\ \mathtt{or}\ \mathtt{inr}(\mathbf{x}_2).e_2 : \tau]\!]\\
&\qquad \circ \big\langle\!\big\langle \mathrm{id}, [\![\Theta,\Gamma \vdash e' : \tau']\!]\big\rangle\!\big\rangle.
\end{aligned}
$$

- $e \equiv \langle e_1, e_2 \rangle$:

$$
\begin{aligned}
&[\![\Theta, \Gamma \vdash \langle e_1, e_2\rangle[\mathbf{x} \mapsto e'] : \tau_1 \times \tau_2]\!] \\
&\quad = [\![\Theta, \Gamma \vdash \langle e_1[\mathbf{x} \mapsto e'], e_2[\mathbf{x} \mapsto e']\rangle : \tau_1 \times \tau_2]\!] \\
&\quad = \langle\!\langle [\![\Theta, \Gamma \vdash e_1[\mathbf{x} \mapsto e'] : \tau_1]\!], [\![\Theta, \Gamma \vdash e_2[\mathbf{x} \mapsto e'] : \tau_2]\!] \rangle\!\rangle \\
&\quad = \langle\!\langle [\![\Theta, \langle \Gamma, \mathbf{x} : \tau' \rangle \vdash e_1 : \tau_1]\!] \circ \langle\!\langle \mathrm{id}, [\![\Theta, \Gamma \vdash e' : \tau']\!] \rangle\!\rangle, \\
&\qquad\quad [\![\Theta, \langle \Gamma, \mathbf{x} : \tau' \rangle \vdash e_2 : \tau_2]\!] \circ \langle\!\langle \mathrm{id}, [\![\Theta, \Gamma \vdash e' : \tau']\!] \rangle\!\rangle \rangle\!\rangle \\
&\quad = \langle\!\langle [\![\Theta, \langle \Gamma, \mathbf{x} : \tau' \rangle \vdash e_1 : \tau_1]\!], [\![\Theta, \langle \Gamma, \mathbf{x} : \tau' \rangle \vdash e_2 : \tau_2]\!] \rangle\!\rangle \circ \langle\!\langle \mathrm{id}, [\![\Theta, \Gamma \vdash e' : \tau']\!] \rangle\!\rangle \\
&\quad = [\![\Theta, \langle \Gamma, \mathbf{x} : \tau' \rangle \vdash \langle e_1, e_2 \rangle : \tau_1 \times \tau_2]\!] \circ \langle\!\langle \mathrm{id}, [\![\Theta, \Gamma \vdash e' : \tau']\!] \rangle\!\rangle.
\end{aligned}
$$

- $e \equiv \mathtt{fst}(e_1)$:

$$
\begin{aligned}
&[\![\Theta, \Gamma \vdash \mathtt{fst}(e_1)[\mathbf{x} \mapsto e'] : \tau]\!] \\
&\quad = [\![\Theta, \Gamma \vdash \mathtt{fst}(e_1[\mathbf{x} \mapsto e']) : \tau]\!] \\
&\quad = \pi_1 \circ [\![\Theta, \Gamma \vdash e_1[\mathbf{x} \mapsto e'] : \tau \times \tau_2]\!] \\
&\quad = \pi_1 \circ [\![\Theta, \langle \Gamma, \mathbf{x} : \tau' \rangle \vdash e_1 : \tau \times \tau_2]\!] \circ \langle\!\langle \mathrm{id}, [\![\Theta, \Gamma \vdash e' : \tau']\!] \rangle\!\rangle \\
&\quad = [\![\Theta, \langle \Gamma, \mathbf{x} : \tau' \rangle \vdash \mathtt{fst}(e_1) : \tau]\!] \circ \langle\!\langle \mathrm{id}, [\![\Theta, \Gamma \vdash e' : \tau']\!] \rangle\!\rangle.
\end{aligned}
$$

- $e \equiv \mathtt{snd}(e_2)$: analogous to the previous case.

- $e \equiv \lambda \mathbf{x}'. e_1$:

$$
\begin{aligned}
&[\![\Theta, \Gamma \vdash (\lambda \mathbf{x}'. e_1)[\mathbf{x} \mapsto e'] : \tau_1 \Rightarrow \tau_2]\!] \\
&\quad = [\![\Theta, \Gamma \vdash \lambda \mathbf{x}'. e_1[\mathbf{x} \mapsto e'] : \tau_1 \Rightarrow \tau_2]\!] \\
&\quad = p\lambda([\![\Theta, \langle \Gamma, \mathbf{x}' : \tau_1 \rangle \vdash e_1[\mathbf{x} \mapsto e'] : \tau_2]\!]) \\
&\quad = p\lambda([\![\Theta, \langle \Gamma, \mathbf{x}' : \tau_1, \mathbf{x} : \tau' \rangle \vdash e_1 : \tau_2]\!] \circ \langle\!\langle \mathrm{id}, [\![\Theta, \langle \Gamma, \mathbf{x}' : \tau_1 \rangle \vdash e' : \tau']\!] \rangle\!\rangle). \quad \text{(C.3)}
\end{aligned}
$$

Since, by the permutation lemma,

$$
\begin{aligned}
&[\![\Theta, \langle \Gamma, \mathbf{x}' : \tau_1, \mathbf{x} : \tau' \rangle \vdash e_1 : \tau_2]\!] \\
&\quad = [\![\Theta, \langle \Gamma, \mathbf{x} : \tau', \mathbf{x}' : \tau_1 \rangle \vdash e_1 : \tau_2]\!] \circ \langle\!\langle \pi_1, \ldots, \pi_n, \pi_{n+2}, \pi_{n+1} \rangle\!\rangle
\end{aligned}
$$

and, by the contraction lemma,

$$
[\![\Theta, \langle \Gamma, \mathbf{x}' : \tau_1 \rangle \vdash e' : \tau']\!] = [\![\Theta, \Gamma \vdash e' : \tau']\!] \circ \langle\!\langle \pi_1, \ldots, \pi_n \rangle\!\rangle
$$

it follows that

$$
\begin{aligned}
&[\![\Theta, \langle \Gamma, \mathbf{x}' : \tau_1, \mathbf{x} : \tau' \rangle \vdash e_1 : \tau_2]\!] \circ \langle\!\langle \mathrm{id}, [\![\Theta, \langle \Gamma, \mathbf{x}' : \tau_1 \rangle \vdash e' : \tau']\!] \rangle\!\rangle \\
&\quad = [\![\Theta, \langle \Gamma, \mathbf{x} : \tau', \mathbf{x}' : \tau_1 \rangle \vdash e_1 : \tau_2]\!] \\
&\qquad \circ \langle\!\langle \pi_1, \ldots, \pi_n, \pi_{n+2}, \pi_{n+1} \rangle\!\rangle \circ \langle\!\langle \mathrm{id}, [\![\Theta, \Gamma \vdash e' : \tau']\!] \circ \langle\!\langle \pi_1, \ldots, \pi_n \rangle\!\rangle \rangle\!\rangle \\
&\quad = [\![\Theta, \langle \Gamma, \mathbf{x} : \tau', \mathbf{x}' : \tau_1 \rangle \vdash e_1 : \tau_2]\!] \circ (\langle\!\langle \mathrm{id}, [\![\Theta, \Gamma \vdash e' : \tau']\!] \rangle\!\rangle \otimes \mathrm{id}_{[\![\tau_1]\!]}). \quad \text{(C.4)}
\end{aligned}
$$

Finally, from (C.3) and (C.4),

$$\begin{aligned}
&[\![\Theta, \Gamma \vdash (\lambda \mathbf{x}'.\, e_1)[\mathbf{x} \mapsto e'] : \tau_1 \rightharpoonup \tau_2]\!] \\
&\quad = p\lambda\big([\![\Theta, \langle \Gamma, \mathbf{x} : \tau', \mathbf{x}' : \tau_1 \rangle \vdash e_1 : \tau_2]\!] \circ (\langle\!\langle \mathrm{id}, [\![\Theta, \Gamma \vdash e' : \tau']\!] \rangle\!\rangle \otimes \mathrm{id}_{[\![\tau_1]\!]})\big) \\
&\quad = p\lambda\big([\![\Theta, \langle \Gamma, \mathbf{x} : \tau', \mathbf{x}' : \tau_1 \rangle \vdash e_1 : \tau_2]\!]\big) \circ \langle\!\langle \mathrm{id}, [\![\Theta, \Gamma \vdash e' : \tau']\!] \rangle\!\rangle \\
&\quad = [\![\Theta, \langle \Gamma, \mathbf{x} : \tau' \rangle \vdash \lambda \mathbf{x}'.\, e_1 : \tau_1 \rightharpoonup \tau_2]\!] \circ \langle\!\langle \mathrm{id}, [\![\Theta, \Gamma \vdash e' : \tau']\!] \rangle\!\rangle.
\end{aligned}$$

- $e \equiv e_1(e_2)$:

$$\begin{aligned}
&[\![\Theta, \Gamma \vdash e_1(e_2)[\mathbf{x} \mapsto e'] : \tau]\!] \\
&= [\![\Theta, \Gamma \vdash e_1[\mathbf{x} \mapsto e']\,(e_2[\mathbf{x} \mapsto e']) : \tau]\!] \\
&= \varepsilon \circ \langle\!\langle [\![\Theta, \Gamma \vdash e_1[\mathbf{x} \mapsto e'] : \tau'' \rightharpoonup \tau]\!], [\![\Theta, \Gamma \vdash e_2[\mathbf{x} \mapsto e'] : \tau'']\!] \rangle\!\rangle \\
&= \varepsilon \circ \\
&\qquad \langle\!\langle [\![\Theta, \langle \Gamma, \mathbf{x} : \tau' \rangle \vdash e_1 : \tau'' \rightharpoonup \tau]\!] \circ \langle\!\langle \mathrm{id}, [\![\Theta, \Gamma \vdash e' : \tau']\!] \rangle\!\rangle, \\
&\qquad\quad [\![\Theta, \langle \Gamma, \mathbf{x} : \tau' \rangle \vdash e_2 : \tau'']\!] \circ \langle\!\langle \mathrm{id}, [\![\Theta, \Gamma \vdash e' : \tau']\!] \rangle\!\rangle \rangle\!\rangle \\
&= [\![\Theta, \langle \Gamma, \mathbf{x} : \tau' \rangle \vdash e_1(e_2) : \tau]\!] \circ \langle\!\langle \mathrm{id}, [\![\Theta, \Gamma \vdash e' : \tau']\!] \rangle\!\rangle.
\end{aligned}$$

- $e \equiv \mathtt{intro}(e_1)$:

$$\begin{aligned}
&[\![\Theta, \Gamma \vdash \mathtt{intro}(e_1)[\mathbf{x} \mapsto e'] : \mu \mathrm{T}.\, \tau_1]\!] \\
&\quad = [\![\Theta, \Gamma \vdash \mathtt{intro}(e_1[\mathbf{x} \mapsto e']) : \mu \mathrm{T}.\, \tau_1]\!] \\
&\quad = I \circ [\![\Theta, \Gamma \vdash e_1[\mathbf{x} \mapsto e'] : \tau_1[\mathrm{T} \mapsto \mu \mathrm{T}.\, \tau_1]]\!] \\
&\quad = I \circ [\![\Theta, \langle \Gamma, \mathbf{x} : \tau' \rangle \vdash e_1 : \tau_1[\mathrm{T} \mapsto \mu \mathrm{T}.\, \tau_1]]\!] \circ \langle\!\langle \mathrm{id}, [\![\Theta, \Gamma \vdash e' : \tau']\!] \rangle\!\rangle \\
&\quad = [\![\Theta, \langle \Gamma, \mathbf{x} : \tau' \rangle \vdash \mathtt{intro}(e_1) : \mu \mathrm{T}.\, \tau_1]\!] \circ \langle\!\langle \mathrm{id}, [\![\Theta, \Gamma \vdash e' : \tau']\!] \rangle\!\rangle.
\end{aligned}$$

- $e \equiv \mathtt{elim}(e_1)$:

$$\begin{aligned}
&[\![\Theta, \Gamma \vdash \mathtt{elim}(e_1)[\mathbf{x} \mapsto e'] : \tau_1[\mathrm{T} \mapsto \mu \mathrm{T}.\, \tau_1]]\!] \\
&\quad = [\![\Theta, \Gamma \vdash \mathtt{elim}(e_1[\mathbf{x} \mapsto e']) : \tau_1[\mathrm{T} \mapsto \mu \mathrm{T}.\, \tau_1]]\!] \\
&\quad = E \circ [\![\Theta, \Gamma \vdash e_1[\mathbf{x} \mapsto e'] : \mu \mathrm{T}.\tau_1]\!] \\
&\quad = E \circ [\![\Theta, \langle \Gamma, \mathbf{x} : \tau' \rangle \vdash e_1 : \mu \mathrm{T}.\, \tau_1]\!] \circ \langle\!\langle \mathrm{id}, [\![\Theta, \Gamma \vdash e' : \tau']\!] \rangle\!\rangle \\
&\quad = [\![\Theta, \langle \Gamma, \mathbf{x} : \tau' \rangle \vdash \mathtt{elim}(e_1) : \tau_1[\mathrm{T} \mapsto \mu \mathrm{T}.\, \tau_1]]\!] \circ \langle\!\langle \mathrm{id}, [\![\Theta, \Gamma \vdash e' : \tau']\!] \rangle\!\rangle. \qquad \square
\end{aligned}$$

Lemma 9.1.3 In any model of FPC,

$$\text{if } \Theta, \Gamma \vdash e \rightsquigarrow v : \tau \text{ then } [\![\Theta, \Gamma \vdash e : \tau]\!] = [\![\Theta, \Gamma \vdash v : \tau]\!].$$

PROOF: By induction on the derivation of $e \rightsquigarrow v$.

Assume that $\Theta, \Gamma \vdash e \rightsquigarrow v : \tau$.

- $e \equiv \mathbf{x}_i$ $(1 \leq i \leq |\, \Gamma \,|)$: vacuous.

- $e \equiv \mathtt{inl}(e_1)$:
  Then, $v \equiv \mathtt{inl}(v_1)$ where $\Theta, \Gamma \vdash e_1 \rightsquigarrow v_1 : \tau_1$ and

$$\begin{aligned} [\![\Theta, \Gamma \vdash e : \tau_1 + \tau_2]\!] &= \amalg_1 \circ [\![\Theta, \Gamma \vdash e_1 : \tau_1]\!] = \amalg_1 \circ [\![\Theta, \Gamma \vdash v_1 : \tau_1]\!] \\ &= [\![\Theta, \Gamma \vdash v : \tau_1 + \tau_2]\!]. \end{aligned}$$

- $e \equiv \mathtt{inr}(e_2)$: analogous to the previous case.
- $e \equiv \mathtt{case}\ e_0\ \mathtt{of}\ \mathtt{inl}(\mathbf{x}_1).e_1\ \mathtt{or}\ \mathtt{inr}(\mathbf{x}_2).e_2$:
  - $\Theta, \Gamma \vdash e_0 \rightsquigarrow \mathtt{inl}(v_1) : \tau_1 + \tau_2$:
    Then, $\Theta, \Gamma \vdash e_1[\mathbf{x}_1 \mapsto v_1] \rightsquigarrow v : \tau$ and

$$\begin{aligned} [\![\Theta, \Gamma \vdash e : \tau]\!] &= \big[[\![\Theta, \langle \Gamma, \mathbf{x}_1 : \tau_1 \rangle \vdash e_1 : \tau]\!], [\![\Theta, \langle \Gamma, \mathbf{x}_2 : \tau_2 \rangle \vdash e_2 : \tau]\!]\big] \\ &\quad \circ \delta \circ \langle\!\langle \mathrm{id}, [\![\Theta, \Gamma \vdash e_0 : \tau_1 + \tau_2]\!] \rangle\!\rangle \\ &= \big[[\![\Theta, \langle \Gamma, \mathbf{x}_1 : \tau_1 \rangle \vdash e_1 : \tau]\!], [\![\Theta, \langle \Gamma, \mathbf{x}_2 : \tau_2 \rangle \vdash e_2 : \tau]\!]\big] \\ &\quad \circ \delta \circ \langle\!\langle \mathrm{id}, \amalg_1 \circ [\![\Theta, \Gamma \vdash v_1 : \tau_1]\!] \rangle\!\rangle \\ &= \big[[\![\Theta, \langle \Gamma, \mathbf{x}_1 : \tau_1 \rangle \vdash e_1 : \tau]\!], [\![\Theta, \langle \Gamma, \mathbf{x}_2 : \tau_2 \rangle \vdash e_2 : \tau]\!]\big] \\ &\quad \circ \amalg_1 \circ \langle\!\langle \mathrm{id}, [\![\Theta, \Gamma \vdash v_1 : \tau_1]\!] \rangle\!\rangle \\ &= [\![\Theta, \langle \Gamma, \mathbf{x}_1 : \tau_1 \rangle \vdash e_1 : \tau]\!] \circ \langle\!\langle \mathrm{id}, [\![\Theta, \Gamma \vdash v_1 : \tau_1]\!] \rangle\!\rangle \\ &= [\![\Theta, \Gamma \vdash e_1[\mathbf{x}_1 \mapsto v_1] : \tau]\!] \qquad \text{, by the substitution lemma} \\ &= [\![\Theta, \Gamma \vdash v : \tau]\!]. \end{aligned}$$

  - $\Theta, \Gamma \vdash e_0 \rightsquigarrow \mathtt{inr}(v_2) : \tau_1 + \tau_2$: analogous to the previous case.
- $e \equiv \langle e_1, e_2 \rangle$:
  Then, $v \equiv \langle v_1, v_2 \rangle$ where $\Theta, \Gamma \vdash e_i \rightsquigarrow v_i : \tau_i$ $(i = 1, 2)$ and

$$\begin{aligned} [\![\Theta, \Gamma \vdash e : \tau_1 \times \tau_2]\!] &= \langle\!\langle [\![\Theta, \Gamma \vdash e_1 : \tau_1]\!], [\![\Theta, \Gamma \vdash e_2 : \tau_2]\!] \rangle\!\rangle \\ &= \langle\!\langle [\![\Theta, \Gamma \vdash v_1 : \tau_1]\!], [\![\Theta, \Gamma \vdash v_2 : \tau_2]\!] \rangle\!\rangle \\ &= [\![\Theta, \Gamma \vdash v : \tau_1 \times \tau_2]\!]. \end{aligned}$$

- $e \equiv \mathtt{fst}(e')$:
  Then, $\Theta, \Gamma \vdash e' \rightsquigarrow \langle v, v' \rangle : \tau \times \tau'$ and

$$\begin{aligned} [\![\Theta, \Gamma \vdash e : \tau]\!] &= \pi_1 \circ [\![\Theta, \Gamma \vdash e' : \tau \times \tau']\!] \\ &= \pi_1 \circ \langle\!\langle [\![\Theta, \Gamma \vdash v : \tau]\!], [\![\Theta, \Gamma \vdash v' : \tau']\!] \rangle\!\rangle \\ &= [\![\Theta, \Gamma \vdash v : \tau]\!] \qquad \text{, because } [\![\Theta, \Gamma \vdash v' : \tau']\!] \downarrow. \end{aligned}$$

- $e \equiv \mathtt{snd}(e')$: analogous to the previous case.
- $e \equiv \lambda \mathbf{x}.\, e'$: vacuous.

- $e \equiv e_1(e_2)$:
  Then,
  - $\Theta, \Gamma \vdash e_1 \leadsto \lambda\mathbf{x}.e' : \tau' \rightharpoonup \tau$,
  - $\Theta, \Gamma \vdash e_2 \leadsto v' : \tau'$,
  - $\Theta, \Gamma \vdash e'[\mathbf{x} \mapsto v'] \leadsto v : \tau$

  and

$$\begin{aligned}
[\![\Theta, \Gamma \vdash e : \tau]\!] &= \varepsilon \circ \langle\!\langle [\![\Theta, \Gamma \vdash e_1 : \tau' \rightharpoonup \tau]\!], [\![\Theta, \Gamma \vdash e_2 : \tau']\!] \rangle\!\rangle \\
&= \varepsilon \circ \langle\!\langle [\![\Theta, \Gamma \vdash \lambda\mathbf{x}.\, e' : \tau' \rightharpoonup \tau]\!], [\![\Theta, \Gamma \vdash v' : \tau']\!] \rangle\!\rangle \\
&= \varepsilon \circ \langle\!\langle p\lambda([\![\Theta, \langle \Gamma, \mathbf{x} : \tau' \rangle \vdash e' : \tau]\!]), [\![\Theta, \Gamma \vdash v' : \tau']\!] \rangle\!\rangle \\
&= [\![\Theta, \langle \Gamma, \mathbf{x} : \tau' \rangle \vdash e' : \tau]\!] \circ \langle\!\langle \mathrm{id}, [\![\Theta, \Gamma \vdash v' : \tau']\!] \rangle\!\rangle \\
&\qquad\qquad\qquad\qquad\qquad\qquad \text{, because } [\![\Theta, \Gamma \vdash v' : \tau']\!] \downarrow \\
&= [\![\Theta, \Gamma \vdash e'[\mathbf{x} \mapsto v'] : \tau]\!] \qquad \text{, by the substitution lemma} \\
&= [\![\Theta, \Gamma \vdash v : \tau]\!].
\end{aligned}$$

- $e \equiv \mathtt{intro}(e')$:
  Then, $v \equiv \mathtt{intro}(v')$ where $\Theta, \Gamma \vdash e' \leadsto v' : \tau'[\mathrm{T} \mapsto \mu\mathrm{T}.\, \tau']$ and

$$\begin{aligned}
[\![\Theta, \Gamma \vdash e : \mu\mathrm{T}.\, \tau']\!] &= I \circ [\![\Theta, \Gamma \vdash e' : \tau'[\mathrm{T} \mapsto \mu\mathrm{T}.\, \tau']]\!] \\
&= I \circ [\![\Theta, \Gamma \vdash v' : \tau'[\mathrm{T} \mapsto \mu\mathrm{T}.\, \tau']]\!] \\
&= [\![\Theta, \Gamma \vdash v : \mu\mathrm{T}.\, \tau']\!].
\end{aligned}$$

- $e \equiv \mathtt{elim}(e')$:
  Then, $e' \leadsto \mathtt{intro}(v)$ and

$$\begin{aligned}
&[\![\Theta, \Gamma \vdash e : \tau'[\mathrm{T} \mapsto \mu\mathrm{T}.\, \tau']]\!] \\
&\quad = E \circ [\![\Theta, \Gamma \vdash e' : \mu\mathrm{T}.\, \tau']\!] \\
&\quad = E \circ [\![\Theta, \Gamma \vdash \mathtt{intro}(v) : \mu\mathrm{T}.\, \tau']\!] \\
&\quad = E \circ I \circ [\![\Theta, \Gamma \vdash v : \tau'[\mathrm{T} \mapsto \mu\mathrm{T}.\, \tau']]\!] \\
&\quad = [\![\Theta, \Gamma \vdash v : \tau'[\mathrm{T} \mapsto \mu\mathrm{T}.\, \tau']]\!] \qquad \text{, because } E \circ I = \mathrm{id}. \qquad \square
\end{aligned}$$

D Propositions D.0.1 and D.0.2

Proposition D.0.1 In the situation (9.6) of page 176, for symmetric **Cpo**-functors F' and G' such that

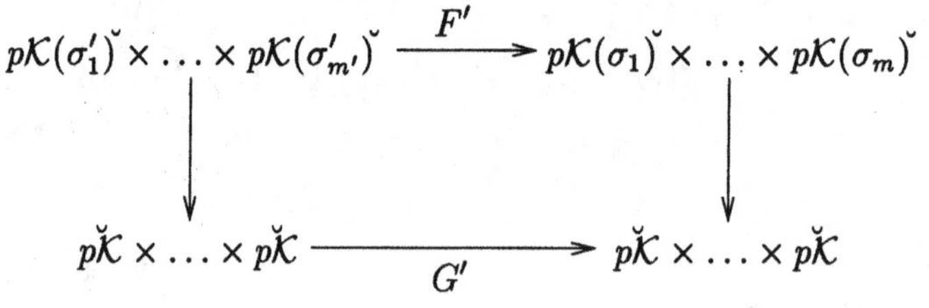

$p\mathcal{K}(\sigma'_1)\check{} \times \ldots \times p\mathcal{K}(\sigma'_{m'})\check{}$
F'
$p\mathcal{K}(\sigma_1)\check{} \times \ldots \times p\mathcal{K}(\sigma_m)\check{}$
$p\check{\mathcal{K}} \times \ldots \times p\check{\mathcal{K}}$
G'
$p\check{\mathcal{K}} \times \ldots \times p\check{\mathcal{K}}$

,

if

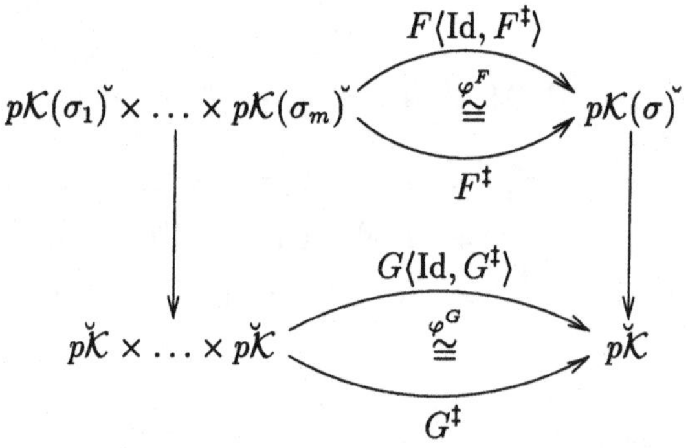

$F\langle \mathrm{Id}, F^{\ddagger}\rangle$
$p\mathcal{K}(\sigma_1)\check{} \times \ldots \times p\mathcal{K}(\sigma_m)\check{}$
φ^F
$\cong$
$p\mathcal{K}(\sigma)\check{}$
$F^{\ddagger}$
$G\langle \mathrm{Id}, G^{\ddagger}\rangle$
$p\check{\mathcal{K}} \times \ldots \times p\check{\mathcal{K}}$
φ^G
$\cong$
$p\check{\mathcal{K}}$
$G^{\ddagger}$

and, for $S = F(F' \times \mathrm{Id})$ and $T = G(G' \times \mathrm{Id})$,

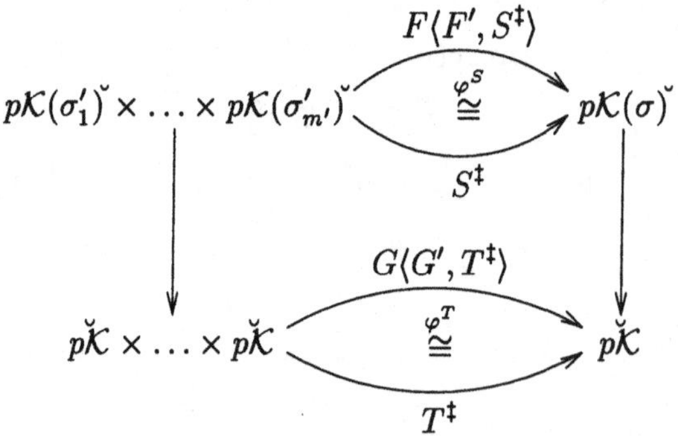

$F\langle F', S^{\ddagger}\rangle$
$p\mathcal{K}(\sigma'_1)\check{} \times \ldots \times p\mathcal{K}(\sigma'_{m'})\check{}$
φ^S
$\cong$
$p\mathcal{K}(\sigma)\check{}$
$S^{\ddagger}$
$G\langle G', T^{\ddagger}\rangle$
$p\check{\mathcal{K}} \times \ldots \times p\check{\mathcal{K}}$
φ^T
$\cong$
$p\check{\mathcal{K}}$
$T^{\ddagger}$

then

$$
\begin{array}{ccc}
p\mathcal{K}(\sigma_1')\check{} \times \ldots \times p\mathcal{K}(\sigma_{m'}')\check{} & \underset{F^\ddagger F'}{\overset{(F(F' \times \mathrm{Id}))^\ddagger}{\underset{\longrightarrow}{\overset{\longrightarrow}{\psi^{F,F'} \cong}}}} & p\mathcal{K}(\sigma)\check{} \\
\Big\downarrow & & \Big\downarrow \\
p\check{\mathcal{K}} \times \ldots \times p\check{\mathcal{K}} & \underset{G^\ddagger G'}{\overset{(G(G' \times \mathrm{Id}))^\ddagger}{\underset{\longrightarrow}{\overset{\longrightarrow}{\psi^{G,G'} \cong}}}} & p\check{\mathcal{K}}
\end{array}
.
$$

PROOF: Recall from page 124 that

$$
\begin{array}{ccc}
F(F'X, S^\ddagger X) & \xrightarrow{\varphi_X^S} & S^\ddagger X \\
{\scriptstyle F(F'X, \psi_X^{F,F'})}\Big\downarrow & & \Big\downarrow{\scriptstyle \psi_X^{F,F'}} \\
F(F'X, F^\ddagger F'X) & \xrightarrow[\varphi_{F'X}^F]{} & F^\ddagger F'X
\end{array}
.
$$

Then, writing W for $({U_{\sigma_1}}^{op} \times U_{\sigma_1}) \times \ldots \times ({U_{\sigma_m}}^{op} \times U_{\sigma_m})$, V for ${U_\sigma}^{op} \times U_\sigma$ and W' for $({U_{\sigma_1'}}^{op} \times U_{\sigma_1'}) \times \ldots \times ({U_{\sigma_{m'}'}}^{op} \times U_{\sigma_{m'}'})$, and applying V to the above diagram it follows that

$$
\begin{array}{ccc}
G(G'W'X, T^\ddagger W'X) & \xrightarrow{V\varphi_X^S = \varphi_{W'X}^T} & T^\ddagger W'X \\
{\scriptstyle G(G'W'X, V\psi_X^{F,F'})}\Big\downarrow & & \Big\downarrow{\scriptstyle V\psi_X^{F,F'}} \\
G(G'W'X, G^\ddagger G'W'X) & \xrightarrow[V\varphi_{F'X}^F = \varphi_{WF'X}^G = \varphi_{G'W'X}^G]{} & G^\ddagger G'W'X
\end{array}
$$

and therefore $V\psi^{F,F'} = \psi^{G,G'}W'$. □

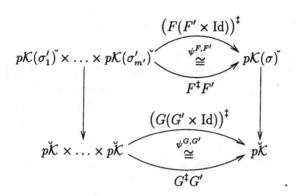

Proposition D.0.2 For symmetric **Cpo**-functors F_i, G_i $(i = 1, 2)$ such that

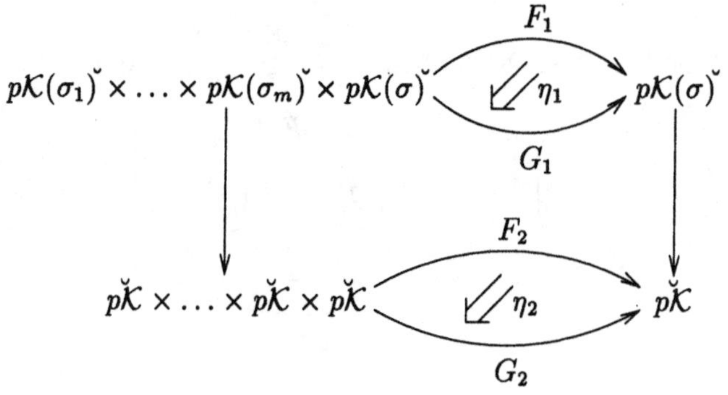

,

if, for $H = F, G$,

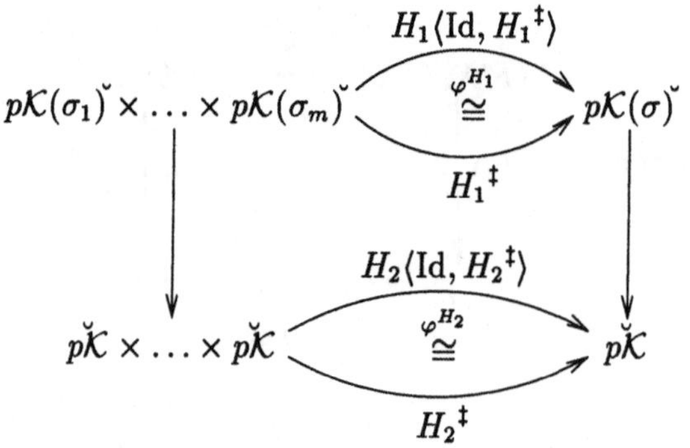

then

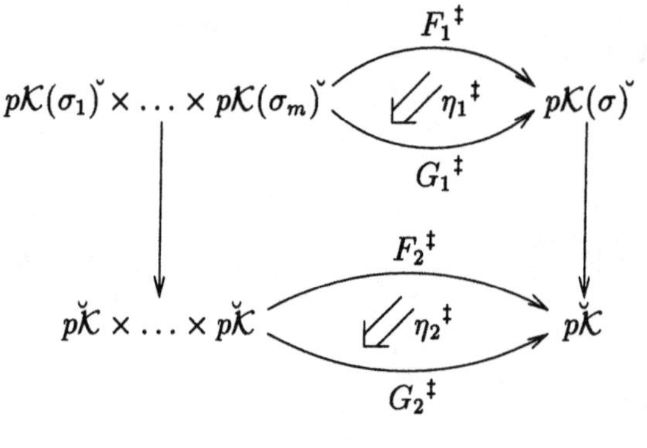

.

Proof: Recall from page 110 that

$$
\begin{array}{ccccc}
F_1(X, F_1{}^{\ddagger}X) & & \xrightarrow{\quad \varphi_X^{F_1} \quad} & & F_1{}^{\ddagger}X \\
\Big\downarrow{\scriptstyle F_1(X, \eta_1{}^{\ddagger}_X)} & & & & \Big\downarrow{\scriptstyle \eta_1{}^{\ddagger}_X} \\
F_1(X, G_1{}^{\ddagger}X) & \xrightarrow[\eta_{(X, G_1{}^{\ddagger}X)}]{} & G_1(X, G_1{}^{\ddagger}X) & \xrightarrow[\varphi_X^{G_1}]{} & G_1{}^{\ddagger}X
\end{array}
.
$$

Then, writing W for $(U_{\sigma_1}{}^{op} \times U_{\sigma_1}) \times \ldots \times (U_{\sigma_m}{}^{op} \times U_{\sigma_m})$ and V for $U_{\sigma}{}^{op} \times U_{\sigma}$, and applying V to the above diagram it follows that

$$
\begin{array}{ccccc}
F_2(WX, F_1{}^{\ddagger}WX) & & \xrightarrow{\quad V\varphi_X^{F_1} = \varphi_{WX}^{F_2} \quad} & & F_2{}^{\ddagger}WX \\
\Big\downarrow{\scriptstyle F_2(WX, V\eta_1{}^{\ddagger}_X)} & & & & \Big\downarrow{\scriptstyle V\eta_1{}^{\ddagger}_X} \\
F_2(WX, G_2{}^{\ddagger}WX) & \xrightarrow[\substack{V\eta_{(X, G_1{}^{\ddagger}X)} \\ \| \\ \eta_{2(WX, G_2{}^{\ddagger}WX)}}]{} & G_2(WX, G_2{}^{\ddagger}WX) & \xrightarrow[V\varphi_X^{G_1} = \varphi_{WX}^{G_2}]{} & G_2{}^{\ddagger}WX
\end{array}
$$

and therefore $V\eta_1{}^{\ddagger} = \eta_2{}^{\ddagger}W$. □

Bibliography

[Abr87] S. Abramsky. *Domain Theory and the Logic of Observable Properties.* PhD thesis, University of London, 1987.

[Abr90] S. Abramsky. The lazy λ-calculus. In D.A. Turner, editor, *Logical Foundations of Functional Programming*, pages 65–116. Addison-Wesley, 1990.

[Adá93] J. Adámek. Data types in algebraically ω-complete categories. To appear in Information and Computation, 1993.

[AJ94] S. Abramsky and A. Jung. Domain theory. To appear in the Handbook of Logic in Computer Science, 1994.

[AMR94] S. Abramsky, P. Malacaria, and Jagadeesan R. Full abstraction for PCF (extended abstract). In M. Hagiya and J.C. Mitchell, editors, *Theoretical Aspects of Computer Software*, pages 1–15. Springer-Verlag, 1994.

[AT90] J. Adámek and V. Trnková. *Automata and Algebras in Categories.* Klumer Publ., 1990.

[Bar92] M. Barr. Algebraically compact functors. *Journal of Pure and Applied Algebra*, 82:211–231, 1992.

[BCL85] G. Berry, P.-L. Curien, and J.-J. Lévy. Full abstraction for sequential languages: the state of the art. In M. Nivat and J.C. Reynolds, editors, *Algebraic methods in semantics*, pages 89–132. Cambridge University Press, 1985.

[Car86] A. Carboni. Bicategories of partial maps. *Cahiers Topologie Géom. Différentielle*, 1986.

[CF58] H.B. Curry and R. Feys. *Combinatory Logic*, volume 1 of *Studies in Logic and the Foundations of Mathematics.* North-Holland, 1958.

[CGW89] T. Coquand, C.A. Gunter, and G. Winskel. Domain theoretic models of polymorphism. *Information and Computation*, 81:123–167, 1989.

[CM93] P. Cenciarelli and E. Moggi. A syntactic approach to modularity in denotational semantics. In *CTCS-5 (Category Theory and Computer Science Fifth Biennial Meeting)*, pages 9–12. CWI, September 1993.

[CS93] R. L. Constable and S.F. Smith. Computational foundations of basic recursive function theory. *Theoretical Computer Science*, 121:89–112, 1993.

[Ers73] Y. Ershov. Theorie der numerierungen I. *Z. Math. Logik*, 19, 1973.

[Fio93a] M.P. Fiore. A coinduction principle for recursive data types based on bisimulation. In *8th LICS Conf.*, pages 110–119. IEEE, Computer Society Press, 1993.

[Fio93b] M.P. Fiore. **Cpo**-categories of partial maps. In *CTCS-5 (Category Theory and Computer Science Fifth Biennial Meeting)*, pages 45–49. CWI, September 1993.

[FJM+96] M.P. Fiore, A. Jung, E. Moggi, P. O'Hearn, J. Riecke, G. Rosolini, and I. Stark. Domains and denotational semantics: History, accomplishments and open problems. To appear in the Bulletin of the European Association for Theoretical Computer Science. (Technical Report CSR-96-2, The University of Birmingham, School of Computer Science —available from ftp://ftp.cs.bham.ac.uk/pub/tech-reports/1996/CSR-96-02.ps.gz), 1996.

[FK72] P.J. Freyd and G.M. Kelly. Categories of continuous functors, I. *Journal of Pure and Applied Algebra*, 2:169–191, 1972.

[FMRS92] P.J. Freyd, P. Mulry, G. Rosolini, and D.S. Scott. Extensional PERs. *Information and Computation*, 98:211–227, 1992.

[FP92] M.P. Fiore and G.D. Plotkin. On compactness and **Cpo**-enriched categories. In G. Winskel, editor, *Proceedings of the CLICS Workshop (23-27 March 1992)*, volume 397-II of *DAIMI PB*, pages 571–584. Computer Science Department, Aarhus University, May 1992.

[FP94] M.P. Fiore and G.D. Plotkin. An axiomatisation of computationally adequate domain theoretic models of FPC. In *9th LICS Conf.* IEEE, Computer Society Press, 1994.

[Fre90] P.J. Freyd. Recursive types reduced to inductive types. In *5th LICS Conf.*, pages 498–507. IEEE, Computer Society Press, 1990.

[Fre91] P.J. Freyd. Algebraically complete categories. In A. Carboni, M.C. Pedicchio, and G. Rosolini, editors, *Category Theory*, volume 1488 of *Lecture Notes in Mathematics*, pages 131–156. Springer-Verlag, 1991.

[Fre92] P.J. Freyd. Remarks on algebraically compact categories. In M.P. Fourman, P.T. Johnstone, and A.M. Pitts, editors, *Applications of Categories in Computer Science*, volume 177 of *London Mathematical Society Lecture Note Series*, pages 95–106. Cambridge University Press, 1992.

[GMW79] M.J.C. Gordon, A.J.R. Milner, and C.P. Wadsworth. *Edinburgh LCF*, volume 78 of *Lecture Notes in Computer Science*. Springer-Verlag, 1979.

[GS90] C.A. Gunter and D.S. Scott. Semantic domains. *Handbook of Theoretical Computer Science*, pages 633–674, 1990.

[Gun92] C.A. Gunter. *Semantics of Programming Languages: Structures and Techniques.* The MIT Press, 1992.

[HO94] J.M.E Hyland and C.-H.L. Ong. Full abstraction for PCF: dialogue games and innocent strategies. Preprint, 1994.

[How80] W.A. Howard. The formulae-as-types notion of construction. In *[HS80]*, pages 479–490. Academic Press, 1980.

[HP90] H. Huwig and A. Poigné. A note on inconsistencies caused by fixpoints in a cartesian closed category. *Theoretical Computer Science*, 73:101–112, 1990.

[HS80] J.R. Hindley and J.P. Seldin, editors. *To H.B. Curry: essays in Combinatory Logic, lambda calculus and Formalisms.* Academic Press, 1980.

[Hyl91] J.M.E. Hyland. First steps in synthetic domain theory. In A. Carboni, M.C. Pedicchio, and G. Rosolini, editors, *Category Theory*, volume 1488 of *Lecture Notes in Mathematics*, pages 95–104. Springer-Verlag, 1991.

[Jay91] C.B. Jay. Partial functions, ordered categories, limits and cartesian closure. In *Workshops in Computing*, IV Higher Order Workshop, Banff, pages 151–161. Springer-Verlag, 1991.

[Joh77] P.T. Johnstone. *Topos Theory.* Academic Press, 1977.

[Kel82] G.M. Kelly. *Basic Concepts of Enriched Category Theory.* Cambridge University Press, 1982.

[Kel89] G.M. Kelly. Elementary observations on 2-categorical limits. *Bull. Austral. Math. Soc.*, 39(2):301–317, 1989.

[Koc70] A. Kock. Strong functors and monoidal monads. Various Publications Series 11, Aarhus Universitet, August 1970.

[KS74] G.M. Kelly and R. Street. Review of the elements of 2-categories. In G.M. Kelly, editor, *Proceedings Sydney Category Theory Seminar 1972/1973*, pages 75–103. Springer-Verlag, 1974.

[Lam68] J. Lambek. A fixpoint theorem for complete categories. *Math. Zeitschr.*, 103:151–161, 1968.

[Law73] F.W. Lawvere. Metric spaces, generalized logic, and closed categories. *Rend. del Sem. Mat. e Fis. di Milano*, 43:135–166, 1973.

[Law90] F.W. Lawvere. Some thoughts on the future of category theory. In A. Carboni, M.C. Pedicchio, and G. Rosolini, editors, *Category Theory*, volume 1488 of *Lecture Notes in Mathematics*, pages 1–13. Springer-Verlag, 1990.

[LM84] G. Longo and E. Moggi. Cartesian closed categories of enumerations for effective type-structures. In G. Kahn, D. MacQueen, and G. Plotkin, editors, *Symposium on Semantics of Data Types*, volume 173 of *Lecture Notes in Computer Science*. Springer-Verlag, 1984.

[LM92] S. Mac Lane and I. Moerdijk. *Sheaves in Geometry and Logic: A First Introduction to Topos Theory*. Springer-Verlag, 1992.

[LS81] D.J. Lehmann and M.B. Smyth. Algebraic specification of data types: A synthetic approach. *Math. Systems Theory*, 14:97–139, 1981.

[Mac71] S. MacLane. *Categories for the Working Mathematician*. Springer-Verlag, 1971.

[Mar76] G. Markowsky. Chain-complete posets and directed sets with applications. *Algebra Univ.*, 6:53–68, 1976.

[MC88] A.R. Meyer and S.S. Cosmadakis. Semantical paradigms: Notes for an invited lecture. In 3rd *LICS Conf.*, pages 236–253. IEEE, Computer Society Press, 1988.

[McC84] D.C. McCarty. *Realizability and Recursive Mathematics*. PhD thesis, University of Oxford, 1984. Also CMU-CS-84-131, Carnegie-Mellon University.

[Mil77] R. Milner. Fully abstract models of typed lambda calculus. *Theoretical Computer Science*, 4:1–22, 1977.

[Mit90] J.C. Mitchell. Types systems for programming languages. *Handbook of Theoretical Computer Science*, pages 366–457, 1990.

[ML83] P. Martin-Löf. The domain interpretation of type theory. In Programming Methodology Group, editor, *Workshop on the Semantics of Programming Languages*, pages 21–48, 1983. University of Göteborg and Chalmers University of Technology.

[Mog86] E. Moggi. Categories of partial morphisms and the partial lambda-calculus. In *Proceedings Workshop on Category Theory and Computer Programming, Guildford 1985*, volume 240 of *Lecture Notes in Computer Science*, pages 242–251. Springer-Verlag, 1986.

[Mog88] E. Moggi. Partial morphisms in categories of effective objects. *Information and Computation*, 76:250–277, 1988.

[Pho90a] W. Phoa. *Domain Theory in Realizability Toposes*. PhD thesis, Trinity College, Cambridge, 1990. Also CST-82-91, University of Edinburgh.

[Pho90b] W. Phoa. Effective domains and intrinsic structure. In 5th *LICS Conf.*, pages 366–377. IEEE, Computer Society Press, 1990.

[Pho93] W. Phoa. Adequacy for untyped translations of typed λ-calculi. In *8th LICS Conf.*, pages 287–295. IEEE, Computer Society Press, 1993.

[Pit92] A.M. Pitts. A co-induction principle for recursively defined domains. Technical Report 252, Cambridge Univ. Computer Laboratory, September 1992. To appear in Theoretical Computer Science.

[Pit93a] A.M. Pitts. Relational properties of domains. Technical Report 321, Cambridge Univ. Computer Laboratory, December 1993.

[Pit93b] A.M. Pitts. Relational properties of recursively defined domains. In *8th LICS Conf.*, pages 86–97. IEEE, Computer Society Press, 1993.

[Plo77] G.D. Plotkin. LCF considered as a programming language. *Theoretical Computer Science*, 5:223–256, 1977.

[Plo81] G.D. Plotkin. A structural approach to operational semantics. Technical Report DAIMI FN-19, Computer Science Department, Aarhus University, September 1981.

[Plo83a] G.D. Plotkin. Domains. Department of Computer Science, University of Edinburgh, 1983.

[Plo83b] G.D. Plotkin. A metalanguage for predomains. In Programming Methodology Group, editor, *Workshop on the Semantics of Programming Languages*, pages 93–118, 1983. University of Göteborg and Chalmers University of Technology.

[Plo85] G.D. Plotkin. Denotational semantics with partial functions. Lecture at C.S.L.I. Summer School, 1985.

[Plo93a] G.D. Plotkin. Second order type theory and recursion. Slides of a talk given at the Scott Fest, February 1993.

[Plo93b] G.D. Plotkin. Type theory and recursion (extended abstract). In *8th LICS Conf.*, page 374. IEEE, Computer Society Press, 1993.

[Rey74] J. Reynolds. Towards a theory of type structure. In B. Robinet, editor, *Programming Symposium '74*, volume 19 of *Lecture Notes in Computer Science*. Springer-Verlag, 1974.

[Rey83] J. Reynolds. Types, abstraction, and parametric polymorphism. IFIP Congress, 1983.

[Rob87] E. Robinson. Logical aspects of denotational semantics. In *Category Theory and Computer Science*, number 283 in Lecture Notes in Computer Science, pages 238–253. Springer-Verlag, September 1987.

[Rom89] L. Román. On partial cartesian closed categories. In *Proc. AMS Conf. on Categories in Comp. Sci. and Logic (Boulder 1987)*, volume 92, 1989.

[Ros86] G. Rosolini. *Continuity and Effectiveness in Topoi.* PhD thesis, University of Oxford, 1986.

[RR88] E. Robinson and G. Rosolini. Categories of partial maps. *Information and Computation*, 79:95–130, 1988.

[RT93] J. Rutten and D. Turi. On the foundations of final semantics: Non-standard sets, metric spaces, partial orders. In J.W. de Bakker, W.P. de Roever, and Rozenberg, editors, *Proc. of the REX workshop, Semantics: Foundations and Applications*, volume 666 of *Lecture Notes in Computer Science.* Springer-Verlag, 1993.

[Rut93] J. Rutten. A structural co-induction theorem. In *Proc. of the 9th Conference on the Mathematical Foundations of Programming Semantics*, Lecture Notes in Computer Science. Springer-Verlag, 1993. To appear.

[Sco69] D.S. Scott. A type-theoretical alternative to CUCH, ISWIM, OWHY. Also [Sco93], 1969.

[Sco70] D.S. Scott. Outline of a mathematical theory of computation. Technical Report PRG-2, Oxford Univ. Computing Lab., 1970.

[Sco72] D.S. Scott. Continuous lattices. In F.W. Lawvere, editor, *Toposes, Algebraic Geometry and Logic*, volume 274 of *Lecture Notes in Mathematics*, pages 97–136. Springer-Verlag, 1972.

[Sco76] D.S. Scott. Data types as lattices. *SIAM Journal of Computing*, 5:522–587, 1976.

[Sco79] D.S. Scott. Identity and existence in intuitionistic logic. In M.P. Fourman, C.J. Mulvey, and D.S. Scott, editors, *Applications of Sheaves*, volume 753 of *Lecture Notes in Mathematics.* Springer-Verlag, 1979.

[Sco80] D.S. Scott. Relating theories of the λ-calculus. In R. Hindley and J. Seldin, editors, *[HS80].* Academic Press, 1980.

[Sco82] D.S. Scott. Domains for denotational semantics. In M. Nielsen and E.M. Schimdt, editors, *9th Colloquium on Automata, Languages and Programming*, volume 140 of *Lecture Notes in Computer Science*, pages 577–613. Springer-Verlag, 1982.

[Sco93] D.S. Scott. A type-theoretical alternative to CUCH, ISWIM, OWHY. *Theoretical Computer Science*, 121:411–440, 1993. Reprint of a manuscript.

[Sim92] A.K. Simpson. Recursive types in Kleisli categories. Department of Computer Science, University of Edinburgh. Draft, 1992.

[Smy77] M.B. Smyth. Effectively given domains. *Theoretical Computer Science*, 5:257–274, 1977.

[SP82] M.B. Smyth and G.D. Plotkin. The category-theoretic solution of recursive domain equations. *SIAM Journal of Computing*, 11(4):761–783, November 1982.

[Sto77] J.E. Stoy. *Denotational Semantics: The Scott-Strachey Approach to Programming Language Theory.* The MIT Press, 1977.

[Tay91] P. Taylor. The fixed point property in synthetic domain theory. In *6th LICS Conf.*, pages 152–160. IEEE, Computer Society Press, 1991.

[Vic89] S. Vickers. *Topology via Logic.* Cambridge University Press, 1989. Volume 5 of Tracts in Theoretical Computer Science.

[Wag94] K.R. Wagner. Abstract pre-orders. In M. Hagiya and J.C. Mitchell, editors, *Theoretical Aspects of Computer Software*, pages 598–617. Springer-Verlag, 1994.

[Wan79] M. Wand. Fixed point constructions in order-enriched categories. *Theoretical Computer Science*, 8:13–30, 1979.

[Zha91] G.-Q. Zhang. *Logic of Domains.* Birkhäuser, 1991.

Index

Symbol Index

Chapter 1

Chapter 2

Chapter 3

Chapter 4

Chapter 5

Chapter 6

Chapter 7

Chapter 8

Printed in the United States
By Bookmasters